Shaping Childcare Practice in Scotland
Key papers on adoption and fostering

Shaping Childcare Practice in Scotland
Key papers on adoption and fostering

Edited by Malcolm Hill

Published by
British Association for Adoption & Fostering
(BAAF)
Skyline House
200 Union Street
London SE1 0LX
www.baaf.org.uk

Charity registration 275689

© Malcolm Hill 2002

British Library Cataloguing in Publication Data
A catalogue record for this book is available
from the British Library

ISBN 1 903699 14 2

Project management by Miranda Davies,
Production Editor, *Adoption & Fostering*,
BAAF
Photographs on cover posed by model
by John Birdsall
www.JohnBirdsall.co.uk
Designed by Andrew Haig & Associates
Typeset by Avon Dataset Ltd, Bidford on Avon
Printed by Russell Press Ltd. (TU),
Nottingham

Contents

Foreword

The genesis of this anthology was a discussion between practitioners and researchers about the way in which fostering and adoption were developing in Scotland. In the course of conversation people were reflecting on the very significant contribution made by Scottish practitioners, researchers and policy makers during the last two decades. Inevitably the passage of time, changes in personnel and local government reorganisation have led to the dissipation of knowledge and a lack of awareness of what work has gone before. However, the debate and dilemmas remain surrounding the best way to secure the future welfare of children who cannot live within their birth families. Often, rather than building on past work, individuals and agencies find themselves starting from scratch.

This anthology is intended to fulfil the role of the family member who remembers events and history, and passes the information on to new and younger members. It brings together key articles making them available to today's practitioners and managers, and to students – the practitioners of tomorrow.

In the years covered by the anthology, new legislation has been enacted in Scotland relating not just to children and families but establishing the Parliament itself. This offers an exciting opportunity for social policy and social work practice to be developed to meet the needs of children and families in Scotland.

Adoption practice has changed, becoming more open and flexible. Fostering now embraces a wide range of situations, from short-term and respite to life-long commitment. Debates in the future are likely to be about the scope and place of adoption, the range of fostering provision and how support can be provided to all concerned over a lifetime. Pragmatically, how can significant numbers of prospective parents be recruited, supported and sustained to meet the complex and life-long needs of children who have experienced pain, separation and loss?

1

BAAF Scotland has played a significant role in the 21 years of its existence, providing practical services such as child linking, training, advice and information, as well as contributing to public debate and policy formation. It has been supported by many people, including those whose contributions appear in this anthology. As new challenges emerge, we hope to continue working to promote the welfare and future of Scottish children and their families, and that a future anthology will bring together tomorrow's practice developments and innovations.

Barbara J Hudson
Director, BAAF Scotland

Introduction: adoption and fostering in Scotland – contexts and trends

Malcolm Hill

This book is an anthology of key articles, originally published in the journal *Adoption & Fostering,* which are concerned with the placement of children in families other than those they were born to. This takes two main forms. Adoption involves the permanent inclusion of children in new families, where the adopters acquire all the legal rights and responsibilities of parents on a life-long basis. Fostering embraces a wide range of situations where a couple or individual looks after a child 24 hours a day for a matter of days, months or years, without any legal transfer of parenthood to the foster carers. Private fostering occurs when an arrangement is made directly between parents and foster carers (Holman, 2002), but this book covers the more common situation where a local authority is responsible for the child.

The articles in the book were chosen because they were either about adoption or fostering in Scotland or were written by authors in Scotland about broader issues which have shaped policy and practice.[1] This means that the book combines accounts of relevant practice and legal developments, summaries of research and reviews of changing ideas about adoption and fostering. Some of the matters dealt with are particular to Scotland, but many of the contents refer to trends that are comparable to those elsewhere in the UK and so have implications for readers there and elsewhere, in addition to those located in Scotland.

Like any journal, *Adoption & Fostering* does not necessarily cover all the topics of the day, since the articles that are published depend on the choices of individuals to take the trouble to write and submit a paper, as well as editorial and peer review judgements about relevance and quality. The articles deal with an important range of topics, but are not fully

---

[1] References in the text given in bold print are to articles that have been included as chapters in this book. The other references are provided at the end of the book.

comprehensive. Therefore this introductory chapter describes the background to adoption and fostering in Scotland, while each section of the book has its own short introduction to summarise and contextualise the chapters that follow. It is helpful to begin with a brief account of more general services for children and families in Scotland, of which alternative family placements are a part, as well as those elements of the law and legal system relevant to fostering and adoption.

Services for children

There are slightly over one million children in Scotland (NCH Scotland, 2002). Many services, such as nurseries, schools and youth provision, cater for any child or young person of the relevant age and have open access. This book is concerned with children and young people who require particular services on account of temporary, long-term or permanent separation from their families. However, it is important to emphasise that these are children first and so are entitled to make use of universal services, as indeed nearly all do.

The main responsibility for children requiring substitute family care rests with local authorities, which have duties to assess and assist children in need of care and protection. This duty is normally carried out by social work staff in area or neighbourhood children and family teams. Policy and practice are moving towards a position where all parts of the authority work corporately for the sake of fostered children, who have education and health difficulties well out of proportion to their numbers. Those on the threshold of adulthood have major employment and housing needs (Convention of Scottish Local Authorities, 2000). Local authorities must also provide an adoption service, which is quite often organised on a more centralised basis.

Commonly families have received other kinds of practical and counselling help (family support) from the local authority before their children become fostered or adopted. Authorities have a particular duty to provide such help to "children in need", whose health or development would suffer if services were not provided, together with children who are disabled or are affected by disability in the family (Scottish Office, 1997; Hill et al, 1998).

Local authority social workers also investigate situations of suspected child abuse, often jointly with the police. If a child is thought to be at risk, then a case conference is held to bring together all the key professionals, usually with the parents, in order to share information and formulate a plan for the child's safety. When there are continuing concerns about a child's safety within the family home, that child's name will be placed on a Child Protection Register. In recent years enquiries have been made about more than 7,000 children each year and at any one time just under 2,500 children in Scotland have been on a register (Scottish Executive news release, October 2000).

In only a minority of situations does it happen that children referred for possible abuse leave home, but it is the case that a growing proportion of those who are fostered and adopted have been abused or seriously neglected (Minnis *et al*, 2001). This has major implications for the children and the new carers, since the children need to make a double recovery from their ill-treatment and from their separation from familiar people and surroundings, while the carers must have the skills to help the child with the complex adjustments. On top of this may well be a number of other challenges such as stigma and shame associated with being in an "abnormal" situation, understanding their past and sorting out a sense of who they are against a background of having lived in more than one family.

A large number of voluntary agencies provide a wide range of services for children and their families. Certain larger children's agencies like Barnardo's and NCH run fostering schemes, usually of a specialist nature (Barnardo's, 2001; Walker *et al*, 2002). Independent fostering agencies proliferated in England during the 1990s, some having been set up by former local authority carers. At the start of the new millennium, a few began operating in Scotland.

The law in relation to fostering and adoption (see also Section III)

The main statute currently governing arrangements for fostering is the Children (Scotland) Act 1995. This Act integrated previously separate legislation dealing with public law affecting children and private law (e.g. divorce). It covers children's rights and parental responsibilities in general, but most of its sections concern three overlapping groups of children:

- "children in need" for whom local authorities have particular duties to provide services;
- children who may need compulsory measures, for their own care and protection and/or on account of their behaviour;
- children who are "looked after"[2] by local authorities, including those who are fostered.

The 1995 Act also prescribes circumstances in which a local authority may apply to a court for parental rights and responsibilities to be transferred to itself by means of a Parental Responsibility Order (PRO).

Several core principles are embodied in the Act:
1. the *welfare principle* – a child's welfare throughout childhood must be a paramount consideration when decisions are made;
2. the *minimum necessary intervention principle* – compulsory orders should not be made unless less intrusive measures have been considered and are inadequate to safeguard or promote the child's welfare;
3. the *participation principle* – children's views should be heard and taken into consideration, according to their age and understanding;
4. the *sensitivity to identity principle* – decisions should take into account a child's religious persuasion, racial origin and cultural and linguistic background.

On the whole, the Act does not single out fostering, but prescribes the circumstances in which children may be looked after either in a family placement or residential care and sets out local authority duties with

---

[2] The term "looked after" was introduced into England and Wales by the Children Act 1989 to describe those children formerly (and still sometimes informally) referred to as "in care", who are mostly living away from home. The phrase "looked after" was also used by the Children (Scotland) Act 1995, but refers to a wider category since it covers those on home supervision as well as those "accommodated and looked after" away from home.

respect to all looked after children. For instance, within the context of the key principles outlined above, authorities are required to promote contact between looked after children and their parents or people with parental responsibilities.

The Children (Scotland) Act 1995 is accompanied by three volumes of Regulations and Guidance (Scottish Office, 1997). These cover:
1. support and protection for children and their families;
2. children looked after by local authorities;
3. Adoption and Parental Responsibilities Orders.

The Fostering of Children (Scotland) Regulations 1996 require all local authorities to appoint a panel to approve foster carers and specify how authorities should decide about placing a child in foster care, keep records and establish foster carer and placement agreements. Children in foster care (and residential care) should have an individual care plan and the child's circumstances and needs must be systematically reviewed within six weeks of placement, within a further three months and then at six-monthly intervals. Volume 2 of the Guidance gives detailed attention to the fostering service. Among the issues covered are recruitment and approval of foster carers, assessment, training and support, allegations, placement arrangements and introductions (Scottish Office, 1997).

The principal statute in relation to adoption is the Adoption (Scotland) Act 1978 (McNeill, 2000). Among other things, this defines adoption and its effects, specifies who may adopt and sets out requirements for court procedures (further detailed in associated Rules of Court). At the time of writing, only a married couple or a single person may adopt. Unmarried heterosexual or gay couples may not adopt, although removal of this restriction is being considered for the English Adoption and Children Bill in order to widen the availability of adoption for children.

In the majority of cases, birth parents give their consent to adoption. However, some do not consent and some actively oppose adoption. The consent of birth parents may be dispensed with by the court on one or more of four grounds, which may be summarised as follows (BAAF, 2001a). The parent:
• is not known, cannot be found or is incapable of giving agreement;
• is withholding consent unreasonably;

- has persistently failed without reasonable cause to fulfil parental responsibilities;
- has seriously ill-treated the child and is unlikely to have the child returned.

It is possible for a court to make a Freeing Order. This means that the matter of parental consent for adoption is dealt with separately from the question of adoption itself, either by obtaining parental agreement or by satisfying the sheriff that such agreement should be dispensed with. The child thereby becomes "free for adoption" and the adoption agency is then able to place a child with adopters or help existing carers apply to adopt without anxiety that parents may change their mind or a court not accept a request to dispense with parental agreement (Lambert *et al*, 1990; McNeill, 2000).

All adoption agencies (local authorities or voluntary) that assess adopters must have an adoption panel. The functions of the panel are to consider the information about adopters and children, then make recommendations to the agency about the approval of adopters and the suitability of a proposed placement for a particular child (Scottish Office, 1997, Volume 3; BAAF, 2001a).

The Adoption (Scotland) Act 1978 was amended by the Children (Scotland) Act 1995 in various ways. For instance, it required adoption agencies to provide a post-adoption support service, while all local authorities must make available adoption allowances, which are payable subject to criteria related to the child or family circumstances and income. When making decisions about adoption, courts and agencies must consider as the paramount consideration the need to safeguard and promote the welfare of the child throughout the child's life. They shall also take into account the child's views 'so far as is practicable' (section 6) (BAAF, 2001a).

Intercountry adoption is regulated under the Adoption (Intercountry Aspects) Act 1999. This requires that the same adoption practice and standards with regard to information, assessment and support be applied to intercountry adoption as to domestic adoption.

During the 1990s a worldwide trend in adoption was towards "openness". Earlier policy and practice had normally severed any knowledge by birth parents about their child's whereabouts or progress following adoption. Also birth parents and adopters did not meet. This secrecy and segregation has now been opened up in various ways. In particular, birth parents quite often now meet adopters before the adoption, while infrequent ongoing but indirect contact by exchanging letters, cards and photos has become common, although face-to-face contact remains rare. The law neither encourages nor discourages contact, which operates at the discretion of adopters. The Children (Scotland) Act 1995 Guidance does however, promote certain forms of openness, such as involving birth parents in meeting prospective adopters, though it is more guarded on post-adoption contact (Scottish Office Volume 3, pp 12 & 39). The law does promote secrecy in one respect by stating that the records of the adoption hearing must be kept confidentially at Register House in Edinburgh for 100 years, except that an adopted person may have access on reaching the age of 17.[3]

In 2002 a set of National Care Standards were issued, including one each covering (i) adoption and (ii) foster care and family placement services (Scottish Executive, 2002a, b). The Standards are to be used by the Scottish Commission for the Regular of Care when registering and inspecting services. The 32 Adoption Standards apply to adopted people (1–12), birth families (13–17), prospective and actual adoptive parents (18–31) and adoption agencies (32). The 13 Fostering Standards relate to services for children (1–4), services for foster carers (5–12) and management and staffing (13).

The main principles informing both sets of Standards are:
- dignity;
- privacy;
- choice;
- safety;
- realising potential;
- equality and diversity.

---

[3] A few other exceptional circumstances are included in the Act.

The legal system

In most countries, children for whom judicial action may be required are dealt with by a court. Often there are separate types of court for dealing with child protection and the child's behaviour (chiefly crimes), such as the family and youth courts respectively in England and Wales (Hallett *et al*, 1998; Pitts, 2001). In Scotland, however, decisions about whether compulsory measures are required are made by Children's Hearings, informal tribunals which have the power to make compulsory disposals (Martin *et al*, 1981; Cowperthwaite, 1988; Lockyer and Stone, 1998; Kearney, 2000). Three lay people (children's panel members) make the decision at the Hearing and one of them acts as chair. Panel members are not legally qualified, but ordinary members of the public who have received relevant training. The main disposal they can make is a supervision requirement, which can include a condition that the child resides in a particular place, such as a foster home. Hearings deal with any cause for concern that might require compulsory action, whether that involves the child's need for "care and protection" or the child's behaviour (notably offences and school non-attendance).[4] When making decisions, the Children's Hearing has the child's best interests as its primary consideration, although with respect to offences it should also take into account public safety (section 16(5)). Hearings also review supervision cases at least once a year.

Besides the lay Hearings, sheriff courts also deal with some cases. If facts are disputed (a minority of cases), the case must go to court for proof, after which it returns to the Hearing to make a disposal. The courts also deal with emergency child protection cases and appeals. Most significantly for present purposes, only a sheriff may make an adoption order or take the intermediate step of freeing a child for adoption. Adoption cases may be dealt with in the sheriff's chambers, rather than in full court. When local authorities plan adoption for a child who is subject to a supervision requirement, it is necessary for a Children's Hearing to be held before an application is made to the sheriff, so that the

---

[4] The specific grounds for referral to Children's Hearings are set out in section 52(2) of the Children (Scotland) Act 1995.

panel members can consider the plan. When a local authority decides to move towards a PRO, freeing or adoption for a child on supervision, they must request a Review Hearing where the panel can discuss the plan (section 73). If the Hearing does not approve of an adoption plan, the authority may still go ahead, but must formally reconsider within 28 days and must notify the reporter. The Hearing must make advice to the local authority (informing the child and relevant persons) and this must be put in a written report (Scottish Office, 1997).

Fostering in Scotland

Scotland has a strong and long tradition of fostering. Its history reveals the lengthy roots of modern concerns (e.g. about recruiting enough foster carers, the role of money, the best ways of ensuring proper standards of care). State involvement in substitute family care in Scotland originated in Poor Law arrangements to "board out" children with families. Under the Poor Law Act of 1579, it was possible for 'a beggar's bairns' to be looked after by a person of 'honest estate' by direction of a magistrate or justice (Ferguson 1948, pp 286–7). By the early 19th Century it had become common for larger urban parishes to board out the majority of children who were orphaned or deserted or whose parents were in poorhouses (Lamond, 1892). Indeed, the Scottish system inspired similar developments in England (Heywood, 1978; Levitt, 1988). Typically children from urban areas were placed with "guardians" in the countryside. This was seen to be not only physically healthier, with more wholesome food available, but also socially desirable by protecting the children from contamination and "demoralisation" by adults in the poorhouse. As a contemporary wrote:

The practice of boarding out the pauper children with cottars in country and at the seaside is one of the peculiar and redeeming features of the Scottish system. (Lamond, 1892, p 261)

In Glasgow during the later 19th Century about 300–400 children were boarded out at any one time. Some were placed 'as far removed as possible from the evil influences of city life' (p 264).

As Abrams (2001) has written, it was often the aim 'to give children a fresh start with new identities', but 'the experience of being a boarded-out child could be fraught with tensions and anxieties which were, in no small part, the result of being denied information about biological parenthood and social origins' (p 212). The strong emphasis on a clean break from disapproved parents still has some echoes today, but on the whole it is at odds with a current recognition of the importance to children of continuity. As we shall see later in the book, fostered children are now usually encouraged to have contact with their birth families. In adoption, too, awareness of origins is now promoted, while ongoing contact is no longer exceptional. Also there is now greater understanding of the role of poverty and family history in poor parenting.

The selection of carers in Victorian times was not systematic and inspection visits were infrequent (McKay, 1907; Ferguson, 1948). Initially placements were only made with parental consent; the alternatives were for children to stay in workhouses with their parents or for the family to receive no financial support. As time went by, there was a greater preparedness to override parental wishes and even to stop contact (Levitt, 1988), measures which were to be echoed over a century later in the very different context of the 1980s. Inspection reports stated that most of the fostered children appeared happy and certainly more so than children in poorhouses. Among the other outcome criteria used at the time were children entering respectable jobs, learning new habits and melting into the population (Lamond, 1892; Ferguson, 1948). There were accounts of ill-treatment, though. Interestingly, then as now, worries were expressed about the low educational input children were thought to receive in foster homes (Ferguson, 1948). Critics also wondered if families were more interested in the allowances they received for upkeep and clothing than the children themselves (Hill *et al*, 1991). The Children Act 1908 tightened up the fostering inspection system with a view to preventing families "baby farming", i.e. taking in many children for the income (Levitt, 1988).

Recurrent concerns about the quality of care given by some carers eventually led to the establishment of children's departments in Scotland from 1948 onwards. These were charged with more careful assessment of foster carers, more frequent monitoring and regular reviews (Levitt, 1988; Murphy, 1992; Holman, 1996). Staff were increasingly likely to have a professional social work qualification.

After 1970, local authority duties towards looked after children and adoption passed to generic social work departments. Since the Children (Scotland) Act 1995, local authorities have taken a more corporate approach, but social work services retain the primary responsibility for dealing with cases day to day. Apart from a small number of babies who may be placed directly with adopters, children who cannot be looked after by their birth families usually go either to foster care or residential care (children's homes, residential units and schools). Overall the total numbers in foster and residential care fell considerably in the 1980s, but there has been a small rise since 1993 (Scottish Executive, 2001; NCH, 2002):

1988	5,264
1993	4,698
1999	4,939
2000	4,766

This represents just over four per 1,000 of the population aged 0–17. In Glasgow the numbers grew by nearly 20 per cent between 1997 and 2000. These are the numbers at any one time: evidently the numbers of children who become looked after during the course of any one year are larger. About two per cent of fostered children have a minority ethnic background, with the largest group being of mixed parentage (Triseliotis *et al*, 2000).

For some time, the numbers of children in foster care have been growing and the numbers in residential care reducing. The total number of children fostered at any one time grew by a quarter between 1993 and 1999 to more than 3,000 and they now make up nearly two-thirds of those who are looked after in public care (Scottish Office, 1996, 2000). Foster care is therefore now dealing with some young people who were formerly thought to require residential care and who tend to be more testing in their behaviour. The sample of foster children assessed by Minnis *et al* (2001) had the following characteristics:

- 93 per cent had experienced some kind of abuse or neglect;
- 77 per cent had been sexually abused;
- 60 per cent had clinical mental health problems.

Generally residential care caters for young people aged 11 and over, although one in ten are younger than this (Scottish Executive website). Nearly all pre-school children accommodated away from home are fostered, but four-fifths of children and young people in foster care are of school age and slightly more than half are aged 11 and over (Triseliotis *et al*, 2000). Thus although the type of placement is related to age, foster care does provide for large numbers of adolescents. It is important not to generalise about young people's attitudes to foster and residential care. Some have a definite preference for residential settings, because of family loyalties or, conversely, strong disillusion with families. On the other hand, as many have a definite wish to live in a family household (Triseliotis *et al*, 1995a; Hill, 1996).

Children can be fostered for a range of reasons, but the most common include family stress or conflict, abuse and neglect, and parental illness (Convention of Scottish Local Authorities, 2000). They may be accommodated on a voluntary basis (i.e. with parental consent), but somewhat more than half are fostered on a compulsory basis by means of a supervision requirement of the children's hearings (Statistical Bulletin, February 2000).

Local authorities are responsible for recruiting and supporting most foster carers, but voluntary and independent agencies have a growing role. Two strong and linked trends over the last 20 years have been specialisation and professionalisation. Tendencies for foster carers to prefer or be more suited to fostering for particular lengths of time or ages of children have become formalised. Thus about 40 per cent concentrate on placements of less than three months (emergency, respite, pre-adoption and short-term). About a quarter foster adolescents, typically for one to two years (Triseliotis *et al*, 2000). From the 1970s onwards, agencies developed separate specialist schemes, especially to cater for teenagers or children with disabilities. Carers received a fee or salary in addition to the usual allowance, as well as extra training and support. In turn they were expected to care for more challenging children and take on more "treatment", family support or administrative tasks. The Community Alternative Placement Scheme in Glasgow (run by NCH) was a particularly innovative project, which has enabled young people to live in the community who would otherwise be in secure accommodation or residential school. Some have thrived, though others had poorer outcomes (Walker *et al*, 2002).

A different trend in the 1990s was to make all the carers in the same authority professional, in recognition of the complex tasks undertaken **(Ramsay, 1996)**. Not only do the children require care and attention, but also increasingly foster carers take on support roles with birth family members. A number of authorities now make differential payments according to the qualifications and skills of the carers rather than the characteristics of the child.

Local authorities now usually assign a link or support worker to each foster family, with a role complementary to that of the social worker responsible for the child and birth family. Generally, link workers are very highly regarded by foster carers, children's workers somewhat less so and the administrative aspects of local authorities less still (Triseliotis *et al*, 2000).

A growing concern in the 1990s was the increase in allegations of child abuse made against foster carers (Bray and Minty, 2001). Agencies now usually prepare carers for "safe caring", which entails examining and adjusting the details of everyday life to avoid situations where children could be harmed or might make an allegation (Rose and Savage, 1999; Brown, 2002).

Adoption in Scotland

Informally, adoption has existed for centuries and often fostering arrangements shaded into adoption. Out of 268 children boarded out by the Barony Parish between 1884 and 1889, two were reported as having been adopted by their guardians (Lamond, 1892).

The first adoption statute for Scotland was enacted in 1930. This introduced the total transfer of legal parenthood. At the time, adoption tended to be a semi-secret event and status, on account of the stigma associated with unmarried parenthood and to some degree adoptive parenthood. Hence, birth families did not know where their adopted child had gone to and the adoptive records were made confidential. However, Scotland was unusual at that time in enabling adopted people to see their records and obtain a copy of their original birth certificate once they reached adulthood, with the potential to seek out their birth families from the identifying information there (Triseliotis, 1973). According to Triseliotis (1980), this right is a significant means of enabling adopted people to establish a sense of identity, completeness and citizenship. He argued that the primary motivation for most people was curiosity, although this might be enhanced by particular stresses or trigger events. In practice, few people took up this option, partly because they were not always aware of their entitlement to do so, but the numbers increased as a result of publicity about the introduction of similar rights in England. The first Adoption Act also forbade payments to adopters, because of fears that otherwise people would take in children mainly for the money. This restriction remained until the introduction of adoption allowances in the 1980s (Scottish Association for the Adoption of Children, 1983; Hill *et al*, 1989).

Adoption can take place within the family, as when a step-parent or grandparents adopt. This has been discouraged by professionals as it is seen to disguise or distort family relationships and may exclude a birth parent, but adoptions by relatives are nevertheless the most common form of adoption, since the family members concerned see it as providing legal security and confirming the status of the relative or step-parent who is adopting. Relative adoptions do not need to be arranged by an agency, although a report is required by a local authority (**Phillips, 1992**).

Applications to adopt by non-relatives must be approved by a local authority or voluntary adoption agency, of which there are several in Central Scotland. In 1999, just over 200 adoption applications were made through local authorities (just over 150) and voluntary agencies (just under 50) (Scottish Executive, 2002). All but a few of each year's applications for adoption are granted. The number of children adopted each year is thus much smaller than those fostered. Consequently most children's social workers have much less experience of adoption than fostering.

The number of freeing orders granted rose by a half from 70 to 116 between 1996 and 2000. Whereas 17 per cent of freeing applications did not succeed in 1996, this was true for only three per cent of applications in 2000 (Scottish Executive, 2002).

Since the 1960s, there has been a sharp reduction in the numbers of babies placed for adoption by lone mothers, due to a number of factors related to changed attitudes to single parenthood, more support and contraception. It has also become more common for children to be adopted from foster and residential care, although still only a small minority of these. As a result of these trends, the ages of children at adoption have been rising. In 1999 only one in five were babies (aged under one year). The majority were aged under five, but 40 per cent were of school age, which runs counter to the still popular image of adoption as associated with infancy.

Over the last 20 years an increased proportion of adoptions has been without parental agreement and a number are now actively contested. This has usually occurred when the local authority believes that the parents are not capable of caring for the child adequately or safely, despite help to change (Lambert *et al*, 1990; Hill *et al*, 1993).

Although many childless couples would gladly adopt a healthy infant, the number of people willing and able to adopt looked after children is much lower, on account of their age, difficult histories and often educational or behavioural problems. A BAAF survey of 28 of the 32 Scottish local authorities revealed that somewhat over 600 children were registered as requiring a permanent placement (46 per cent for adoption and 54 per cent some other kind of permanent placement). Thus adoption and fostering were equal options for permanent placement. Two-hundred-and-seventy-eight children were waiting for adoption and during 1999–2000 somewhat fewer new families were approved for adoption (244). Connected with this shortfall, a significant number of children waited over 12 months for a placement, especially among the over five years age group. A growing number of children were being registered for adoption, but those still waiting for a placement at the year-end also increased (BAAF, 2001b).

About four-fifths of adopters are recruited by local authorities and the remainder by voluntary organisations (BAAF, 2001b). Voluntary agencies tend to specialise, for example with respect to placements for younger children or in Catholic families, and offering post-adoption advice and support. Barnardo's provides a specialist fostering and adoption service for children that local authorities find hard to place and established the Khandan Initiative to recruit carers with Asian backgrounds (**Singh, 1997**; Social Work Services Inspectorate, 1998).

Much effort is required to recruit suitable adopters and there is a high drop-out rate among enquirers (80–90 per cent). Considerable numbers of people are interested in adopting, but relatively few of these "stay the course" from expressing an interest right through to adoption. For example, Glasgow City Council received 285 enquiries about adoption between 1998 and 2000. This led to 85 families attending an information meeting, of whom 30 were approved as adopters (Glasgow City Council, 2001).[5] This pattern may in part result from dissatisfaction with procedures and delays, but probably more important is that many people realise they are not suited to adopt the kinds of children available for adoption, who are mostly older or have disabilities.

Adoption has been promoted by the Government in recent years as the best arrangement for many children who are looked after in public care, when their birth families have little or no prospect of providing a satisfactory long-term home. The respective roles and merits of fostering and adoption have been long debated within the context of changing ideas about children's needs (Thoburn, 1994; Triseliotis, 2002). The next section of this anthology examines some of the principles underpinning service development and placement choices.

---

[5] Annual Review of Children's Services Plan.

Section I
Trends in child placement philosophy

In the last 25 years, the most vibrant approach to services for looked after children has been that of permanency planning, i.e. seeking to ensure that all children have a caring family for life. This was rooted partly in strong values about family life, but also bolstered by research evidence about the crucial importance to children of receiving both current and life-long commitment within a family setting, as well as evidence of the poor outcomes of looked after children. Permanence ideas have been closely related to attachment theory (Howe, 1995).

Permanency planning has emphasised efforts to keep children's stays in state care as short as possible. The ideal has been to return the majority quickly home after a period of help, support or respite, while arranging permanent alternative families for the minority for whom this is not possible or desirable. The latter aspect has put adoption in central place. Fostering has remained the most common option for looked after children and has been given an expanded role to provide not only daily care, but also parental support, life-story or therapeutic help to emotionally damaged children and preparation for moving back home or on to adoption (Triseliotis *et al*, 1995b). Nevertheless much of the key thinking and research until recently focused on adoption rather than fostering – a trend reflected in the journal articles.

In 1980, the journal published a seminal article by **McKay (1980)**. This described a new policy recently introduced in Lothian Region, which set out virtually for the first time in the UK a coherent approach for permanency planning for children aged up to ten years. It was recognised that arrangements for teenagers needed to be different. The paper set out three clear principles in relation to young children in care:

1. All children should grow up with their own parents or permanent substitute parents.
2. Those parents or parental figures should provide at least "good enough care".
3. The child's welfare should be the first consideration in making any plans.

These seemingly simple and uncontentious ideas marked a sharp break with previous practice. From now on, planning should be directed at returning children to their birth parents or placing them for adoption or fostering on a permanent basis within a framework of tight time limits. The hitherto common option of long-term fostering on an open-ended and legally insecure basis was seen as unsatisfactory. The main role for foster care would be to offer time-limited and clearly focused placements with a contract or more enduring "supplementary care" usually for adolescents or disabled children in frequent contact with parents. Drawing on English research evidence about the low chances of children returning home after being away more than six months, the policy entailed intensive work to reunite children within six months if at all possible. Unless there were clear signs of progress in achieving this, plans for an alternative permanent family should be made.

This policy was implemented in Lothian (**O'Hara and Hoggan, 1988**) and influenced to varying degrees most other authorities in Scotland (and elsewhere) during the 1980s. As McKay noted, a key element of the strategy was to recruit foster carers and adopters with a clear understanding of what their roles and timescales should be. There was a greater readiness by local authorities to use legal powers to terminate parental rights (Millham *et al*, 1989), while the introduction of adoption allowances allowed many foster carers to adopt and also assisted smaller number of new families adopting a child or sibling group (Hill *et al*, 1989). Permanency planning, whether it followed the Lothian model or operated somewhat differently, was seen as effective in attracting new types of family willing to offer a permanent home to children and in arranging from more children to be adopted from care (see Section VII in this book). However, across the UK critics of permanency planning argued that it underestimated children's ties with birth families and produced an oppositional rather than partnership stance towards birth parents (Holman, 1988; Harding, 1991; Ryburn, 1994).

Triseliotis (1991) reviewed the position at a time when debates about permanency were at their height. He supported the ideal of permanency in the sense that all children should have a base for life or a family they can call their own. Triseliotis reviewed evidence for the considerable success of permanency planning policies in achieving stable placements for many children with special needs, including some with very challenging behaviour. He noted, however, the strong link between poverty and the circumstances of families who relinquished a child for adoption. Therefore measures to tackle poverty should also be an important strand of policies to ensure all children had a secure future in a family, while some of the expertise and models used to support adoptive families could also be used for work with birth families.

Triseliotis also questioned the rigid use of time limits and ready use of the law to override parental wishes. He challenged especially the notion of a "clean break", which had become central to permanency policies.[1] This was based on the principle that children had to give up their existing family ties if they were to attach themselves effectively to a new family. Triseliotis stressed that, *whenever possible*, adoption should be arranged on a voluntary basis and in a manner that allowed children to retain existing loyalties and identities. Moreover, it was important that the stress on adoption did not sideline fostering as a good option for many children, especially adolescents, which might lead on to adoption through open rather than pre-determined planning. Nevertheless he asserted that in some situations where children have been persistently abused adoption is best for children's safety and well-being, regardless of the amount of help available for the birth family. He warned that the pendulum might swing too far back towards a point where children who could benefit from adoption were not given that opportunity.

Taking up the link between children's services and poverty **Giltinan (1995)** opposed the use of adoption as a generalised solution for lone-parent families on low incomes, as had been advocated by certain "new right" individuals and organisations. He expanded the argument to consider the general impact of market-oriented policies in the welfare state. He welcomed the emphasis on providing services on the basis of consumer wishes, but expressed concern about the apparent view of welfare as a commodity. The shift to more service provision by voluntary organisations on behalf of local authorities had the potential for innovation, but also the risk of agencies having to carry out closely prescribed activities on behalf

---

[1] Sometimes referred to as the "child rescue" approach, which has been a persistent strand in childcare history (Holman, 1988; Hendrick, 1994).

of the state. Giltinan also argued that a radical change was needed in the justice system in Scotland. He suggested that the Children's Hearings system was based on laudable principles (putting children's needs first) and was by and large working well, but the adversarial and time-consuming procedures in courts caused confusion, distress and delays. In 2002, the Justice Department accepted the need to make changes to court situations where children are key witnesses.

As Triseliotis indicated was likely to happen, the trend in child welfare policy in Scotland and the UK during the 1990s was largely to emphasise family support and partnership. Towards the end of the decade **Triseliotis (1998/9)** examined how far "permanency through adoption" was in decline. Both English and Scottish statistics suggested a reduction had taken place in the numbers of children adopted from care in the middle of the decade. He examined various factors contributing to this. They included the legislative shift brought about by the Children Act 1989 in England and Wales and to a considerable degree repeated in the Children (Scotland) Act 1995 towards family support and greater protection of parental rights. Also experience and research had shown that placements for the adoption of older children often had poor outcomes. In some instances, this meant that placements had perhaps been made when the risk of breakdown was too high, but also that the support given to adoptive families taking on very challenging children had not been adequate (see Sections IV and VII of the book). Triseliotis again advocated a balanced and measured approach. Just as he had previously described the dangers of an excessive and inappropriate resort to adoption, now it was important to set alongside this the value and success of adoption for many children.

The late 1990s saw a renewed interest by the UK government in adoption as a route out of public care, with the Prime Minister and his newly established Policy Innovation Unit taking a lead role. Many of the arguments and counter-arguments of the 1980s are being revisited 20 years on (Selwyn and Sturgess, in press).

Fox Harding (1991) characterised the permanency movement as having a paternalist, "state as parent" approach, since at its heart was the view that the state in the form of local authorities should be interventionist to pursue their vision of what was best for looked after children, seeking support from the courts when parents were opposed. Fox Harding outlined three alternative perspectives: *laissez-faire* (minimal state intervention), kinship defenders (supporting birth families) and children's rights (stressing children's participation). While much of the debate about permanency has concerned the respective powers, roles and rights of birth parents and the state, each side has appealed to a notion of children's rights, whether it be entitlements to family life, continuity, identity or long-term belonging. These kinds of rights are based on children's developmental needs, but another kind of right is participatory, i.e. the right to influence decisions affecting oneself. **Hoggan (1991)** argued that it is vital to maximise children's own involvement in plans for their future, but also states that their capacity to do so is in part reliant on "benign adult power" enabling them to do so. She favoured encouraging and helping children to express their wishes and feelings, so they could be taken effectively into consideration in accordance with the Adoption (Scotland) Act 1978. Hoggan supported the use of interactive techniques, exercises and tools for communication with children, but stressed that these should be used to create genuine dialogue and not simply to persuade children to accept adult views. The paper gives examples from preparation groups to show how children's contributions can be facilitated. Hoggan also highlighted the need to handle constructively children's pain from past experiences and the workers' potentially distressing responses, rather than avoid these negative feelings (see also Fahlberg, 1994; Howe, 1995).

Of Fox Harding's four approaches, that of kinship defenders was seen as in direct opposition to permanency planning and indeed these two positions prompted her initial analysis of the arguments and evidence underlying tensions in child welfare policy (Fox Harding, 1982). During the 1990s, the term "family support" came to represent the kinds of practical measures that kinship defenders advocated. This entailed policies prioritising assistance to birth families so they could continue to provide a permanent family for their children, or resume doing so. Backing from both central and local government was fortified by reactions against what were seen as excessively zealous and legalistic approaches to child protection, which resulted in numerous investigations but little help being offered to families, whether or not the concerns about possible abuse were substantiated (Department of Health, 1995; Canavan *et al*, 2000). This led to "refocusing" towards more supportive services. A linked notion was that of partnership, which suggested that local authorities should be less confrontational and seek to work openly and jointly with parents. Partnership is not mentioned in the Scottish legislation, but does feature in the preceding White paper (Social Work Services Group, 1993) and in the Guidance to the Children (Scotland) Act 1995. Among the sections of the Act that promote "partnership" are those requiring local authorities to consider parental views when making decisions and to promote parental relations and contact with their children (see also **Tisdall and Plumtree, 1997**).

Hill (2000) identified four dimensions of partnership between authorities and parents: communication, decision-making, contact arrangements with the child and shared care. He examined British research evidence to show the persistence of obstacles to co-operation and failures to tackle or resolve differences. On the other hand, several trends did mark progress towards a more partnership approach. These included a move towards greater involvement of parents in decision-making, increased contact between parents and their children in foster homes, and the growth in post-adoption contact, mainly indirect. Hill noted the importance of taking a long-term view, since initial contacts between workers and families can establish patterns that favour or inhibit open communication and participative decision-making. Echoing the reservations expressed by Triseliotis about "clean breaks", Hill also observed that even when parents prove unable to carry out certain parental functions, notably full-time care, it remains important to consider what other roles they can still usefully perform in the child's best interests. Similarly, decision-making and planning should not be seen as simply divided into the extremes of joint or unilateral, because several intermediate forms of involvement are possible according to the need and circumstances. The most important thing is that all concerned acknowledge openly what kind of co-operation is desirable and consistent with legal requirements. Hill concluded that the term partnership may disguise and simplify complex interactions and differences in perspective, so that it may be helpful to think of agencies, professionals and carers "working at" ways of "working together" with birth parents and other family members.

An important concept that gained currency around the turn of the millennium was that of resilience. Writing in Ireland, Gilligan (1997) suggested that permanency planning, especially insofar as it was identified with adoption, was not relevant to the great majority of children and young people in care, whose age, wishes and/or family loyalties precluded adoption. Drawing on research from psychology and psychiatry on resilience, he argued that this provided a framework for young people in foster and residential care which was both widely applicable and optimistic in outlook. The associated ideas have been influential in Scotland (Daniel *et al*, 1999b).

A resilience approach shares with permanency planning a recognition of the deep and damaging impact on children of loss and negative parenting, and the importance for children to have secure attachments. However, it also emphasises children's capacities to overcome adversity by a combination of personal strengths and external supports. While some resilient children benefit from largely innate characteristics, it is also possible for children to learn coping skills and for adults to identify and capitalise on children's specific abilities and interests (Gilligan, 2001). Whereas permanency planning and attachment theory have tended to focus on children's needs for a strong positive relationship with one or two crucial adults, a resilience approach pays much attention – *in addition* – to children's talents and active roles, the importance of informal support networks and the centrality in children's lives of school as a venue for both academic and social learning and support. Such ideas promote a wide, holistic perspective on foster care. They are also compatible with adoption. As Clarke and Clarke (2000) observed, adoption is one of the most powerful means of fostering resilience in the sense of triumph over adversity. It offers a radical environmental change, not only of family but of home and community, which can give new opportunities children with traumatic birth parental treatment.

1 Planning for permanent placement

Margaret McKay

This article was first published in Adoption & Fostering *99:1, 1980.*

At a time when there is increasing emphasis on homefinding, with the appointment in many areas of specialist childcare resource workers, it is important to clarify what we mean by fostering and to place substitute home-finding in the context of planning for children. In particular there is a need for a redefinition of long-term fostering, which for too long has been a form of care fraught with insecurity and uncertainty for children. This paper is a contribution to the current examination of childcare practice based on work in East Lothian; a more comprehensive, descriptive analysis of substitute family care is contained in *Fostering in the 70s and Beyond*, published by the Association of British Adoption and Fostering Agencies (ABAFA, now BAAF, 1977).

In many areas up and down the country there seems to be agreement that more foster parents are needed. Foster parents to do what? For whom? For how long? With what aim in mind? Unless we are able to define the nature and tasks of fostering then our efforts in the recruitment, assessment, and support of substitute families will be at best inconsistent, at worst counterproductive. Probably we have all encountered situations where the foster family's understanding of its role conflicted with the worker's expectations. Most commonly these differences in perception revolve around the question of plans for the children and contact with the natural parents.

For example, long-term fostering may be seen by the social worker as open-ended and impermanent, with a plan of return home sometime hovering on the horizon. The foster parents, however, may be committed to retaining the child as a permanent member of their family. Alternatively the social worker may recognise that the child is unlikely ever to return home and hope to extend the fostering placement indefinitely because the child has settled down happily. The foster parents in turn initially understood that they would be providing short-term, temporary care and never intended to add permanently to their family. But the longer the placement continues the more difficult it becomes for them to assert their own rights and needs. The child in both situations experiences insecurity and a fluctuating level of commitment. It is not surprising that so many long-term placements eventually collapse under the strain of uncertainty and ambivalence.

The principles

Before embarking on substitute home-finding we need to make explicit the principles and philosophy which underlie our work with children in care, namely:

1 No child should grow up without people whom he looks on as his parents, either his own natural parents or permanent parent substitutes.
2 His parents (or parent figures) must be able to provide 'good enough care' (Pringle, 1974); to meet his need for love, security and responsibility appropriate to his stage of development, and stimulation.
3 In planning for children in care the local authority should give first consideration to the need to safeguard and promote the welfare of the child throughout his childhood (Children Act 1975, section 59).

Consequences for practice

If we accept these principles, what are the consequences for practice and the provision of services?

1 We commit ourselves to family-based care for a child, either in his own family, or in a substitute home. We recognise the difference between biological and psychological parenting and acknowledge that over time the people who care for a child come to be viewed by him as his parents. The younger the child, the more quickly will this happen.
2 We develop skills (including using the skills of others) in assessing a child's needs, which will vary in emphasis according to his age and previous experiences. We must be able to assess whether his natural parents or parent substitutes can meet his needs and identify what assistance they require to do so. Equally, we are prepared to help parents and children to separate permanently when it is clear that they have no future together.

3   We acknowledge that conflicts of interest can arise between the needs of parents and the needs of children and that in resolving any such conflict the long-term welfare of the child must be our first consideration. We take account of the wishes and feelings of the child when planning his future.

Foster care and home-finding

Where and how do foster care and substitute home-finding fit into the above framework of services for children in care? Firstly, they serve as a time-limited, task-focused, therapeutic service for children and their natural families. The aim is either to effect rehabilitation of children with their families by preserving existing meaningful relationships, helping to repair and restore damaged relationships, or in situations where rehabilitation is unlikely or impossible to help natural parents and children to separate from each other and to move on to new unions, including permanent substitute care.

Foster parents undertaking this short-term contract work are assuming a caring role towards the child but not a full parental role. They need to be closely involved in the plans for the child and the nature and degree of their involvement with parents must be clearly stated at the outset. Only families able to include natural parents, to co-operate in an agreed plan for the child, and to manage the pain of helping parents and children separate where necessary should be engaged in this task. Other essential features of such foster care are that the families involved can engage in a contract based on partnership with the department and that they perceive their task as contributing to the working out of the plans for the child's future. The department for its part must be active in the partnership, formulating and maintaining the contract and ensuring that short-term placements do not drift on through lack of decisions about the next step for children in care.

Secondly, there is a need for permanent substitute families (a description which encompasses adoptive homes and long-term foster homes). Families in this category assume a full parental role but have the capacity to tolerate legal uncertainties where either parental consent to adoption is withheld and where the time limit provisions of the Children Act

1975 would apply, or where for financial reasons full legal adoption is not feasible. In these situations child, substitute family and local authority are committed to ensuring that the child remains with his substitute parents. An example might be a case where children had experienced multiple admissions to care and it had been impossible to stabilise the natural family environment despite practical and counselling help. Another example might be the child in care whose parents' stated intentions of receiving him home were not translated into reality, again even though they had been given help. Normally children would only move on to permanent substitute homes after a period spent working out their future in a contract foster family or short-term residential care.

Thirdly, foster parents are required who can provide supplementary care for children who still have meaningful contacts with parents who are unable to accept full responsibility for them. These are cases where supplementary parenting on a long-term basis is necessary. For example, there is the single parent whose children are in care on a five-day or weekend basis; the severely handicapped or sick parents; the teenager who needs to be away from home but who identifies strongly with his natural family and is able to take the initiative in maintaining the links; the family with a handicapped child where regular relief breaks are required. This form of care is only appropriate for families in close, regular contact.

Deciding which plan

How do we decide which form of substitute care a child needs when? We decide by linking our knowledge of the needs of children with the evidence of what happens to children in care and planning our intervention accordingly. Rowe and Lambert's study *Children who Wait* (1973) showed that once a child has been in care for more than six months his chances of returning home to his natural family reduce to one in four. After two years in care the chance of return home is minimal. We need to integrate this evidence into our practice and share with parents the knowledge that the work done in the six months following reception into care is crucial if rehabilitation is to be effected. We need to invest resources of time and skill in working with parents, children and contract foster parents during that vital period and we need a rigorous, positive review at the six months stage to evaluate the progress made and to begin formulating alternative plans for children if there is no evidence of real progress towards returning home.

Obviously the suggested timescale of six months to return children home is meant as a framework and not a rigid strait-jacket. Factors such as the age of the child at admission to care, previous separations, the quality and quantity of parental contact whilst in care have to be weighed when assessing the likelihood of return home. It is important to remember, however, that a preschool child out of contact with his natural parents for even a short time will begin to form significant attachments to the acting parent figures. Another point to bear in mind is that separating parents and children permanently arouses strong feelings of pain and perhaps guilt in all of us. In order to deal with these inner feelings when the child's welfare requires such separation, we need to feel confident that all reasonable measures to reunite parent and child have been taken. This is another reason for working intensively in the period following admission to care.

Rowe and Lambert's study and Newman and Mackintosh's *A Roof Over their Heads* (1975), which was carried out locally, demonstrated that there are significant numbers of children in care who have little or no contact with their natural families. These are the children for whom long-term foster parents have traditionally been sought. What are we asking children and long-term foster parents to do in these situations? We are asking them to simulate the relationship of parents and children but without making a full, lasting commitment to each other; to assume a full parental role without the backing either of legal security or a firm decision about the permanency of the placement from ourselves. How does one meet a child's need for security in circumstances of such ambivalence?

In conclusion, therefore, our recruitment of foster parents should be informed by the needs of children. We should be seeking:

a) short-term foster families who can work as part of a team to an agreed plan for the children, involving the natural parents;

b) permanent substitute families for those children who are unlikely to return home even though this fact may not be acknowledged by their natural families;

c) foster parents who can supplement parenting for natural parents on an interim or longer term basis according to need. Essential prerequisites of such placements are the existence of a real relationship between natural parents and child and the maintenance of close links over time.

References

Association of British Adoption and Fostering Agencies (October 1977), *Fostering in the 70s and Beyond*, London: ABAFA.

Newman N and Mackintosh H (1975) *A Roof Over their Heads*, Edinburgh: University of Edinburgh, School of Social Administration.

Pringle M K (1974) *The Needs of Children*, London: Hutchinson.

Rowe J and Lambert L (1973) *Children who Wait*, London: Association of British Adoption Agencies.

2 Perceptions of permanence

John Triseliotis

This article was first published in Adoption & Fostering *15:4, 1991.*

It is tempting to start by saying that permanency through adoption for children with special needs is on the defensive, and that adoption policy and practice are at the crossroads because of the challenges they face. The fact is that adoption, as an institution, has always been at the crossroads, as it mirrors the society within which it is practised. Because society is not static but changes all the time, so adoption changes and adapts to new needs and challenges. For example, over the last 20 or so years there have been radical changes in patterns of living, including changes in personal, sexual, couple and family relationships. What is understood by the concept of family has been re-defined to take account of diverse life-styles, divorce, reconstitution and single parenthood. These changes are here to stay and adoption has had to respond to them.

In considering the various ways in which families are constituted now, and how atypical they are of our traditional image of the family, it is hard not to claim that adoptive parenthood has been a pace-setter in this direction. Psychological parenting is no longer confined largely to adoption but is becoming far more common, along with step-parenting and parenting through various forms of assisted reproduction.

Changes in personal and social relationships have always been the main dynamic underlining the evolution of the practice of adoption throughout history. Had I been writing on this topic five years ago, I might have been tempted to say that, for reasons that have not escaped you, adoption as an institution was moving towards its sunset. Permanence through adoption, for children with special needs, was then seen as the final remnant of what was once a big field of social work policy and practice. The end of this final form of adoption was expected to come with the provision of better preventive and supportive services to families to ensure permanence for children within their own families.

Two new issues have surfaced in the meantime, however, to give adoption a new dimension. Open adoption, which was previously characteristic of mainly non-European cultures, is gradually coming into prominence, along with intercountry adoption which Britain, compared to some other countries, resisted for a long time. Concepts of permanence cannot be examined in isolation from these other recent developments.

The concept of permanence

There is no agreed definition of the concept of permanence. Perceptions, therefore, are bound to vary. Different protagonists, depending on the ideologies and value positions they hold about the place of the family and the role of the state in relation to families and children, place different emphases on what is good for families and children. Polarised positions between the so-called "defenders of the family" and those who are perceived as "savers of children" can only delay the development of an agreed and coherent theoretical framework, based mainly on what empirically is known to be good for children. Insights gained from empirical studies can only illuminate part of the debate because research is still lacking in many areas of practice. Some things we will also never know about because of the ethical objections to certain types of research involving human beings. Neither can the ethical dilemmas surrounding some of the issues be resolved totally by empiricism. For example, can permanence outside the family of origin be justified solely on the grounds that it works? Or would, for example, the moral issues surrounding inter-country adoptions disappear, if research were to show that the children eventually do well or even very well?

It could be reasonably argued that in a world of instability with high divorce rates, marital reconstitution, step-parenting and a large number of single-parent families, it is somewhat paradoxical to talk of permanence for children coming into public care. Thus the concept of permanence can only be examined in relative terms and in the context of the society within which it is being pursued. At the same time, when planning for children who have already experienced a chequered background, there is perhaps an extra responsibility to ensure, if not guarantee, an added form of stability in their lives.

My own studies have led me to define permanency in practical terms, these being to provide each child with a base in life or a family they can call their own, and more hopefully a family for life (Triseliotis, 1983; Triseliotis and Russell, 1984).

Studies have been showing that the difference between those who manage to cope in adult life and those who don't is closely related to the kind of support systems they continue to enjoy and whether or not they have a base in life they can call their own and turn to for practical and emotional support when needed. This applies even more so to individuals who have spent a large part of their childhood in public care. Our own studies have shown that those who had no birth families to return to, but were fortunate to secure relative permanence within foster or adoptive homes, fared infinitely better in adult life compared to those who left the care system with no such base. This empirical reality is one of the concepts which underpins the policy to secure permanence for children with special needs.

Few would disagree that it is in every child's interests that a strenuous effort is made to achieve permanence first and foremost within the child's own family and country of origin, where biological and psychological parenting, including ethnic identification, can occur simultaneously. Where this is not possible, and in the light of what has been said earlier, permanence may have to be pursued outside the family of origin. It would be hard to argue that everything possible was done to achieve permanence within their own families for all the children with special needs who have been adopted over the last two decades. For many though, adoption has provided the base which was missing from their lives.

Whether permanence for special needs children is on the defensive or not it is difficult to say. It is proper, though, that after 20 or so years we take stock and look at both the successes and blemishes. In the following pages an attempt will be made to identify the various forces that gave the impetus to the adoption of children with special needs, examine the permanency movement's achievements and challenges, and briefly look at outcomes and the future.

The forces which gave the impetus to the adoption of children with special needs

A number of events seem to have coincided in the early 1970s to stimulate interest in permanence through adoption for children with special needs. First, the dwindling number of babies being available for adoption and, second, the realisation that there were large numbers of children in public care whose families were unable to have them back or who had no families to return to. Neither were there any realistic plans for the future of these children. Attention then was drawn to the needs of these children for continuity of care and for a family to call their own. It is doubtful, though, whether this new "move" would have taken place if it wasn't for the declining number of baby adoptions.

The third factor was an empirical one. Besides research, already referred to, concerning the plight in adult life of those who were formerly in public care, and who grew up in unstable arrangements, two other types of studies provided added impetus and optimism. First, a small but increasing number of studies were beginning to demonstrate the reversibility of early psychological trauma which came about through separations and deprivations. In other words, that children could overcome early adversities, provided suitable new conditions could be ensured (Kadushin, 1970; Clarke and Clarke, 1976; Triseliotis and Russell, 1984; Bohman and Sigvardsson, 1980). Second, that psychological parenting such as adoption and long-term fostering were a reality. Those who matter to children are generally the people who bring them up and not necessarily those who give birth to them (Triseliotis and Russell, 1984; Hill *et al*, 1989).

In this new type of adoption, the future psychological well-being of these children was dependent, not only on the accomplishment by adoptive parents of the traditional tasks associated with adoption, but adoptive parents were now expected to take on a treatment type role with many of the children.

If Britain responded to the decline in baby adoption by going all out for securing adoptive families for older children and children with disabilities that were previously thought unadoptable, a number of countries on the continent of Europe responded by turning mainly towards intercountry adoptions. It can be assumed that older children and those with disabilities or learning difficulties with no birth families to return to were either found long-term foster homes or kept in residential homes. This may be a somewhat simplified picture, but if the adoption statistics coming out of these countries are correct, then the adoption of own-country children with special needs has hardly featured in recent years. One explanation of why intercountry adoption did not develop in similar numbers in Britain, as on the continent, was possibly the stance taken by many black and white social work practitioners, the prohibition of non-agency adoptions and stricter immigration laws. A second explanation is the close links maintained by researchers, trainers and practitioners in Britain with the USA. It was the USA where the first ideas and service programmes for children with special needs were developed and these quickly crossed the Atlantic. Though the United States were pioneers in this field, eventually they followed a middle path to that of Britain and the continent of Europe by paying attention to both children with special needs and to intercountry adoptions.

Achievements and challenges

After more than a decade of pursuing a policy of permanency through adoption for children with special needs, there have been some astounding successes, but equally challenges and blemishes.

1 Achievements

Families for life
The policies formulated and the practices developed seem to have had considerable success. If studies are right, within a period of three to five years following placement, something like eight out of every ten children with special needs seem to stabilise with their new families (Thoburn and Rowe, 1988; Borland *et al*, 1991). This may not be a long enough period to judge outcomes. As we shall also see later these figures hide significant variations in outcome, depending on age at placement, and sometimes on the agency making the placement. On the earlier definition of permanency, these children were provided with a possible base in life. This has not been achieved easily and the cost to some families has been consider-

able. We are not talking about older children only, but children displaying serious emotional and behavioural problems, children who have been physically or sexually abused, children with learning and physical disabilities and children who are HIV positive. For a variety of reasons, today's "special needs" displayed by children who need new families appear more intense and intractable compared to those of ten or 15 years ago. The question arises as to whether we have reached the limits of what can reasonably be expected of permanent new families, without a much more comprehensive network of supportive treatment-oriented services being made available.

A body of new knowledge and expertise

As a result of the challenge to place children with special needs with new families, childcare practitioners have developed a large body of new knowledge and expertise covering the preparation, assessment and post-placement support of new families and of the children involved, using both individual and group methods. This body of knowledge and expertise is now being recognised more widely and is being transferred to other areas of childcare work. The permanency movement has also demonstrated what can be achieved by agencies who develop coherent policies with accompanying services in this area.

Empowerment and partnership

A less recognised achievement is the realisation that through organised, explicit and collaborative forms of preparation and assessment, adoption workers have provided 'the script for the expected behaviour for adoptive parenthood' (see also Kirk, 1987). The role of adoptive parents and the parenthood tasks to be carried out were not only better defined, but an explanation for the rationale behind them was also offered. This has included information and help to adoptive parents to understand and use child development theory, particularly as it emerged from the studies of separated children. This was an empowering approach and far removed from the "all powerful" adoption social worker image. Adoptive parents were being prepared, trained and supported to become their own experts within realistic limits. As a result a climate of increased partnership began to develop between adoption workers and adoptive parents well before the word "partnership" became fashionable in social work. This type of relationship formed the background against which post-placement support was provided. I am aware that this shift in practice is not yet uniform across the country. Far from being complacent, we have to be reminded that some applicants still complain of long waits to obtain a response or to be prepared/assessed. Worse is the way that non-accepted applicants are left with little or no support following a long period of preparation/ assessment.

Intensified rehabilitation efforts

Because of the need to make the case before the courts to free some children for adoption, studies suggest that after about the mid-1980s the pursuit of permanence sharpened, and efforts for the rehabilitation of children with their own families intensified (Lambert et al, 1990).

2 Challenges

A number of recent challenges seem also to have put the pursuit of perm-anency outside the family of origin on the defensive. These challenges have to do with the legitimacy of adoption, the setting of time limits and the clean-break approach, and the role of the birth parents.

The legitimacy of adoption

The first challenge concerns the legitimacy of adoption for children who enter public care without their parents having originally asked for adop-tion. As an example, approximately 40 per cent of children adopted each year in Scotland, England and Wales have been in public care. In England the percentage leaving care through adoption has been rising since the late 1970s. The critics of adoption argue that this is because not enough is being done to enable children to stay or return to their families of birth.

Some critics also contrast the attention being paid to children with special needs for new families, including the pre-placement and post-placement support offered, with the negligible help offered to children and their families before and during admission to care or following return home from public care. The payment of adoption allowances, to secure permanence for children with "special needs", is also quoted as an example which has exposed the weakness of general social provision for

39

ordinary families and children. If similar allowances and attention were paid to birth families, it is argued, these might have helped to keep families and children together.

The legitimacy of adoption will continue to be challenged so long as much of childcare need is generated as a result of extremes of poverty and homelessness in relation to the rest of the population. The lack of adequate provision and of supportive services undermines the coping resources of many parents. An acceptable policy of child care, and therefore of adoption, has to include adequate resources at the general, the preventive and tertiary levels to enable families to raise their own children, before permanency through adoption can be legitimised. While Teague's (1990) argument that adoption represents a deliberate childcare policy for "ideological mastery" or "social control" is extreme, the critics of adoption have to be taken seriously. Ideological domination are the words used by opposing sides to accuse each other either of excesses in the separation of children from their families or in unfounded professional optimism about the chances of rehabilitation.

The close relationship that exists, though, between poverty and the relinquishment of a child for adoption, whether voluntarily or involuntarily, cannot be dismissed easily. It is mainly improved social conditions that have reduced own country adoption to almost nil in some northern European countries such as Scandinavia and Holland. It is, equally, the extremes of poverty in some Third World countries that force parents to part with or sell their children. If we are serious about children's best interests, then concepts of permanence have to start with permanency in family of origin and country of origin, moving away from a position 'of viewing all children admitted to care as potentially free for adoption'.

The provisions in the Children Act 1989 for support to families are to be welcomed, but the test will be its implementation and how the resourcing of preventive and rehabilitative services will be achieved. It is also the view that, with "child protection" capturing the headlines and resources, little is left for mainstream childcare work. Is it not a paradox that a few dramatic cases of child abuse capture the attention of both the profession and the media, but not the extreme conditions of poverty and homelessness affecting thousands of children?

We have to accept, however, that even in the best regulated societies, of which we are not one, there will always be situations where, irrespective of how much provision there is and how well services are delivered, some parents for personal or social reasons, or most likely for both, will be unable to continue or resume the care of their children. Worst still is the fact that where children are concerned, social workers have to act from how the situation stands now, instead of how it might have been if past mistakes had not been made. The dilemma is how to respond to an existing situation, knowing that to be able to grow up and face the demands of adult life, children require stability, security and continuity of care with a base in life to call their own. They should obviously have the right to attain these conditions within their own families, but in my view they also have a right to achieve permanence with new families, when everything else has failed. The example of the harsh circumstances of children who leave public care without a base in life has already been referred to and does not offer an attractive alternative.

Farmer and Parker (1991) found that one in five children in care were unlikely to return home and long-term arrangements seemed desirable. Furthermore, they found that for 38 per cent of the children return home broke down and the outlook for second and third attempts was not good.

Obviously we have to satisfy ourselves that the children and their families had the best possible help to resume the care of their children, and had adequate support following the children's return home. We have not yet used with birth families the experience gained from supporting new families to maintain placements. Dingwall *et al* (1983), though, observe that it is right and reassuring that social workers think the best of parents but wonder if sometimes they are over-optimistic about achieving rehabilitation.

It is a sad fact that we lack a shared philosophy of childcare policy and practice which explicitly, rather than implicitly, also includes permanence through adoption. This can result, as McMilland and Wiener (1988) argue, in 'resistance, often mute, to permanent care plans (outside the family of origin). At worst, this will show in deliberate sabotage of the plan . . .' As a result, in their view, plans to move children on to permanent homes are often not realised and they continue to drift through the care system and placement. Information is also emerging that with devolved and tight budgets in some social services departments, adoption allowances receive less sympathetic attention than before.

Time limits and the "clean break" approach
Rigid time limits and the "clean break" policy, which went alongside permanency planning through adoption, and possibly still does, has been one of the big blemishes in the permanency movement's short history. While many children moved into new families without leaving behind important links, others had meaningful ties severed before joining their new families. The significance of the emotional links between especially an older child and a mother or a father or a grandparent were often underestimated and some children were cut off from emotional life-lines before they had established new ones. Some of the examples are too painful to relate here. Margaret Forster's recent book (1991), *The Battle for Christabel*, should become compulsory reading for all adoption workers with regard to this topic.

I challenged this policy in 1985 and I would like to think that each child's meaningful ties to past figures are assessed and maintained in a form of open adoption. A range of studies suggest that contact does not threaten the stability of the placement, provided the new family have agreed to it. On the contrary, contact seems to help stabilise the arrangements. I am not saying that all contacts are worth preserving, but as Fratter (1989) has also shown, it is possible to provide legal and emotional security to children through adoption without cutting them off from earlier important links.

Why and how such a situation came about is difficult to explain. There are those who attribute it to the legacy of the poor law with a strong desire to "save children" from what are seen as neglectful parents. Like a hundred or more years ago, the importance and meaning of parents to their children have again been underestimated. Older children, particularly, quickly lose their sense of identity and self-concept when communication with their biological parents is suddenly altered or terminated (Gibson and Noble, 1991). Jenson and Whitaker (1978) add that the bond that unites parent and child does not totally dissolve when a child is placed with another family. This does not mean that children cannot develop psychological bonds with a new family, but they can do this more easily when their earlier attachments are recognised and, where necessary, maintained. Not surprisingly, arranging adoption with contact is a far more complex process compared to closed adoption.

Both the concept of adoption with contact and open adoption, used appropriately, should help to expand the boundaries of adoption. With few exceptions, such as where the law has to protect children, parting with a child through adoption should be a voluntary act and free of pressures. Tentative research findings suggest that some parents of both younger and older children within the public care system who are unable to care for their own children would not be unwilling to agree to adoption, provided the links were maintained. When it comes to baby adoption, openness could give rise to increased altruism. Altruism, as a motivating factor in adoption, already operates in some societies where adoption is seen as a donation without severing contact. However, altruism, openness and contact have also to be shown to be in a child's interests, irrespective of the adults' intentions and preferences.

A sense of altruism, though, can only develop if birth parents come to feel equal, have a choice, are in control and own the adoption decision. It could be rightly argued that there is no such thing as pure altruism without some self-interest. In this case the satisfaction for the birth parent comes not only from the knowledge that she/he can be of service to other human beings, but also from safeguarding the well-being of her child without the feeling of total loss if it includes contact or continued updating. No doubt there is still much more that needs to be learned about the long-term impact of open adoption. In the meantime, social workers are not only facing the emotional challenge of finding families for children with special needs, but also families that can accept contact and openness.

The role of birth parents
One shift in attitude that seeking new families for children with special needs has brought about has been the recognition that such families offer a service. This has helped to lower the barriers between professionals and adoptive families and contribute to a climate of greater collaboration and partnership. Sadly, this has not been matched with a similar change in relationships between many birth parents and social

workers. Increasingly we are faced with angry birth parents and stressed social workers experiencing a gap in communication and in constructive relationships.

During the early part of the permanency movement, conflict featured very little, if at all, because many of the children had been in public care for a long time and most parents had disappeared or lost interest in their children. As those children moved on, a new generation of parents and children emerged, but with different needs and expectations. More parents are readier now to challenge social work decisions, including the use of the courts. At the same time, social workers' awareness of the need to plan early to prevent drift in children's lives has increased the likelihood of conflict with parents, resulting sometimes in bad feeling, acrimony and stress. The handling of the increasingly conflict-ridden nature of adoption work seems to have contributed to some of the disillusionment towards permanency planning currently found among practitioners. Around 600 parental consents to adoption are dispensed annually by the courts in England and Wales as having been 'unreasonably withheld'. [Source: Report to parliament on the operation of the Children Act, 1975 (1979)].

Like other users of services, parents of children in public care are readier now than before to challenge social work decisions at every stage and especially when adoption is being considered, and this is likely to increase under the concept of "parental responsibility" provided for in the Children Act of 1989. Social workers are rightly encouraged to look upon parents as partners and to try to plan jointly with them, but partnership does not always stand the strain arising from different perceptions of what is good for a child and especially as the parents' power does not match that of the worker. As an example, conflict is inevitably generated when freeing procedures are used which give parents the right to defend themselves before a court of law, and some have successfully done so. Yet social workers mirror in some ways the parents' agony and stress in their experience of protracted and stressful court procedures, something for which they have little preparation or support. There are no clear criteria for decision-making when the children are not free for adoption. In addition, the adversarial aspects of many proceedings before the courts often exacerbate rather than reduce conflict.

Outcomes

Do the outcomes achieved so far justify the pursuit of permanency through adoption for children with special needs, or do the challenges referred to earlier call for a much more cautious approach? Similarly, are the breakdowns experienced unacceptably high or within acceptable limits? To answer some of these questions we have to turn to outcome studies. The studies themselves are far from unproblematic. Inconsistencies and contradictions abound, but some agreement is also beginning to emerge about specific issues and circumstances.

I am not alone in recognising the complexities and hazards of trying to assess and compare outcome studies involving children placed for adoption or foster care. This is not the place to discuss in detail the methodological complexities but some of these include: not comparing like with like; failure to establish children's baselines on entering the system; questions of definition and measurement about such concepts as "satisfaction", "well-being" and "self-esteem", and variations in the length of time between placement and the studies taking place. Where long-term criteria are used to assess outcome, the intervening variables can distort the picture. Finally, long-term or follow-up retrospective studies have not yet emerged.

A simple example of how outcomes for older children can be distorted is whether those children who are adopted by their long-term foster parents are included in the sample. Foster parents don't usually proceed to adoption before considerable stability in the placement has been achieved. An additional point to be borne in mind is that an increasing number of British studies now refer in their findings to both permanent family foster care and to adoption because of the many overlaps between these two types of substitute parenting. A further complication with adoption studies is that some have concentrated on disruption before and after the adoption order was granted, while others focus only on what happened following the granting of the adoption order.

In assessing satisfactory or unsatisfactory outcomes, studies have used the rather crude criterion of the placement continuing or breaking down following a certain period of time after the arrangement is made. Of course continuity of a placement is not always synonymous with success. Nor is a disruption or breakdown always disastrous for the child.

Highlighting the dangers of comparing outcome studies is not meant to paralyse thinking and action but it serves to add caution to the making of too definitive statements. We have to start somewhere though, if we are ever to be able to build more sophisticated and sensitive measures.

Children with special needs

A spate of studies which have been monitoring and evaluating perm-anency through adoption for children with "special needs" began to emerge in the 1980s, and are still doing so. These have been appearing, mainly in the USA and Britain, where such policies and practices have been pursued. While in the case of baby adoptions the characteristics of the adopters were found by earlier studies to be the most crucial factor, when it comes to children with special needs the picture is much more complex. In this instance both the characteristics of the child and of the adopting family seem crucial to outcome, including what Belsky (1981) calls 'the context within which parenting takes place'.

On average, something like eight out of every ten children seem to settle down with their new families reasonably well. Looking at the figures, though, in greater detail, they show that children placed when under about the age of ten have a consistently lower rate of breakdown than those who are placed when older. For the under ten-year-olds the rate may be as low as ten per cent, but it rises from between 15 and 50 per cent for those who are older, depending on which study is examined. The breakdown rate for the age group of ten and over is not monolithic but varies, usually rising with increased age and increased difficulties dis-played by the child. A breakdown rate of between 25 and 40 per cent may, therefore, be accepted as usual. What happens to those who are adopted in adolescence presents a complex tableau of benefits and losses with breakdowns reaching sometimes 50 per cent and over. Older age is not infrequently accompanied by emotional and behaviour difficulties which many carers find difficult to handle. The child's ambivalence about commitment to the placement is often a further factor posing a threat to the placement.

Other pointers from the studies are that adoption with contact does not seem to threaten the stability of the placement, provided the adoptive family has agreed and has been prepared for this. Similarly, siblings placed together seem to experience fewer disruptions than when they are split, though other factors may be more important than the sheer fact of being a member of a sibling group, such as the quality of relationships between siblings. Children with learning difficulties and physical disabilities have been found to do very well by more than one study and they demonstrate consistently low breakdown rates. The main explanation for this is that such children are mostly adopted by people with previous experience of caring for children or adults with some disability.

Placing young children with families who have other children near the new child's age continues to carry a high risk for the placement. While childless couples were found in our recent study to be more successful in parenting young children, experienced parents were more successful in parenting older children who were disturbed (Borland *et al*, 1991).

Who can successfully parent a child and which children can be parented by new families is still far from clear, but a crucial variable contributing to disruptions, and mentioned by several studies, is the failure of the child to bond or attach itself. This is not always a one-way process, but can relate to characteristics in both the child and the carer. Without some form of attachment to provide a degree of mutuality and satisfaction in the relationship, the arrangement usually breaks down from between 12 and 18 months. In other words, when no rewards begin to emerge after a period of time, carers tend to give up. As in marital relationships, and in line with "exchange" theory, something is expected back at some point. Similarly, breakdown is more likely if carers find that the adjustment and well-being of other children in the family is threatened as a result of the new child's behaviour. Estimating, however, the possibilities of attachment when matching family and child is far from easy. It is an area where much more refinement in assessment processes is required. Though commitment and perseverance by the new parents is essential for successful outcome, a realistic view from the start of what the parents are taking on can also be decisive. Combining temporary optimism with realism from the outset is not always easy.

It remains difficult to predict which individual children will settle well with their new families, but certain features of the social work service increase the likelihood of stability for children of all ages. These are: more accurate assessment; better planning and preparation; the provision of adoption allowances; and a wide range of post-placement support services with specialist staff being available for use and consultation by families as the need arises. Staff who are knowledgeable and experienced in the field of child care seem to be more successful in making more stable arrangements compared with others.

The adoption of adolescents

As already pointed out, permanency through adoption for adolescents carries many risks, with breakdown ranging between 30 and 50 per cent. A number of agencies, possibly discouraged by the high rate of breakdowns among older children, including the high investment demanded in human and physical resources and the distress that usually follows from breakdowns, are either far more cautious and discriminating, or have given up altogether considering adolescents. Yet a blanket approach is not in the children's best interests. After all, even among the most difficult to place groups, at least half the children settle down in their new families.

How do practitioners distinguish between those who are going to succeed from the rest? Good assessment and good preparation of both children and families are again emerging as important variables that contribute towards placement stability. Above all, especially with adolescents, it is important to listen to them, obtain their views and establish their wishes and feelings. In the past, we have perhaps not always listened carefully and enough to what they had to say, or failed to involve them more fully in planning and decision-making. Some of them may not want adoption, but something different; others may want security through adoption but without severing links with their birth families; others still may want to commit themselves fully to an adoptive family.

It is too early to predict how the concept of "parental responsibility" built into the 1989 Children Act is going to affect adoption, but a possible unwelcome outcome would be to deprive, especially older children, of a badly needed secure base in life through adoption.

Based on our studies here, adoption as an option should not be ruled out for older children and for those who wish to retain links with members of their birth families. Possibly the best chance for older children entering care, and who cannot return to their families, is fostering with a view to adoption, even if it takes some time. Otherwise such children will be condemned to a life of rootlessness. Adoption through foster care has achieved considerable success in the past, but the move by many agencies towards contractual, time-limited placements could jeopardise this route unless more flexible placement policies are developed.

It is the legality of adoption and the emotional security that goes with it that sets it apart in the minds of the children and their adoptive parents from other forms of substitute parenting. A second tier of adoption order will only be perceived as a second-class type of adoption. A second tier adoption may have worked, for example, in France, though I am not familiar with any French studies in this area, but the historical backgrounds and contexts between Britain and France are not the same. Other ways could be found to provide security for children who cannot return to their families and where adoption, as we understand it now, cannot be pursued.

The way forward

The permanency movement has demonstrated what can be achieved in the placement of children with special needs. A small group of practitioners and managers can take a lot of credit for these achievements. Many of the children who found new families were emotionally damaged and often displayed behavioural difficulties. There is a lot of evidence now which points to the capacity of many children to overcome deprivation and emotional damage. For some very damaged children we may be unable to undo all the earlier damage but we could provide a range of compensating experiences. Mistakes have also been made in the past – taking stock can only help to produce a more measured response. It would be a retrograde step, though, to relax the efforts and the impetus developed in finding new families for children who have no-one to turn to. Social workers cannot be held responsible for the defects in social policy and for its failure to provide supportive and rehabilitative services to all families and children.

Caring for children with special needs has also proved stressful and painful. Besides offering care, many adoptive and foster parents are also expected to provide therapy to some very disturbed children without having been trained or equipped to do so. More attention must therefore be paid to how to furnish them with problem-solving skills and with a network of treatment services they can call upon without being labelled as dysfunctional. Permanence can be achieved through a number of routes and care arrangements. Joining a new family through adoption still remains the preferred option for some vulnerable children with no one else to turn to. There are strong pressures here and in other countries to see the abolition of adoption, especially for older children, for the wrong reasons. This should be resisted. Adoption will phase itself out only when every child can live with his or her own family and in his or her own country, thus maintaining continuity and stability. This position has not yet been reached. Its discouragement could prove detrimental to many children who would be condemned to a life of rootlessness for ideological reasons.

Postscript

Since this article was written permanence through adoption for children with no realistic prospects of returning to their families has been in some decline. There are many reasons for this making adoption for looked after children more complicated and more difficult to achieve than in the past. Long-term fostering has a definite place as a form of substitute care, but the recent trend of using the term "permanence" to describe it is misplaced because, unlike adoption, the term is inconsistent with the legal realities.

References

Belsky J (1981) 'Early human experience: a family systems perspective', *Developmental Psychology* 17, pp 3–23.

Bohman M and Sigvardsson S (1980) 'Negative social heritage', *Adoption & Fostering* 101:3, pp 25–31.

Borland M, O'Hara G and Triseliotis J (1991) 'Placement outcomes for children with special needs', *Adoption & Fostering* 15:2, pp 18–28.

Clarke A M and Clarke A D B (eds) (1976) *Early Experience: Myth and evidence*, London: Open Books.

Dingwall R, Eekelar J and Murray T (1983) *The Protection of Children*, Oxford: Blackwell.

Farmer R and Parker R (1991) *Trials and Tribulations*, London: HMSO.

Forster M (1991) *The Battle for Christabel*, London: Chatto & Windus.

Fratter J (1989) *Family Placement and Access*, Ilford: Barnardo's.

Gibson D and Noble D N (1991) 'Creative permanency planning: residential services for families,' *Child Welfare* 70:3.

Jenson J and Whitaker J (1978) 'Parental involvement in children's residential treatment', *Children and Youth Services Review* 9:2.

Kadushin A (1970) *Adopting Older Children*, New York: Columbia University Press.

Kirk D (1981) *Adoptive Kinship*, Canada: Butterworth.

Lambert L, Triseliotis J and Hill M (1990) *Freeing Children for Adoption*, London: BAAF.

McMillan and Wiener R (1988) 'Preparing the caretaker for placement', *Adoption & Fostering* 12:1, pp 20–22.

Teague A (1990) *Social Change, Social Work and the Adoption of Children*, Aldershot: Avebury/Gower.

Thoburn J and Rowe J (1988) 'A snapshot of permanent family placement,' *Adoption & Fostering* 12:3, pp 29–34.

Thoburn J (1990) *Success and Failure in Permanent Family Placement*, Aldershot: Gower.

Tizard B (1977) *Adoption: A second chance*, London: Open Books.

Triseliotis J and Russell J (1984) *Hard to Place*, Aldershot: Gower.

Triseliotis J (1983) 'Identity and security in adoption and long-term fostering', *Adoption & Fostering* 7:1, pp 22–31.

3 Child care at the end of the millennium

Donal Giltinan

This article was first published in Adoption & Fostering *19:3, 1995.*

There are three issues that deeply concern me and which, in my view, have a huge impact on social work with young people and families at the end of this millennium. The first is the delivery of social welfare in a market economy. Do the market principles, that some agencies aspire to and some have had forced upon them, enhance or enfeeble social work to children and families?

The second issue is the reality and the destructive power of manufactured poverty. We are a rich nation – one of the richest in the world – and yet have a huge population of young people and families living in abject poverty. At the Scottish Association of Directors of Social Work (ADSW) conference in 1994, Cardinal Winning asked, 'What are you doing about the victims of a society that is structurally unjust?' I want to revisit that question as I do not think that our profession has adequately answered it.

The final point I want to raise is this: Is our system of justice in Scotland truly capable of making the welfare of children its paramount consideration, or, as Lord Gill recently argued (*The Scotsman*, 12 April 1995), is it a legal relic that is failing to do us justice?

Social welfare in a market economy

Local government reorganisation is not the only change that has been taking place in social work service delivery in Scotland. For 35 years, the post-war welfare state remained relatively unchanged and unchallenged. However, the Thatcher Government, influenced and in some cases *driven* by the political and economic philosophies of Friedman, Hayek, Popper and others, began to regard the increasing share of public expenditure which was being devoted to welfare services as unsustainable. The growing demand of a rapidly increasing ageing population, combined with the high unemployment caused by the slimming and trimming of the Thatcher years, put huge pressure on public spending. The argument against public spending was developed not only in economic terms, but also in moralistic terms. Spending on welfare was viewed as creating a dependency culture; an underclass of people who were becoming reliant on welfare handouts and who were devoid of any personal initiative or commitment to work.

It would be naive and untrue to suggest that all of this happened as a result of the appointment of a Conservative Government in 1979. The Barclay Report (1982) spoke about the vast untapped reservoir of volunteers who could complement social work in the statutory services. There was also consideration at that time of transferring a large volume of public social services to some of the major voluntary organisations, a move which was, by and large, resisted by the voluntary agencies on the grounds that it would compromise their independence and weaken the welfare state.

By the late 1980s, the climate was right and could no longer resist the introduction of market principles for the delivery of welfare services. The dogma of 'marketism' was unshakeable and there was no sector of life which could not be subjected to it. Welfare, whether it be statutory or philanthropic, would have to be delivered according to market principles. At last year's ADSW conference, Bob Holman reminded us that few can now dispute that Britain is dominated by the market culture. I quote:

> The establishment of a near untrammelled free market was executed by the Thatcherite governments, but its ideology has been propagated, brilliantly, by the new right.

There were some lone voices of horror and resistance but, by and large, local government and the voluntary sector decided that this was a philosophy and a theology that they could no longer avoid. The Griffiths Report (1988) provided the mandate for the development of a mixed economy of care with an increasing share being delivered by the private 'for profit' sector and the voluntary sector, arguing that this would give choice (choice being a basic principle of the market philosophy) and would create innovation in a competitive environment.

Many, including myself, rushed off to familiarise ourselves with the new jargon in this lexicon of the market. I learned much about the purchasers and providers, about internal and external customers, and indeed was much enriched by that brief academic experience. However, nowhere during that enthusiastic imparting of knowledge about the wonders of the market place did anybody subject to rigorous scrutiny how philanthropy and welfare would behave when delivered according to market principles.

For four centuries markets have dealt effectively and efficiently with commodities and they will continue to do so, but the trouble is that welfare is not a commodity that can be purchased by the highest bidder and subjected indiscriminately to a culture of supply and demand. There is little doubt in my mind that some aspects of service provision have been enhanced by subjecting them to some aspects of market principles: for example, having resources determined and designed by service demand rather than trying to fit client need to predetermined and value-laden resources has been a major and important change in the delivery of social work.

During the past few years, Scottish local authorities have moved from a state system of welfare to a market system of welfare. It is clear, however, that although welfare is going down the market road, it still has a long way to go before it approximates anything like a free market in the sense that there are a multitude of suppliers operating in a competitive environment. It needs to take stock of how much further along that road it should go. Other countries which have gone down this route are now trying to reverse their way out of it because the most profitable services have been "creamed off" while the least profitable or less fashionable have been abandoned. The fact is that Scotland has always had a mixed economy of welfare, especially in child care. The majority of the list D schools were run by the churches; adoption services were run by the voluntary societies; and children's homes were largely run by the voluntary sector.

In the Victorian era, welfare relied on philanthropy from the rich to the poor and the state was the residual provider. This balance changed in the mid-40s and, from then until the late 1980s, the state became the major provider of welfare, with the voluntary and private sectors becoming residual providers. But a mixed and pluralist economy is not and does not have to be a market economy. Free markets and pure markets are about competitive advantage and the survival of the fittest; welfare is about supporting the least fit. Welfare pluralists have argued for an increasing role for the voluntary sector, while their protagonists on the new right champion the market as the mechanism for controlling welfare expenditure and offering choice. The past five years have seen a deliberate shift in emphasis to the state taking on, not so much a residual role, but the role as a purchaser of services, while the voluntary and private sectors have taken a higher profile as providers.

There is growing evidence that the voluntary sector is getting locked into a provider role as servants of the state welfare system. While the larger agencies within the sector, such as Barnardo's and NCH, have the strength, financial power and wisdom to retain adequate space for innovative projects, smaller agencies are becoming increasingly preoccupied with meeting their contract specifications, with little room for manoeuvre. For these agencies, the barriers to entry into the welfare market have been removed, but the option of exit from the market has also been removed from their control. The result may be stifled growth and lack of innovation.

Social work in general, and child welfare in particular, needs a new social encyclical, a new 'Rerum Novarum' that guarantees quality services of the highest standards, that are neither market-led nor inspection-controlled, but needs-led and user-controlled.

Manufactured poverty

If markets are about commodity and wealth, welfare is about human need and poverty.

It has been said that politicians use research like a drunk person uses a lamp-post, more for support than illumination. The Government's response to the recent Rowntree Report (1994) on income and wealth would suggest that they could find neither support nor illumination in its two volumes, which draw on a series of research projects funded by the Foundation. It is a scholarly report which sadly confirms the worst fears regarding the insidious effect of fiscal and social policy on children and families in the UK during the past two decades. The tragedy is that the promised cascade of wealth started to flow. The population as a whole is

50 per cent better off compared with the late 1960s; indeed the top ten per cent is twice as well off, but the number of people living in households below *half* the national average income has risen from *three* million in the mid-1970s to a staggering *eleven* million in 1991.

The so-called cascade of wealth has been absorbed not by the single mothers and the benefit scroungers as suggested by a recent social security minister and a former Welsh Secretary, but by couples with two incomes and by single people without children – that is, those who least need it. The frightening thing is that the disparity between rich and poor has grown faster in Britain than in any other country in the world for which data is available, other than New Zealand. In the UK, the poorest tenth of the population has twice as many children as the richest tenth, and single mothers with children have experienced the greatest disparity of wealth in the entire spectrum. The rich are locked in a virtuous cycle where more begets more and the poor in a vicious circle where less begets less.

For me, the free market in welfare reached its nadir at the beginning of March with reports in The *Independent on Sunday* (5 March, 1995) and the *Daily Telegraph* (8 March, 1995) that the Institute of Economic Affairs is promoting adoption as a major method of child care. This bastion of the new right, together with Professor Richard Whitfield, the former UK Child Care Director of an international childcare organisation, are concerned about the impact on society of the increasing numbers of children brought up by single mothers living on benefit in poor housing. In particular, they fear that this rise will lead to the development of a delinquent underclass.

Cocooned in self-righteousness, they seem to be driven by the belief that money and wealth are prerequisites of good parenting and good citizenship. Not everyone can have money and wealth and not everyone can have children, and so the ideology of the free market provides an elegant solution . . . *and the rich shall inherit the babies*.

Where are compassion and concern, self-esteem and individual worth? The fundamental flaw in the philosophy of the Institute of Economic Affairs and the others of the new right is that it does not have the breadth and the depth to withstand the challenges thrown up by life, nor is it able to satisfy aspirations and hopes that are not money driven. If cash is all, then to have none is nothing. A pitiless preoccupation with markets and incentives is put forward as a national consensus, paradoxically over-looking the fact that the foot-soldiers of this wealth are the single parents and low-income families who leave their houses before dawn in order to wash the cups and freshen the offices of those at the top of the pyramid of wealth who promise us that, if we wait long enough, this wealth will cascade down. The rhetoric was: 'there are good times coming'; the reality, 'you will never live to see them.'

Wealth is cascading, paradoxically, upwards. With the abandonment of a minimum wage and devices such as the National Lottery, wealth is redistributing from the poor to the rich. Among the few who benefit are those who own our media and dominate the debate. It is incumbent on child welfare agencies, whether in the voluntary sector or in the local authority, to ensure that this poverty, manufactured by fiscal policy, does not become a significant reason for the reception of children into care and subsequently for the rights and responsibilities of their parents being transferred to the state.

What is the relevance of this growth in inequality to childcare agencies? Barnardo's recent report (1994), *Unfair Share,* argues very persuasively that what causes poor health, a shorter life expectancy and even suicide is not absolute living standards, but inequality. Individuals measure their worth in relation to the average; despondency and despair seeps into the souls of children and families at the bottom of the pyramid. Meanwhile the Government and the royal household antiphonally recite their mantra 'absolute poverty has been abolished'. Like all mantras, this one's strength lies in its repetition rather than in its inherent truth.

Poverty in an affluent economy such as ours is directly related to lack of income or wealth and can only be effectively dealt with by the govern-ment's fiscal policies. Just as in the last century it was in the interests of all to introduce public health measures to combat the spread of infectious physical disease fostered by poverty, so in this century it is in the interests of all to remove the factors which are fostering the social diseases of drugs, crime, political extremism and social unrest.

The Children Act 1989 and the Children (Scotland) Act 1995 give enabling powers to local authorities to deal with the worst aspects of poverty as it affects children and young people. Local authorities should

The background of children who enter local authority care

Child 'A' aged 5–9
no dependence on social security benefits
two-parent family
three or fewer children
white
owner occupies home
more rooms than people
Odds are 1 in 7,000

Child 'B' aged 5–9
household head receives income support
single adult household
four or more children
mixed ethnic origin
privately rented home
one or more persons per room
Odds are 1 in 10

(*Bebbington and Miles*, 1989, p 349)

think twice about their role in relieving central government of its income maintenance responsibilities because this is a burden that local government cannot bear. Welfare rights projects have been one of the most effective responses of local government to central government's income maintenance policies. They have been the poor person's Touche Ross and Price Waterhouse rolled together.

I am concerned at the silence among directors of social work, directors of social services and directors of childcare voluntary organisations in response to the Government's fiscal policy regarding the distribution of wealth. It is incumbent on directors and senior managers, both in the voluntary and statutory sectors, to be advocates for their clients. This is not a peripheral duty that they should adhere to if so inclined, or if the political ethos in which they operate will be benign in its response to criticisms from statutory and voluntary welfare bodies. Senior officers in the voluntary and statutory sector, as well as elected representatives, must shoulder part of the responsibility for ensuring an equitable distribution of the wealth of the nation.

Child welfare and the justice system

My 20 years' experience of social work in Scotland have left me in no doubt about its commitment to rekindle the embers of hope and equip families and young people with the skill to participate as valued members of neighbourhoods, communities and societies. In our democratic society, we rely heavily on a concept of justice and a system of justice to achieve this. I would therefore like to comment finally on our civil justice system, with particular reference to how it affects children and families and child care agencies at the end of this millennium.

Lord Gill, in his recent article in *The Scotsman* (12 April, 1995), argued that our system of civil procedure is a contemporary relic of a vanished age. He was not specifically referring to the treatment of children within the civil court system, but his remarks summed up for me many of the concerns expressed by our profession about the inadequacies of the system to deal with the inexorably complex issues of the conflict between the rights of children and the responsibilities of adults, and the needs of both. The system exists to serve the public, and children and young people constitute a vital part of the public, and the public have a right to demand that it serves their needs.

The basic structure of civil procedure in Scotland has changed little since the Court of Session Act 1825 – an adversarial system of petition or appeal, and answers, debate or proof. The system faithfully applies a tradition of nearly 200 years of amazing indifference to the delays, criticism, and frustration of those whom it serves. It was designed by adults (mostly male) for adults (male and female) and there is grave doubt that it serves even them well.

It is the hallmark of a civilised democratic society that we have confidence in the laws that form the framework of its system of justice. The Lord Justice General of Scotland and Lord President of the Court of Session said recently in a maiden speech to his fellow peers that Scotland can look forward into the next century with confidence that it has a system of family law which is in keeping with the needs of modern society. There are some young people who are growing up in public care in Scotland who do not share this confidence in our system of justice. Unless the current piecemeal approach to reform gives way to a comprehensive review of the law as it affects young people, with no assumption in favour of the *status quo*, then young people will merit our understanding and sympathy if they hold the guardians of the civil justice system in the same regard as Will Caning holds the Rugby Football Union.

Blame for the crisis in law cannot be placed at the door of the judges or any one group of people. Nor is there any conspiracy afoot. It is the nature of the beast that needs reassessment, and the attitudes which support the survival of the *status quo*; creating a legal framework that is truly equitable means a fundamental overhaul of our legal thinking. For too long the legal system has escaped scrutiny and resisted criticism because of its mystical position at the centre of our social order. The institution itself will have to change. Only then will confidence in our justice system be restored.

Social work, health care and the police cannot and should not bear the burden of a justice system designed for adults and applied to young people. Young people cannot be made the hostages of flawed evidence in a flawed justice system. I am mindful of the role of the Children's Hearing as part of our civil justice system. In its 25 years, it has generally served young people faithfully and well, but the difference is that it was designed for young people with a focus on need rather than deed and with a goal of serving the deprived rather than dealing with the depraved. The Children's Hearing is an important and major part of the civil justice system but young people have the right, as do all people, to have the entire system of justice work on their behalf, not just part of it.

Conclusion

There are major changes afoot in the way social welfare is administered in Scottish society and our profession has a key role to play in those changes. Unpopular as it is, local government reorganisation is about to happen and we have to live with it, mould it to the advantage of our clients, identify the opportunities it presents and take advantage of them. These changes will, in themselves, create a cultural shift but redressing the injustices of the system requires radically reforming not only the body politic, but also the body legal.

Postscript

As far as social welfare in Scotland is concerned, the seven years since the publication of this article have been the "best of times and the worst of times".

The rapid spread of "manufactured poverty" has slowed down and in some instances halted but has not been reversed. Welfare services have been protected from the worst excesses of the free market economy but the inexorable shift of responsibility from the public to the private sector continues. Our court system still operates in adult mode and the law takes precedence over justice and child welfare.

References

Barnardo's (1994) *Unfair Shares*, Ilford: Barnardo's.

Bebbington A and Miles J (1989) 'The background of children who enter local authority care', *British Journal of Social Work* 19:5, pp 349–68.

Griffiths R (1988) *Community Care/Agenda for Action: A report to the Secretary of State for Social Services*, London: HMSO.

Joseph Rowntree Foundation (1994) *Enquiry into Income and Wealth Vols 1 & 2*, York: Joseph Rowntree Foundation.

4 Is permanency through adoption in decline?

John Triseliotis

This article was first published in Adoption & Fostering *22:4, 1998/99.*

Introduction

The main purpose of this paper is to examine recent concerns about the alleged decline in the proportion of looked after children leaving care through adoption and to seek possible explanations for this. What came to be known as the permanency "movement" through adoption, with its emphasis on the placement of older children and of those with "special needs" originated in the United States in the mid-1970s before it was introduced in Britain. The key underlying principles that informed it were that:

- the children would be free for adoption or have no realistic chance of a return to their families of origin, following sustained but unsuccessful efforts to establish permanency within their own families;
- placement in a new family would be in the interests of the child;
- the goal should be for a permanent, secure and nurturing environment.

The main research and theory that underpinned this form of adoption came from:

- the proportion of children found to be drifting within the public care system with no realistic chance of returning to their families (Rowe and Lambert, 1973);
- studies suggesting that, given a new nurturing environment, older children and those with special needs could be reintegrated and do well in new families (Kadushin, 1970; Tizard, 1977; Triseliotis and Russell, 1984);
- the theoretical/clinical approach expounded by Goldstein, Freud and Solnit (1973; 1980) urging for continuity and stability in children's lives.

(For a more detailed account of the rationale, achievements and some of the blemishes associated with this form of adoption see Triseliotis, 1991.)

Evidence for the decline of adoption

Around two-thirds of the 7,000 or so children adopted annually in Britain are adopted by relatives, mainly step-parents. The remaining are non-relative adoptions and almost all of these involve children looked after by local authorities. It is to the care system statistics, therefore, that we have to turn to establish whether there has been a decline or not. Evidence for the possible decline in the number of those adopted out of care first came in a Social Services Inspectorate (SSI) report (1996) which expressed real concern, referring to:

- the low status given to child placement services in some local authorities, with a quarter of children needing adoption having to wait more than three years for placement;
- the lack of detailed assessments and care plans on many children's files;
- delays in identifying new families.

The Department of Health must have taken these findings seriously because it convened two consultation meetings to consider the issues – the first in London in December 1997 and the second in York the following May. The House of Commons Health Committee Report (1998) also accepted the evidence put before it and concluded that (Vol 1, para 153, p 38):

> ... local authorities too often do fail to take adoption sufficiently seriously as an option; that unnecessary delays occur, and that insufficient support is offered to adoptive parents.

Establishing and contrasting the amount of adoption activity within local authorities is a complex matter. Apart from the absence of detailed statistics, it could be claimed that fewer children leaving care by adoption signifies higher proportions being restored to parents, relatives and friends. It can also depend on whether children adopted are seen as a proportion of all looked after children or of annual discharges.

A BAAF survey (1997) which covered the period up to 1995 showed that on average 3.5 per cent of children left care through adoption, but there were very wide discrepancies between authorities in the number of looked after children adopted as a proportion of all in care. Some authorities, mostly shires, reported up to seven per cent placements, while others cited only a tiny percentage. In another study, one local authority agency approved as many as 67 adoptive families in one year and three agencies none (Lowe, 1997). Similar variations are to be found in the Statistical Reports published annually by the Department of Health. When the same figures are examined as a proportion of all discharges (Table 1), they show that in two-fifths of authorities those discharged by adoption were under 4.9 per cent, in just over two-fifths the discharge rate was between 5.0 and 9.9 per cent and in the remaining agencies (N 19 or 16 per cent) it was over ten per cent.

Table 1
Percentage of all discharges which were by adoption, 1997

%	No. of authorities	% of authorities
Under 4.9	46	40.7
5.0–9.9	48	42.5
10.0 +	19	16.8
Total	113	100

Source: Based on calculations made by Professor Roy Parker (private communication).

Table 2 examines the number of children adopted annually, first as a proportion of all children looked after and then as a proportion of all discharges from care. It shows that in recent years both the proportion and numbers of those adopted kept rising until 1993. Actual adoption numbers rose from 1,700 in 1981 (or 1.8 per cent of all children looked after) to 2,500 (or 4.8 per cent) in 1993. After that there has been a steady drop, reaching 1,900 in 1997 (or 3.7 per cent of all children looked after). However, the statistical picture somewhat changes when adoption numbers are seen as a proportion of annual discharges (Table 2). The proportion of discharges by adoption kept rising from 4.2 per cent in 1981 to seven per

Table 2
Children leaving care through adoption and children placed for adoption

	1981	1987	1993	1994	1995	1996	1997
Adopted	1,700	2,038	2,500	2,300	2,000	1,900	1,900
% of all in care	1.8	3.1	4.8	4.7	4.0	3.7	3.7
% of all discharges	4.2	6.3	6.8	7.0	6.0	5.9	6.2
Placed for adoption	Not known	935	2,600	2,200	2,200	2,300	2,500
% of those in care	Not known	1.4	4.9	4.5	4.4	4.5	4.8

Source: DoH annual statistics on children looked after by local authorities.

cent in 1994. After that they fell to around six per cent, though there was a slight increase in 1997 but not back to the 1994 level.

The statistical picture concerning children "placed for adoption", as different from "being adopted", is also more mixed. The numbers and proportion kept rising until 1993, went down in the three subsequent years but started rising again in 1997, though it did not reach the 1993 level. Of course not all the children placed are subsequently adopted. The recent House of Commons Health Committee Report (Vol 1, 1998) claimed that because of the increasing problems displayed by the children, a significant number of new families do not proceed to adopt.

The overall conclusion that can be drawn from Table 2 is that there has been some decline in adoptions over the last three to four years, but not as serious as it was perhaps thought. We do not know whether this trend will continue or be reversed in the coming years. Nevertheless, both the SSI (1996) and the House of Commons Health Committee reports (1998), which examined records and/or heard evidence on the matter, concluded that a number of children needing adoptive placement cannot be or are not placed.

Possible explanations for the decline

We can only speculate about the possible reasons for the partial decline in the proportion of children leaving care by adoption. A few of the following factors, supported by various evidence, offer some explanation, but the precise contribution of each would be mere supposition. They include:

1 the impact of the Children Act 1989;
2 the pressures facing social services departments (SSDs);
3 mixed outcomes resulting from the more negative 'baggage' carried by the children;
4 failure to provide adequate post-placement support services;
5 the emergence of new forms of "permanence";
6 the advent of adoption with contact;
7 adverse publicity;
8 fewer people coming forward to adopt.

Impact of the Children Act 1989

The Children Act for England and Wales was not an accidental piece of legislation and many factors contributed to it, including some of the excesses of the permanency "movement". The Act also reflected the periodic swing of the pendulum by shifting the balance of rights from local authorities towards the courts and parents, and perhaps from children to parents. Among other things, it placed the emphasis on family support, the exercise of parental responsibility and restoring children to their parents or wider family. It is worth asking whether, intentionally or otherwise, the implementation of the Children Act has made adoption more complicated and more difficult to achieve due to some of its requirements, for instance: the number of people now to be consulted before a placement is made; the concept of parental responsibility emphasising the parents' continuing duties, obligations and interests in their children, unless it is overruled by the court; and the power of the courts to make contact orders when hearing applications for adoption orders.

The overruling of parental responsibility may be becoming more difficult to achieve and it may be creating a climate of uncertainty among adoption workers whether to put a case forward or not. In a letter to *The Times* (28 March 1998) Ruth Staines, who described herself as an adoption worker, wrote that:

The major issue is finding couples or single people who are prepared to consider adopting or long-term fostering of children who are beyond babyhood and those who have remained in abusive families because of the stringent requirements of the Children Act.

Judge Paul Collins wrote back to say that there is nothing in the Children Act 1989 which obliges social workers to devote limitless time and resources 'to even the most hopeless and abusive parents' (*The Times*, 3 April 1998). However, and possibly as a reaction to some of the excesses of the 1980s, Sir William Utting (1998) in his evidence to the House of Commons Health Committee said that his review team had found evidence that (p 37, 1998):

. . . authorities are too careful and painstaking in their regard for parental rights and are less active in protecting children against known or suspected harm.

The pressures facing SSDs

A number of recent developments within social services departments have also been identified as having contributed to the decline in the number of adoptions. The House of Commons Health Committee Report (Vol 1, 1998) acknowledged that the resources available to SSDs do not match up with demand. Among other things, this gap led to delays in the placement of children and the provision of support to them and their carers. The British Association of Social Workers in its evidence to the same Committee (p 37) said that:

. . . there was legitimate concern that some placements are delayed because local authorities cannot afford to pay inter-agency fees.

Furthermore, the SSI (1996) claimed that part of the explanation for a significant proportion of children having to wait for three years before placement was that departments lacked staff with expertise in adoption. In most authorities it is the children's social workers, rather than the family placement staff, who are responsible for identifying those children who need more permanent homes and putting them forward. Yet because of the demands made on their time, these workers are mostly preoccupied with child protection work, assessments and coping with emergencies, with insufficient attention paid to the needs of children already looked after (Rushton *et al*, 1997; Bullock, 1998; Triseliotis *et al*, 1998). In a study of children's services, the Audit Commission (p 16, 1994) also observed that:

> *Because of the pressure of child protection work field social workers have little spare time for work with other children in need who require support other than child protection.*

Another area that has apparently suffered because of devolved budgets and financial constraints is the reluctance, in some agencies, to give information about practical financial support available, such as adoption allowances (Lowe, 1997).

Finally, there is evidence that the training of social workers working with children and families is not adequate, especially in the area of direct work with children (Marsh and Triseliotis, 1996; House of Commons Health Committee, 1998; Triseliotis *et al*, 1998). In the words of Kahan (1977):

> *Training does not offer the extensive knowledge they [social workers] need to make wise decisions about complex child care situations.*

As yet another illustration of the downgrading of this type of work, of the 37 post-qualifying and advanced courses approved by the Central Council for the Education and Training of Social Workers (CCETSW) in relation to children and families, 25 were found to be in child protection and only two in family placement work. The remaining ten were courses in general child welfare or child care work. No doubt institutions offering courses respond to market forces (*The PQ Directory*, CCETSW, London, 1997).

Mixed outcomes resulting from the more negative "baggage" carried by the children

Another reason suggested for the alleged decline of permanency through adoption is the very negative "baggage" carried by the children and the increasing demands made on the adoptive parents, possibly leading to more breakdowns and poorer outcomes than in the past (Howe, 1997). (Because of space limitations, outcomes are considered here mainly in relation to breakdowns in placement arrangements, rather than within the wider context of satisfaction with the adoption experience. To complicate matters, many studies have not distinguished between breakdowns before and after the adoption order was made.)

British studies covering the placement of children during the early stages of the permanency "movement" in the 1980s found an overall breakdown rate of around 20 per cent, but considerable variations existed between different age groups. For children under the age of ten when placed, the breakdown rate was less than ten per cent, but for older children it could be up to 50 per cent (Thoburn, 1990; Borland *et al*, 1991; Fratter *et al*, 1991; Strathclyde Social Services Department, 1991). The proportion of breakdowns following the making of the adoption order are much lower compared to those which occur before (Fratter *et al*, 1991; Lowe, 1997). Fewer breakdowns were also reported by studies concentrating on the adoption of children displaying physical or learning disabilities (Gath, 1983; Macaskill, 1985; Fratter *et al*, 1991).

It has been suggested that after the initial successes of the permanency "movement", increasingly more "difficult", "disturbed" and "complex" children were put forward, either making it very difficult to find new families or increasing the possibility of a breakdown in the arrangements. However, this is not borne out. A survey covering more recent placements identified only nine per cent breakdowns among local authority placements, and only 3.5 per cent for the voluntary sector (Lowe, 1997). (It is possible that the low rate found was due to the poor level of returns of questionnaires, but we will never know.) Also, unlike most other studies referred to above, this one found that most breakdowns (54 per cent) occurred in the five to nine age group and only 22 per cent in the ten and over. Another recent study shows the high levels of success achieved by single people adopting children with 'special needs' (BAAF, 1998).

A question to be asked is whether the association found by most studies between older age and breakdowns has deterred practitioners from placing children aged ten and over. Table 3 shows that there has been a drop, from 21 per cent adopted in 1986 to 14 per cent in 1997, but this does not amount to full statistical significance. A more detailed examination of

Table 3

Age group at placement of children adopted by non-relatives between the mid-1980s and 1997

| | Year and Numbers | | | | | |
| | 1986 | | 1993 | | 1997 | |
Age group	N	%	N	%	N	%
0–4	1,144	56	1,240	50	1,020	55
5–9	472	23	840	34	580	31
10+	421	21	390	16	250	14
Total	2,037	100	2,470	100	1,850	100
Average age at placement	Not known		5.8 yrs		5.5 yrs	

Source: DoH annual statistics on children looked after by local authorities

the figures also reveals that those aged under one went down from 27 per cent in 1986 to eight per cent in 1997. If these two age groups decreased, there was a corresponding increase in those aged one to nine. More than half (55 per cent) of all children adopted from care in 1997 were under five, the mean age being 5.5. This is only slightly different from 1993 when the mean age was 5.8.

Failure to provide adequate post-placement support services

Much attention in both practice and research is usually reserved for break-downs because they can be very traumatic and distressing for all con-cerned. Although general findings such as those outlined earlier show that far more placements succeed than break down, these have to be qualified. As an example, a number of studies have highlighted the heavy demands made by some children on their new parents, the exhaustion of some adopters and the few rewards which often arrive very late (Thoburn, 1990; Holloway, 1997; Howe, 1997).

Adopting such challenging children would require, in most cases, consistent and continued support, yet other studies suggest that the provision of such services is patchy and lacking strategic coherence and consistency (see Hughes, 1995; Watson and McGhee, 1995; SSI, 1996; House of Commons Health Committee Report, 1998). These families may have spread by word of mouth the difficulties, including the absence of support, putting off others from contemplating adoption.

The emergence of new forms of "permanence"

Both the Children Act 1989 and the Review of Adoption Law (Department of Health, 1993) were keen to identify new forms of "permanence" for children within their immediate and wider families, and for those in long-term foster care who either did not want adoption or for whom adoption was not suitable. These forms included:

- permanence within own family;
- residence orders living with relatives;
- residence order in "permanent" foster care with or without contact;
- support towards independent living;
- adoption with or without contact.

Even though their actual extent has not been empirically tested or demonstrated, the Children Act rests on the principle that family networks are generally strong enough to undertake long-term substitute family care roles. Nobody would possibly argue with the general aim, but the question could also be asked whether, as a result of this emphasis, the tension between the focus on biological lineage and the blood tie on the one hand, and the psychosocial rearing of children through adoption on the other, has been intensified, creating a more hostile environment within SSDs towards adoption. A group of adoptive parents giving oral evidence to the House of Commons Committee thought so, claiming that many social workers were biased against adoption, a point reiterated by Morgan (1998), but concrete evidence was not produced.

Long-term foster care or adoption? Not all children who are in long-term foster care want adoption, especially if they are well settled, nor is it always in their interests to move to adoption. Others, however, do and they should be offered the chance. The recent tendency in many local authorities to equate long-term fostering with "permanent" placement only clouds, rather than clarifies, the issues. This designation goes beyond semantics in that, not only is there no such thing in law as "permanent" fostering, but practitioners may be resorting to it to avoid complex legal procedures associated with adoption.

While there are overlaps between adoption and long-term fostering, there are also significant qualitative differences. I know of eight studies which compare adoption with long-term fostering. All comparisons of this kind have their problems as it is rarely possible to compare like with like. Six of the studies found clear advantages for adoption over long-term fostering. The findings of several of these are based on the comments of those who experienced these forms of substitute parenting and not simply on breakdown rates (Raynor, 1980; Triseliotis, 1983; Dumaret, 1985; Hill et al, 1989; Bohman and Sigvardsson, 1990; Holloway, 1997). The main advantages identified in favour of adoption are:

- legality: 'It is something permanent and by law';
- security: 'I belong';
- continuity and permanence: 'You cannot be taken away'.

The above were typical comments made by children adopted by their long-term foster carers (Hill et al, 1989). When it came to foster care, these children described it as:

> . . . in-between and I wanted a safe home.

> As a foster child you can still worry about what is going to happen to you.

A group of American researchers (McDonald et al, 1996) who examined 29 studies from different countries to assess the effects of long-term foster care concluded (p 149) that:

> Adoption, when available as an option, should generally be pursued rather than long-term foster care.

In contrast, Fratter et al (1991) and Gibbons et al (1995) found no difference in breakdown rates between those placed for adoption and those fostered. In fact Gibbons and colleagues concluded that the foster care group did best. This may not be surprising as breakdown rates and satisfaction with the experience are not the same.

The advent of adoption with contact

Contact between the placed child and members of the birth family is now becoming far more widespread than before, with one recent survey claiming that continuing contact of some kind with the birth mother occurred in 49 per cent of cases (Lowe, 1997). Though some would point to the recent increase in intercountry adoption as a wish on the part of would-be adopters to avoid contact, there is no specific evidence that contact has been discouraging people from coming forward to adopt. The main British study on the subject found that where difficulties occurred contact was not the main factor. Contact, though, appeared to be just another complication, among too many already, to have to manage (Fratter, 1996).

Adverse publicity

Politicians and the media seem to like adoption, even if its recent diversity has eluded them. Their predominant images continue to be of infants being adopted by childless couples. Adoption to them seems to represent stability, continuity and commitment at a time when the average family is going through so much change and instability. At the same time they dislike the idea of detailed regulation and of extensive investigations being carried out into the background and circumstances of those wishing to adopt. In line with other recent market developments, there has even been talk not only of partially deregulating adoption, but of allowing the setting up of profit-making agencies to organise both domestic and intercountry adoption (see Triseliotis *et al*, 1997). To paraphrase one political philosopher, total freedom for adults to pursue their interests allows the possibility for oppressing the weak, in this case the children (Berlin, 1991).

Over the same period, adoption workers and their practices came under a barrage of criticism and attacks from the same sources for what was described as their "political correctness". As an example, when the previous Prime Minister decided to launch a new policy initiative towards the end of December 1996, he chose adoption as his first theme with the promise to root out "political correctness" in its ranks. Broadly similar statements were recently made by Paul Boateng, former Junior Health Minister, before and on the introduction of new adoption guidelines (see *The Times*, 29 August 1998).

Much of the criticism has been directed against ethnic matching, though other forms of matching are seen not only as desirable but necessary for the preservation of the placement. In fact, in spite of the Junior Minister's statements to the press and the press headlines that greeted it, the guidelines issued by his Department do not do away with ethnic matching. On the contrary, they recommend that children should ideally be placed in families with a similar ethnic, religious and cultural background. It is only where it is not possible to find, with proper effort, families of similar ethnic parentage that they should be placed in other families (DoH LAC (98) 20, 1998).

The importance of children being able to maintain links with their ethnic group, culture and heritage is summed up in a recent review (Rushton and Minnis, 1997) of all the relevant studies on the subject which concluded that (p 11):

> ... despite the fact that limited research evidence tends to give positive support for transracial placements, we find ourselves continuing to argue that ethnically matched placements will be in the best interests of both the child and the community in most instances. (See also Triseliotis et al, 1997.)

By picking on the practices of a tiny minority of social workers, and sometimes quoting out of context, some politicians and the media have conveyed the misleading impression of adoption being fraught with complications and problems and managed by uncaring and insensitive staff. At no stage has any credit been given to the remarkable achievements of the last 20 or so years. We don't know the impact of these criticisms on the public, but it should come as no surprise if, after all this, the morale of adoption workers has dropped, turning their attention to alternative and less contentious forms of substitute care.

Fewer people coming forward to adopt?

Finally, it is said that fewer people put themselves forward to adopt now than before but, again, concrete evidence is lacking. There are many reasons, though, why this could be so, including: the children's problems resulting in fewer rewards for their parents; the protracted and often adversarial nature of the proceedings; adverse publicity; lack of adequate post-placement and post-adoption support; insufficient or incorrect information about the children's background; and greater access than before to intercountry adoption. Demographic changes, too, may have played their part, such as expanding or creating a family through divorce, new partnerships and reconstitution.

Concluding remarks

This paper set out to answer the question of whether "permanence" through adoption is in decline. Though this view is strongly supported by the House of Commons Health Committee Report (1998) and the SSI (1996) report, the statistical evidence available offers only partial support.

A series of events seems to have contributed to some decline, including policy directions and organisational changes within social services, the children's difficulties and the negative treatment of adoption by sections of the press and politicians.

The kind of adoption pursued in Britain over the past two decades or so has been more diverse than before, both in terms of the children adopted and the families who adopt them. However one looks at the outcomes, adoption has recently provided a social base for over 40,000 children who would otherwise have grown up without a family to call their own. (The figures are based on the DoH Annual Statistics on Looked After Children.) This has not been easy to achieve, either for the children or their new families. Studies advise that the scars of earlier separations, emotional traumas and conflict do not heal readily. As a result expectations need to be tempered. Nevertheless, the evidence also suggests that this kind of adoption does work well for the majority of the children placed. The following is a reminder of what happens to children who grow up being looked after by the local authority and without a firm social base in life:

- They are four times more likely to be unemployed.
- They are 60 times more likely to be homeless.
- They constitute a quarter of the adult prison population (Paul Boateng MP, reported in the *The Times*, 14 April 1998).

It is appropriate to seek alternative forms of placement to suit the children's needs, but the stability, continuity and legality that go with adoption will continue to have a firm place in child placement policy and practice. While taking rigorous stock of some of the mistakes made in the past, such as the time limits imposed and the "clean break" approach, we also need to be reminded of the remarkable achievements. On the basis of the research evidence, many children's needs still find fulfilment through adoption.

References

Audit Commission (1994) *Seen But Not Heard*, London: HMSO.

Berlin I (1991) *The Crooked Timber of Humanity*, London: Fontana Press.

Bohman M and Sigvardsson S (1990) 'Outcome in adoption: lessons from longitudinal studies', in Brodzinsky D M and Schecter M D (eds), *The Psychology of Adoption*, New York: Oxford University Press.

Borland M, O'Hara G and Triseliotis J (1991) 'Permanency planning for children in Lothian region', in Social Work Services Group (ed), *Adoption and Fostering*, Edinburgh: Scottish Office.

BAAF (1997) *Focus on Adoption – A snapshot of adoptions in England, 1995*, London: BAAF.

BAAF (1998) 'Single-parent adoptions', Preliminary results given to *The Times* newspaper, 12 October.

Bullock R (1998) *Evidence to the House of Commons Health Committee*, Vol 1, p 19, London: The Stationery Office.

Department of Health (1993) *Review of Adoption Law*, London: HMSO.

Dumaret A (1985) 'Scholastic performance and behaviours of sibs raised in contrasting environments', *Journal of Child Psychology & Psychiatry & Allied Disciplines* 26:4, pp 553–80.

Fratter J, Rowe J, Sapsford D and Thoburn J (1991) *Permanent Family Placement: A decade of experience*, London: BAAF.

Fratter J (1996) *Adoption with Contact*, London: BAAF.

Gath A (1983) 'Mentally retarded children in substitute and natural families', *Adoption & Fostering* 7:1, pp 35–40.

Gibbons J, Gallagher B, Bell C and Gordon D (1995) *Development After Physical Abuse in Early Childhood: A follow-up study of children on protection registers*, London: HMSO.

Goldstein J, Freud A and Solnit A J (1973) *Beyond the Best Interests of the Child*, New York: Free Press.

Goldstein J, Freud A and Solnit A J (1980) *Before the Best Interests of the Child*, New York: Burnett Books.

Hill M, Lambert L and Triseliotis J (1989) *Achieving Adoption with Love and Money*, London: National Children's Bureau.

Holloway J S (1997) 'Foster and adoptive parents' assessment of permanent family placements', *Archives of Disease in Childhood* 76, pp 231–35.

House of Commons Health Committee Report, Vols 1 & 2 (1998) *Children Looked After by Local Authorities*, London: The Stationery Office.

Howe D (1997) 'Parent reported problems in 211 adopted children: some risk and protective factors', *Journal of Child Psychology & Psychiatry* 38, pp 401–12.

Hughes B (1995) *Post-placement Services for Children and Families: Defining the need*, London: Department of Health.

Kadushin A (1970) *Adopting Older Children*, New York: Columbia University Press.

Kahan B (1997) 'None so deaf', *Child Care Forum* 26:16.

Lowe N (1997) 'Some perspectives from national research', in James G (ed), *Post-placement Services in Adoption and Fostering*, London: Department of Health.

Macaskill C (1984) *Against the Odds*, London: Batsford.

McDonald T, Allen R, Westerfelt A and Piliavin I (1996) *Assessing the Long-term Effects of Foster Care: A research synthesis*, Washington: Child Welfare League of America.

Marsh P and Triseliotis J (1996) *Ready to Practise?*, Aldershot: Avebury.

Morgan P (1998) *Adoption and the Care of Children: The experience in Britain and America*, London: Institute of Economic Affairs.

Raynor L (1980) *The Adopted Child Comes of Age*, London: George Allen & Unwin.

Rowe J and Lambert L (1973) *Children Who Wait*, London: BAAF.

Rushton A, Quinton D, Dance C and Mayes D (1997) 'Preparation for permanent placement: evaluating direct work with older children', *Adoption & Fostering* 21:4, pp 41–48.

Rushton A and Minnis H (1997) 'Annotation: transracial family placements', *Journal of Child Psychology & Psychiatry* 38:2, pp 147–59.

Social Services Inspectorate (1996) *For Children's Sake: An SSI inspection of local authority adoption services*, Parts 1 & 2, London: Department of Health.

Strathclyde Social Work Department (1991) 'The outcome of permanent family placement', in Scottish Office (ed), *Adoption and Fostering*, Edinburgh: Central Research Unit Papers.

Thoburn J (1990) *Success and Failure in Permanent Family Placement*, Aldershot: Avebury.

Tizard B (1977) *Adoption: A second chance*, London: Open Books.

Triseliotis J (1983) 'Identity and security in long-term fostering and adoption', *Adoption & Fostering* 7:1, pp 22–31.

Triseliotis J and Russell J (1984) *Hard to Place: The outcome of adoption and residential care*, London: Gower.

Triseliotis J (1991) 'Perceptions of permanence', *Adoption & Fostering* 15:4, pp 6–15.

Triseliotis J, Shireman J and Hundleby M (1997) *Adoption: Theory, policy and practice*, London: Cassell.

Triseliotis J, Borland M, Hill M (1998) *Fostering Good Relations: A study of foster care and foster carers in Scotland*, Part 1, Edinburgh: Scottish Office.

Utting W (1998) *Evidence Given to the House of Commons Health Committee on Children Looked After by Local Authorities*, London: The Stationery Office.

Watson L and McGhee J (1995) *Developing Post-placement Support*, Edinburgh: BAAF.

5 The role of children in permanency planning

Pauline Hoggan

This article was first published in Adoption & Fostering *15:4, 1991.*

Although the theme of this article is "the role of children in permanency planning", it is of course actually about the role which adults enable or indeed permit children to have in being involved in a genuine way in decisions that affect their lives and their futures. To help focus our concern on the needs of children, rather than with adoption as a measure which provides for the social interest of adults, it may help to heed these words from Roald Dahl, the writer much disapproved of by adults and enthused over by children. In a recent survey of British primary school-age children, however, 30 per cent named him as their favourite writer (The *Observer*, 22 September 1991). 'I am totally convinced that most grown-ups have completely forgotten what it was like to be a child between say the age of five and ten. They all *think* they can remember. Some of course actually can, but very few' (Dahl R, 1991).

Main stances on children's rights

Debates about children's rights are often conducted within a framework which contains three main stances – protectionist, parentalist and child libertarian (Adler, 1985). The protectionist view, that of the middle ground, argues that the healthiest position society can take towards its children is to allow them increasing responsibility in proportion to their age, understanding and stage of development. The parentalist view would be, crudely, that parents should have more or less total authority over children. This is open to the challenge that such a rigid stance is counter to ideals of natural justice, and that it is unsound to expect that children forced to be dependent on adult authority till a certain age will then be able to take on responsibility if they have not been given the opportunity to practice self-determination as they grow up. The third position, that of libertarian, argues that children should have rights completely equal to those of adults. This position appears to me to deny that benign adult power is needed to nurture and stimulate children to develop from a position of infant dependency to adult independence. Such a view only exposes children to further exploitation by adults. For example, we recently heard a story about an infant being placed for adoption in a country which seems to have a law requiring all children to consent to their own adoptions. The scene, therefore, which was described was one in which the infant concerned gave his consent by putting his thumb print on the necessary form – it was of course being put there by an adult who was arranging the adoption.

Lothian experience

It would seem to me that the broad "consensus stance" in contemporary Scottish society would be one of some form of protectionism – the middle ground – and this is reflected in our adoption law (in section 6 of the Adoption (Scotland) Act 1978):

> . . . in reaching any decision relating to the adoption of a child, a court or adoption agency shall have regard to all the circumstances, first consideration being given to the need to safeguard and promote the welfare of the child throughout his childhood, and shall so far as practicable ascertain the wishes and feelings of the child regarding the decision and give due consideration to them, having regard to his age and understanding.

During the last decade Lothian has been able to show a positive outcome for the small proportion of the children in our care who have been placed permanently away from their families of origin, and we should feel reasonably satisfied at our efforts to act in the best interests of the children throughout their childhoods. We have also made a sustained effort to provide staff with training in communication with children by, for example, using the excellent material which BAAF has been instrumental in disseminating, in particular the work of fine teachers and practitioners such as Vera Fahlberg (1988), Claudia Jewett (1984) and Jane Aldgate (Aldgate and Simmonds, 1988). Every child being placed permanently in Lothian Region is expected to have some form of life-story book and virtually all children over the age of about four will, before placement, at least take part in a series of groups with other children in similar circumstances, run by experienced and able practitioners. Nevertheless, in reflecting on our involvement with the five to 12 age group in permanency planning, my view is that these children experience a more parentalist stance from adult authority than the legal framework and general social attitudes would imply are acceptable. I would argue that there *are* a number of factors which contribute to this dynamic and that they are significant in reducing the potential of our efforts to act in the best interests of the children.

Rationalisation and pragmatism

The first factor, I would suggest, is the tendency towards rationalisation and pragmatism in making childcare decisions. We rationalise that a measure is truly the best one for a particular child rather than being honest that we do not have the resources which would genuinely be fitting – for example, in convincing ourselves that a group of siblings really "need" to grow up separately, when in fact we know we don't have a suitable place for them all together. In such situations, surely it would be healthier for the children's future development if we were able to create honest relationships between adults and children, and acknowledge that perhaps we are having to compromise between what we feel is really right for them and what we can actually offer.

There are now many excellent publications and videos which supply ideas on techniques in communication with children, but we need to be sure that our motive in using these often effective methods is to open up real dialogue between adults and children, rather than to persuade children to accept our adult decisions.

It is also important that our mode of communication is one which is comfortable for the individual child, not for us. For example, analogies with animals are a favoured tool used by adults and can be tremendously useful, but we should be careful about their meaning for the developmental stage of the child, and also about possible symbolism. Bruno Bettelheim gives some examples of insensitivity in his book *On*

Learning to Read (1991), in which he argues that many early language teaching programmes patronise children and seriously dampen their motivation to achieve true literacy. He criticises reading books which depict animals who continually indulge in silly human behaviour or which use as positive characters an animal, such as the rat, which is one of the few animals which attacks young children. The thoughtlessness of this example was compounded by the fact that the particular series of books was aimed at groups of disadvantaged children who were likely to be living in slum areas where rat infestation was a real problem.

Avoiding pain

The second factor is the ever present tendency among us all to avoid pain. Reputable teaching on communication with children places such work in a clear context of dealing with loss and bereavement, and emphasises how essential it is that workers are aware of what this will mean for them at a personal level. As Claudia Jewett (1984) comments, 'The helping adult must understand that the recovery to healthy living involves pain. There is no short cut'. Several years ago a student participated in one of our children's groups which had four weekly sessions and included five children between the ages of about nine and 12. One of the exercises we used was developed from Vera Fahlberg's workbook on attachment and separation. We had written out on separate cards a large number of adjectives which described different feelings which were placed face up around the room, and the children were asked to take their time to pick out any cards which described the feelings they thought they might have when they heard that there was an adoptive family available for them. The aim of the exercise was to help the children realise that they are likely to have very mixed feelings. On this occasion the exercise led to a very open discussion among the children of some of the distressing situations they had been in. After the group the student expressed her concern that we were encouraging children to raise such issues, but when the children arrived for the next week's group asking if they could carry on with the same discussion she acknowledged that the learning for her was about her own distress when faced with such powerful feelings.

Claudia Jewett also cautions us that the developmental stages such as magical and concrete thinking are 'never completely eradicated and tend to recur in times of crises, even in adults'.

Adult power

The third factor is the function of adult power itself, especially in a process such as adoption which involves the transfer of parental rights (and therefore the body of the child) from one group of adults to another, often in an adversarial way. It is likely that many of the children will already have experienced a high level of conflict and inconsistent adult behaviour. Professor Thomson (1991) asserts that the assumption of parental rights by local authorities is a drastic step, not only because it deprives the birth parents of their rights but because it also deprives the child concerned of his or her liberty. I think it is sometimes difficult to acknowledge that a child's relationship with society's systems is severely altered by the status of being in care on a long-term basis, and that their links with institutions are not filtered through relationships with parents or guardians.

Believing children

Children in long-term care can be placed in a "no-win" situation by care workers. Because they have suffered loss, neglect or abuse they often have developmental delays or display difficult behaviour. We sometimes assume that these labels equate with a child being unable to express or hold *any* valid view. To go back to the example of our children's group exercise, we deliberately used a large number of cards and variety of words in order to demonstrate to the children the many ways in which feelings can be described:

Devastated	*Anxious*	*Sad*	*Happy*	*Excited*	*Hopeful*
Depressed	*Joyful*	*Scared*	*Terrified*	*Optimistic*	*Tearful*
Exhilarated	*Pleased*	*Ecstatic*	*Awful*	*Nauseous*	*Proud*
Ashamed	*Guilty*	*Relaxed*	*Thoughtful*	*Confused*	

We did not expect that the children themselves would understand all of the words we had used, and originally intended to try to use the explanation of the meaning of some of the words to progress discussion about the feeling itself. However, to our surprise, a high proportion of the children attempting this exercise were able to pick out a series of cards which perfectly described a number of mixed feelings that one might have in such a situation. To our further surprise, children who had been profiled as having learning disabilities, serious lack of concentration and very immature behaviour seemed to be able to pick out three- or four-syllable words such as devastated and exhilarated.

Another illustration of the inaccuracy of labels concerned a thorough developmental assessment of a four-year-old girl who had been in care for a high percentage of her life with one foster carer. As the child's parents were alcoholic and the child showed some of the physical characteristics of "foetal alcohol syndrome", it was assumed that she may also be affected by other characteristics such as a degree of learning disability. The developmental test, however, showed her as in fact being above average in four out of five areas, which cast a different light on her future needs.

In any case, should we as adults assume that if we do our assessments properly, we will necessarily have more sound views than children? A research study of children's and adult's perceptions of stressful life events, covering six different countries, raises this question (Yamamoto et al, 1987). In the study children aged between about seven and 13 were given a list of 20 undesirable life events chosen by the researchers, and asked to place them in order of worry. The children rated 'losing a parent' at the top; also high on the list, but reported as the most frequently occurring event, was 'telling the truth but no-one believing me'. What was striking for the researchers was the remarkable degree of agreement in the stress ratings and in reported incidents of stressful events, regardless of gender, race, class or culture, thereby giving 'credence to the presence of wide-spread, common perceptions and attitudes among children'. Even more remarkable was that the outcome of the same research with adults again showed a significant degree of agreement in their rating of stress in life events across cultural and professional boundaries – but the adults' agreed ratings were significantly different from those of the children. For example, the adults rated the arrival of a sibling in the family fairly high, whereas this was rated lowest by children. These findings would suggest that adult judgements may be used 'on a prevalent set of normative expectations or a sort of folklore, rather than upon accurate assessments of children's perceptions and attitudes'.

Conclusion

Workers who take a parentalist or "welfare" view express fears that children, if given a degree of real power, will make decisions which are harmful to them. I hope that the young people placed by us in Lothian during the 1980s will be asked to reflect on their experience in a further research project. However, I would speculate that many of them may feel that, in the circumstances, being placed in a family which provided a lifetime base, was to their advantage. I am sure, though, that they will have much to teach us about how our approach can improve, for example, in enabling young people to keep certain relationships going (or not) and in being more realistic about the degree of challenge the new relationships bring. A recent article by John Triseliotis (1991) provides us with some helpful signposts in this direction.

For those children who strongly disagree with our plans for them, are we certain that our reasons for carrying on regardless are sound? Or are they affected by issues of convenience, cost or unwillingness to lose face?

The children with whom we are concerned already feel worthless and different from other children in the community. The Scottish poet, Norman McCaig (1979) has said, 'man, whether he like it or not, can't climb down from his genealogical tree and scramble up another of his own choice'. Yet this is what we ask of children placed permanently away from their family of origin – the price they must pay to achieve the same status as other children in the community. We owe it to them that the systems to which we contribute operate with the highest level of integrity.

References

Adler R (1985) *Taking Juvenile Justice Seriously*, Edinburgh: Scottish Academic Press.

Aldgate J and Simmonds J (1988) *Direct Work with Children*, London: BAAF/ Batsford.

Bettelheim B and Zelan K (1991) *On Learning to Read: The child's fascination with meaning* (second edition), London: Penguin.

Dahl R (1991) *Guide to Railway Safety*, British Railway Board.

Fahlberg V (1988) *Fitting the Pieces Together*, London: BAAF.

Jewett C (1984) *Helping Children Cope with Separation and Loss*, London: Batsford Academic.

McCaig N (1979) 'My way of it', autobiographical essay, in Lindsay M (ed) *As I Remember*, London: Robert Hare Ltd.

Thomson J (1991) *Family Law in Scotland*, Butterworth: Law Society of Scotland.

Triseliotis J (1991) 'Maintaining the links in adoption', *British Journal of Social Work* 21, p 401–14.

Yamamoto I, Soliman A, Parsons J and Davies Jnr O L (1987) 'Voices in unison – stressful events in lives of children in six countries', *Journal of Child Psychology & Psychiatry* 28, pp 855–64.

6 Partnership reviewed: words of caution, words of encouragement[1]

Malcolm Hill

This article was first published in Adoption & Fostering *24:3, 2000.*

Introduction

As the 1990s have given way to the new millenium, it is timely to re-evaluate one of the key terms and guiding principles that informed child welfare policy and practice in the UK during that decade – partnership. This became popular partly as a reaction to what were seen as excessively confrontational and legalistic elements of permanency planning in the 1980s. Partnership with birth parents was advocated with the intention and hope of producing a more co-operative ethos for relationships between statutory services and families in difficulties.

This article reviews research evidence about progress and short-comings in the way British child welfare agencies, particularly local authorities, have sought to work with parents in relation to family placements. After a brief review of partnership principles, research evidence will be reviewed about types and degrees of co-operation in practice. The implications are then discussed in terms of a spectrum of co-operation and the need for honesty about what degree of co-operation is desirable or feasible when the primary goal is promoting child's welfare.

The meaning of partnership with birth parents and associated aspirations

The roots of working collaboratively with birth families extend back many years, but the idea of "partnership" with parents was introduced in the

---

[1]This article is based on a presentation made to the BAAF Research Symposium in November 1999. It was accepted for publication before the author resumed editorship of the journal.

mid-1980s to contrast with working in opposition to parents or dealing with them as if they were not full citizens (Fisher *et al*, 1986; Freeman, 1994). The term was not explicitly included in the 1989 Children Act, nor indeed the Children (Scotland) Act 1995 or the Children (NI) Order 1995. However, the guidance to this legislation did emphasise partnership with parents as a key principle, as did many contemporary commentators (Allen, 1996).

Two main aspects to partnership with parents were described in government guidance and the research literature:

- maximum involvement of parents in planning and decision-making;
- minimum intrusiveness – avoidance of compulsory orders unless necessary in the child's interests.

During the 1990s the main principles and elements of partnership were more clearly articulated (Freeman, 1994; Kaganas *et al*, 1995). These may be summarised as follows:

- Recognise and promote continuing parental responsibility.
- Include parents in decision-making at all stages.
- Be open and honest.
- As far as possible, work in agreement with parents.
- Whenever possible, avoid legal action.
- Consider and respect family, community and cultural contexts, strengths as well as weaknesses.

All these considerations are subject to the welfare principle which is enshrined in British legislation and the UN Convention on the Rights of the Child. In other words, a partnership approach should have as its goal the best interests of the child.

The role of research in illuminating partnership

Research has a number of potential parts to play in elucidating partnership. In particular it can:

- describe and analyse the nature and processes of the relationships;
- identify variations by area, placement type, family circumstances, gender, etc;

- examine the impact on the key parties, especially the children and parents.

In considering the nature of "partnership" relationships, it is necessary to recognise that the agency side is represented by two key players: the child's social worker and the carers. They have the main direct contact with parents, although they are affected by a host of other people, such as team managers and fostering link workers. When two or more parental figures are involved with a child, they may well have different attributes and interests.

Four main features of the relationship are relevant for assessing the nature of partnership when a child is looked after away from home:

1 Communication
How often does this occur? What information is passed to and from parents? How openly are expectations, rights, options and constraints discussed?

2 Decision-making
To what extent and in what ways are parents enabled to express their views? How much influence do parents have on decisions?

3 Contact with the child
How often does the child see the parent(s)? What is the quality of contact?

4 Shared care
To what extent, if at all, do parents continue to look after the child some of the time?

Sometimes it may be enough to know how far partnership is occurring in a specific way, but often it is vital to understand the consequences too.

In practice, existing research has tended to focus on assessing elements of partnership and gaining the perspectives of those affected. Measurable evidence about outcomes is sparser. In any case, it is not easy to demonstrate conclusively how, through a complicated chain of events, communication with parents and taking account of their views in decision-making affects a child's behaviour or happiness. Also, research like practice has largely focused on mothers rather than fathers, especially with respect to adoption.

In the remaining sections, findings from research are reviewed, with an examination of:

- obstacles and absence of partnership;
- progress in partnership;
- what helps working together;
- the consequences of "partnership".

Obstacles and absence of partnership

Here we consider the evidence about the stages that lead up to and beyond a child's placement in a foster or adoptive family.

Child abuse investigations are commonly a route for children admitted to foster care or adoption. During care proceedings, many children experience interim placements in foster care. A major change in British child protection compared with the 1980s has been the shift from case conferences consisting only of professionals to an expectation that parents should normally be included (Thoburn *et al*, 1995). In a number of areas, decision-making has been shared with kin networks through the use of Family Group Conferences (Jackson and Nixon, 1999a, 1999b). Despite these new participative arrangements, parents, and especially men, still feel marginalised in decision-making meetings in relation to child protection (Bell, 1999; Whitfield and Harwood, 1999). Whether or not abuse is established, most parents feel aggrieved, which makes partnership difficult. They also resent supervised contact (Cleaver and Freeman, 1995; Freeman and Hunt, 1998).

Even if family placements do not start in such a context of tensions or conflict between social worker and parents, there is generally little time to clarify and agree mutual expectations about future communication and contact. Admissions to foster care are rarely planned, unless the child is moving from a previous placement (Triseliotis *et al*, 1995a, 2000; Barn *et al*, 1997).

Divergence or conflict of viewpoints is very common between agencies and parents, both in relation to admission *per se* and to particular placements. In a study of accommodated children, 'Participation of a significant minority of parents and a rather smaller proportion of children was said to be "difficult"' (Packman and Hall, 1998, p 261). For only a quarter of admissions were parents, children and social services all in favour. Triseliotis *et al* (1995a) found similar disparities in viewpoint. Lack of consensus occurs not only when local authorities are intervening to remove children from resistant parents, but also when they are seeking to keep families together. Both studies found that in a number of cases, parents were frustrated by social workers' reluctance to remove children from home when the parents thought this was the best or only solution.

At the time of admission, parents often feel they have little influence over what happens. Few are given a chance to comment on their preferred placement, partly because there is usually little choice anyway (Triseliotis *et al*, 1995a; Freeman and Hunt, 1998; Triseliotis *et al*, 1998). The emergency nature of many placements also means that there is little scope to match parents with carers who appear most compatible. Furthermore, parents may receive little information about the legal situation, their rights and what has happened to the child (Barn *et al*, 1997). The work demands on social workers are among the reasons they give for not being able to act as co-operatively with parents as they would wish (Masson *et al*, 1997).

There is evidence that white workers find it harder to engage effectively with black families and this may be linked to the over-representation of black children in care (Barn, 1993). Improvements have occurred in the recruitment of black and minority ethnic staff in parts of England, but in Scotland low levels are found almost everywhere and considerable ignorance has been identified among white staff concerning racism and minority cultural backgrounds (Singh *et al*, 2000). When it is necessary to use interpreters this can hinder as much as aid communication, unless very carefully handled and prepared for (Humphreys *et al*, 1999).

Both guidance and practice have stressed the need for regular planning and reviews, which should normally include birth parents (and older children). Nevertheless, the use of care plans is still not universal (Social Services Inspectorate, 1996). One study found that significantly fewer Asian and mixed parentage children had care plans than others (Barn *et al*, 1997). Similarly, many review meetings do not have parents attending, though apparently more than in the past (Berridge, 1996; Social Services Inspectorate, 1996).

Official guidance and textbooks (Triseliotis *et al*, 1995b) highlight that most foster carers should see their role as working not only with the child, but also with relevant family members. This is particularly the case in specialist or professional schemes.

However, most foster carers receive little help for this complex task. Preparatory training for foster carers, especially outside specialist schemes, is short, while continuing training is not available or attended by many (Triseliotis *et al*, 1998; Lowe, 1999). This links to the issue of payment: it is only reasonable to expect foster carers to take on a broader task than direct care of the children if they have commensurate remuneration. Many foster carers do not see themselves as being fully respected and involved by the agency, so this diminishes their willing-ness and capacity to work closely with parents (Waterhouse, 1999). Evidently it is difficult to promote good co-operation between carers and parents if the sense of partnership between carers and the local authority is lacking.

Many foster carers are ambivalent about the involvement of parents, especially when the parents have difficult personalities, drink problems or have abused or neglected the children (Triseliotis *et al*, 1998, 2000; Waterhouse, 1999). In the recent Scottish evaluation of fostering services, work with parents was not prominent in foster carers' motivations or their descriptions of their experience as foster carers (Triseliotis *et al*, 1998). In relation to current foster children's birth parents, one in six reported no contact. For the majority of cases where contact occurred, just half stated that this was easy. Nearly one in five reported that it was rarely or never easy. The remainder had mixed experiences.

Even when parents and their children remain in touch, this does not necessarily entail significant engagement between the child's two families. Much contact takes place away from the foster home, which is less disruptive for foster families but can lead to a sharp division in children's lives (Cleaver, 1999; Waterhouse, 1999). In the Scottish fostering study, for 30 per cent of the cases the contact was neither in the foster home nor parental home (Triseliotis *et al*, 1998). The proportion of access visits occurring in foster carers' homes ranged from 16 to 50 per cent between authorities. Even though distance may play a part, this suggests that agency policy and practice influence the nature of contact.

Turning to adoption, a survey of 50 statutory and voluntary agencies carried out by Lindley (1997) identified several stages and aspects of the adoption process where birth parents had little or no involvement. Few of the agencies let birth family members see the completed assessment forms or had a birth parent on the adoption panel. Most agencies encouraged adopters to meet with birth parents but nearly all did not wish to reveal the whereabouts of the adoptive home. Only one-quarter provided post-adoption support to birth parents.

High proportions of adoptions are now contested and nearly half of orders follow dispensing with mothers' consent (Department of Health, 1999). Hence in such cases 'during the prelude to adoptions arrangements for contact will be made under duress' (p 50).

Many adopters are willing for indirect contact to take place, but are opposed to direct contact (Lambert *et al*, 1990; Department of Health, 1999). There is a hierarchy of anxiety, fathers causing greatest concern, mothers next, with siblings and grandparents less threatening. Concerns include managing the contact, fear of destabilising the placement, worries about adverse impact on the child (especially when ill-treatment has occurred) and difficulty in handling family events and present-giving. An English study of adoptive or permanent foster families found that relatively few children still had contact with their birth parents, but where it occurred a number of new parents reported the children to be unsettled by the contact (Quinton *et al*, 1998). A third of the new parents said they needed help in negotiations with birth parents.

Birth parents, too, may not take up opportunities to collaborate. Logan (1999) found that a number of birth parents did not collect information made available by adopters. Even when communication did occur, this rarely involved birth fathers.

The evidence from all these studies is that there are often inherent obstacles to partnership in family placement. Often birth parents have resented social work involvement and opposed the placement in the first place. Many carers are suspicious about contact with the child's parents. Particularly in short-term and emergency placements, which are the majority, there is little time to talk and work through the differences of perspectives and expectations.

Progress in partnership

Although the preceding section showed that working together with birth parents remains a difficult enterprise, research has also documented a variety of ways in which progress has been made towards more shared planning and a less restrictive approach to parental contact in both foster care and adoption.

In child protection greater efforts are now made to include birth parents in decision-making. There is considerable evidence that parents are much more involved in planning in situations of alleged or proven child abuse (Thoburn *et al*, 1995). Moreover, although many parents are understandably hostile about initial abuse referrals, their attitudes often mellow over the years (Cleaver and Freeman, 1995).

The influence of the minimal intrusion principle can be seen in the decisive shift away from use of court orders in England and Wales towards a higher proportion of voluntary accommodation (Packman and Hall, 1998). Compared with the 1980s, British foster children are now much less likely to have their contact with parents compulsorily terminated or to be freed for adoption against parental wishes (Department of Health, 1999).

The majority of black and minority ethnic children in many areas are now being placed with families of similar backgrounds (Sellick and Thoburn, 1996; Barn *et al*, 1997; Singh *et al*, 2000). This is likely not only to assist children's identity but also encourage parental contact (Rashid, 2000). Barn (1993) found that black children were more likely to have frequent parental contact than white children. However, in some parts of the UK transracial placements remain common. In the Barn *et al* study, the proportion of African-Caribbean foster carers in different areas ranged from ten to 41 per cent, of Asian foster carers from none to 31 per cent.

It is hard to track changes in attitudes over time, but researchers who were active in both the 1980s and 1990s believe that workers are putting more effort into maintaining a child's family links (Bullock *et al*, 1998; Cleaver, 1999). It appears that contact between looked after children and their parents is greater than formerly, so that it is no longer a predictor of those going home. In other words, even when children are in long-term care, contact is more likely to be maintained than formerly (Bullock *et al*, 1998). However, contact frequencies for children in foster care are lower than for residential care, even when age is allowed for (Bilson and Barker, 1995).

Parents still often lack confidence when invited to participate in planning and review meetings. However, Packman and Hall (1998) found that some became more at ease over time and so better able to contribute more fully.

Significant efforts to include birth parents more in key processes and decisions are also evident with respect to adoption. In a survey of adoption agencies in England and Wales, 80 per cent had policies that birth family members should be involved in recruitment and selection. Most agencies encouraged adopters to meet with birth parents before the adoption proceeded (Lindley, 1997).

Contact following adoption has increased substantially and is now standard expectation in nearly all adoption agencies (Lindley, 1997; Department of Health, 1999). Written agreements are increasingly common so that all parties are clear about the purpose and nature of contact (Lowe *et al*, 1999).

In the main, the contact is indirect, with face-to-face communication still exceptional after an adoption order is granted. So-called letterbox schemes have become the norm (Lindley, 1997; Rajan and Lister, 1998). Usually the exchange is of letters, cards and photos. Most often the contact is annual and it is unusual to exchange items more often than two or three times per year, typically on birthdays and at Christmas (Ryburn, 1994; Carter *et al*, 1999). These schemes seem to be widely accepted but researchers have also identified issues that have often not been well thought out. For instance, how do adopters and birth parents get adequate preparation and support without infringing their privacy? How do adoption agencies best manage the growing flow of letters, cards and presents? Which aspects are clerical and which require professional oversight (Department of Health, 1999)?

Despite the expansion of letterbox schemes, it must be remembered that some birth parents remain excluded from knowledge and contact even though they would like to stay in touch (Mason and Selman, 1998).

What helps working together

Research has shown wide variations between agencies with regard to some indicators of partnership with parents, such as frequency of parent–child and parent–foster carer contact or adoption contact agreements (Lowe *et al*, 1999; Triseliotis *et al*, 2000). It has been much more difficult to specify conclusively which elements of agency policy and practice are responsible, since there are so many factors to consider.

Feedback from birth parents does indicate the kinds of qualities in individual workers that help them feel valued and involved. Just like children and young people (Hill, 1999), they value willingness to listen, honest information-giving and respectful attitudes (Masson *et al*, 1997). Work in relation to child protection processes (Department of Health, 1995; Thoburn *et al*, 1995; Bell, 1999) indicated a number of key factors which facilitate the involvement even of reluctant or hostile parents. The main requirements were:

- clear information provided in advance to parents in writing;
- positive attitudes, honesty and creative negotiation skills of the individual worker;
- supportive agency policies and a positive desire to involve parents throughout the agency.

When children are placed in foster care, parents welcome being asked about their children's special needs and preferences (Freeman and Hunt, 1998). This should now happen routinely with the Looking After Children materials (Ward, 1998). It is important that the type of placement is one that parents feel they can approve of and work with. Carers need to be able to reassure parents that they are not usurping their role and to discuss openly issues of discipline, which concern many parents (Triseliotis *et al*, 1995b). Later on in longer-term placements, providing parents with detailed up-to-date information about their children is very important (Masson *et al*, 1997). Again, like young people, parents need prior information to be able to participate productively in discussions. The meetings need to be held at times and in places that suit parents (Masson *et al*, 1997). When parents have drink, drugs or behaviour problems or have a history of child abuse, foster carers welcome social worker presence during contact visits (Triseliotis *et al*, 2000), though, as noted earlier, birth parents themselves often dislike this.

In adoption, specific plans for contact need to be thoroughly negotiated and agreed in advance with birth parents and adopters. This may help avoid contesting and so promote better feelings in the long run (Department of Health, 1999; Lowe *et al*, 1999). The nature and frequency of contact should be negotiated individually rather than prescribed and there ought to be mechanisms for identifying exchanges that become one way (Logan, 1999). For indirect letterbox contact, adopters welcome guidance and sample documents but not many currently receive them. These could be given to birth parents too (Department of Health, 1999). Adopters (and presumably birth parents) also want to know what vetting of letters takes place, if any. Birth parents welcome acknowledgement of their messages so they know their communication arrived (Carter *et al*, 1999). Both sides want the agreement kept to.

Face-to-face contact after adoption seems to work better when previous contact was good, notably where foster carers adopted (Hill *et al*, 1989; Department of Health, 1999). Agency policies and practices that carefully explain and promote contact seem to be influential in enabling this to happen (McRoy, 1991). It is also helpful if adopters understand the reasons for contact, are prepared for how to manage it, have pre-court contact and have the skills and support to facilitate contact (Ryburn 1994; Department of Health, 1999). Neutral settings for contact can help when there are anxieties on one or both sides. In a recent study, adopters welcomed being able to make contact outside their own homes, but noted the artificiality and low level of birth parent–child interaction. Some adopters are reassured by social worker presence; others resent the restriction on freedom (Department of Health, 1999). A number of older children only agree to adoption if contact continues and this appears to work well when the adopters are content about it and do not encourage guilt or divided loyalties (Triseliotis *et al*, 1997).

Whether having post-adoption contact face to face or by letterbox, many adopters and birth parents find it very helpful to have an agency as an intermediary to provide distance, to help negotiate plans and to sort out difficulties if they arise (Carter *et al*, 1999). According to Logan (1999, p 35), 'the agency provides a safeguard reassuring all parties that boundaries are in place'. Similarly, adult adoptees like the protection of having an agency that can inform them if their birth relatives wish to make contact, so they can decide themselves how to respond (Stanaway, 1996/7).

Mediation may help birth parents and adopters reach a clear joint decision in advance. The London-based Post Adoption Centre set up a mediation service in 1994 (Kedward *et al*, 1999). A small survey of users revealed that both sets of parents felt listened to and most thought the agency was impartial. Some mediation did not result in contact because the adopters vetoed it. In other cases where contact was agreed, the mediator also helped manage as well as plan this.

Although local authorities and their social workers are learning how to work better with birth parents when there is conflict over child protection or contested adoption, it is not easy to offer or receive genuine support in situations of strong conflict. An evaluation by Mason and Selman (1998) showed that a complementary voluntary sector service could be very helpful for birth parents in these circumstances. Important factors were independence from the local authority, careful listening and willingness to act as an intermediary.

The consequences of "partnership"

As indicated above, we have little evidence about the impact of local authority moves towards closer co-operation with parents. Research has shown that many foster carers and adopters are very anxious about this, particularly because they do not see it as fitting with their role and expectations and because they fear or witness adverse effects on the child (Department of Health, 1999; Triseliotis *et al*, 2000). Yet there is also evidence that careful recruitment and preparation can increase open and participative attitudes (Triseliotis *et al*, 1995b, 1997).

It is generally assumed that increased participation and contact will help the birth parents of looked after children, but we know little about how their well-being or parenting capacity is actually affected. The main evidence consists of subjective feedback. Understandably, parents report dissatisfaction about being left out of decisions and plans (Barn *et al*, 1997) and conversely respond favourably when they are involved

(Triseliotis *et al*, 1995a; Packman and Hall, 1998). Parents who were included in training for foster carers felt valued and developed more of a shared understanding with foster carers (Gilchrist and Hoggan, 1999). Masson *et al* (1997) found that reunions with children after long gaps were often difficult, but parents nonetheless usually felt relief and pleasure.

In adoption, cessation of contact has been the norm for many years in the UK, although openness has stronger roots in many cultures (Dutt and Sanyal, 1998). Studies have repeatedly shown the intense and prolonged despair that can result from losing a child to adoption, whether voluntarily or compulsorily (Winkler and van Keppel, 1984; Logan, 1996). Likewise, research has indicated the benefits that can come when birth parents stay in touch, though the samples in most of the studies have been small. Being involved in choosing adopters reduced birth parents' sense of powerlessness and guilt. It also helped comfort them about their decision (Ryburn, 1994; Fratter, 1996). An evaluation of a letterbox exchange in Hampshire found that birth parents valued knowing about their children's progress and gained peace of mind (Carter *et al*, 1999). Logan (1999) also found positive responses, though the information could be upsetting at the same time as being welcome.

Commonly birth parents want more information about the progress of their adopted children. Many of those who placed their children for adoption before openness was customary believe they are entitled to receive non-identifying information and many yearn for telephone or personal contact (Mullender and Kearn, 1997).

The data available about the impact on children of partnership with birth parents are sparse. In relation to child protection conferences, the effects on children of including birth parents have not been systematically assessed. It is interesting that Bell (1999) found that most social workers thought they acted in a participatory way, but only a minority thought the child benefited. Assessments of Family Group Conferences indicate that in the great majority of cases, decisions made largely by kin are thought by professionals to be acceptable and in the child's interest.

Two-thirds of Scottish foster carers thought that children benefited from seeing their parents and only one in ten did not, though overall a third registered a qualification (Triseliotis *et al*, 1998). Many US and

British studies of children in foster and residential care have shown positive long-term results when they have regular and frequent contact with parents. Compared with those not in contact, they tend to have better personal well-being, a lower incidence of behaviour problems and greater likelihood of return home (Fanshel and Shinn, 1978; Millham *et al*, 1986; Berridge and Cleaver, 1987; Bullock *et al*, 1993). This appears to hold true, even for older and more difficult children (Sellick and Thoburn, 1996). However, parents who maintain regular contact tend to have more favourable circumstances and dispositions, so that it does not follow that all children will benefit from greater contact, though most probably will.

Masson *et al* (1997) examined the effects on children of concerted efforts by social workers and others to re-engage with parents who had lost touch. In most cases some information was found. Benefits included obtaining letters and photos, when previously there were none. For about half the sample of 62 children, meetings or more regular contact took place. Some were glad to have the opportunity to have questions answered about the reasons for having to leave home or their parents' background.

The findings on adoption with face-to-face contact similarly indicate that where it happens it is usually experienced positively by the children (Fratter, 1996), but that is at least partly because the circumstances are favourable (e.g. prior adopter–birth parent familiarity and parental support for the adoption plan). Of the 12 children with face-to-face contact in the Fratter study, six were content with the amount of contact and five wanted to see their mothers more often. However, the research evidence on adoption with face-to-face contact remains small in scale and duration, so that those who have reviewed the literature warn against over generalising; it can work well, but is not suitable for all children (BAAF, 1999; Department of Health, 1999).

Adopted children not in touch with birth parents show a wide spectrum of views, from curiosity and a wish or thirst for information to strong hostility and a desire not to think about birth parents (Howe, 1996). Thomas *et al* (1999) found that out of 26 children seven explicitly said they did *not* want contact, 12 seemed content without it and seven did want it.

Discussion

Partnership with birth parents was one of the main childcare principles of the 1990s in the UK. This ideal of co-operation is highly laudable, but may also be misleading and can have negative as well as positive consequences. Research indicates that there have been positive developments in practice, but tensions and difficulties remain. Studies continue to document either active conflict or more passive lack of involvement by birth parents at each stage of a child's care career. To understand both the opportunities and limitations of a partnership approach, it is necessary to unravel what is meant by partnership with parents and acknowledge that it is a guiding principle that needs to be balanced alongside other considerations.

We have seen that partnership is particularly relevant at several key points in the career of a child looked after away from home. These range from initial assessment or investigation, via admission to family placement and initial care planning, to reviews and possibly placement for adoption. The kinds of relationship established with parents at early stages of contact or placement will affect the chances of later co-operation, yet often this phase is characterised by a social work focus on short-term issues, hurried responses and divergent viewpoints.

Partnership is also a multiple concept, embracing several broad attitudes such as openness, voluntarism and respect, which are expressed through communication by social work staff and carers, in decision-making and by the degree of parental contact and involvement in care of the child. In favourable circumstances, the aim will be to maximise parental involvement at all stages and in all aspects, but this will not be the case when parental behaviour or wishes run contrary to the child's welfare. If it is thought to be in the child's best interests not to return home or to have contact restricted, then partnership may not be able to extend to contact or care. However, parents still have rights legally and ethically as both parents and citizens to give and receive information and to participate in decision-making.

There are elements of a partnership approach which are justified as ends in themselves. Even parents who are partly or wholly being excluded from their children's lives are entitled to information, explanations and courtesy. In other respects, partnership is a means to a different end, i.e. the child's welfare. This can involve many ways of helping the child directly, for example, by providing shared care, demonstrating continued love or interest and helping with issues of loss and identity. Parents can also help the child indirectly through giving carers information, understanding, validation or support. Thus contact should not be viewed simply in terms of a parent's needs or even the child's immediate physical and emotional needs, but considered in long-term perspective with regard to all dimensions of the child's development.

The term partnership appears to offer an equal and intimate relationship, as in marriage or business, but in child welfare, power differentials and the various ways to achieve possible closeness need to be recognised. Local authorities have greater legal and resource power than parents 'judged to be irresponsible' (Kaganas *et al*, 1995, p 9). This will often overlay extended and possibly lifelong experiences of *powerlessness* by parents within society, on account of social exclusion, racism, gender or disabling attitudes (Boushel and Lebacq, 1992; Barn *et al*, 1997; Booth and Booth, 1998; Kedward *et al*, 1999). The implication is not that power can simply be divested, since it is inherent to the situation. Rather, a subtle analysis is required to distinguish the necessary or helpful aspects of authority from the unnecessary and unhelpful aspects, with the intention of ensuring that agency and worker power 'can be made more humane and accountable' (Healey, 2000, p 94). This means in practice that workers and carers should strive to reconcile plans for the child with parental wishes, but also acknowledge legal constraints or incompatibilities with the child's interests, so that parents are not given false expectations of a greater say than is realistic. Conversely, the local authority's view of the child's interests should only be used as a reason for disregarding parents when their view is well grounded in all the available evidence.

Recognising the spectrum of possible co-operative relationships would assist understanding of partnership and open acknowledgement with parents of its potential and limitations. A framework applied by the Social Services Inspectorate (SSI) to inter-agency co-operation can be adapted and extended for agency–parent relations (SSI, 1996; Tisdall *et al*, 2000). Co-operation may range from simply communicating with each other about one's own actions and plans, right through to joint planning and action, which tends to be what partnership entails. This can be seen in many ways as corresponding with the spectrum of family placement, with expectations of co-operation being greatest with brief foster placements and least after adoption.

Table 1
Type of co-operation in relation to spectrum of care

Type of co-operation	Spectrum of care
Joint activity (shared care)	Respite and some short-term fostering
Bi-lateral or joint planning	Intermediate fostering
Collaboration	Longer-term fostering
Consultation	Choice of adopters
Communication	Open adoption
No communication	Conventional Western adoption

In practice, both actual and desirable degrees of co-operation will vary from this pattern. What is important is that both sides to an agreement are clear about what degree of co-operation is expected, specify limitations on their negotiating position and are also honest about their differences in perspective and interest. In many cases of foster care the level of fully joint planning may be desirable and possible, but sometimes local authorities (or indeed the courts) may decide to override parental wishes and use their power to do so. Or the two parties may simply not be able to agree, so that consultation may be the best that can be achieved. Adopters may welcome communication, but be concerned or alarmed if they think birth parents want joint planning or activity. The adopters may be reassured if they realise that consultation may be all that birth parents want.

Conclusions

Unless carefully integrated in practice, the language of partnership may disguise rather than resolve tensions between agencies, carers and parents, distract from real differences of opinion about what is best for children and gloss over differences in power and resources. The onus should be on agencies and workers to be open, honest and respectful to parents, and seek wherever possible to negotiate agreements, but at times that means recognising and accepting differences of goals and plans. It may mean mutual acknowledgement that fully joint planning may not be possible, so that consultation or collaboration may be more appropriate. Equally, the legal power of local authorities or adopters should not be used to limit communication when this is in the child's interests or even when it is neutral as regards the likely impact on the child.

Research confirms that significant changes have occurred towards greater partnership in several respects, for instance in participation at meetings and in care plans, with more use of written agreements, increased promotion of parental contact in foster care and of post-adoption communication. Social workers can make a difference in re-establishing contact, which may sometimes fulfil parents and/or children's rights and wish to know about each other and sometimes lead to resumed contact. Mostly efforts have been focused on mothers, with very little attention to fathers or other birth relatives, especially in adoption.

In the main, the research and practice indications are that these developments are positive for birth parents themselves. The consequences for children are less clear. We still know very little about the impact of parental involvement in decision-making and planning on children. This is justifiable in terms of parents' rights as citizens and service users, so long as it is not detrimental to children, but we still need to know more about the consequences. Usually participation in decisions does go hand in hand with contact but this is not invariably so. In relation to foster care, the evidence suggests that the great majority of children benefit from ongoing involvement but not all. For adoption, the jury is still out since we know that small numbers gain from significant levels of contact, but it is uncertain how far this conclusion can be extended to the great majority who have minimal or no contact. Research is needed, not only to examine outcomes as well as processes and opinions, but to help differentiate those circumstances in which particular kinds of co-operation and contact are beneficial or not. We should beware generalisations, since the nature and effects of co-operation among any parties in the fostering or adoption network are very much affected by the other people concerned, as well as the particular circumstances.

It is evident that engaging productively with birth parents for the sake of their separated children requires resources, i.e. time, thought and skills on the part of workers and carers. Time may be needed to help parents with their own difficulties, involve them in key meetings and reviews, assist them in contact and sometimes arrange supervised contact – all this in addition to work with the child and carers. Not all birth parents and carers want preparation and help but many do. Carers and adopters require information, preparation and assistance to communicate well with birth parents. This has already meant considerable expansion of services devoted to supporting contact in foster placements or following adoption, but much more is required.

During the 1990s, partnership reflected and spurred attempts by British local authorities to work more co-operatively with parents in relation to child care and protection. However, the term tends to disguise the complex balancing of interests, views and perspectives that this often entails. The phrase "working together" conveys this process better, since it does not presuppose a particular degree of co-operation and suggests the need for active and thoughtful "working at" the issues with parents.

References

Allen N (1996) *Making Sense of the Children Act*, Chichester: John Wiley & Sons.

Argent H (1995) *See You Soon*, London: BAAF.

BAAF (1999) *Contact in Permanent Placement*, London: BAAF.

Barn R (1993) *Black Children in the Public Care System*, London: BAAF/ Batsford.

Barn R, Sinclair R and Ferdinand D (1997) *Acting on Principle*, London: BAAF.

Bell M (1999) 'Working in partnership in child protection: the conflicts', *British Journal of Social Work* 29:3, pp 437–56.

Berridge D (1996) *Foster Care: A research review*, London: HMSO.

Berridge D and Cleaver H (1987) *Foster Home Breakdowns*, Oxford: Blackwell.

Bilson A and Barker R (1995) 'Parental contact with children fostered and in residential care after the Children Act 1989', *British Journal of Social Work* 25:3, pp 367–81.

Booth T and Booth W (1998) *Growing up with Parents who have Learning Difficulties*, London: Routledge.

Boushel M and Lebacq M (1992) 'Towards empowerment in child protection work', *Children & Society* 6:1, pp 38–50.

Bullock R, Little M and Millham S (1993) *Going Home*, Aldershot: Dartmouth.

Bullock R, Gooch D and Little M (1998) *Children Going Home*, Aldershot: Ashgate.

Carter V, Magee S and Thoday R (1999) 'Adoption information exchange: evaluation of a letterbox system in a local authority', *Adoption & Fostering* 23:1, pp 24–30.

Cleaver H (1999) 'Contact: the social worker's experience', in Hill M (ed.), *Signposts in Fostering*, London: BAAF.

Cleaver H and Freeman P (1995) *Parental Perspectives in Cases of Suspected Child Abuse*, London: HMSO.

Department of Health (1995) *Child Protection: Messages from research*, London: Department of Health.

Department of Health (1999) *Adoption Now: Messages from research*, Chichester: John Wiley & Sons.

Dutt R and Sanyal A (1998) 'Openness in adoption or open adoption – a black perspective', in Hill M and Shaw M (eds), *Signposts in Adoption*, London: BAAF.

Fanshel D and Shinn E B (1978) *Children in Foster Care: A longitudinal investigation*, New York: Columbia University Press.

Fisher M, Marsh M, Phillips M and Sainsbury E (1986) *In and Out of Care*, London: BAAF/Batsford.

Fratter J (1996) *Adoption with Contact*, London: BAAF.

Freeman M D A (1994) *Children, Families and the Law*, London: Macmillan.

Freeman P and Hunt J (1998) *Parental Perspectives on Care Proceedings*, London: HMSO.

Gilchrist A and Hoggan P (1999) 'Involving birth parents in foster care training', in Hill M (ed.), *Signposts in Fostering*, London: BAAF.

Healey K (2000) *Social Work Practices*, London: Sage Publications.

Hill M (1999) 'What's the problem? Who can help? The perspectives of children and young people on their well-being and on helping professionals', *Journal of Social Work Practice* 13:1, pp 135–46.

Hill M, Lambert L and Triseliotis J (1989) *Achieving Adoption with Love and Money*, London: National Children's Bureau.

Howe D (1996) *Adopters on Adoption*, London: BAAF.

Humphreys C, Aktar S and Baldwin N (1999) 'Discrimination in child protection work: recurring themes in work with Asian families', *Child & Family Social Work* 4:4, pp 283–92.

Jackson S and Nixon P (1999a) 'Family Group Conferences: A challenge to the old order', in Dominelli L (ed.), *Community Approaches to Child Welfare*, Aldershot: Ashgate.

Jackson S and Nixon P (1999b) 'Family Group Conferences: users' empowerment of family self-reliance – a development from Lupton', *British Journal of Social Work* 29:4, pp 621–30.

Kaganas F, King M and Piper C (eds) (1995) *Legislating for Harmony: Partnership under the Children Act 1989*, London: Jessica Kingsley.

Kedward C, Luckock B and Lawson H (1999) 'Mediation and post-adoption contact', *Adoption & Fostering* 23:3, pp 16–26.

Lindley B (1997) *Secrets or Links?*, London: Family Rights Group.

Logan J (1996) 'Birth mothers and their mental health: uncharted territory', *British Journal of Social Work* 26:5, pp 609–25.

Logan J (1999) 'Exchanging information post-adoption', *Adoption & Fostering* 23:3, pp 27–37.

Lowe K (1999) 'Training for foster carers', in Wheal A (ed.), *The Companion to Foster Care*, Lyme Regis: Russell House Publishing.

Lowe N and Murch M, Borkowski M, Weaver A, Beckford V with Thomas C (1999) *Supporting Adoption: Reframing the approach*, London: BAAF.

Mason K and Selman P (1998) 'Birth parents' experiences of contested adoption', in Hill M and Shaw M (eds), *Signposts in Adoption*, London: BAAF.

Masson J, Harrison C and Pavlovic A (1997) *Working with Children and 'Lost' Parents*, York: Joseph Rowntree Foundation.

McRoy R (1991) 'American experience and research on openness', *Adoption & Fostering* 15:4, pp 99–111.

Millham S, Bullock R, Hosie K and Haak M (1896) *Lost in Care*, Aldershot: Gower.

Mullender A and Kearn S (1997) *'I'm Here Waiting': Birth relatives' views on Part 2 of the Adoption Contact Register for England and Wales*, London: BAAF.

Packman J and Hall C (1998) *From Care to Accommodation: Support, protection and control in child care services*, London: The Stationery Office.

Quinton D, Rushton A, Dance C and Mayes D (1998) *Joining New Families*, Chichester: John Wiley & Sons.

Rajan P and Lister L (1998) 'Nottinghamshire's letterbox contact service', *Adoption & Fostering* 22:1, pp 46–52.

Rashid S (2000) 'The strengths of black families: appropriate placements for all', *Adoption & Fostering* 24:1, pp 15–22.

Ryburn M (1994) 'Contact after contested adoptions', *Adoption & Fostering* 18:4, pp 30–7.

Sellick C and Thoburn J (1996) *What Works in Family Placement*, Ilford: Barnardo's.

Singh S, Patel V K P and Falconer P (2000) 'Confusion and perceptions: social work conceptions regarding black children in Scotland', in Iwaniec D and Hill M (eds), *Child Welfare Policy and Practice*, London: Jessica Kingsley.

Social Services Inspectorate (1996) *Inspection of Local Authority Fostering 1995– 6: A national summary report*, London: Department of Health.

Stanaway E (1996/7) 'Birth parent-initiated contact: views and feelings of adult adoptees', *Adoption & Fostering* 20:4, pp 22–8.

Thoburn J, Lewis A and Shemmings D (1995) *Paternalism or Partnership*, London: HMSO.

Thomas C and Beckford V with Murch M and Lowe N (1999) *Adopted Children Speaking*, London: BAAF.

Tisdall E K M, Monaghan B and Hill M (2000) 'Communication, co-operation or collaboration? Voluntary organisations' involvement in the first Scottish Children's Services Plans', in Iwaniec D and Hill M (eds), *Child Welfare Policy and Practice*, London: Jessica Kingsley.

Triseliotis J, Borland M, Hill M and Lambert L (1995a) *Teenagers and the Social Work Services*, London: HMSO.

Triseliotis J, Borland M and Hill M (2000) *Delivering Foster Care*, London: BAAF.

Triseliotis J, Sellick C and Short R (1995b) *Foster Care: Theory and practice*, London: BAAF.

Triseliotis J, Shireman J and Hundleby M (1997) *Adoption: Theory, policy and practice*, London: Cassell.

Triseliotis J, Borland M and Hill M (1998) *Fostering Good Relations*, Edinburgh: The Scottish Office.

Ward H (1998) 'Using a child development model to assess the outcomes for social work intervention with families', *Children & Society* 12:3, pp 202–9.

Waterhouse S (1999) 'How foster carers view contact', in Hill M (ed.), *Signposts in Fostering*, London: BAAF.

Whitfield K and Harwood L (1999) 'Parents' experience of child protection', *Practice* 11:2, pp 49–58.

Winkler R C and van Keppel M (1984) *Relinquishing Mothers in Adoption*, Melbourne: Institute for Family Studies.

Section II
Children's legislation in Scotland

Since it was implemented in 1996, the Children (Scotland) Act 1995 has been the primary legislation affecting both private and public law in relation to children. One of the main intentions behind the Act was to integrate and update different elements of the law according to a common set of principles. Thus, in a single statute it covered certain universal features of family relations (e.g. parental rights and responsibilities), legal arrangements for children affected by parental separation and divorce, child protection, Children's Hearings and looked after children. For the most part, the Act replaced existing relevant legislation, but the sections with respect to adoption were treated as amendments to the Adoption (Scotland) Act 1978, which remains the key statute with respect to adoption. Three sets of Guidance were issued to accompany the Act (Scottish Office, 1997).

The Act itself does not mention let alone incorporate the UN Convention on the Rights of the Child, but the Guidance makes clear that core principles from the Convention do inform the contents and inter-pretation of the Act. The UN Convention, containing 54 Articles, was adopted by the UN General Assembly in 1989 and has subsequently been ratified by the great majority of nation states, including the UK (with a few reservations). Among the key rights embodied in the Convention are those to survival, health, education, protection and service provision. Article 12 affirms the rights of children to express their views and for those views to be taken into account according to the age and maturity of the child. The Convention applies to everyone below the age of 18 (unless majority is reached earlier under national law). The Convention stipulates that respect for children's rights should not discriminate according to a child's characteristics or background.

Plumtree (1995) described the main features of the Children (Scotland) Act 1995 and outlined many of its sections. She notes that four main principles inform the Act and accord with key Articles in the UN Convention. The principles are:

- When decisions are made about a child, the welfare of the child should be the paramount consideration. Agencies and courts are now obliged to take a long-term perspective, considering the child's best interests *throughout childhood* and in relation to adoption *throughout life.*
- The child's views shall be taken into account, allowing for the age and maturity of the child.
- No order should be made by a court or Hearing unless it is better for the child to do so than not making an order. (This is sometimes known as the *minimum necessary intervention* principle or, misleadingly, as the *No Order* or *minimum intervention* principle – see Skinner and McCoy, 2000.)
- There shall be regard to the child's religious persuasion, racial origin and cultural and linguistic background.

To help agencies fulfil their responsibilities with regard to children's heritage, the Scottish Office commissioned the production of a booklet with guidelines and examples of good practice (Chakrabarti *et al,* 1998).

Plumtree noted that Part 1 of the 1995 Act embodied an important change in emphasis by indicating that parental rights are associated with parental responsibilities and in some respect derive from the exercise of responsibilities, not inherent possession of the child. The Act introduced three new emergency protection orders, including the Exclusion Order, which was new to the UK. This enables courts to order the removal of an (alleged) abuser from the home instead of needing to remove the child. Such orders have been applied for and made very infrequently.

Prior to the 1995 Act, local authorities had been able to assume parental rights for children in their care without the need to go to court, unless a parent appealed. This had been used quite widely in Scotland, especially as a first step for authorities wishing to place children for adoption when parents would not agree or could not be found. However, it had come to be seen as an inappropriate power, so the new Act required that any authority wishing to take over parental rights and responsibilities has to apply to a court for a Parental Responsibilities Order. The Act also made consistent the grounds for dispensing with parents' agreement with respect to applications for a Parental Responsibilities Order, Freeing Order or Adoption Order.

Plumtree observed that the Act included only five sections on adoption. These did, however, include important changes. For instance the courts and adoption agencies, when making their decisions, now had to consider the child's welfare "throughout life" and the child's religious, racial, cultural and linguistic background. Although considerable dissatisfactions had been expressed about the principles and practicalities of freeing for adoption (Lambert *et al*, 1990; Hill *et al*, 1993; Lowe *et al*, 1999), the Act retained freeing, but introduced tight timetables for the procedures. Local authorities were given the duty to provide post-placement support for adoptive families and all were required to have an adoption allowance scheme.

In several respects the 1995 Act may be seen as representing a shift away from permanency planning towards partnership. This is seen in changes with respect to parental rights and the *No Order* provisions, as well as the new requirement for local authorities to consult with Children's Hearings about adoption plans when children were under supervision. Such changes reflected wider concerns that social work agencies had acted in a too high-handed manner with respect to parents and Hearings (Clyde, 1992; Kearney and Mapstone, 1992). Nevertheless, the Act reaffirmed the importance of adoption as an appropriate solution when assessments indicate this is in the child's life-long interests.

Tisdall and Plumtree (1997) compared the Scottish 1995 Act with the Children Act 1989, which applied only in England and Wales, apart from elements related to early years services that did have effect in Scotland. Since the 1989 Act came first and was generally well received, it is not surprising that some of the principles and details were adapted or even directly copied in the 1995 Act. For example, the phrase "looked after" was introduced by both (though with a wider compass in Scotland), while the focusing of preventive services on "children in need" was also a shared characteristic (but with the additional category of "children affected by disability" in Scotland). However, as **Plumtree (1995)** emphasised, the contrasts were also significant, taking account of the differences in legislative history, immediate influences and current context. This was most evident in relation to the Children's Hearings system, which is very different from the Family Proceedings and Youth Courts in England (Pitts, 2001) and whose functions, powers and duties were incorporated in the 1995 Act from previous legislation with certain modifications. Whereas the "children in need" category arguably represented in England and Wales a broadening of the circumstances where local authority help should be provided, in Scotland many saw it as a narrowing compared with section 12 of the Social Work (Scotland) Act 1968, which it replaced with respect to children. Tisdall and Plumtree also observed that in many parts of England and Wales services continued to be allocated on the basis of children being "at risk" of significant harm, rather than "in need" (see also Colton *et al*, 1995).

An interesting development in the 1995 Act was that local authorities were held to be responsible for children in need and looked after children *corporately*. In other words, all departments and not just social work services are covered and obliged by the Act. Also Children's Services Plans are now required to involve all relevant agencies. These ideals have been much easier to state in theory than to operationalise in practice. Nevertheless, the Act did both respond to and extend efforts to improve co-operation among in particular social work, education and housing services (Tisdall *et al*, 2000; Lloyd *et al*, 2001). New Labour policies, including its Children's Strategy and Action Plan (Scottish Executive, 1999, 2001), have further encouraged inter-agency co-operation.

7 The Children (Scotland) Act 1995

Alexandra Plumtree

This article was written in 1995. The Act came into force on 1 November 1996 (Part I) and 1 April 1997 (Parts II, III and IV).

The article was first published in Adoption & Fostering *19:3, 1995.*

It is worth making two preliminary points. Despite recent Reports and Enquiries (SCCLR, Orkney, Fife, etc) this Act is not a re-writing or codification of the law; some bits of existing law are repealed, some re-stated, some changed in part. There will be as many different statutes to consider as before, only the list will be changed.

This Act is *not* the Children Act 1989 restated for Scotland. The law and procedure in Scotland remain very different from those in England and Wales. Some of the ideas in the 1989 Act occur in this Act, and some of the same language, but the legislation is not the same.

Layout of the Act

The Act has four Parts, and five Schedules. Part I deals with parental responsibilities and rights. These provisions are private law, but have implications for those dealing with children under public law. The provisions of this Part inter-relate with the rest of the Act, and there are cross references between public and private law.

Part II is the biggest one, with four Chapters. Part III deals with Adoption, but only has five sections. The bulk of changes to adoption law are contained in Schedule 2.

Part IV has miscellaneous provisions. Schedule I deals with Children's Panels, Schedule 2, Adoption, Schedule 3, transitional provisions, and Schedule 4, minor amendments. One or two of these are very important. Schedule 5 deals with repeals.

There are no over-arching principles set down at the beginning of the Act, as there are in the Children Act 1989. Attempts were made to introduce amendments which would provide such a list of principles, but these were resisted by the Government. They took the view that there are definite principles set out in the Act, applying in all appropriate places, and that there was no need to have a list at the beginning. Certainly, there are various principles throughout the Act, but many feel it would have been helpful to have a list at the beginning.

The principles are an attempt to incorporate the UN Convention on the Rights of the Child into our law. The main ones are:

- That the welfare of the child should be paramount.
- That the child's views shall be regarded, taking into account his/her age and maturity.
- No order should be made unless it is better for the child that the order be made rather than not.
- That there shall be regard for the child's religious persuasion, racial origin, and cultural and linguistic background.

The last principle is not contained in all parts of the Act but only in relation to the local authorities' duties, and to adoption. Further, there is no statement of the general principle that delay should be avoided, although it is clear from the debates in Parliament that all those involved in using the Act will be expected to minimise delay.

There is no overall interpretation section for the Act, but instead an interpretation section (15) at the end of Part I, and a similar one (93) at the end of Part II. This has to be borne in mind when working with the Act.

Part I: Parents, children and guardian

Sections 1 and 2 deal with parental responsibilities and parental rights respectively. There is an attempt here and elsewhere in the Act to empha-sise that parents have responsibilities towards their children, as well as rights over them, with a view to moving away from the traditional legal concept of a child as a "possession" of the parent. The parent is expected to safeguard and promote a child's health etc, to provide direction and guidance, to maintain contact if not living with the child, and to act as the child's legal representative. A parent has the right to have the child living with him, or otherwise to regulate the child's residence, to control, direct or guide the child's development, to maintain contact if the child is not residing with him, and to act as the child's legal representative.

With regard to the legal representation of children, an important amendment to the law in this area is contained in Schedule 4, para 53(3). This amends the Age of Legal Capacity (Scotland) Act 1991, giving a child under 16 the capacity to instruct a solicitor in civil matters where the child 'has a general understanding of what it means to do so'. Generally speaking, a child of 12 or over will be presumed to have such an understanding.

Section 3 restates who have parental responsibilities etc automatically, replacing section 2 of the Law Reform (Parent & Child) (Scotland) Act 1986. The position remains the same, that a mother always has parental rights, and a father has them if married to the mother at the time of conception, or subsequently.

Section 4 introduces a new process by which a father without parental rights may acquire them, by agreement with the mother, without having to go to court.

Section 5 allows those with care or control of a child, but without parental responsibilities etc, powers to safeguard the child's health etc and particularly to consent to medical treatment in certain circumstances. This will be particularly helpful in day-to-day matters where children are with foster parents, or with relatives.

Section 6 states that a person reaching a major decision involving parental responsibilities etc is to have regard, so far as is practicable, to the views of the child. This is one of the statements of the principle, already mentioned, of considering the child's views.

The longest section in Part I is section 11, which deals with Court Orders in relation to parental responsibilities etc. This gives the court (Sheriff or Court of Session) the power to make 'such order . . . as it thinks fit', in relation to parental responsibilities, rights, guardianship or the administration of property of a child. There is a list of orders which the court may make, including residence and contact orders. The list is not exclusive, so a court could still make a custody order. This would give a parent more than a residence order, which relates only to arrangements as to with whom a child is to live.

Section 3 of the 1986 Act has been repealed, but Section 11(3) of this Act allows "a person" to make an application whether or not they have or have had parental responsibilities etc, in relation to the child. There are some exceptions, including a parent whose child has been adopted or freed.

In making any order, the court has to consider the welfare of the child as its paramount consideration, is not to make an order unless it considers it would be better to do so than not to do so, and is to take account of the child's views. The practicalities of how this last principle will work in the Act will be dealt with by Rules of Court.

It is worth mentioning section 54 here, although it is in Part II. This gives a court the power to refer a child directly to the Reporter, with a ground for referral established. The Reporter considers whether it is appropriate to have a Hearing. This power is open to the court in a wide range of proceedings, including adoption. This replaces the existing provisions in the Matrimonial Proceedings (Children) Act 1958 and the Guardianship Act 1973.

Part II: Promotion of children's welfare by local authorities and by Children's Hearings, etc.

Chapter 1: Support for children and their families

Chapter 1, sections 16–38, is primarily concerned with the duties of local authorities in relation to children living in their area. The definition of local authority is clearly stated (section 93) as a council constituted under Section 2 of the Local Government etc (Scotland) Act 1994. In other words, it does not just mean the social work department.

Section 16 states that throughout this Part a Children's Hearing or a court making a decision about a child must treat the child's welfare as the paramount consideration. They must take account of the child's views, and should make no order if that is preferable to making an order.

Section 17 deals with the duties of local authorities to children "looked after by them". The duties include safeguarding and promoting welfare which is to be their paramount concern, the promotion of regular contact between the child and parent, etc, and taking into account the views of the child, parent and others, and of the child's religious, racial, cultural and linguistic background. These duties may be disregarded if they consider it is necessary to do so to protect members of the public from "serious harm" (section 17(5)).

The children covered by this section are those who are looked after under section 25, children subject to supervision requirements, children under warrants or authorisations, (e.g. Child Protection Orders), children subject to parental responsibilities orders, and children from other jurisdictions. There is no distinction between those children on supervision who remain at home and those who do not.

This section introduces the concept of children being "looked after" by the authority, as opposed to the current phraseology of "in care". The Government wished to move away from the stigma which they felt attached to the phrase "in care". It remains to be seen what difference this will make to the way in which children are dealt with by local authorities.

This Chapter of the Act then goes on to provide for many other duties and powers of the local authority. Section 25 gives a duty to "provide accommodation for" children who cannot be cared for by parents (section 15 of the Social Work (Scotland) Act 1968 is repealed). Section 22, the promotion of welfare for children in need, is the replacement for the duties in section 12 of the 1968 Act, towards children. Section 12 is *not* repealed, but is amended (Schedule 3, paragraph 15(11)), so that the duty remains to those over 18. This means that section 12 of the 1968 Act and section 22 of the 1995 Act may often need to be considered together.

Other provisions include section 38, short-term refuges for children at risk of harm. Children may be provided with refuge for seven days with a possible extension to 14 days.

Chapter 2: Children's Hearings

This Chapter (sections 39–51) deals with some of the Children's Hearing provisions, the remaining provisions being in Chapter 3. Part III of the 1968 Act is repealed entirely with the exception of the section 31(1) and (3). Much of the system remains the same, although restated with some important changes.

The Secretary of State is given the power to make the procedural rules for Children's Hearings, as has been done in the past. Children's Hearings are still to be conducted in private, and, while the right of the press to attend is retained, they may now be excluded from any part of the Hearing if it is considered necessary to do so. There is still a prohibition on publication of proceedings at Children's Hearings, etc., with an offence created, but this prohibition can be dispensed with if considered necessary "in the interests of justice".

The rights and duties of attendance at Children's Hearings are changed from the 1968 Act, in that children and parents now both have a duty and a right to attend. Further, a parent may be excluded by a Hearing. The Chairman has to explain the substance of what happened at the end of the exclusion. There is no power to exclude a child from a Hearing, which means that, as a child now has a right to attend as well as a duty, the child, if she or he wishes to remain, cannot be excluded although an adult can.

Section 51 deals with appeals and makes a couple of significant changes to the existing law. It will now be possible to appeal from the Sheriff to the Sheriff Principal as well as directly to the Court of Session. More controversially, section 51(5)(c)(iii) provides that a Sheriff may substitute for the disposal of the Hearing any other supervision requirement that it could have imposed under section 70. This is seen as a breach of the principle that the court deals with assessment of evidence but the Hearing decides about welfare.

Chapter 3: Protection and supervision of children
This Chapter contains further provisions for the Children's Hearing system, and also covers various types of Orders which may be made: Child Assessment Orders (CAO), Child Protection Orders (CPO) and Exclusion Orders (EO).

Section 52 restates the grounds for referral previously contained in section 32 of the 1968 Act. They are much the same as before, with the exception of a new ground for the misuse of alcohol or drugs. The Act then goes on to provide, in section 53, for a duty on the local authority to investigate and refer to the Reporter, a duty on the police to refer when they have such information, and the power to anyone else to refer. The Reporter requires to investigate and make decisions (section 56). If a Reporter refers a child to a Hearing, proceedings are dealt with in section 65. The Children's Hearing's powers to make warrants are in sections 66 and 67, and the Sheriff's involvement in the establishment of grounds for referral is in section 68. Sections 69 and 70 deal with disposal of referrals by Children's Hearings, including the making of supervision requirements. The review of supervision requirements is dealt with in section 73, which again demonstrates the cross-over between the different parts of this Act by giving a duty to local authorities to refer for review any child subject to a supervision requirement and for whom they wish to seek a PRO, or a Freeing or Adoption Order. The Hearing, as well as considering the supervision requirement, then needs to prepare a report to go to the court which deals with the application. This does at least mean that Hearing members will be able more easily to discuss adoption and plans for permanency.

Section 63 introduces new procedures for children arrested by the police under the Criminal Procedure (Scotland) Act 1975 and detained in a place of safety. Section 85 allows application to the Sheriff to re-hear grounds of referral which were previously established. This provision follows the recent Ayrshire case where the Court of Session allowed evidence to be re-heard. It allows the child or parent to apply to the Sheriff to review a previous finding for grounds of referral, provided certain criteria are met.

Interspersed through these provisions are those for the three types of orders mentioned, although Hearings have no direct involvement in CAOs and EOs.

The Child Assessment Orders are dealt with in section 55. An application is made to the Sheriff by the local authority and she or he must be satisfied that there is reasonable cause to suspect that a child's treatment or neglect has caused or is likely to cause "significant harm"; that assessment is required to establish whether there is reasonable cause for the belief; and that such assessment is unlikely to be carried out without the order. This is a completely new tool in child protection terms in Scotland, and must not be confused with assessment when a Children's Hearing is considering the best plans for a child. The application may or may not lead to a referral to the Reporter. Such orders can only be for up to seven days and may authorise removal of the child from home.

Child Protection Orders and ancillary matters are dealt with in sections 57–62. There are complicated timescales and rights of review and appeal involved but the basic points are that application has to be made to a

Sheriff, can be made by any person, and, where an order is made, notification of the order given forthwith to the Reporter. The Sheriff shall not grant an order unless satisfied that there are reasonable grounds to believe that the child is being treated or neglected so as to be suffering 'significant harm' or that this will be suffered if the child is not removed (or left where she or he is) and that the order is necessary to protect the child from harm (section 57(1)). Section 57(2) gives the local authority a right to apply to the Sheriff with slightly different tests to be satisfied. A local authority can apply for a Child Protection Order under section 57(1) or section 57(2).

A Sheriff can attach conditions to a CPO, including contact. If the Reporter decides not to liberate a child (section 60(3)), a Hearing must take place on the second working day after the CPO is implemented.

Under section 61, if a Justice of the Peace is satisfied that the conditions in section 57(1) are present, and that it "is not practicable" to make an application to the Sheriff, an emergency authorisation can be made. This can be on the application of any person including a local authority. Under sub-section (5) a police constable may also remove a child to a place of safety, if satisfied as the JP would be. Either type of authorisation falls if not followed up with an application for a CPO within 24 hours. Detailed regulations, rules of court and guidance still require to be made to indicate how all the provisions for CPOs are likely to work, and in particular when it will not be "practicable" to apply to the Sheriff.

Exclusion Orders are dealt with in sections 76–80. Only a local authority can apply to the Sheriff for an order excluding from the child's home any person named in the order. The conditions are that the child has suffered, is suffering, etc., "significant harm" as a result of conduct, etc., of the named person; that the making of an Exclusion Order against the named person is necessary to protect the child and would safeguard the child's welfare better than removing the child; and that, if an order is made, there will be an adult able to care for the child in the home. This type of order is a complete departure in child protection terms, and the sections have been largely based on the existing exclusion orders in the Matrimonial Homes (Family Protection) (Scotland) Act 1981. Unlike those provisions, however, the Government accepted during the progress of the Bill that, in order to provide emergency protection for children, it should be possible for the Sheriff to grant an EO *without* notice being given to the named person beforehand. Section 76 now allows a Sheriff to grant an exclusion order without notice to the named person, pending a fuller Hearing, with notice, within a specified time. We do not know what the specified time will be until regulations are produced. These provisions mean that it may be possible to exclude an adult from the home, rather than removing the child, although there will be difficult assessment decisions to be made about which interim order is more appropriate, particularly if the family's history is not known. If an EO has been made, and the named person given notice, the Sheriff may attach powers of arrest.

All in all, the provisions for CAO, CPO, and EO give a range of tools for child protection. A lot of the details await regulations etc, but there will be considerable changes in child protection practice.

Chapter 4: Parental Responsibilities Orders, etc.

This Chapter deals with PROs, but there are some miscellaneous sections at the end. In particular, the child's right to consent to medical treatment in terms of section 2(4) of the Age of Legal Capacity (Scotland) Act 1991 is stated as being unaffected by anything in this Act (section 90). The interpretation of this Part of the Act is also in this Chapter, section 93.

The provisions for PROs in sections 86–89 are straightforward, allowing a local authority to seek the parental responsibilities etc. for a child. These provisions replace sections 16 and 17 of the 1968 Act. Local authorities apply to a Sheriff thus answering the current concerns about the procedures under section 16. A parent will be able to consent to a PRO, and if she or he does not consent, the local authority must ask the Sheriff to dispense with consent. The procedure thus resembles an application for freeing or adoption, and the similarity is increased because the grounds for dispensation of consent are exactly the same as those for dispensation in adoption and freeing petitions.

In making a PRO the Sheriff can attach any conditions. A child shall be allowed reasonable contact (section 88(2)) with or without a specific condition from the court. A PRO lasts until the child is 18, but the child, the local authority, the former parent or "any other person claiming an interest" can apply to the court at any time for variation or discharge of the order.

Part III: Adoption

Part III is very short, with only five sections. Adoption law is amended quite considerably by this Act, but most of the provisions are in Schedule 2, and the legislation for adoption will remain the 1978 Act, as amended by the 1995 Act.

Section 95 states that in any decision relating to adoption a court or adoption agency shall have regard to the welfare of the child "throughout his life" as the paramount consideration, and shall have regard to the child's views, and to his religious, racial, cultural and linguistic background. Section 96 provides a duty on adoption agencies to consider whether there is an alternative to adoption and is complemented by para 16 of Schedule 2 (amending section 24 of the 1978 Act), giving the court a duty not to make an order unless it considers that it would be better for the child.

Section 97 introduces a very welcome provision allowing a step-parent to adopt a child of his or her spouse on his or her own, without the need for the natural parent to adopt his or her own child.

Looking at Schedule 2, there are a considerable number of detailed amendments. Section 1 of the 1978 Act is amended to include a specific duty on local authorities to provide post-placement support, although these are not the words used in the statute. There are provisions for different types of regulation in the area of adoption, giving time limits to adoption agencies to process cases where adoption is planned, but parental agreement is not forthcoming. Again, the details will be contained in the regulations, but it is expected that agencies will have quite tight time limits within which they will be obliged to apply for freeing orders for adoption, the object being to minimise delay in planning for children.

Paragraphs 8 and 9 change the rules about who may adopt. Applicants will be able to seek adoption if they have been habitually resident for a period of at least one year.

As already indicated, the grounds for dispensing with consent in adoption and freeing are the same by which the local authority assumes parental responsibilities. The grounds in the 1978 Act remain much as before, but they are restated in paragraph 10, Schedule 2, amending section 16 of the 1978 Act.

Paragraph 18 inserts a new section 25A in the 1978 Act giving courts a duty to draw up timetables in adoption and freeing cases, where there are disputes. Paragraph 21 provides for repeal of sections 32–37 of the 1978 Act, which relate to protected children.

Paragraph 25 inserts a new section in the 1978 Act, section 51A, for adoption allowances schemes. This clause was directly the result of amendments by BAAF, and basically provides that adoption agencies who are local authorities must have a scheme. Regulations as to how such schemes are to be drawn up, altered etc. will follow, but all 32 of the new local authorities will be required to have them.

Conclusion

In this article I have touched on only some of the provisions, but attempted to give a reasonable overview of the Act. A lot of the fine tuning and the procedures to be followed depend on what regulations and rules of court etc are issued. At present, it is not anticipated that the Act will come into force until at least October 1996. A lot remains to be done to make this Act work, and work well for the children of Scotland, and we await further developments with interest.

Postscript

This piece on the 1995 Act was written in 1995, before the supporting regulations and court rules were finalised and before it came into force: Part I on 1 November 1996, and the rest on 1 April 1997. The Act has now been in force for five years, so it is beginning to "bed down" as a piece of working legislation.

The Part I provisions have led to fewer private law orders and to an increased awareness by courts of the importance of children's views. Residence and contact have replaced custody and access. Race, religion, culture and language do need to be considered by courts in private cases even if section 11 does not specifically mention them, following the appeal court decision in Osborne v Matthan *1998 SC 682.*

In the public law provisions, "looked after" has replaced "in care" although the same labelling seems to occur with the new term. By far the biggest issue for children and families, however, is an ever-increasing lack of local authority resources, with budgets more and more stretched.

The system of Child Protection Orders operates well to protect children, despite a lot of initial worries about court procedures. The other two orders are not used a great deal, but are there as options when needed.

In permanency planning, the introduction of Advice Hearings on plans for adoption, etc. has made discussion more open, but there are some serious operational difficulties, especially with contact being an issue in an increasing number of cases. Similar problems have arisen with the detailed timescales for adoption agencies in disputed cases. These are issues which will need further legislative changes.

8 The Children Act 1989 and the Children (Scotland) Act 1995: a comparative look

Kay M Tisdall and Alexandra Plumtree

This article was first published in Adoption & Fostering *21:3, 1997.*

In the past six years, children's legislation has been revised across the UK. England and Wales received their children's legislation first, with the Children Act passed in 1989 and implemented in 1991. Northern Ireland and Scotland had to wait several years for their parallel children's legislation, and it was not until 1995 that the Children (Northern Ireland) Order and the Children (Scotland) Act made their ways through Parliament. Their implementation has been swift: Northern Ireland implemented its Order in November 1996 and Scotland has had a staggered timetable with full implementation by 1 April 1997.

The three pieces of legislation have similarities. They all bring together aspects of family, childcare and adoption law that affect children. They all attempt to set out basic principles, common to the different fora children find themselves in; all three have been held up by the government as putting the United Nations Convention on the Rights of the Child into law. Shared terminology can be found across the legislation, such as "children in need" and "looked after" discussed below – although the exact meanings may be different. Much can be learnt from comparing the different legislation and, more importantly, from their implementation.

At the same time, the three pieces of legislation are not exact replicas of each other. The Children Act 1989 and the Children (Northern Ireland) Order 1995 are the closest, as many sections of the 1989 Act are repeated verbatim in the Northern Ireland Order. But as described by Kelly and Coulter (1997), Northern Ireland has a different structure for children's services from that of England and Wales: Northern Irish social services are amalgamated within health structures, so that Health and Social

Services Boards assess needs and commission services from Health and Social Services Trusts or the voluntary/private sectors. Local authorities have the primary responsibility for statutory childcare services in England, Wales and Scotland.

The Scottish legislation is even more distinct from elsewhere in the UK, because of its substantially different law, procedures and traditions. For example, the Scottish Children's Hearings system, which deals both with children in need of care or protection and with children who offend, is unique in the UK (see below for description). The new Act has been implemented just shortly after local government reform in Scotland, which changed the two-tier structure into 32 unitary authorities – so that the Act has been implemented in a time of great insecurity as well as opportunity. Thus, there are strong similarities between UK children's legislation, but also fundamental differences both in the law itself and the contexts of its implementation.

Introducing the Children Act 1989 and the Children (Scotland) Act 1995

The Children Act 1989 was hailed by virtually all commentators, the Government and professionals alike, as one of the greatest reforms of children's legislation this century. Its creation had been spearheaded by an influential 1984 report from the House of Commons Social Services Committee, which had advocated a thorough review of law and regulations so as to produce a 'simplified and coherent body of law comprehensible not only to those operating it but also to those affected by its operation' (House of Commons, 1984, para 119). A working party was quickly established by the Department of Health and Social Security, and pro-duced a Review in 1985 of Child Care Law, which was then followed by a 1987 White Paper (Department of Health and Social Security, 1985, 1987). The recommendations contained in these documents had been heavily influenced by a series of research reports on the childcare system and intensive consultation among professionals. Meanwhile by 1988 the Law Commission had completed its review of private law affecting children (Law Commission, 1988). The Children Bill drew on both these sets of proposals. Beyond this measured approach to policy making, the Children Bill was influenced by numerous scandals and enquiries over the 1970s and 1980s. Child abuse enquiries proliferated, with the Cleveland Report (Butler-Sloss, 1988) produced in 1988 in time to affect the legislation. The drama over child protection at times overshadowed other, perhaps more far-reaching, provisions of the legislation.

The Children (Scotland) Act 1995 had a not dissimilar history, with a time lapse of approximately five years. A Child Care Law Review was set up by the Scottish Office in 1988, and it reported in 1990 (Social Work Services Group (SWSG), 1991). Many expected a White Paper and new legislation shortly thereafter. But the smooth path of policy reform was rocked by a number of scandals and enquiries, such as the Fife Enquiry (1992) into Fife Council's childcare policies and the Clyde Enquiry (1992) into the removal of children, under child protection procedures, in Orkney. (For a further discussion of these and other reports, see Tisdall, 1996, 1997.) The White Paper, *Scotland's Children* (SWSG, 1993a), was not produced until 1993 and even then it took considerable pressure in order to gain parliamentary time for the promised legislation. Finally, a bill was put forward in 1994, which included changes recommended by the Scottish Law Commission on Family Law (1992) and following from the adoption law consultation (SWSG, 1993b), and was influenced by the Children Act 1989 itself.

The Children (Scotland) Act 1995 replaces most of the Social Work (Scotland) Act 1968 as it applied to children. Thus the legislative basis for the Children's Hearings system can now be found in the 1995 Act. At a Hearing, three trained members of the public (who are part of a local "children's panel") meet with the referred child, the parents and other professionals. Unlike elsewhere in the UK, there are no care orders, only supervision requirements. The Hearing decides whether a child needs compulsory measures of supervision and, if so, what measures are needed. The system had been established with a basic division of powers: issues of "justice" (whether fact or legal) should be determined by the court whereas "welfare" decisions (i.e. what happens to the child) should be made by the Hearing. Such a division, however, is a generalisation some-what belied by the actual workings of the system: courts do take account of "welfare" and hearings do on occasion determine a disputed issue of fact. (For a more detailed description of the current Children's Hearing system, see Hill *et al*, 1997.)

Most of the system has been retained by the 1995 Act but with certain critical alterations. For example, children now have the right (and not only the duty) to attend their own Hearings; parents and the press can be excluded from a Hearing, under certain criteria to do with the child's welfare; and "safeguarders" (who report on a child's best interests) can be appointed in a broader range of circumstances. A controversial change has been introduced to give the court additional powers on appeal. A Sheriff will now be able to substitute his or her own decision for that of the Hearing, thus eroding the basic division between welfare and justice decision-making jurisdictions. This change was justified by the Government as protecting the Children's Hearings from adverse rulings from the European Court of Human Rights.

The 1995 Act is based on the following fundamental legal principles:

- The welfare of the child shall be the paramount consideration in making decisions affecting the child. Sections 11(7), 16(1), 17(1), 95, Sch. 2 para 16.
- Due regard shall be given to children's views, subject to their age and maturity; while any child has this right, children aged 12 or older are presumed to have sufficient age and maturity. Sections 6(1), 11(7), 16(2), 17(3) and 95.
- No order should be made unless it is better than making no order. Sections 11(7), 16(3), 96, Sch. 2 para 16.
- Due regard shall be given to a child's religious persuasion, racial origin and cultural and linguistic background. Sections 17(4), 22(2) and 95.

These principles have been applied to adoption decisions, with one extension. The welfare of the child *throughout his or her life* is paramount in adoption decisions.

The legal principle of avoiding unhelpful time-delays is not as comprehensively stated in the 1995 Act as it is in the 1989 Act, although it is raised in relation to adoption and has been addressed in rules and regulations.

The new legislation contains numerous other significant changes. For example:

- a conceptual shift from parental rights to parental responsibilities;
- new procedures for unmarried fathers to obtain parental responsibilities;

- revised procedures and orders in family law, e.g. with a change from "custody" and "access" to "residence" and "contact" orders;
- new duties on local authorities to publish Children's Services Plans and information;
- a change in terminology from "in care" to "looked after" (see below);
- new duty on local authorities to provide services and support for "children in need";
- new duties on local authorities for children with and affected by disabilities (e.g. assessments);
- the duty on local authorities to help young people who have been "looked after" has been slightly extended up to the age of 19 if the young person had been "looked after" at compulsory school-leaving age (local authorities have the power to provide such aftercare until the young person is 21);
- the possibility for young people to seek "refuge" in designated short-term "safe refuges";
- new orders in child protection: an emergency Child Protection Order (CPO), a Child Assessment Order (CAO) and an Exclusion Order (EO) for an alleged abuser;
- a new order whereby local authorities go to court to gain parental responsibilities (PRO).

A summary of the legislation can be found in the previous article (Plumtree, 1995).

Several of these changes have direct parallels with the Children Act 1989. The 1989 Act uses the term "parental responsibilities", but leaves it ill-defined; the 1995 Act has been commended for having a more detailed list of parental responsibilities. Both Acts contain such provisions as: the unmarried fathers' agreement; changes in family law orders; and the terminological change to "looked after" children. This last change applies to children who would have previously been termed "in care" of a local authority, but attention must be given to the width of categories of children who are included in the Scottish definition of "looked after". For example, children on a supervision requirement from a Children's Hearing, even if they are living at home, are "looked after" children. The provisions on child protection in both Acts use the concept of "significant harm", a subject for considerable judicial definition in England and Wales (see Hardiker, 1996; Rodgers, 1996). The use in the Scottish legislation, however, is restricted to short-term measures for child protection and there are likely to be substantial differences in how Scottish courts define the term. No statutory definition exists in the 1995 Act and Scottish judges will not consider themselves bound by such 1989 Act decisions. "Children in need" was a category first devised for the 1989 Act, and its definition is largely replicated in Scotland (see below for further discussion). The parallels between the two pieces of legislation allow for Scotland to learn a great deal from the English and Welsh experience.

The Children (Scotland) Act 1995 made more revisions to adoption legislation in Scotland than the Children Act 1989 did for England and Wales, by amending the Adoption (Scotland) Act 1978. Changes in Scottish law include:

- a birth parent no longer has to adopt when a step-parent is adopting the child;
- local authorities have a duty to provide post-placement support;
- attempts are made to co-ordinate the Children's Hearings system and permanency planning;
- the grounds for dispensing with parental consent in adoption are slightly modified, and are the same as when local authorities seek a PRO;
- an adopted person can apply for information from the adoption court records and the Registrar at the age of 16, rather than 17.

Fostering itself is given little direct mention in the 1995 Act, and the impact on fostering largely arises from the revised regulations. Children who are fostered through local authorities, for example, will be "looked after" children and, because of this status, will have specified rights, requirements for review and the possibility of after-care.

Conceptual changes

Both the 1989 and 1995 Acts introduce major conceptual changes. Children's rights have risen on the political and policy agendas, so that the Children Act 1989 begins with key principles about children's rights and welfare while the Children (Scotland) Act has a very similar list threaded through its provisions. (For a discussion of tensions and gaps, see: Bell, 1993; Houghton-James, 1995; Tisdall, 1997.) The emphasis on children's rights can explain the conceptual shift to parental responsibilities: parents have responsibilities *towards* children, and only have rights in order to operationalise those responsibilities. Children are no longer considered the property or extensions of their parents.

The principle of minimum necessary intervention can be traced in both pieces of legislation. For example, in applications for family law court orders, courts cannot make an order unless it is better than making no order. This has similarities to the obligations on courts and adoption agencies to look at all alternatives to adoption, before making or seeking an order. Such a principle complies with Article 9 of the UN Convention, which states that children should not be separated from their parents ("parents" are left undefined in the Convention) unless it is *necessary* for the child's welfare. Further, the legislation supports contact with *both parents*; joint parenting is emphasised even when marriages break up, through the change to "residence" and "contact" orders, and unmarried fathers can make a (supposedly easy-to-do) legal agreement with mothers to gain full parental responsibilities.

While parents are supposed to be partners with each other in the best interests of their children, so are local authorities supposed to be partners with parents. The term "partnership" itself cannot be found in the legislation, but is laid out in the Scottish White Paper principles (SWSG, 1993), SWSG Guidance on the Act (1997) and in the 1989 Act Guidance (Department of Health, 1991). When a child is "looked after", local authorities have a duty to consider parents' views when making decisions and promote "personal relations and direct contact" where appropriate (section 17, 1995 Act). The terminological change itself to "looked after" hopes to emphasise that partnership should be maintained. Local authorities should take on parental responsibilities only as required and parents do not lose theirs unless this is formally decided by courts (see House of Lords, Hansard, 6 June 1995, Col. 30). While "partnership" has at times been found difficult in areas such as child protection conferences, good practice has been found in England and Wales (Thoburn, 1995). (For further discussion of "partnership", see: Calder, 1995; Kaganas *et al*, 1995.)

Both pieces of legislation can be seen as tightening legal proceedings, giving courts greater involvement in certain decisions (see Parton, 1991). For example, in the 1995 Act courts have increased powers in emergency child protection decisions. CPOs have their duration tightly controlled, and variations on "significant harm" are set as the tests for them and other orders. There are extra rights of review by courts in the CPO process. As mentioned, local authorities have to apply to courts for PROs.

Just as legal proceedings have been tightened, so has access to services. The new category of "children in need" is defined by the Scottish legislation (section 93(4(a)) as:

(i)   the child is unlikely to achieve or maintain, or to have the opportunity of achieving or maintaining, a reasonable standard of health or development unless there are provided for him, under or by virtue of this Part, services by a local authority;

(ii) his health or development is likely significantly to be impaired, or further impaired, unless such services are so provided;

(iii) he is disabled; or

(iv) he is affected adversely by the disability of any other person in his family.

The same wording can be found in the 1989 Act, except for the addition of children adversely affected by disability in its own sub-category. Since (i) and (ii) of the "children in need" category are so wide, English and Welsh local authorities could include children affected by disabilities as "children in need". But the specific inclusion in the Scottish definition strengthens the right of children affected by disabilities to services and could potentially apply to a large number of children.

The "children in need" category was introduced in England and Wales ostensibly to allow for more preventive services, and thus in some ways to discourage targeting solely on crisis child abuse situations (Department of Health, 1995). However, the practice has been far less preventive in many local authorities (see below). In Scotland, the new category was seen as narrowing the possibilities for children's services, compared to the general welfare duty contained in section 12 of the Social Work

(Scotland) Act 1968 (which requires local authorities to promote the welfare of people in their area by making available advice, guidance and assistance) (Tisdall, 1996). The Government's intention to target was clear:

I believe we need a suitable trigger. We do not want a local authority to have carte blanche to intervene when it is not necessary. Some assessment of need is surely appropriate and we cannot expect local authorities to promote the welfare of children where such action is not required, and, perhaps more importantly where it is not desired by the child's family. (Lord Fraser of Carmyllie, Hansard, 6 June 1995, Col. 51).

Despite the deletions of specific mention of children in section 12, the Scottish Office has affirmed that this general duty can still apply to children (SWSG, 1997) and indeed "children in need" is so vaguely defined in the Act as to give the potential to be inclusive and providing open-access services. (For further discussion, see Tisdall, 1997.)

Under the 1995 Act, the definition of local authority is corporate. Previously, the references to local authorities in the Social Work (Scotland) Act 1968 had been interpreted to mean "social work departments", and the change to a corporate definition potentially has great significance. For example, local authorities will be *corporately* responsible for "children in need", for implementing Children's Hearing decisions and for drawing up Children's Services Plans. Such services as housing, education and recreation are included in this corporate responsibility. Will educational services have to give due regard to children's views, if a child is "looked after"? Will recreational services be called upon to implement certain types of decisions made by Children's Hearings? Such a corporate structure is not necessarily found in English and Welsh local authorities and, even if so, responsibilities are not always recognised across departments. Thus section 27 of the 1989 Act specifically lists local education and housing authorities as certain of the "outside" agencies which can be asked to co-operate with local authorities, alongside health; the parallel section in the 1995 Act (section 21) does not because it has no need to with "corporate" and unitary local authorities.

Children's Services Plans, recently added to the Children Act 1989 by SI 1996 No. 785 and required in the 1995 Act, have a specific aim to promote interagency co-operation and collaboration. The English guidance was not only issued jointly between the Department of Health and the Department for Education and Employment (1996), but was also sent by the NHS Executive to health authorities and trusts. As yet, no such intention has been evident for the Scottish guidance. The increased emphasis on planning, which has been promoted elsewhere in health, housing and community care (see Percy-Smith, 1996), can be seen in these new legislative requirements.

Both pieces of legislation, then, display certain conceptual trends. The principles of children's rights, parental responsibilities, planning and interagency co-operation can be traced in both. Some procedures have been tightened and the judiciary has an increased decision-making role. Whether the legislation promotes a more preventive or a targeted approach to children's services is disputable, but clearly both Acts rely on categories to determine access to services.

How might these trends develop in practice? In particular, what can Scotland learn from the English and Welsh experiences? In the sections below, two areas will be focused upon: 'children in need' and inter-agency co-operation.

Children in need

The reported experiences of England and Wales have been less than reassuring. Local authorities have been implementing the provisions with scarce resources; the situation for many Scottish local authorities is even worse. While there is a legal definition of "children in need", it is itself so vague that local authorities themselves must make decisions about definition and priorities – which the SWSG guidance (1997) itself clearly expects local authorities to do.

When the 1989 Act was first implemented, some local authorities interpreted the category "children in need" to be synonymous with "children at risk". The Department of Health had to give a clear message that this was not permitted. Still, research found several local authorities concentrating their efforts on children at risk of abuse and neglect (Aldgate and Tunstill, 1995; Colton et al, 1995). Research on child protection found that many children were only able to access "children in need" services through "at risk" procedures (Department of Health, 1995;

Aldgate and Tunstill, 1995; Brandon *et al*, 1996). The intention of "children in need" to move away from "crisis" intervention towards "preventive" services was not flourishing in many areas.

While making individual decisions, Colton *et al* (1995) found that social workers were still struggling with a lack of specific guidance on how to define "need". A "gate-keeping" category such as this can be particularly difficult to utilise when children move in and out of being "in need". Because of resource constraints, most managers interviewed by Colton *et al* (1995) did not believe that open-access, non-stigmatising "children in need" services would survive. The only hope, as the managers saw it, lay in collaboration with the voluntary sector. On the flip side, social workers could face the dilemma of services that were provided being *higher* than community standards; some parents felt that bad behaviour was being rewarded, and siblings could be resentful or jealous.

As local authorities have the power to refine the definition of "children in need" for their own areas, the definition provides considerable flexibility to meet local needs and demands. Scotland has even more flexibility than England and Wales because far fewer services are specified for "children in need". While Schedule 2 of the 1989 Act lays out numerous duties for local authorities to provide specific services, the 1995 Act only specifies ones for day-care, after-school care and holiday care. Such flexibility, though, has some disadvantages. Children in one area might be eligible for a service, but not eligible in another. In 82 English local authorities surveyed in 1992, only 73 per cent identified children in care as a predetermined "children in need" group and 38 per cent identified privately fostered children as one (Aldgate and Tunstill, 1995). Given the smaller size of most local authorities in Scotland, migration between local authority areas may increase and local authorities with good services for particular needs (e.g. for children with disabilities, or young people who are homeless) may have increasing demands on their services.

Inter-agency co-operation
"Children in need" has provided a new contentious area for inter-agency co-operation and collaboration. The Audit Commission (1994) found that the definition of "in need" itself was a source of confusion and

disagreement among English agencies, particularly between social services, education and health. Similarly, housing and education can have very different concepts of need, based on their respective pieces of legislation. Certainly the Audit Commission (1994) suggested the Children's Services Plans must begin with a joint definition of needs that should, or can, be addressed.

Children's Services Plans have been heralded as a great opportunity to improve not only planning for children's services, but also inter-agency co-operation and collaboration. Research on English and Welsh planning experience has emerged in the past two years (Aldgate and Tunstill, 1995; Social Services Inspectorate, 1995; Sutton, 1995). These found several gaps such as:

- unclear purpose and intention;
- limited ascertainment of need, with some local authorities only assessing need based on past referrals;
- limited data collection and analysis;
- poor methods for determining priorities;
- inter-agency collaboration and consultation sometimes lacking, particularly with regard to the voluntary sector and groups representing people from ethnic minorities. Without shared definitions of need, common databases, and agreed structures for collaboration, inter-agency collaboration was poor;
- cursory consultation with service users and elected members;
- insufficient attention to commissioning services;
- lack of monitoring and evaluating outcomes;
- failure to link with other plans and reviews.

Positive progress was noted, however, on improving co-operation across social services, housing, education and health, both in planning and service delivery (Aldgate and Tunstill, 1995).

Children's Services Plans may well be the best mechanism to promote interagency co-operation and collaboration: legal tests of section 27 in the 1989 Act have demonstrated its weaknesses in requiring collaboration. For example, one department in a local authority cannot use it to force another department within the same authority to provide a service: when social services sought to use section 27 to access housing services, the

Court of Appeal decided that the section could not apply to unitary local authorities: 'You cannot ask yourself for help' (*R v London Borough of Tower Hamlets, ex parte* Byas (1993) 25 HLR 105). Because the section says that an authority does not have to comply with a request if it 'unduly prejudice[s] the discharge of any of their functions', requested agencies/departments may find it easy to point to waiting lists and limited resources as justifications for refusing. English interpretation does not directly apply to Scotland, but the Scottish equivalent to section 27 (section 21) may be more powerful in rhetoric than it will be legally.

Learning from experience

The research from England and Wales on the Children Act 1989 has shown many difficulties. The Children (Scotland) Act has incorporated several of the provisions which have proven problematic or weak in the 1989 Act. However, so many hopes were placed on the 1989 Act that perhaps some disappointment was inevitable. The resource constraints on local authorities were considerable, particularly as other legislation like community care was also being implemented.

Scotland also has similar problems in resources and change, but it has at least three major advantages: a more favourable ideological climate; a tradition of welfare approaches; and the opportunity to learn from England and Wales. All the deficits found in defining "children in need" and working co-operatively can be translated into key questions to address: On what information should Children's Services Plans be based? How will "children in need" be defined, and who will be involved in that definition? Who should local authorities consult with for plans? How wide should Children's Services Plans be? As an adopter, a foster carer, or a child who is "looked after" or adopted, how can you be involved in planning services for your local authority? How will children's and parents' rights to be consulted and involved be operationalised? Service planners, providers and other professionals will need to struggle with the translation of more abstract principles and concepts into practice – for example, making "due regard to a child's view" meaningful. They will need to translate rights and duties specified for the individual – such as due regard to a child's religious persuasion, racial origin and cultural and linguistic background – into considerations for planning and service delivery.[1]

With the Scottish crisis generated by huge financial shortfalls in many new authorities and the trauma of local government restructuring, learning from the experience of England and Wales is particularly important: to ensure that mistakes are not repeated, that the best of good practice is considered, and that the transition is as smooth as possible for children and their families. For ultimately, the new children's legislation should be a platform to provide the best possible support and services for children and their families – and that aim must not be forgotten in the turmoil of change.

Postscript

Children's legislation in the UK now sits in a very different context, with various gradations of devolved responsibility to new forms of government in Wales, Northern Ireland and Scotland and changes in the political parties in power. There is now immense activity within children's services, new conceptual drives such as the war on "social exclusion" and "joined-up government" and a flurry of new initiatives, new targets and new legislation to support them.

These changes have picked up certain of the unresolved, and certainly undelivered, aspects of the children's legislation. The push towards preventive rather than crisis-driven social work with families largely failed to materialise in the 1990s (Aldgate and Statham, 2001), in times of tight budgets and local government reform. Variations on children's strategies are emerging throughout the UK (e.g. Children and Young People's Unit, 2001; National Assembly for Wales, 2000; Scottish Executive Education Department, 2001; see http://www.northernireland.gov.uk/ for discussion of), that are stressing a holistic view of children, that agencies simply must work together and that families need to be supported before crisis occurs. The negative outcomes for "looked after" children, the lack of "safe refuges" and failures to protect children continue to make headline news and feature in research reports. New attention is being placed on

---

[1] An anonymous referee for this paper provided these helpful ideas in linking principles, concepts with planning and practice.

addressing them but concerns remain about tight budgets, inadequate staffing levels and poor morale in social work's children and family services in many local authorities.

Did Scotland learn from elsewhere in the UK, when it implemented its legislation? The first Children's Services Plans suffered from many of the same deficits found in the original English and Welsh ones (Scottish Office, 1999; Tisdall et al, 2000), although elements of good practice emerged. Most local authorities concentrated on trying to obtain corporate agreement and to bring in other statutory partners such as health. These aims have become a mantra of children's services, with For Scotland's Children recommending 'a single service system for children's services' (Scottish Executive, 2001, p 72) and a range of plans affecting children being brought together. Compared to England, however, the research programme evaluating implementation has been limited to date, particularly in child care.

The children's legislation was highly successful at putting children's rights on the policy agenda. The UN Convention on the Rights of the Child is now common currency; the need (if not always the practice) to listen to children's views has risen on the political agenda, with numerous initiatives at both national and local levels. The principles are slowly winding their way into other pieces of legislation, such as the requirement for schools to give due regard to children's views in the Standards in Scotland's Schools, etc. Act 2000, and into legal decisions (see Cleland and Sutherland, 2001). Some "leftovers" that were too contentious to go into the children's legislation are now being looked at, with the devolved legislature frequently being more radical than Westminster: e.g. limiting the physical punishment of children by their parents; the establishment of children's commissioners; and legal representation in Children's Hearings. These issues have partially risen up the policy agenda because of the UK's incorporation of European Convention on Human Rights into domestic law.

Research and other evidence continue to demonstrate that the UK, in its policy and practice, fails to meet the needs and rights of children, young people and their families. But the attention is now considerable to these issues and New Labour has promised to eradicate child poverty in 20 years. Will the commitment be sustained – and ultimately deliver?

References

Aldgate J and Tunstill J (1995) *Making Sense of Section 17*, London: HMSO.

Aldgate J and Statham J (2001) *The Children Act Now: Messages from research*, London: The Stationery Office.

Audit Commission (1994) *Seen But Not Heard*, London: HMSO.

Bell V (1993) 'Governing childhood: neo-liberalism and the law', *Economy and Society* 22:3, pp 390–407.

Brandon M, Lewis A and Thorburn J (1996) 'The Children Act definition of "significant harm" – interpretations in practice', *Health and Social Care in the Community* 4:1, pp 11–20.

Butler-Sloss, Rt. Hon Justice E (1988) *Report on the Inquiry into Child Abuse in Cleveland 1987*, Cmnd. 412, London: HMSO.

Calder M C (1995) 'Child protection: balancing paternalism and partnership', *British Journal of Social Work* 25, pp 749–66.

Children and Young People's Unit, Department for Education and Skills (2001) *Tomorrow's Future*, can be found at http://www.cypu.gov.uk/corporate/publications.cfm

Cleland A and Sutherland E (Eds) (2001) *Children's Rights in Scotland* (second edition), Edinburgh: W Greens.

'Clyde Inquiry' (1992) *The Report of the Inquiry into the Removal of Children from Orkney in February 1991*, Return to an Address of the Honourable the House of Commons, 27 October 1992, chaired by Lord Clyde, London: HMSO.

Colton M, Drury C and Williams M (1995) 'Children in need: definition, identification and support', *British Journal of Social Work* 25, pp 711–28.

Department of Health (1991) *The Children Act 1989: Guidance and Regulations*, London: HMSO.

Department of Health (1995) *Child Protection: Messages from research*, London: HMSO.

Department of Health and Department for Education and Employment (1996) *Children's Services Planning: Guidance*, London: DoH.

Department of Health and Social Security (1985) *Review of Child Care Law and Family Services*, London: HMSO.

Department of Health and Social Security (1987) *The Law on Child Care and Family Services*, Cmnd. 62, London: HMSO.

'Fife Inquiry' (1992) *The Report of the Inquiry into Child Care Policies in Fife*, Return to an Address of the Honourable the House of Commons, 27 October 1992, chaired by Sheriff Kearney, London: HMSO.

Hardiker P (1996) 'The legal and social construction of significant harm', in Hill M and Aldgate J (eds) *Child Welfare Services: Developments in law, policy, practice and research*, London: Jessica Kingsley.

Hill M, Murray K and Tisdall K (1997) 'Services for children and their families', in English J (ed) *Social Services in Scotland* (revised edition), Edinburgh: Mercat Press.

Houghton-James H (1995) 'Children divorcing their parents', *Journal of Social Welfare and Family Law* 17, pp 185–99.

House of Commons (1984) *Children in Care: Second report from the Social Services Committee (Short Report)*, Vol. 1, pp 360–1, 1983–84, London: HMSO.

House of Lords (1995) *Hansard Committee of the Whole House off the Floor of the House: Children (Scotland) Bill*, First sitting, 6 June 1995, Westminster: HMSO.

Kaganas F, King M and Piper C (eds) (1995) *Legislating for Harmony: Partnership under the Children Act 1989*, London: Jessica Kingsley.

Kelly G and Coulter J (1997) 'The Children (Northern Ireland) Order 1995: a new era for fostering and adoption services?', *Adoption & Fostering* 21:3, pp 5–13.

Law Commission (1988) *Review of Child Law, Guardianship and Custody*, 172, London: HMSO.

National Assembly for Wales (2000) *Children and Young People: A framework for partnership*, http://www.wales.gov.uk/subichildren/toc-e.htm

Parton N (1991) *Governing the Family: Child care, child protection and the State*, Basingstoke: Macmillan.

Percy-Smith J (ed) (1996) *Needs Assessment in Public Policy*, Buckingham: Open University Press.

Plumtree A (1995) 'The Children (Scotland) Act 1995', *Adoption & Fostering* 19:3, pp 30–35.

Rodgers M E (1996) 'Standard of Proof in Care Order Applications under the Children Act 1989', *Web Journal of Current Legal Issues*, 2, http://www.ncl.ac.uk/~nlawwww/1996/issue2/ rodgers2 .html

Scottish Executive Education Department (2001) *For Scotland's Children: Better integrated services*, http://www.scotland.gov.uk/library3/education/fcsr-00.asp

The Scottish Office, Social Work Services Group (1999) *Children (Scotland) Act 1995: Review of children's services*, Letter 11 January.

Scottish Law Commission (1992) *Report on Family Law*, No. 135, London: HMSO.

Social Services Inspectorate (1995) *Children's Services Plans: An analysis of Childrens' Services Plans 1993/94*, London: Department of Health.

Social Work Services Group (1991) *Review of Child Care Law in Scotland*, Report of a Review Group appointed by the Secretary of State, chaired by J W Sinclair, London: HMSO.

Social Work Services Group (1993a) *Scotland's Children: Proposals for child care policy and law*, Cmnd. 2286, London: HMSO.

Social Work Services Group (1993b) *The Future of Adoption Law in Scotland*, Consultation Document, Scottish Office.

Social Work Services Group (1997) *Scotland's Children: The Children (Scotland) Act 1995 Regulations and Guidance*, Vol. 1: Support and Protection for Children and their Families, London: The Stationery Office.

Sutton P (1995) *Crossing the Boundaries – A discussion of Children's Services Plans*, London: National Children's Bureau.

Thoburn J (1995) 'Social work and families: lessons from research', in Kaganas F, King M and Piper C (eds) *Legislating for Harmony: Partnership under the Children Act 1989*, London: Jessica Kingsley.

Tisdall K (1996) 'From the Social Work (Scotland) Act 1968 to the Children (Scotland) Act 1995: pressures for change', in Hill M and Aldgate J (eds) *Child Welfare Services: Developments in law policy, practice and research*, London: Jessica Kingsley.

Tisdall K (1997) *Children (Scotland) Act 1995 – Developing law and practice for Scotland's children*, London: The Stationery Office.

Tisdall K, Hill M and Monaghan B (2000) 'Communication, co-operation or collaboration? Voluntary organisations' involvement in the first Scottish Children's Services Plans', in Iwaniec D and Hill M (eds), *Child Welfare Policy and Practice: Issues emerging from current research*, London: Jessica Kingsley.

Section III
Perspectives on adoption

The Children Act 1975, all of which applied in Scotland as well as in England and Wales, introduced a number of major innovations in adoption. Several of these were intended to make it easier for children to be adopted from care, either by their existing foster carers or by new adopters. Although the Act did strengthen the position of local authorities and to a much smaller degree foster carers vis-à-vis parents, just as important for subsequent developments was the greater willingness of agencies to go to court to override parental wishes in order to achieve permanence via adoption or greater security for foster carers.

Most unusually, the Children Act 1975 included provision for evaluation. Two measures (adoption allowances and freeing for adoption) evoked much controversy in the period leading up to the Act, so research was commissioned by the then Scottish Office to assess their implementation and impact. Interestingly, attitudes to each have subsequently developed in contrasting ways. Adoption allowances were originally opposed heatedly by many people, but have now come to be widely accepted and available all over Scotland. By contrast, freeing orders appeared to have more extensive support at the start, but since being put into effect have been dogged by considerable dissatisfaction as well as some success.

Adoption allowances were intended to make it possible for children to be adopted, who otherwise would not be, by giving adopters financial support, usually until the child reached adulthood. Allowance schemes were initially an option that local authorities could take up, but were not required to do so. In practice, though, all Scottish authorities moved to the introduction of an allowance scheme within three years, in contrast to the more piecemeal development in England (Hill *et al*, 1989). Schemes varied considerably in detail, but in broad terms made allowances available to enable foster carers to adopt or were payable to new adopters caring for a child with special needs or a sibling group. Later, allowances were made compulsory by the 1995 Act.

Allowances were originally opposed for several reasons, including concerns that they would alter the nature of adoption, blur the distinction from fostering and provide unfair assistance to adopters when birth parents could not receive the same help. It was also feared that children would resent the fact that they were being "paid for" or doubt the motivation of the adopters. Several of these fears were reminiscent of comments about families with boarded out children in Victorian times (see Introduction). Hence the research carried out in Scotland on allowance sought to assess these matters, in particular about the effects on children's feelings and identity. Based on interviews with children adopted with an allowance or just about to be, **Triseliotis and Hill (1987)** produced reassuring findings that nearly all did not think the payment affected their relationship with their adopters. For a minority, this was because they did not know about the allowance. The majority did realise their adoptive parents receive a payment, but it was not salient in their lives and they denied that it bothered them. Most simply accepted it as a practical means of enabling the family to keep them or to do things they otherwise could not afford. Whatever their understanding about the allowance, many affirmed that adoption was something they were very pleased about and that they valued the allowance for making this possible. Even those who had been fostered for many years and had no doubts that they would have stayed with their foster carers anyway, still welcomed the confirmation of their status or name within the family. Most had already felt a strong sense of security within the family, but treasured the external recognition. One qualification of this positive picture was that the children generally did not want people outside the family to know about the payment.

The idea of freeing for adoption originated in times when adoptions commonly involved single mothers giving up babies, who expected to have no further contact. It was seen as desirable to have an early interim stage in court proceedings when a child could be "freed" for adoption before particular adopters had been identified or applied. At the freeing stage, the issue of parental consent would be dealt with so the parent(s) were then also "free" to get on with their lives. When the freeing provision was introduced the context had changed with the advent of permanency planning, so that more older children were being considered for adoption, sometimes against parental wishes. A study of the early years of freeing by **Lambert** *et al* **(1990)** indicated that many practitioners and managers looked forward to the opportunity to use freeing as a speedier route to adoption for older, looked after children. As expected, most freeing of infants was with parental consent, but a considerable proportion of applications for freeing of looked after children asked that parental agreement be dispensed with. Both types of application turned out to take a long time, as a result of lengthy processes in both local authorities and the courts. Also, initially, applications that were actively contested by parents were often fraught for all concerned and did not lead to success by the local authority. This led to widespread disillusionment with freeing among local authority staff. Partly as a result of the research, the Children (Scotland) Act 1995 and its associated Regulations introduced specific timetables for each stage of freeing procedures.

While most writing and research has concentrated on adoption by "strangers", for many years a quite different form of adoption accounted for a growing proportion of adoptions (half in the year 2000). These were adoptions by relatives, of which the main type was step-parent adoption whereby parents (normally mothers) adopted their own children jointly with a new marital partner. For a long time, practice wisdom towards this form of adoption has been discouraging since it is seen to distort family relationships and deny the position of the separated parent (usually the father). Particularly paradoxical was that a birth parent had to adopt her own child to enable her spouse to do so. This anomaly was removed by the Children (Scotland) Act 1995 (section 97), which allows step-parents to adopt in their own right their spouse's child **(Plumtree, 1995)**.

Prior to that change, **Phillips (1992)** carried out a study of local authority reports on step-parent adoptions and interviewed members of the adoptive families and professionals. Before they began the application, most of the parents and step-parents had a very limited understanding of the implications of adoption or possible legal alternatives, including custody and official name changes. When they became aware of these options, they rejected them as not giving the legal security they gained from adoption. All the adopters were glad to have adopted, though those who were the birth parents were not happy that they had had to give up their existing parental status in order to become an adoptive parent. As with freeing, there were complaints about the slowness of the process. None of the social workers had received specific training in this area and many voiced concerns about their role, which seemed to be often rubber stamping.

As noted in Section II of this book, the Children (Scotland) Act 1995 required local authorities to produce a Children's Services Plan by April 1997 and subsequently at regular intervals. These were intended to cover all children in the authority and the kinds of services that were available and needed. The Guidance (Scottish Office, 1997) stipulates that consideration should be given to children who have been adopted or are in the process of being adopted. The 1999 Review of plans listed adoption as one of four core services (with fostering, child protection and after-care), but also noted that many plans gave little or no attention to adoption services. Even where adoption was referred to there was usually little assessment of need, numbers or costs (Scottish Office Review of Children's Services Plans, January 1999). The Review invited authorities to ensure proper coverage in future.

Clark and McWilliam (1999) undertook a thorough analysis of adoption coverage in all the 27 published plans plus drafts of the remaining five unpublished plans. Most commonly adoption was coupled with looked after children and only nine authorities had adoption in a separate section. Adoption was rarely linked to the main strategic objectives given in the plan. The most frequent goal, present in half the plans, was to develop post-adoption support, but this was usually to take the form of information and counselling for adopted adults, not support for adopted children and their families.

Few of the plans provided details of the number of children with current or future needs for adoption. One-third of authorities purchased at least some of their adoption services from voluntary agencies. Several were working with other authorities to share placements or were planning to do so. No plans included financial projections for adoption services, but a few indicated difficulties in affording adoption allowances or providing reports with respect to intercountry and step-parent adoptions.

Although the primary focus of the analysis by Clark and McWilliam was on adoption, they compared attention to fostering and residential care. They concluded that these areas were dealt with more fully and with a greater sense of direction. The authors expressed concern about the marginalisation of adoption within plans, presumably reflecting a more general low profile on the policy agenda.

Another example of neglect in the literature centres on the birth fathers of children relinquished for adoption. Quite a lot is known about birth mothers' reactions to loss and separation, thanks to a number of studies carried out in Australia, North America and England (e.g. van Keppel, 1991) and one in Scotland (Bouchier et al, 1991). These mainly relate to adoptions of babies that took place some time ago, though recently some attention has been given to the parents of looked after children who were adopted, often against their parents' wishes (Ryburn, 1992; Mason and Selman, 1997).

The main thrust of the literature has been that birth mothers do not usually forget nor easily get on with their lives, as commentators, advisors and sometimes mothers themselves hoped at the time of the adoption. Many experience a deep and enduring sense of loss, often coupled with a wish to know how the child is doing and sometimes also a desire to see the child. They reported persistent complex feelings of distress, resentment and anger (Winkler and van Keppel, 1984; Bouchier et al, 1991; Logan, 1996). With this in mind, **Clapton (2001)** set out to examine birth fathers' experience and see what similarities and differences there were with the women's accounts. Most of the men in this study described strong feelings of trauma and anguish, as well as a continuing interest in the child, just like birth mothers. Also similar to mothers' experiences, the men found that key dates such as birthdays instigated intense feelings and thoughts about the child. Curiosity, concern, loss and regret for the child were common longer-term reactions, while several identified a sense of responsibility or parenthood towards the absent child. Clapton concluded that birth fathers are likely to respond in a similar way to mothers when losing a child to adoption. The idea of connectedness felt by men to a child they have not parented challenges certain gender stereotypes and suggests that more priority should be given to fathers' feelings, role and responsibilities before adoption.

Before 1990 virtually all adoptions in Scotland were domestic, i.e. they involved children born in Scotland or occasionally elsewhere in the UK. This contrasted with many countries in Western Europe and North

America where many adoptions were intercountry, with most of the children coming from Asia or Latin America (Andersson, 1991; Hoksbergen, 1996). Professional opinion in the UK has largely been unfavourable to intercountry adoption. The reasons include a wish to focus on the needs of looked after children in the UK rather than of childless couples wanting a baby; concerns about identity and racism; and preference for helping children to live with families in their country of origin (Dutt and Sanyal, 1991; Triseliotis, 1991). The situation changed considerably in response initially to publicity about children in Romanian "orphanages'" (many were not orphans, though) and later about residential nurseries in China, which led to a comparative upsurge in international adoptions to the UK (Beckett *et al*, 1999; Selman, 2000). A national follow-up study indicated that most of the children were progressing very well (Rutter *et al*, 2000). The numbers of intercountry adoptions by families in Scotland are still not large. For instance a survey of 23 adoption agencies (about two-thirds of the Scottish total) revealed that 25 families had been approved for intercountry adoptions in 2001. China was the largest source of children, with Thailand and Brazil also providing several each (BAAF Scotland, 2002).

Triseliotis (2000) reviewed a range of evidence about intercountry adoption on a worldwide basis and concluded that much of the practice is neither moral nor in keeping with international law. Triseliotis recognised that some individual children benefit from intercountry adoption, provided it is carefully regulated. However, he points out that is too small in scale to offer an effective solution to poverty and abandonment in the source countries, so that any adoption programme ought to be accompanied by strategies and resources for local development. Many of the adults concerned avoid formal agencies and any kind of assessment. Contrary to international agreements, many children are obtained for adoption without gaining parental consent or where consent has been bought or obtained under duress. Often little or no attention is given to helping children and families adjust or to sustaining a positive identity for the children that includes their culture of origin. He concludes that intercountry adoption has until now been too often based on market principles and adult motives, but that a commitment is growing to make the child's interests central. Altruism could express itself through providing resources to support children in their own country and ensuring that adoption across continents only occurs when that really is the best available option for the child.

9 Children and adoption allowances

John Triseliotis and Malcolm Hill

This article was first published in Adoption & Fostering *11:1, 1987.*

When adoption allowances were introduced a number of people expressed reservations because of their possible negative impact on the children's identity. The main argument was that the children might come to feel "stigmatised" for being at the receiving end of what are seen as welfare benefits or come to see themselves as different from other adopted children within the same or another family whose parents adopted them without an allowance attached. They might even think that their parents adopted them solely or mainly for the money.

As part of our study of monitoring adoption allowances in Scotland we decided to interview children to find out whether or not they really feel this way. Another important aim of this part of the study was to test an earlier finding by Triseliotis (1983) concerning differences he found between those who grew up adopted and those fostered for most of their childhood life. That study suggested not only qualitative differences between adoption and long-term foster care in favour of the former, but also that long-term foster care carried ambiguities and uncertainties for the child in terms of status, security and sense of belonging which were not found to be present in adoption. Triseliotis put forward then the need to find ways of providing greater security for the child in long-term foster care, if not by means of full adoption, at least something analogous to adoption. As most of the children adopted with allowances were in foster care, some of them aged between 12 and 16, the study presented us with an opportunity to examine what difference, if any, adoption makes to children who are in long-term foster care, especially those nearing the end of their childhood. In *re M* (*minors*) heard in the Court of Appeal on 11 October 1984, Sir Roger Ormrod stated that in his opinion adoption was not designed to cater for children in long-term foster care and custodianship was better.

Interviewing children of varying ages on such a sensitive subject presents many methodological and ethical problems. For example, questions which may seem appropriate for the older or more verbal child are frequently inappropriate and non-productive for the younger or more inhibited child. A further and more difficult problem is obtaining the parents' permission to talk to the children. Though all the parents were known to us through the main interviews of our study, nevertheless some were hesitant or not ready to give their consent at this stage. In addition, in many cases the children were either too young and/or disabled to have been told about the allowances. There were also older children whose parents had not told them about the allowance even though they were of an age to understand. A few who had told their children did not wish them to be interviewed. As we comment in the main report submitted to Social Work Services Group (Scotland) a new "secret" is being born centering on adoption allowances.

Eventually we decided to look upon the interviews as a pilot exercise. In order to ensure that communications would be comparatively straight-forward we decided to concentrate on those aged nine and over. We interviewed nine children, all in different families. This is a small number but we plan to carry out more in the next part of the research. All those we saw were being adopted by people who had fostered them for some time before. Many of the parents who readily agreed for us to have access to the children were also present at the interview. Because of this, doubts may be cast on the reliability of the material obtained and questions may be reasonably asked whether the children were giving the kind of answers that would please their adoptive parents.

The interviews

Our wish from the outset was to carry out exploratory interviews to obtain the children's views about the meaning of adoption to them after a long period in foster care. Also we wanted to understand their views about the payment of adoption allowances to their parents. Three key themes emerged from these interviews: a) Perceived differences between foster care and adoption; b) the symbolism of the adoption order; and c) the meaning of allowances.

Differences between foster care and adoption

Most of the children were clear about their former fostering status and their recent transition to adoption. Most, but not all, had been given some explanation about being fostered but fuller understanding about the meaning of this emerged only gradually. Two of the children were brought up to think of themselves as adopted and it was only recently with talk about adoption allowances that it dawned on them that they were only fostered. Almost all the children said they knew at least one other child who had been fostered, but it was not usual for them to have known other adopted persons. Therefore they had little chance to learn about adoption through someone who had experienced what it meant.

At the time of the interview most of the children had a good idea about the main differences, as they saw them, between fostering and adoption. In their eyes adoption meant "permanence" (their word) and "being part of the family". Fostering was perceived as "temporary". Typical comments were:

- 'In fostering you are there for two or three years. Adoption is for life: you cannot be taken away';
- 'Adoption means you are a proper part of the family';
- 'Adoption is permanent, fostering is for a wee while'.

Other phrases which indicated a sense of belonging were:
- 'Being really their child';
- 'You are just their own child';
- 'Being part of the family and not feeling left out';
- 'Having a family for life'.

When asked to elaborate on some of these comments, most of the children used phrases which conveyed a sense of security, permanence and continuity. For example:
- 'Will be more secure';
- 'No more moves and changes';
- 'It is up to the parents what we do and not up to others'.

In effect, in spite of being fostered by the same family over a lengthy period of time, the children felt some lack of security and full belonging which was eventually provided by adoption. Although the children felt confident of their foster parents' love, they were conscious that their full family membership was brought into question in the eyes of outsiders by their different names and by experiences they had to undergo which other children did not. Therefore they saw adoption as bringing some immediate tangible gains, such as not having to undergo medicals or receive social work visits. The main benefit, however, was the relief of not having to explain to friends and teachers why they had a different surname from that of their adoptive parents.

Goffman (1963) argues that whenever a change in name occurs 'an important breach is involved between the individual and his old world'. This theme was taken up by others to suggest that whenever a change of name takes place this has a negative impact on the person's identity. While this may be so in some instances, no account is taken, as in this case, of feelings of being "different" or of "not belonging" generated in a child whose surname differs from that of the substitute family. Many writers on the subject attribute moves for a change in surname as solely related to expressed or unspoken pressures on the part of the family. No thought is given to the fact that such a step may be to satisfy a child's long-felt wish.

The children felt "good" or "glad" or "pleased" about the change of their status from fostering to adoption. Though their fostering experience was satisfactory, adoption seemed to convey something stronger and more satisfying. It is not as if suddenly the children felt transformed through the transition from fostering to adoption, but unlike fostering, adoption made them feel much more as 'being part of the family and not "different" '. As another one put it: 'Adoption means to me, to mum, and to the rest of the family that I belong now'. Doreen, like some adoptive parents, expressed the paradox that in one way adoption made no difference since she inwardly felt fully wanted and part of the family, yet in another sense it was an important and desired change because it demonstrated to other people outside that she was now a family member like a natural child.

Only Thomas seemed uncertain as to what adoption meant to him. He said that it would take a long time before he felt a "full" member of his adoptive family. This child showed signs of being confused in a more general way and yet there was nothing in his comments to indicate any particular unhappiness.

The symbolism of the law

As interviewers we were struck by the symbolic meaning of the law to these children, something that we had not anticipated. The children seemed to attach a lot of importance to something being "legal", even those who were aged 15 or 16. There was awareness about the legal transfer of powers that adoption brings with it, which meant that other people would no longer be making decisions on their behalf or remove them. Typical comments were: 'It is something permanent and by law', or simply 'It is legal'. Doreen said:

I was wanting to be adopted but it was just really the same, I mean it didn't change anything – yet if I had not been adopted I would have been quite disappointed because by law I wouldn't be here actually.

Thus the making of the adoption order was a symbolic act creating a deep, satisfying psychological feeling for these children. These comments, if confirmed by our follow-up, would demonstrate that a piece of legislation which mostly confirms a *de facto* situation has the capacity to convey a deep sense of security and belonging.

The meaning of allowances

Six of the children knew that their parents were receiving money in the past for looking after them. The rest were told or found out more recently in connection with the adoption allowances. As a result, one of the latter children was confused and unable to understand about adoption allowances. Others had only a somewhat hazy grasp of what they meant. Only one child knew how much money was involved. In some families there was a little more reference to the allowance than in others, but overall not much "fuss" was made of it. Perhaps the absence of consistent explanation accounts for the amount of vagueness we found. It is also possible from what we have found in our interviews with the parents, that they themselves were not yet aware about the exact amount of payments involved or the terms of payment. In addition, it appears that in many families, there is not much talk about money anyway.

In the eyes of the majority of the children, the adoption allowance was like a continuation of the fostering allowance and it was treated in a matter-of-fact way. Although social workers took the trouble to talk to the children about the adoption plans, we learnt that very few had spoken to them directly about the allowance. As we say in another part of the main report, many social workers believed that it was up to the parents to explain or not. A fair number had not considered this issue at all.

With the exception again of one child who was confused both about adoption and about allowances, the rest had no reservations, viewing both the fostering and adoption allowances as necessary and desirable, although one child did say 'I didn't expect that sort of thing coming with adoption . . . I thought once I was adopted that was it.' Nevertheless, he still thought there was value in it.

It would be unrealistic to expect children to unburden deeper feelings at a one-off meeting with a stranger, but even so they seemed to treat the issue in an unemotional, matter-of-fact way. They saw the allowances mainly in terms of their practical value and no other significance was attached to them. Most of them were aware that without the allowance they would not have been adopted and so would have been prevented from "being a full member of the family". Overall they saw the allowance as making it easier for their parents to meet the demands for clothes, food and the like: 'you know it brings clothes and school things and things like that', or 'it would do them a lot of good, it would be their money to spend on us', or 'they need the money to look after us', or 'if your dad is out of work, it can keep the family going'.

One set of brothers and sisters were seen who did not know about the allowances that their new parents were to receive. They spoke enthusiastically of the annual camping holiday they would now have, which would have been impossible without financial assistance. Similarly they were glad that this helped keep them together. Without the allowance, the children would have to go without a number of things to which they were accustomed under the fostering allowance. Normally the children we saw described the money as belonging to their parents or the family as a whole and not themselves personally. Equally they thought it appropriate that the allowance went into the general household budget. In some respects the children did not see the allowance as singling them out from the rest of the family. Emphasis on it being for the whole family reduced the possibility of the rest of the family seeing them as "different". In some respects some of the children looked upon their parents as "luckier" than those adopting without an allowance.

Apart from two children, one of whom felt confused and the other surprised, the rest indicated that they were not troubled by the idea that their parents received an allowance in order to adopt them. Some characteristic remarks were: 'it doesn't bother me', 'it doesn't matter', 'it doesn't really bother me, I mean I knew that they needed it, taking an extra child on', or 'it is a help to start another life'.

Maybe the children were denying negative feelings associated with the arrangement but none volunteered any unfavourable comments. Some children were aware that their adoption was delayed mainly because their parents could not afford to lose the fostering allowance. There was no apparent bitterness for having to wait before they could be adopted. It was also obvious that possibly none of these children would have been adopted if it was not for the allowance.

Did this indicate that they suspected their parents' feelings for not adopting them even without an allowance? No such evidence emerged. The uncertainty and insecurity of long-term fostering was related mostly to the children's "ambiguous" position rather than to the parents' feelings. Nor was there any imputation that money diminished their parents' commitment. Similarly, they did not think that they might feel different from those adopted without an allowance. Respondents dismissed this suggestion with comments such as: 'it doesn't make any difference', 'no difference – they are just brought up the same and they just get the same things' or 'you are still 100 per cent adopted if there is an allowance or not'.

Contrary to fears expressed to the Houghton Committee (1972) we have found no evidence suggesting that the children were resenting the fact that their adoptive parents were paid to care for them. The children were asked whether they would tell other people, including friends, about their adoption or about the allowance. Like their parents, they were generally happy to talk to friends about their adoption but not about the allowance. The latter was seen as a family matter of no concern to outsiders. 'No special reason to tell' or 'It is something that should be kept in the family'.

The boundary line between what belongs to the family and what can be shared with outsiders seemed to exercise the children's minds also in relation to telling about adoption. In the view of some, adoption itself was something to be shared with close friends only. Does this reluctance to tell outsiders about the allowance signify a perceived stigma or shame? This has to be seen within the wider context of what families and their members in general see as private or personal matters and therefore as not something to be shared with outsiders. Studies such as Mayer and Timms (1970) suggest that families feel more shame when they seek material help from social agencies than help with personal problems. This is a point we will return to in the main study when we examine the feelings of both the children and of their adoptive parents.

Conclusion

In this exploratory study we set out to test certain assumptions concerning the meaning of adoption and of adoption allowances to children who until recently were in long-term fostering. We are aware that this was a rather biased sample of children and therefore our observations should be read with caution. We hope to interview a more balanced sample in the follow-up study. It may also be possible to ascertain from some parents who did not tell their children what have been the implications for them of their secrecy. Did they change their minds later and tell? Or did any of the children find out?

On the basis of these findings we have found that even for children who were settled in stable foster homes and would soon become young adults, the change from fostering to adoption was a very important one. It conveyed a sense of security and belonging. These findings, if confirmed in our extended study, would seriously question the validity of Sir Roger Ormrod's comments quoted earlier. Such a view takes no account of the changing nature of adoption and of the significance of adoption to children, or that the adoption order has a symbolic significance for them because of its legality and the certainty it carries. These provisional observations confirm Triseliotis's (1983) earlier findings about the in-secure and "ambiguous" status of children in long-term foster care compared to adoption.

The children in this sample, though not for the most part prepared to talk to outsiders about the adoption allowances, were overall strongly in favour of them. They knew that without an allowance they would not have been adopted but they did not think that this had anything to do with their parents' feelings towards them. The only issue was the practicalities involved of coping financially. Without the allowances, the children could not have been adopted without suffering materially and missing basic things they were accustomed to. Without adoption, they would have been robbed of a full sense of legal and permanent membership in the family they had become attached to and which loved them.

Acknowledgements

The study on which this article is based, was funded by the Social Work Services Group of the Scottish Office. Our thanks also go to all the Scottish Regional Authorities which so splendidly co-operated with us in carrying out the objectives of the whole study. We are very grateful for the contribution of Maureen Buist in carrying out some of the interviewing and analysis in the second half of the research project.

References

Goffman E (1963) *Stigma: Notes on the management of spoiled identity*, Englewood Cliffs, NJ: Prentice Hall.

Houghton Committee Report (1972) *Report of the Departmental Committee on the Adoption of Children*, London: HMSO.

Mayer J E and Timms N (1970) *The Client Speaks*, London: Routledge & Kegan Paul.

Triseliotis J (1983) 'Identity and security', *Adoption & Fostering* 7:1, pp 22–31.

10 Freeing children for adoption: the Scottish experience

Lydia Lambert, Maureen Buist, John Triseliotis and Malcolm Hill

This article was first published in Adoption & Fostering *14:1, 1990.*

Since the implementation in 1984 of section 18 of the Adoption (Scotland) Act 1978, enabling children to be freed for adoption, there has been no systematic information about how the provision has worked out. Cases reported in *Adoption & Fostering* legal notes have highlighted several issues and Bell (1988) offered some helpful observations arising from a small number of cases she had dealt with as a guardian ad litem, particularly concerning access and parents' *versus* children's rights. She also noted the need for further clarification and research. This article seeks to fill part of that gap in knowledge by reporting on a wide-ranging study of freeing in Scotland carried out by the authors.

Origins of freeing

The patterns of childcare and adoption practice operating when the provision which enabled children to be freed for adoption came into force in Scotland in September 1984 (just three months after England and Wales) were very different to those at the time when freeing was proposed by the Houghton Committee (1972). Then the main concern had been the numbers of young unmarried mothers who wanted their babies adopted but found the legal process too drawn out (Triseliotis and Hall, 1971). The Houghton Committee proposed a "relinquishment" procedure for these parents, but it was also aware of 'a sizeable number of children in the care of local authorities and voluntary societies for whom no permanent future can be arranged'. For them, the Committee proposed the temporary transfer of parental rights to an adoption agency after consent had been dispensed with. Both proposals were later included in the legislation for freeing.

During the intervening years, the number of babies offered for adoption fell sharply and the emphasis shifted towards finding permanent placements for children in care who were unable to return to their families (McKay, 1980). The resulting growth in permanency planning led to fewer children lingering in care indefinitely, but conflicts over parental rights were sometimes intense. Until freeing became an option, agencies often used the assumption of parental rights in part to test the strength of grounds for dispensing with consent in a subsequent adoption petition. However, there was always uncertainty about the issue of consent until the adoption hearing. The rising number of contested adoptions meant that increasing numbers of prospective adopters and children were faced with prolonged anxiety about the outcome. At the same time some birth parents and members of the judiciary believed that the use of parental rights legislation, as a prelude to adoption, unfairly loaded the dice against contesting parents. Expectations, therefore, were high in social work circles that freeing would provide new alternatives to enable clearer plans for some children to be made at an earlier stage, in a manner which would also be fairer to birth parents.

Freeing in practice

Yet, when social workers began to prepare freeing applications, they soon realised that the process was not likely to be quick or straightforward. By contrast with adoption, the agency is the petitioner in a freeing application as the effect of a freeing order is to transfer *all* parental rights to the agency until they are handed over to adopters through an adoption order. In cases where the birth parents have chosen freeing, the petition should not present problems. However, in the crucial early days unfamiliarity with the procedure led to delays both within agencies and in courts. The result was that, even with consent, freeing often took as long to process as an adoption application and then had to be followed by another hearing concerning the suitability of the adoptive placement before an adoption order was finally granted.

There have been some occasions when freeing has been used to advantage and a hearing has taken place speedily. These include cases where parents were about to go abroad or where there was domestic conflict over the birth of an extra-marital child which made it advisable to release parents from continued involvement in the adoption once they had given their agreement. Otherwise, the timescales required for making two legal petitions instead of one led to the conclusion that there was usually little advantage in using the freeing procedure where parental consent existed in uncomplicated situations. In addition, as these children were often placed with prospective adopters before the freeing order was granted, the adopters experienced all the familiar anxieties which obtained in the traditional route to adoption.

If the child's parents do not consent to the making of a freeing petition, the legal requirements are more stringent. Previously, in contested adoptions, it had been sufficient for the agency to make a brief statement of the grounds as these would be argued by solicitors acting for the adopters (who were the petitioners). In freeing, the agency has to make a full statement of the grounds for requesting the court to dispense with parental agreement in the freeing report submitted to the court. The preparation of the report for the court therefore required close co-operation with the agency's legal section. Once again, lack of experience with the new provision meant that in the early days procedures for consultation, exchange of documents and the approval of the report in these two departments resulted in difficulties and frustrating delays. Later on in our research we found that many changes had been made to try and speed up the process and ensure that the format of reports corresponded to the requirements of the courts. Nevertheless, writing the freeing report was an arduous exercise in which many local authority personnel took part, as the following quotations illustrate.

I was writing the Freeing Report in parallel with the legal section and I was really surprised about how long that actually took for me physically to prepare. I suppose I am used to writing a number of reports but this seemed to be the longest and the most intense report I had ever written and I think it must have taken me fully a month to do it.

... you show it to your senior, you send it up to legal section, then it goes to your senior and your senior may make some suggestions for a change, then it goes to your area officer. Now my area officer signs the report and we send it up to the Divisional Director who says 'this must

*be your preliminary report?' and I laughed and I thought well! . . .
maybe it is quite a good thing in a way that it has been viewed by so
many different people. You are like a puppet really, there is very little
of your own – what you have originally written.*

The likelihood that the majority of freeing applications will be contested,
and therefore require this degree of agency input before being lodged in
court, is borne out by the results of a national census conducted by the
researchers. This covered all freeing applications lodged in court between
1 April 1987 and 31 March 1988, together with any applications which
had been lodged earlier but were still awaiting an outcome. Replies were
received from all 12 Regions and the number of applications totalled
exactly 100. The majority of the 67 applications decided by the end of
March resulted in freeing orders being granted.

Table 1
Freeing census 1987/8 – applications decided

Total *N (%)*	Granted *N (%)*	Refused *N (%)*	Other outcome *N (%)*
67 (100)	58 (87)	5 (7)	4 (6)

The court was asked to dispense with consent in three-quarters of the
cases where a freeing order was granted and two-fifths of these applications were actively contested. Some parents who disagree with freeing
express this by not signing the papers, rather than go through all the effort
to contest in court. There was an important distinction between being
unwilling to agree to adoption and actively contesting it in court, in terms
of the number of days of hearings and the people called to give oral
evidence. However, our more detailed study of 39 freeing applications
revealed that several parents who did not actively contest them still wished
to attend court and "see that justice was done" in a way which had not
previously been possible.

Four types of freeing

The analysis of 39 cases, selected from four Scottish Regions, consisted of freeing applications lodged in court since 1985 where a court decision had been reached (except for one case where the written judgment took a very long time to come through). Twelve of the children also had a sibling for whom a freeing order was sought and, in these cases, we followed the older child. We started by classifying the 39 cases on the basis of the plan for the children when they were received into care, as this would produce a similar distinction to that made by the Roughton Committee. There were just seven cases where the parent(s) made a decision to have their child adopted shortly before or after the child's birth. The other 32 children had all been received into care initially on a temporary basis as a solution to family difficulties and adoption had become the plan at a later date. In ten of these 32 cases the parents themselves came to accept that adoption was the best plan so that they were eventually in a similar position to the seven parents who wished to relinquish their children. The remaining 22 cases were contested in court and clearly resembled the second Houghton category of "dispensation".

However, further investigation suggested that a two-fold classification as either "relinquished" or "dispensed" would be an oversimplification. There seemed to be a *continuum* between choice (however reluctantly made) at one end and conflict (increasingly hotly pursued) at the other end. Altogether, there appeared to be four groups:

- "Freed by choice" — 7 cases
- "Freed by acceptance" — 10 cases
- "Freed without consent" — 11 cases
- "Contested freeing" — 11 cases
  Total — 39

The use of a combination of the initial plan and the eventual outcome indicates the importance of circumstances which occur while the plan for freeing is put into operation. Some cases are always more likely than others to progress smoothly or to be difficult. The ones which come in between are especially those where the way the case is handled can lead either to an acceptance of the freeing plan or to a more vigorous rejection of it.

"Freed by acceptance"

For example, the existence of freeing and the decision to use this route towards adoption appeared to enable both the parents and the social workers in the "freed by acceptance" group to work at this process of relinquishment in stages. The first step was the issue of parental consent. The child's placement with prospective adopters became the next step *after* freeing in all but one instance. This pattern contrasted with that for children who were "freed by choice", where six out of seven had been placed beforehand. In the "freed by acceptance" group the fact that the children were "held" in their existing foster homes seemed to give parents some feeling of involvement in the process. In "working towards" adoption as the best outcome there was no prior move to an adoptive home and so consideration of the freeing petition in court was not pre-empted. Access to their children was usually still left open, though some parents requested that this should decrease or stop. Two mothers chose to tell their children about the adoption and said "goodbye" to them.

Our interviews with social workers revealed a great deal of contact with parents in this group during this phase. This allowed the parents to talk and receive support in beginning to think through parting with their child and consider changing patterns of access. The parents expressed many painful feelings, including anger and guilt, and the social workers too found the decision to go for adoption difficult. It was evident that much effort had previously been put into attempting to restore the children to their families and, as the following quotation shows, there was still much ambivalence:

> . . . it was the right decision in this particular case . . . it is one of the most difficult things because you are always pulled in two directions when you feel very strongly that children belong with their parents and yet you've also got to be assessing what quality of parenting there is. If there'd been any way that it might have been viable we'd have tried something else. But whichever way I looked there wasn't any viable option.

"Freed without consent"

Although they shared many characteristics with those "freed by accept-ance", the freeing orders for the children "freed without consent" were granted only after the applications had been opposed in court, with varying degrees of vigour. The reasons for seeking freeing were complex and differed in emphasis from case to case but, generally speaking, the family problems which social workers had been attempting to resolve had gone on for longer, more repetitively and intractably than they had for those who were "freed by acceptance". Every mother had at least one problem relating either to low intelligence, illness, or involvement in criminal activity, drug or alcohol abuse, and often two or more of these were present. Where information was available about fathers, they too were often reported to have similar problems. Crucially, there appeared to have been a lack of rapport and sense of "working together" between parents and social workers in this group. Despite considerable efforts to support the children in their families and to restore them, social workers saw situations "going downhill", "efforts falling off" and sensed a "lack of motivation" or the contradictory pull of the parents' lifestyles and associations.

In several cases the assumption of parental rights had been considered previously and for others the decision to use freeing instead was undoubt-edly influenced by expectations that it would be quicker and would involve only one contested court process instead of two. Nevertheless, social workers experienced much anxiety as they realised that obtaining a freeing order was not a foregone conclusion. Unlike parental rights, when parents had to object to a decision already made by the local authority, freeing offered natural parents a fairer chance to put their case before the court from the outset. Parents directed the energy created by their anger and hostility to the plan into openly contesting the freeing applications – in one instance for four days of hearings. Sadly the history of their previous failures to care for their children or to change their lives sufficiently to offer them a reasonable chance of security was weighted against the parents in this group and they were unable to persuade the Sheriffs to refuse to dispense with their consents.

"Contested freeing"

Three parents in the "contested freeing" group were successful in having their children restored to them and the return of a fourth child was being considered by the social work department. None of the court decisions in this group was straightforward and they illustrated some of the surprising outcomes which may result from a freeing application. These unusual cases have probably distorted the view of freeing held by many social workers, solicitors and courts. They formed 28 per cent of our total sample, but their nature and that of similar cases not included in the study, has exerted a far greater influence on attitudes than the relatively more straightforward freeing applications in the other groups.

The eventual outcome, after appeals or custody applications, was that freeing orders were granted for only three of the 11 children in this group. The unmarried father of one of these three children applied for custody and there was a lengthy hearing of this petition before the court considered and granted the freeing order. The other two cases were the subjects of appeals before being freed. Three applications were ultimately refused and two others were abandoned during the court hearings when it became apparent that they were likely to be refused. Two cases were sisted (set aside) for an adoption hearing, one after an appeal, as the children were placed with prospective adopters and the courts decided that all the issues should be considered together. These cases illustrated how placement *before* a contested freeing hearing may negate the point of dealing with consent separately. The final case in this group was the one mentioned earlier where there were long delays and the outcome was still undecided at the end of our fieldwork.

Grounds for dispensation

Although the cases in the "contested freeing" group were especially difficult to resolve, the decision to dispense with parental consent in any of the contested applications was never easy. The most common grounds on which dispensations were sought were that the parent 'has persistently failed . . .' (26 cases) or that the parent 'is withholding his agreement unreasonably' (23 cases). Frequently, these grounds were both listed for the same case. In a freeing petition the rights of a birth parent who is claimed to be withholding agreement unreasonably do not have to be weighed against the claims of the prospective adopters as they should in an adoption petition. Yet Sheriffs and others indicated that deciding on this ground in the absence of a counter-claim was, in fact, no easier. If the child was already placed for adoption, the circumstances were in practice usually taken into account.

Contested hearings showed that it was important for agencies to be able to substantiate the grounds through oral as well as written evidence, especially in relation to the current situation. Freeing applications were clearly seen by the courts as a first stage towards possible adoption and the consequences in loss of parental rights required very careful consideration. The court was becoming a battleground for the resolution of interests involving the State, the parents and the child to a greater extent than had been expected before freeing was implemented (Rowe, 1984).

Court hearings

Social workers said they found these court hearings more stressful than those for custody, parental rights or even contested adoptions. They were conscious of the need for careful consideration of the issues, but were anxious about the questions asked by the Sheriff or the defence lawyer and sometimes found the sheer length of time in the witness box a shattering experience. The appearance in court of the child's parent(s) in contested applications was a further source of stress. These were people the social workers had tried to work with and cared about even though they placed the child's interest first. As one of the social workers put it:

I found it discomforting to have the parents sitting there and, on one or two occasions, interrupting the proceedings and making adverse comments. I think I kept in front of me the fact that this was for the child, it was in his interests and this was the right thing to be doing.

Another said:

It was quite difficult going over the case with the mother sitting there looking as black as thunder. Not very pleasant.

Reactions to freeing process

However, social workers' overwhelming concern was about the length of time usually taken over the freeing process. Some went as far as to say that, with hindsight, using freeing had been a disaster or a mistake which they now regretted having embarked on. They were especially worried about the effects on the children but were also conscious of the implications for birth parents, as the following quotation shows:

I feel children are left in limbo a long time after decisions are made and that has implications for natural families. I think it also has implications for children when you are trying to prepare them for something that is way, way ahead that we may not actually be able to achieve for nine months, a year, 18 months – depending on how long these things go through court.

The consequence of these experiences with freeing was that agencies were re-considering the use of contested adoptions. Social workers were reported to be more openly preparing adopters for this possibility and some were virtually making it a condition of acceptance that adopters should be willing to take this risk. Nevertheless, few of the key personnel with responsibility for freeing whom we interviewed in a follow-up study at the end of our fieldwork went so far as to say that they did not see freeing as a useful option. It was evident that the nature of freeing cases had also led practitioners to review their position in respect of contested adoptions. Although these were seen by some as a "way round" freeing, their understanding of the rights of natural parents had shifted and there had been a growing interest in "open" adoption now that more older children were being placed. This position was interesting in the light of observations made by the few birth parents we were able to talk with during the study. These parents indicated that they might have been less likely to oppose the freeing application if they could have maintained some contact, however minimal, with their children.

Greater priority for freeing

The freeing legislation, as currently framed, does not allow for consideration of "terms and conditions", such as parental contact, since these have been left as part of the adoption hearing. However, this is too late for birth parents as they are no longer parties to the adoption after the freeing order has been granted and therefore cannot state their case on this matter. The ability to include terms and conditions in a freeing order is just one of a list of recommendations made as a conclusion to our study (Lambert *et al*, 1989). Several of our recommendations deal with the need for better timetabling and for greater priority to be given to freeing applications. Others have a wider relevance to work with children and families.

The small number of freeing applications lodged in courts each year, and the difficulties many practitioners have experienced with the provision, have highlighted the fact that they involve some of the most complex childcare cases. The proposal to remove all parental rights and place these children for adoption has usually been taken against parents who are still very much in the picture. Consequently it is not surprising that the conflicts have been painful, or that they have not always resulted in the outcome the social workers intended. As far as birth parents are concerned, freeing has indeed given them a fairer chance of stating their case. However, many of the children have had to wait much longer than expected before plans for their future could be resolved, and explaining the situation to them has proved especially difficult. The study found that social work departments and legal departments have made many improvements to their procedures for freeing applications. If court timetables can also be related more clearly to the needs of the child, freeing may have a better chance of being used, when appropriate, as an alternative route to adoption.

Postscript

In the original study, on which the above article is based, we made a number of recommendations including the ability of the court to include "terms and conditions" in a freeing order. Sadly the opportunity for doing so was missed when the Children (Scotland) Act 1995 was drafted. One consequence has been that, unlike England, a freeing order in Scotland cannot contain a condition for post-freeing contact between a parent and their child, but nothing need stop a vountary agreement between the local authority and a parent. The exact legal position is far from clear but the absence of this provision has already led to some Sheriffs refusing to grant a freeing order if they were satisfied that contact was in a child's best interests. Though such a decision can be legally correct, it can also deprive a child from being freed and moving on to an adoptive family.

Another problem to which we equally drew attention, is that if the court were to make a freeing order and the child not placed within a year, then it can be very difficult for child and parent to pick up the pieces and re-establish the quality of contact that existed before. Examples of this kind have recently surfaced and it can be traumatic for both child and parent(s).

References

Bell M (1988) 'The use of freeing orders', *Adoption & Fostering* 122, pp 10–17.

Houghton Committee (1972) *Adoption of Children* (Report of the Departmental Committee), London: HMSO.

Lambert L, Buist M, Triseliotis J and Hill M (1989) *Freeing Children for Adoption*, Final report to Social Work Services Group, Scottish Office, and Summary (CRU paper).

McKay M (1980) 'Planning for permanent placement', *Adoption & Fostering* 99:1, pp 19–21.

Rowe J (1984) 'Freeing for adoption: an historical perspective', *Adoption & Fostering* 8:2, pp 54–7.

Triseliotis J and Hall E (1971) 'Giving consent to adoption', *Social Work Today* 2:17, pp 21–24.

11 The role of social work departments in step-parent adoptions

Rena Phillips

This article was first published in Adoption & Fostering *16:2, 1992.*

Background to the research

Of the 878 adoptions registered in Scotland in 1989 almost half were step-parent adoptions (Scottish Education Department, 1990). The Adoption (Scotland) Act 1978 introduced some important changes with regard to such adoptions, requiring adoptive applicants to give notice to the local authority of their intention to adopt the child. On receipt of this the social work department must investigate and report on the matter to the court.

There has been quite a dramatic increase in research on stepfamilies, but the bulk of it consists of clinical studies of families who are experiencing major problems (Batchelor, 1988). As Brown (1982) notes, the stepfamily is generally neglected in childcare and social work literature and what stepfamilies think of the adoption process is a matter of speculation, as there is lack of research on this topic. To help fill this gap, I recently undertook research into social work involvement in step-parent adoptions. The research set out to answer:

- How do social workers perceive and carry out their roles in step-parent adoptions?
- What are the views of stepfamilies of the service offered to them by social workers in step-parent adoptions?

Methodology

The research was carried out in three Regions in Scotland (referred to as Region A, B and C), by examining the adoption reports submitted to the courts, and semi-structured interviews were held with:

- twenty-one stepfamilies (seven in each Region) who, except for two still awaiting the court hearing, had their adoption orders granted within two years of the research interview. The initial plan was to interview 30 families, and although 84 were approached, the response rate was low;

- sixteen generic social workers (five in Region A and C and 6 in B) with on average five years' experience of step-parent adoption work.
- six senior staff (two in each Region) with management and supervision responsibility for step-parent adoption;
- eight children (over school age) whose families agreed for them to be interviewed. There were 28 children in the sample (including five sibling groups of two and one of four), seven of whom were under school age at the time of the adoption. Their semi-structured interviews were combined with written and visual aids such as family charts, word choice and sentence completion.

Methodological problems were encountered in Region A, as in many of the step-parent adoptions there was no record kept as to whether the adoption order had been granted or not. Also, in two instances (in Region A and C) families included in the sample turned out to be adoptions by grandparents, which only came to light when the interviewers visited. Overall the impression gained was that attention to departmental records in respect of step-parent adoptions was lax.

The social workers interviewed were not the ones who had written the adoption reports on the 21 families in the sample, as this proved too difficult to arrange. The interviews with the social workers were based on the last step-parent adoption with which they were involved. This provided data on an additional 16 families, and allowed a comparison to be made between the views of families and social workers.

In the following discussion the two parents who are now married to each other will be called the "parent" and the "step-parent", and the non-custodial birth parent "the other parent" (all but one of whom were males).

Lack of procedural and legal information

The BAAF leaflet on stepchildren and adoption stresses the importance of information by saying, 'there are delicate relationships between adults and the children in all families and so it is important to think of human needs, motives and feelings as well as the legal side' (BAAF, 1987). Only two of the families received any information and/or counselling to help them decide whether to adopt (one through a Citizens' Advice Bureau and the other from the social work department). Fifty-seven per cent of the families thought that such information would have been helpful to them. None of the families received any information after their notification to adopt and prior to the social work visit.

Seventy-five per cent of the social workers interviewed felt that before their involvement both the parents and the children's understanding of the adoption process was poor.

Alternatives to adoption

Prior to their application to adopt only two of the families were aware of the power of the court to grant a custody order instead of an adoption order, if this better safeguards a child's welfare (section 53, Children Act 1975). Families reported that only two of the solicitors and less than half of the social workers had discussed this with them, and that only 52 per cent had received written information from the social workers on either step-parent adoptions or custody.

Of the social workers interviewed 75 per cent felt that their understanding of custody was limited. Only 56 per cent raised this with the families and 62 per cent did not provide any written information to the families on custody.

At the time of their application to adopt, most families had informally changed their child's surname. Prior to their application to adopt only four were aware of the official procedure for recording a change of surname (General Register Office, 1987) – only two of the solicitors and 38 per cent of the social workers had discussed this with them. Only two of the social workers interviewed had a good knowledge of this procedure and had raised this with the families.

In giving their reasons for adoption, families put legal status as their prime motivation, followed by the wish to be seen as a "proper family", and security and recognition for the step-parent. In discussion with the interviewers regarding custody and official change of name, all the families rejected these as alternatives to adoption on the ground that it did not provide them with the legal security they were seeking. Managers highlighted the difficulties in deciding when an adoption or when a custody order was more appropriate, which was exacerbated by the lack of written policy guidelines on step-parent adoptions in all three departments. In only one section 22 report was custody suggested as a possible alternative, as the children were in regular contact with the other parent (this case had not come to court at the time of the research), with the rest (except for another case which had not come to court) being granted adoption orders.

Other alternatives relating to parental rights orders were drawn to my attention, after the interviews were completed, by the former legal adviser to BAAF in Scotland (Scott, 1990). One is the power of the court under the Law Reform (Parent and Child) (Scotland) Act 1986 to make a parent and step-parent joint tutors of pupil children (girls under 12 and boys under 14) or curators of older children. Such orders give the step-parent the necessary authority to look after the child in the eyes of the outside world, without cutting off the other parent. Also under section 4 of the same Act a parent can appoint another person, who may be the step-parent, to be tutor or curator with legal responsibility for the child, after the birth parent's death. BAAF has issued a very useful practice note on stepfamilies and adoption (BAAF, 1991b) saying that these sort of orders are not widely used by stepfamilies, perhaps because they are not aware of their possibilities. My discussion with practitioners reveals a similar lack of knowledge.

The parent adopting his or her child

Fifty-seven per cent of the families reported that they were not aware prior to the social worker visiting them of the legal requirement that the parent must first give up her or his rights and become an adoptive parent too, and 33 per cent reported that the social workers had not discussed this with them. Eighty-six per cent of the families expressed negative feelings, sometimes very deeply felt, regarding such a requirement. Words like "confusing", "stupid", "farcical", "unfair" were used, as well as feeling "shocked" and "horrified". Some families felt they were "giving the child away" or "losing a child". Thirty-one per cent of the social workers and most of the managers felt that this was a problem.

Issuing of an adoption certificate

Prior to the social worker visiting them 43 per cent of the families were not aware of the issuing of an adoption certificate, which replaces the birth certificate, showing the birth parent as an adoptive parent. Sixty-two per cent of the families reported that the social workers had not raised this with them and 76 per cent disagreed with this procedure.

Visit by curator and procedure in court

Prior to the social work involvement 48 per cent of the families were not aware of the role of the curator, and in 19 per cent of cases this was not discussed by the social worker. Also, 57 per cent of the families were not aware prior to the social work involvement as to what would happen in court, e.g. would they need to appear in court or not? The same number of families had not been informed of the procedures by the social workers, causing confusion and anxiety.

Contact with solicitors

Whilst this study is concerned with the role of social workers in step-parent adoptions, for most families the first port of call regarding the adoption was a solicitor. Most families approached solicitors they already knew or picked one at random, rather than choosing someone with experience of adoption work. Eighty-one per cent of the families felt that the information given by the solicitors was inadequate, and 56 per cent regarded the service as poor.

As regards the costs involved, 56 per cent had not been informed by the solicitor of this, although only two reported financial difficulties. Sixty-nine per cent of the families applied for legal aid, with two being turned down, and all of them complained of the difficulty in understanding the system and the slowness of the process.

Sixty-two per cent of the social workers thought that the families they visited received a poor service by solicitors. Forty-three per cent of the families felt that the process of step-parent adoption was slow. The mean time to grant an adoption was 15 months in Region A, 12 months in Region B and 21 months in Region C. The mean time for social workers to make contact following the notification of the intention to adopt was two months in Region A and B, and eight months in Region C. As regards the number of visits and the timespan involved, in Region A families received three visits over one month, in Region B four visits over two months and in Region C four visits over four months. The interviews with social workers revealed similar findings in Region A and B, but in Region C the social workers made on average nine visits over seven months.

On the whole most of the delays were due to legal issues, such as legal aid or what families described as "incompetence" on the part of solicitors. For example, in one case the solicitor had not advised the parent that as she was not yet 21 she was not legally qualified to adopt. Some families suggested that solicitors should be "cut out" and a "do it yourself" system substituted, and that better liaison between solicitors and social workers might help to speed up the process.

Social work practice

Interviews

Sixty-two per cent of the parents reported not having been interviewed separately by the social workers. Even though 21 of the children out of the sample of 28 were over school age, 48 per cent of the children were not seen on their own. It is interesting to note in this respect that 48 per cent of the families said they had no knowledge before the social worker visited that the children might be seen on their own, and 38 per cent had some reservations about the possibility of separate interviews.

In contrast to the families, 87 per cent of the social workers reported having seen the parents on their own, but 50 per cent did not see the children separately. While the age of the children was most frequently given as the main factor here, three-quarters of the children in this sample were of school age. Only three of the social workers used play and drawing to communicate with the children, and 62 per cent did not recommend books on step-parent adoptions either for the children or adults.

The statutory provisions relating to protected children (section 32 of the Adoption (Scotland) Act 1978) require social workers to visit families until the adoption order is granted or the application otherwise determined. Seventy-one per cent of the families reported that no visits continued after the social workers completed their reports, but 81 per cent did not see the need for this. Of the social workers interviewed 44 per cent reported not making such visits.

Court reports

All three departments had written guidelines for section 22 reports based on the relevant court rules. While there were variations in the depth of assessments, in Regions B and C the reports on the whole adequately covered the requirements of the rules, except that in Region C only two reports had a discussion on alternatives to adoption. In contrast, in Region A, in compliance with expectations of Sheriffs, reports were extremely brief and stereotyped. There was no discussion of the alternatives to adoption, nor an assessment of the personality of the petitioners or the developmental history of the child. While the latter is not required by law, the BAAF practice note on court reports (1991a) stresses that the court is still obliged to consider all the circumstances, and it is therefore best to be as thorough as possible. Most of the social workers in Region A expressed frustrations at the brevity of the reports.

Out of the 21 families, two had their reports shown to them and four had it read out, and all felt positive about the contents. Those who did not see the reports wished they had been given this opportunity.

Three-quarters of the social workers lodged their reports in court. Over a quarter reported their frustrations at not being notified of the results of the court hearing, sometimes depending on the family for this information.

Views on social work visits

Most of the families saw visits as an opportunity for information, explanations and questions, rather than for support. Opinions were nearly equally divided between seeing such visits in a negative or positive light. Negative feelings centred around contact being a necessary evil, invasion of privacy, the power vested in social workers and the futility of the investigation process. As one parent put it, 'what is the point of looking at whether you are a suitable parent for your own child'.

When social workers were asked about the families' attitude to them, half felt this was negative, a quarter felt it was positive and a quarter felt that the reaction was initially negative but became more positive on further acquaintance. The negatives as perceived by the social workers matched the ones expressed by the families.

The other parent

Out of the 21 parents, 12 had formerly been married to the other parent, one was widowed, four had cohabited, and four did not live together at all. There was continuing contact between the children and the other parent in two families, but the rest had lost touch over many years, and 57 per cent did not know the whereabouts of the other parent. Only one family, on the instructions of their solicitor, had traced the other parent to discuss the proposed adoption. In six cases there was contact with the extended family of the other parent, but in only two was the adoption discussed. In three of the families (all in Region C) the social workers interviewed the other parent. Seventy-one per cent of the families were aware that the effect of the adoption was to sever the legal relation-ship with the other parent, and most were in favour of this – some families expressly said that they had hoped for this result through their application to adopt.

Only one of the social workers interviewed did not discuss the wishes of the other parent with the families, but only two actually made contact with the other parent (one by phone). The main reasons given for not seeking the other parent were that their whereabouts were unknown and that it was the curator's job to make such contact. Only two social workers made contact with the extended family of the other parent. Nearly three-quarters made other enquiries, mainly with schools.

The adopted children

The guiding principle relating to the adoption of a child in section 6 of the Adoption (Scotland) Act 1978 highlights the need to safeguard and promote the welfare of the child and ascertain his/her wishes with due regard to age and understanding. The social workers interviewed felt that the most important element in the social work task was representing the child in the proceedings, and that in relation to work with the children the most important issue was the child's knowledge of the adoption. Yet, as discussed above, a large number of school-age children were not seen on their own by the social workers.

The importance for adopted children of knowing about their origins and the facts of their adoption has been well documented. Yet secrecy operated for quite a few of the children in this study – in five of the families the children had not been told about their origins (two under school age), in 11 families they did know who their other parent was (five under school age), in five families they did not know that their stepfather was not their birth father (three under school age) and in eight families the adoption had not been discussed with the children before the applications were lodged (five under school age). In three of the court reports the social workers mentioned their recommendations to the parents to tell the child about the adoption, in four reports it was mentioned that the parents were aware of the need to tell, and in one report this was not raised at all.

We obtained permission to interview eight children. As outlined above quite a number of families had not discussed the adoption with their children, and others felt anxious about the past being brought up again with the children. One child found it too difficult to cope with the interview, which left seven children seen out of a possible sample of 26 (two were under school age at the time of the research). This, unfortunately, is too small a number to yield meaningful results.

The social worker role

None had any specific training in this area, and 62 per cent felt the need for better information on procedural and legal issues. Eighty-one per cent of the social workers and most of the managers expressed concerns, sometimes deeply felt, about the role of social workers in step-parent adoptions. They felt their involvement made little difference, as it was a legal process in which they were being used as a rubber stamp, with most families having made up their mind for adoption long before the social worker arrived on the scene: 'It's like changing trains after the train has left the station.' This contrasts with the views of some of the families, as discussed above, regarding the power vested in social workers.

In relation to supervision and guidance to social workers some of the difficult issues highlighted were: cutting any legal ties with the other parent; when to recommend custody; need for the children to know about their origins; and what criteria to apply regarding the parenting standards of applicants.

While strong reservations were expressed about the role of social workers, there was also the view that there was scope to provide step-families with a valuable service if better counselling could be provided to families before the notification to adopt and if the public, stepfamilies, the legal profession and social workers were better educated regarding the process of step-parent adoption and its alternatives.

Conclusions

All the families who obtained an adoption order were satisfied with the end result, with the most valuable aspects being the security for the step-parent and achieving legal status. Yet, as this research has highlighted, there are major areas of concern regarding the services provided by social workers and solicitors to families. In particular, information and advice is felt to be lacking; families expressed concern at some of the procedures involved; social workers were dissatisfied with their role in the process, and children either lacked knowledge or experienced secrecy about their origins and adoption. Also, the expectations for custody as an alternative for adoption are not being realised.

The Review of Child Care Law in Scotland (1989) has drawn attention to some of the concerns outlined above, but the only recommendation it makes it that the status of the parent should be observed by recording this on the child's new birth certificate. While the Review acknowledges that it may appear anomalous that a parent should have to become an adoptive parent, it concludes that there is no firm evidence that this presents a major problem for stepfamilies – a view not borne out by this research.

While this study is small and exploratory the findings clearly suggest that services to stepfamilies who wish to adopt need to be reassessed. Further research might look at the views of solicitors and curators ad litem and, bearing in mind the current Adoption Law Review, whether an alternative process to adoption which recognises the role and status of stepfamilies, but avoids some of its pitfalls, might be more appropriate to meet the needs of stepfamilies.

Acknowledgements

The research upon which this article is based was made possible by financial support through the Small Grants Scheme for the Social Sciences of the Nuffield Foundation. Thanks also to Rosemary Brewis, lecturer in continuing education at Stirling University and Monique Ferrie, social worker for Central Region for their help with the interviews of families and social workers.

References

Batchelor J A (1988) *Stepfamilies*, Highlight No 85, London: National Children's Bureau.

Brown D (1982) *The Stepfamily – A growing challenge for social work*, Social Work Monographs, Norwich: University of East Anglia.

General Register Office (1987) *Recording Changes of Name and Surname in Scotland*, Leaflet RCN 1, London: HMSO.

Review of Child Care Law in Scotland (1989) Consultation Document 2, Scottish Child Care Law Review.

Scott J, Private communication (1990).

Scottish Education Department (1990) *Children Act 1975, Third Report to Parliament*, London: HMSO.

BAAF (1987) *Step-children and Adoption: Information for parents and step-parents in Scotland*, London: BAAF.

BAAF (1991a) *Social Work Reports in Adoption Proceedings (Scotland)*, Practice Note 19, London: BAAF.

BAAF (1991b) *Step-families and Adoption: A guide to the law in Scotland*, Practice Note 21, London: BAAF.

12 A review of the first Scottish Children's Services Plans in relation to adoption

Irene Clark and Emma McWilliam

This article was first published in Adoption & Fostering *23:2, 1999.*

Introduction

The statutory requirement for local authorities to produce Children's Services Plans was first introduced in England and Wales by the Children Act 1989 (Amendment) (Children's Services Planning) Order. The purpose of this legislation was to ensure that local authorities undertook strategic planning in relation to children in need, improved the quality of services being provided and made better use of their existing resources.

Under the Children (Scotland) Act 1995, by 1 April 1998 Scottish local authorities were to have "prepared and published" their first plan 'for the provision of relevant services for or in respect of children in their area'. The Scottish Office issued guidance to local authorities in February 1997 which provided the "framework" which local authorities were to use in order to prepare their Children's Services Plans (Chapter 2, Volume 1, The Children (Scotland) Act 1995 Regulations and Guidance). Annex A of the guidance lists the main needs of children which require to be identified in both quantitative and qualitative terms in order to provide a basis from which their priority for service provision can be determined. This specifically includes 'Children who have been adopted (and those who are in the process of adoption)' and reference is also made to looked after children who may need to be adopted. Annex B goes on to list services 'which will figure in action programmes' as a means of responding to identified areas of need. Under the broad service heading of Placement Services, Adoption and Post Placement Support Services are itemised. The writers therefore expected that each local authority's Children's Services Plan would contain an adoption services plan for children.

The authors decided to review the first Children's Services Plans produced in Scotland in relation to adoption in order to determine to what extent they had fulfilled the requirements laid down in the guidance. Our objectives in doing so were threefold: to highlight the welfare of children who need adoption services; to gain an overview at a national level of strategic planning for the future of adoption services; and to seek out examples of best practice in terms of corporate approaches and partnerships with other local authorities, voluntary organisations and service users.

Sample and methods

In October 1998, contact was made with the 32 local authorities to obtain a copy of their Children's Services Plan. By this time there were five authorities whose plans were not published but whose representatives kindly agreed to their final draft version being used. We were informed that it was unlikely that these versions would be changed significantly regarding their adoption plans. We prepared a grid as a basis for evaluating the plans. Ten headings were extracted from the guidance: 1–6 taken from the main criteria and 7–10 based on key elements for planning:

1 strategic objectives for the service and the priority given to resourcing them;

2 a corporate plan with contributions and commitments from education, housing and other local authority services;

3 volume of service and expenditure planned over a three-year period in relation to provision by local authority, voluntary organisations and the private sector;

4 identification of needs, their main features, diversity and relative priority for services;

5 consultation with health boards and trusts, voluntary organisations, principal reporter, chair of the children's panel, housing agencies, service users, previous users and potential users;

6 supply of service – directly, in association with other authorities, purchase from voluntary agencies and private concerns in relation to local need and best value for money;

7 current service provision and policies;

8 projected need over the next three years, changes or developments needed to meet these;

9 action plan including staffing levels, training, IT and other resource requirements;

10 monitoring and review structures, performance indicators, outcomes and how these influence future planning processes.

All the authorities were listed against each heading. The authors then read all the Children's Services Plans independently, systematically recording everything each authority had to say about their adoption service under these headings. From these grids we then collated and assessed the content of the plans. A secondary analysis resulted in grouping the findings into three main areas: strategic planning, a needs-led service and a three-year service plan.

Finally, a comparison was made to evaluate how local authorities performed in relation to adoption as opposed to other relevant services for children. We did so by examining to what extent the Children's Services Plans met these criteria in relation to two other related services for looked after children: fostering and residential care.

Strategic planning

The most recurring theme in the Children's Services Plans regarding objectives for adoption services was in the area of post-adoption support. Fifteen of the plans referred to some aspect of post-adoption support as requiring further development. Much of the focus, however, was on adoption counselling for adults. While this is an important service which, in our opinion, is rightly located within the adoption service as a whole, it is not a service for children and the relevance to Children's Services Plans could be questioned. In addition, four local authorities aimed to establish systems to manage the increasing number of open adoption arrangements.

Some authorities had objectives to recruit more adoptive families but did not seem to be putting forward a strategy linked to their projected needs in terms of numbers and type of resources required. The need to link closely the recruitment of adoption resources with the children requiring placement was identified in a Social Services Inspectorate Report on six English local authorities adoption services. This stated that one characteristic of best practice was 'recruitment of adopters targeted on those children for whom adoption is the plan' (Department of Health, 1996, pp 2–3).

Nine authorities had a separate section on adoption in their plan. It was more usual for adoption to be included in a chapter on looked after children. The latter often led to confusion between objectives for children in long-term foster care and those who were to have new legal parents. This was illustrated by the usage of terms such as "adoptive care" and "adoptive carers", and seemed to indicate a lack of clarity about perm-anency planning.

However, while some authorities identified objectives within their adoption or adoption and fostering service, few plans evidenced that their adoption service was viewed as an integral part of an overall strategic plan for children and families services. The Department of Health Local Authority Circular 20 (1998) stated that adoption should be regarded as a mainstream service. The writers therefore suggest that a strategic objective is required in which adoption forms an essential component, for example, to confine the population of accommodated children to those for whom all other alternatives have been assessed as inappropriate to meet their needs. The four proposed stages to implement this are represented in Figure 1 in terms of volume of service.

Although adoption is a service for a small number of children, its significance within this strategy can be seen in that it provides the only exit from public care for children who are not able to return to their family of origin. Furthermore, it fulfils their right to belong to a family (UN Convention on the Rights of the Child 1989).

It had been hoped that the 1995 Children (Scotland) Act would have provided a further option to legal permanence through foster carers obtaining residence orders and being in receipt of residence allowances. However, this route remains fundamentally flawed on two counts. Firstly, it leads to foster carers facing the prospect of a reduction in their standard of living and consequently in their capacity to provide for a foster child. This is because residence allowances are only paid until a child is 16, as opposed to 18 if they were fostered. Furthermore, unlike fostering allowances they are treated as income which is taken into account for both benefit claims and tax purposes. Secondly, and at least as important a consideration, there is no legal requirement for post-placement support for foster carers who obtain a residence order.

In summary, the difficult challenge facing local authorities in prioritising services in a climate of economic constraint is about 'achieving the right balance' (Department of Health, 1998) between preventive services, services for looked after and accommodated children and adoption services.

A needs-led service

A major difficulty shared by all the Children's Services Plans was that they did not contain an audit of current and future needs in terms of adoption services. Four authorities stated the number of children they currently had registered and awaiting an adoptive placement. Another five specified the number of approved adopters they had waiting for a match. One authority identified that 4.9 per cent of their total population

Figure 1
A strategic objective for Children and Families Services

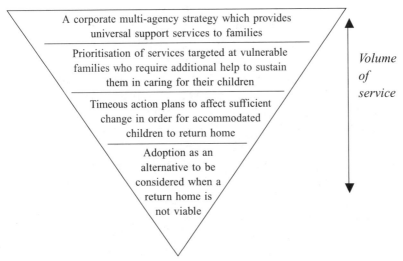

of looked after children were in adoptive placements. A number of authorities said that they needed more resources to pursue adoption as a goal for certain types of children. Various categories were mentioned including older children, sibling groups, children of black or mixed parentage and children with disabilities. References were made to seeking couples or childless couples as potential resources, but no plan stated that enquiries would be equally welcome from single people or one-parent families.

In order to identify projected need for adoptive placements from the existing population of looked after children, local authorities would require, as a minimum, to have the following information:
- children currently registered for adoption at an adoption panel and awaiting placement;
- children where a decision has been made at a childcare review to proceed with adoption as part of their care plan.

This should provide the basis from which to inform a needs-led recruitment strategy. Given the importance now placed on good outcomes and the wealth of research which demonstrates the benefits of adoption on a wide spectrum of measures (Triseliotis *et al*, 1997), adoption should be viewed as a placement of choice for children who cannot return home within acceptable timescales, not as a last resort: 'Authorities need to ensure advice to staff gives positive emphases to adoption as a placement option for children' (Department of Health, 1996, p 39).

When rehabilitation plans fail, local authorities can also promote adoption as a positive outcome by setting a target percentage of the number of these accommodated children they aim to place. Anecdotal information currently available suggests a figure of 90 per cent for pre-school aged children and 60 per cent for children of primary school age. However, this may need further verification.

The most unpredictable factor, especially for the smaller authorities, is the number of babies who will be given up for adoption. Arguably it is more efficient to meet this need through membership of a consortium or through contracting out to voluntary agencies rather than diverting any internal resources away from meeting the needs of older children. Our experience would suggest that while "stretching" baby adopters to consider older children is inadvisable, asking adopters approved for a primary school aged child to consider a younger child often does not present the same difficulties. Three plans identified the need to produce an information leaflet to explain that adoption is no longer a service to meet the needs of childless couples but a service for children. Rather than individual authorities undertaking this task it might be helpful if the Scottish Office commissioned a national leaflet explaining what kind of children need adoption and how to seek further information. In fact, such a proposal could be extended to a range of leaflets to cover criteria for adoption, adoption allowances and post-adoption support. These might present more challenges in incorporating the unique circumstances across all agencies, but it is surely not in children's interests for there to be an increasing divergence of service provision across Scotland. In England such a concern has already been identified in a recent study by Ivaldi (1998):

> These variations are not explained by demographic differences and can only be assumed to be due to a major difference in the use of adoption, reflecting a varying commitment to the priority that is given to adoptions as a means of securing permanent placements for children who cannot live with their birth families. (p 6)

Building up a picture of the overall need for post-adoption support services can be assisted by gathering information on the population of adopted children. Adoption records will indicate how many children were placed for adoption within the authority in the last 18 years and voluntary agencies can provide information on how many children they have placed in different areas. The number of families living within the authority who are in receipt of adoption allowances and the current number of open adoption arrangements will also inform this process.

The authors made contact with the five voluntary adoption agencies in Scotland in October 1998 by means of a letter to a newly established forum where their representatives meet together to discuss issues of common concern. We informed this group about our research on adoption services in relation to Children's Services Plans and asked for any comments they would like to make. In particular we referred them to a summary of stage one of research being carried out by the Centre for the

Child & Society at the University of Glasgow on 'the voluntary sector and children's services planning', in which a main finding was that:

> *The lack of consortium of voluntary agencies or single point contact for local authorities was highlighted. This would have allowed voluntaries . . . to have approached local authorities as a unified group.*

It might assist local authorities in developing their adoption service plans for this group to be more proactive by providing information on what they could contribute to adoption services planning, both as a group and as individual organisations. The feedback from this group was that they would welcome the opportunity to participate in the development of adoption services within Children's Services Plans.

Many Children's Services Plans contained lists of other agencies, voluntary organisations and service users with whom consultation had taken place, either in drawing up the plan or more often by incorporating their responses to a draft plan. It was not possible to determine which statutory agencies, voluntary organisations or service users had been consulted specifically in relation to adoption services. No plan indicated that there had been consultation with adopted children and young people and so their views in relation to adoption services did not appear to have influenced the planning process:

> *The experiences of past users of adoption services are acknowledged as having played a valuable part in helping shape current adoption practice and identifying new needs for service.* (Department of Health, 1996, p 15)

On this basis, it could be valuable for representatives of previous service users such as adopted adults, and current service users, for example, adoptive parents, to be integrally involved in planning, policy development and evaluation of local authorities' adoption services. However, this did not seem to be the case, with the exception of one authority who mentioned service user involvement in devising a recruitment strategy.

In Scotland there are currently no private agencies from which to consider purchasing adoption services. The current options are for authorities to purchase adoption services from the voluntary sector or to form consortiums which serve their mutual interests. In terms of implementing a best value regime, all authorities are obliged to consider which options would provide the most cost-effective services. Nine Children's Services Plans indicated that they currently purchase some of their adoption services from the voluntary sector; these local authorities were all located around Glasgow, Edinburgh and Aberdeen, where the voluntary agencies are based. In addition, three other plans indicated their intention to consider contracting out some or all of their adoption service to the voluntary sector. There was a noticeable move towards working in co-operation with other local authorities, especially in relation to providing a wider range of placement options. This was mentioned in 13 plans as actively ongoing or planned for the future. However, the issue of motivation in respect of authorities with potential for recruiting resources but who do not need these for themselves remains unresolved. A charging policy needs to be introduced between authorities in order to resolve this, which includes the cost of any post-adoption support services by the placing authority. In addition, five authorities spoke of working in partnership with self-help groups for adopted adults or post-adoption support.

Local authorities may also need to consider whether it would be more effective to provide some aspects of their adoption service at a national level. For example, aspects of a post-adoption service such as a helpline, newsletter, ongoing training courses and consultation (Watson with McGhee, 1995). A Scottish Adoption Centre could promote the implementation of national standards for adoption services (Collier, 1998) and assist local authorities in benchmarking their performance and improving practice. Such a resource could be set up in a similar manner to the Centre for Residential Child Care in Scotland in order to ensure that adoption is given its proper place in the development of strategic plans for children's services (Department of Health, 1998, p 14).

Very few authorities specifically indicated that there was a corporate dimension to their adoption plan. Three authorities recognised the need for social work services to work with education and psychological services in order to provide a comprehensive post-adoption support service. However, in the majority of plans where post-adoption support was mentioned it was described as being delivered solely by social work services. Four authorities spoke of having representatives from other services within their council as members of their adoption panel; for example, in order to increase objectivity, one of these also included elected members. Three other authorities mentioned the role of legal services in implementing adoption plans and reviewing their adoption allowances scheme.

As part of implementing continuous improvement in terms of a best value regime, a corporate approach to adoption services needs to be developed further. For example, a public commitment from housing services in relation to providing suitable accommodation for adopters approved to take sibling groups and children with disabilities could contribute to a successful recruitment strategy. Psychological and educational reports on all children being registered for adoption could include an assessment of their emotional, behavioural, cognitive and educational development, identify future needs in terms of schooling and make some prediction about future potential. This would enhance the matching process and the quality of information provided to adoptive parents. A partnership approach is required by education and social services to ensure that adopted children who are manifesting problems at school can be sustained within the education system. School-based problems and the related stress factors present significant difficulties in many adoptive placements:

> Get any group of adopters together and the subject of schools is bound to crop up, reflecting their strong concerns about meeting the educational needs of their adopted children. (Phillips and McWilliam, 1996, p 2)

A needs-led service requires underpinning by a financial plan. This was an area of particular weakness, with no plan projecting future service requirements or providing a three-year financial plan. Two authorities stated their current spending on their adoption service in this financial year and another three what they currently spend on adoption allowances. Several plans indicated that information on expenditure was available elsewhere. Three authorities specified additional sums of money required to undertake specific activities, such as a needs analysis, recruitment and support services.

An analysis of Children's Services Plans by the Social Services Inspectorate in England for 1993/4 states that:

Attention needs to be given to ensure that low, volume-specialised and probably high unit cost services . . . are not overlooked. Because these services may be difficult to provide they require all the more careful planning. (Department of Health, 1996, p 18)

It seems therefore essential to have a separate adoption provisions budget which includes a projected cost for annual recruitment, information leaflets, adoption panel, medical and legal costs, contributions to local authority consortiums, referral and interagency fees, settling in grants, adoption allowances, the contracting out of services to other agencies and post-adoption support. One authority said that it had a charging policy in place in relation to intercountry adoptions. It would be possible to consider extending such a scheme to include step-parent adoption reports in order to meet the costs of sessional staff undertaking these areas of work.

Five authorities said that they planned to review their adoption allowance scheme and there were indications of concern about the cost of adoption allowances, with one urban authority simply stating that they had a £1.5 million expenditure. However, adoption allowances are cost effective when compared with the expense of maintaining the same child in long-term foster care. For example, using the payment rates of an average local authority fee-paying fostering scheme, if a child is long term fostered from the age of eight to 18 the allowances would total £42,538 plus fees of £27,172, amounting to £69,711 for the placement at current costs. This does not take account of after-care costs or of the expense of continuous provision of a social work service for ten years to meet all the statutory requirements for a looked after child. The adoption allowances based on the same scheme minus fees and Child Benefit over this period would cost £40,443 for the same child.

Even taking account of approximately £10,000 for referral and interagency fees if the placement is bought in, and of legal costs, this still meets best value criteria. Adoption allowances can be seen to represent value for money. Information about a local authority's scheme must feature in recruitment so that families know they can afford to adopt sibling groups and children with special needs. Borland and colleagues (1991) found that in a comparative study between those placements which were ongoing, as opposed to those which had disrupted, financial assistance was an important factor: 'Families in the ongoing group were more generously provided for in terms of financial support' (p 27). If authorities are to achieve adoption for hard-to-place children then they will need to be committed to increasing their adoption allowance budget to take account of this.

Our findings suggest that there are many areas requiring further development in order for local authorities to have a corporate, multi-agency, needs-led adoption service with integrated financial planning and service user involvement.

A three-year service plan

Where are we now?
Twenty-two of the plans set out to describe their current adoption service. Five authorities outlined the full range of services while other attempts were less successful owing to significant omissions. This position statement did not need to be lengthy but where it was comprehensive seemed to help provide a basis for future planning.

Where do we want to be?
Twenty-one authorities gave some indication that they had plans for further development of their adoption service over the next three years. The most common proposals were in relation to post-adoption support, with 15 plans including action points in relation to various aspects of this service. Four authorities had plans to set up systems for managing open adoption arrangements and six intended to review their adoption allowance scheme. The need to specifically recruit adoptive parents for hard-to-place children was mentioned in nine plans; other plans to recruit more carers may have been referring to adoptive parents as well as foster carers, but this was unclear.

What do we need to get there?
Planning was greatly hindered by a lack of data on future need, which in turn often led to rather vague and generalised statements of intent which did not readily translate into action plans. Information technology was

not discussed specifically in relation to adoption services, but there was a wider recognition of the importance of developing this within the plans in order to gain management information from which to identify and project needs.

Where there was a financial plan in relation to the cost of implementing action plans, seven authorities stated that this would be carried out 'within existing resources'. Two authorities said that they would increase their current staffing level by appointing another social worker, one to meet increasing demand by adults for adoption counselling and one to increase their efforts to recruit adoptive families. Three plans mentioned training staff in various aspects of adoption work. However, the specialist nature of adoption work may mean that it has been particularly adversely affected by the creation of smaller authorities. 'Single specialist practitioners are lonely individuals. Specialism needs the synergy of a larger group.' (Cheetham, 1995).

How will we know where we have got to?

Eleven authorities placed timescales on their adoption action plans but many plans did not identify performance indicators or criteria for successful outcomes. A model for evaluating achievement in terms of placing children for adoption is outlined in Figure 2.

The Local Authority Circular issued in England and Wales (LAC [98] 20, Department of Health, 1998) also recommends that directors arrange to inform elected members at regular intervals about the current position

Figure 2

Performance indicators and targets in relation to the implementation of adoption plans for children

Age of child	Length of rehabilitation programme	Review decision to adoption panel	Adoption panel to placement	Maximum timescale	Target % of children to be adopted from the population of looked after children who cannot return home
0–5	3–6 months	1 month	3 months	10 months	90%
5–10	6–12 months	2 months	6 months	20 months	60%

of children awaiting placement and that such reports include, as a minimum, certain specified information. Adoption panels can also play an important role in monitoring and evaluating an authority's policies, procedures and performance as an adoption agency. The 1996 Social Services Inspectorate Report, in commenting on the performance of adoption panels, concluded that 'Their quality control function needed reinforcement if they were to play their proper part in promoting improved practice' (Department of Health, 1996, p 66).

Overall findings

In our comparative study, local authorities met the criteria more fully in terms of fostering and residential care. There was a greater sense of direction to these services but a similar lack of integrated financial planning and specific measures of progress. In terms of strategic planning two main objectives were widespread: to reduce the number of accommodated children through developing preventive services and to improve the quality of care. Over 70 per cent had clear statements about the current availability of placements within fostering and residential care, compared to 15 per cent in terms of adoption. There was also significantly greater evidence of corporate and multi-agency planning in relation to meeting educational and health needs. Overall there was a greater sense of direction to these services, but a similar lack of integrated financial planning and specific measures of progress.

The finding from this research that adoption is given a lesser weighting than other relevant services is reinforced in the *Review of Children's Services Plans* (Scottish Office Social Work Services Group, 1999):

> *This important service area is barely covered in the majority of plans and, where it is mentioned, there is usually little assessment of need, numbers and costs.* (p 5)

Conclusions

Our research indicated that nine Children's Services Plans contained an adoption plan for children which succeeded in fulfilling most of the criteria laid down in the guidance, each having particular strengths in different aspects of their plan. They were Aberdeenshire, Angus, City of

Edinburgh, East Ayrshire, East Dumbartonshire, Moray, Shetland, South Lanarkshire and the Western Isles. These authorities are varied in terms of size and other demographic features and provide opportunities for benchmarking for all Scottish local authorities.

Given that so few Scottish local authorities fulfilled the criteria in terms of producing an adoption services plan in comparison with other relevant services, such as fostering and residential care, this review suggests that adoption is at risk of becoming marginalised as a service for children in Scotland. The future planning of adoption services within Children's Services Plans, in our view, will play a critical role in determining whether adoption will continue to exist as a widespread option for looked after children who cannot be brought up within their family of origin.

References

Borland M, O'Hara G and Triseliotis J (1991) 'Placement outcomes for children with special needs', *Adoption & Fostering* 15:2, pp 18–27.

Cheetham J (1995) 'Re-organisation and social work', in Black S, *The Impact of Reorganisation on Particular Services*, Edinburgh: University of Edinburgh, pp 51–53.

Collier F (1998) *Action Plan to Improve Adoption Services*, London: BAAF.

Department of Health (1995) *Children's Services Plans: An analysis of Children's Services Plans 1993/1994*, London: DoH.

Department of Health (1996) *For Children's Sake – An SSI inspection of local authority adoption services*, London: DoH.

Department of Health, LAC (98) 20 (1998) *Adoption – Achieving the right balance*, London: DoH.

Monaghan B, Hill M and Tisdall K, *The Voluntary Sector and Children's Services Planning*, Centre for the Child & Society, University of Glasgow, Personal correspondence.

Ivaldi G (1998) *Children Adopted from Care: An examination of agency adoptions in England 1996*, London: BAAF.

Phillips R and McWilliam E (1996) *After Adoption: Working with adoptive families*, London: BAAF.

The Scottish Office (1999) *Aiming for Excellence*, Edinburgh: The Scottish Office, March.

The Scottish Office (1997) *Scotland's Children: The Children (Scotland) Act 1995, Regulations and Guidance Vol 1.*

Scottish Office Social Work Services Group (1999) *Review of Children's Services Plans*, January.

Triseliotis J, Shireman J, and Hundleby M (1997) *Adoption: Theory, policy and practice*, London: Cassell.

United Nations Convention on the Rights of the Child 1989.

Watson L, with McGhee J (1995) *Developing Post Placement Support*, London: BAAF.

13 Birth fathers' lives after adoption

Gary Clapton

This article was first published in Adoption & Fostering *25:4, 2001.*

Introduction

For over 35 years professionals in the field have been calling for information about the experiences of birth fathers in adoption. In 1965 Anglim
argued that:

> ... we have actually been guilty of contributing to the myth that suggests
> that a child born out of wedlock has only one natural parent. (p 340)

While understanding has slowly grown in respect of the experiences of
birth mothers, it remains the case that we know very little of birth fathers
(Clapton, 1997). Insight as regards these "shadowy figures" (Mason,
1995) has been made ever more relevant by two recent government
initiatives. These are, firstly, the introduction of a raft of measures designed to increase the involvement of men in their families. Over the last
two years increased paternity leave has been advocated, the rights
of unmarried fathers are under review and the National Family and
Parenting Institute has been established, with one of its aims being the
increased involvement of men in their families (Family Policy Unit, 1998;
Department of Health, 1999). Secondly, a series of publications and
briefings in 2000 has sought to raise the profile of adoption (Department
of Health, 2000; Performance and Innovation Unit, 2000). However, once
the question of fathers is linked to adoption, it becomes apparent that our
knowledge of the experiences of birth fathers remains almost as poor
today as it was 35 years ago.

My research began in 1996 and set out to redress this imbalance. The
following discussion is derived from a study of the experiences of 30
birth fathers. The men either responded to an appeal printed in a variety
of adoption publications or were approached because they were in touch
with post-adoption agencies or had registered on the Adoption Contact

Register for Scotland. The men ranged in age from 35 to late 60s. They were invited to give accounts of their birth father life courses, starting with news of the pregnancy through to later-life experiences of searching for and contact with their child who had been given up for adoption, where applicable. The adoptions took place between 1954 and 1985, with most having happened towards the end of the 1960s when the men were in their late teens. The study included an exploration of the nature of fatherhood without the child in question. This was examined in the cases both of men who went on to have other children and those who did not (nine of the group had no further children). The men's hopes for contact in later life and what this signified were also discussed. At the time of the interview ten of the men (one-third) had met their son or daughter. This varied from just one meeting to two years of being in touch. The study also aimed to compare the men's experiences with those of birth mothers (see Clapton, 2000).

This paper is offered as an overview of the men's lives and thoughts following the adoption – principally the period immediately afterwards – and the nature of their thoughts of the child in the subsequent years. Some analysis of the findings and implications for practice are also included. It should be borne in mind that while valuable in providing a glimpse of an unknown experience, this article deals with only part of a lengthier life course – these birth father narratives span many decades and a variety of events. A comprehensive presentation and discussion of the men's experiences from the pregnancy to contact, where appropriate, is forthcoming (Clapton, 2002).

The immediate post-adoption period

Research findings from studies of women's experiences indicate that the immediate 12-month period following the adoption is a significant chapter in birth mother narratives. It is a time that may be marked by intense feelings of loss and pain (Winkler and van Keppel, 1984). Bouchier *et al* (1991) found a range of reactions to the adoption in the year after the relinquishment of the child. These included feelings of "anger and resentment" and "inadequacy and frustration" (pp 50–51). A birth mother is quoted:

I needed to tell somebody how I felt. I was being torn apart and I felt death would have been easier. To say how bad I felt about it and how I could never forgive myself, how hurt I was and how unwanted by anybody. (p 52)

Mindful of the importance of this post-adoption period in the birth mother literature, I wondered whether there was any parallel set of experiences for the 30 birth fathers in the present study. Had there been any impact on them in the weeks and months after the adoption? Did the child continue to "exist" in their thoughts in subsequent years? If so, how?

Twenty-six of the group were in a position to discuss their lives immediately after the adoption. The other four men only became aware of the adoption some time after the event and so could not substantively discuss their feelings relating to the immediate post-adoption period.

Reports of the year following the adoption were divided between the great majority who experienced distress (21) and five men who reported that the adoption had had little emotional impact upon them. Of the 21 men who reported some degree of discomfort or distress, 14 said that this levelled off. The other seven said that feelings of distress such as anger and bitterness persisted; this last group may be under-represented in the sample, since it is reasonable to assume that men with strong feelings would be more likely to participate in the research.

Strong post-adoption feelings that subside

The 14 men in this group reported various feelings of loss, anger and powerlessness in the weeks and months after the adoption, but eventually these subsided. For them the year following the adoption included a range of adoption-related feelings. The report of one father expresses a common experience. When asked how he had felt during the period after the adoption, he said:

Awful really. Very, very sad. Very mixed feelings. Something I wouldn't have intrinsically done under any other circumstances. There was high emotions of all sorts. There was so much going on at that period of time. I think I was shell-shocked when I look back.

A second became 'very depressed . . . it was a lonely time . . . I could have committed suicide'. Others said that they had "lost part of me", it was "like a bereavement" and during this "traumatic period" they had felt "anguish".

One man indicated the impact less directly. He responded that the adoption had had no effect on him because:

I shut it out. I literally put it behind me. I'd never known anyone in that situation before. There had always been kids around. It [having children] was a natural thing. But it was always there.

However, the last part of the above verbatim quotation tends to belie his declaration that he was not affected by the adoption.

Although such initial high emotions levelled off, these men also spoke about a regular presence of the child in their thoughts in the following years. Accounts of the child's continuing "existence" for the men were diverse but typically, as one man put it, his child 'was always in mind. I have a kid out there. I always remembered his birthday.'

Another said that he had:

. . . never stopped loving him or caring for him. It's like I have a son somewhere out there and it can bring a smile to my face and other times it's like a glow. I just feel good. At other times I feel sad when I think about him.

One man recounted that he had once been struck by feelings that something untoward had happened:

I had this weird apprehension that something had happened to him during childhood. And I had to let him go. I had to pretend that he was dead.

This mechanism was apparently necessary because, to all intents and purposes, his son's welfare was beyond his control. This man also spoke of feelings that drew comparison between the son who was adopted and a second son who had been brought up by him. His relationship with his second son was not as close as he would have hoped. He sometimes speculated that he and the adopted son would have been closer:

I suppose the bit that I feel about M is that a bit of me feels, well, I would love to have somebody who's, you know, possibly just that bit closer, somebody who would take me out for a pint.

One man's feelings subsided to a much greater extent than that of the others. Recurrent thoughts of his daughter were less marked than for many in this group. He simply said that he sometimes 'wondered how she had turned out'.

Persistent feelings of distress

There were seven men in this group. They described emotions that either remained at the same intensity or increased. At the time of the interview some of these men were engaged in extended attempts to locate their child. One man said that the pain that he had felt immediately after the adoption "never gets any better". Another reported that his feelings had never changed and added:

It was terribly difficult to cope with. In the intervening years you wonder what she's like. It's her birthday. She's three. How is she getting on? Even to the fact that you wonder 'Is she still alive?'. Something could have happened to her. Not everybody survives childhood. 'Was the adoption successful?' Things triggered it. Suddenly seeing a little girl of that age . . .

Another man, in similar terms to those quoted above, kept an account of his child's development via her birthdays:

As time went by, when I'd see a child I'd think 'B must be that age'. This feeling has become more pronounced as I've got older. There has never been a time when I was completely free.

In the case of another, he reported a similar regularity with regard to the child's presence in his life. In his case this was "every day" and his thoughts consisted of "wanting to know" his daughter.

Some men reported that they had experienced a growth in the intensity of their feelings. One man stated that the pregnancy and birth events had had little impact upon him; he had become involved with another woman who was expecting his (second) child and he had bought a flat for them. However, during the adoption arrangements, he had become progressively more agitated as to the welfare of his child who was to be adopted. He opposed the adoption unsuccessfully and was then left with considerable feelings of regret that remained permanently close to the surface:

My stack of emotional baggage has always meant that I have been unable to think of her without feeling tearful and emotional.

One man reported that, five years after the adoption, ongoing distress had led him to undertake a search of all the primary schools in the area where his daughter was likely to be residing. Another explained that he married soon after the adoption, so the subject of children inevitably arose and he began looking in prams for the son who had been adopted. Another said that the subject arose during counselling:

It was actually on the day of his birthday. I had never seen it [the adoption] as my loss. Always only Y's [the birth mother]. I completely broke down and cried.

No impact in the immediate post-adoption period

A minority of five men reported little emotional impact. For these fathers, thoughts and feelings in relation to the child emerged for the first time a number of years later. Their accounts were diverse as to why they felt little or nothing immediately after the adoption and demonstrated varying degrees of denial. One man said that he did not feel anything because the adoption experience had rendered him "emotionally blocked". The second man stated that his feelings concerning the adoption "weren't a major problem". However, three years after the event:

It started to grate on my mind. It was just there in your brain. The not knowing. Whether she [his daughter] is alive, whether she's alright.

The third man, when asked about his feelings after the birth and adoption, explained these in terms of what he saw as gender differences:

I suppose I blanked it. Yeah, I suppose I was disappointed. I never saw her [the child], there was no hands on. Psychologically it was a different kettle of fish from a man and a woman. We're not the same as women, are we? I was disappointed. I wasn't hurt. I had N [step-daughter], another daughter. I had hands on with her.

This man went on to suggest that his step-parenting role took the place of any activity that would have happened with his first daughter, thus alleviating any negative feelings that may have endured as a result of her adoption. His views and feelings provide a counterpoint to any suggestion that birth fathers will inevitably feel a sense of loss after adoption. This man, as he indicates, seemed to have had his need to parent a daughter satisfied with a second child. Even so, at the time of interview, he was among a number of those who were determinedly searching for their children. This suggests that having a replacement focus for feelings for his adopted daughter had not been sufficient.

Congruences with the experiences of birth mothers

It can be seen from the above accounts that for a large number of the birth fathers the period immediately following the adoption was an emotionally turbulent one, with many reporting feelings of distress and pain. Furthermore, thoughts of the child featured prominently within these accounts. It is therefore suggested that the immediate impact of adoption on birth fathers may have been overlooked by professionals and that there are similarities between the experiences of the men in this study and those reported in the birth mother literature.

Congruence between the two sets of experiences can be seen when a birth mother's report is set between those of two of the birth fathers in the study, with the expression of anger towards self and others:

I became a very angry person after she was born. I used to go to dance halls looking for trouble. I just turned violent for a long time. I used to go out with quite a few guys. We used to get into trouble. Just being stupid. Hitting other people. I turned to drink sometimes. A couple of times I tried drugs. I was having trouble sleeping. I was having back pain. I wasn't mentally ill but I ended up at the Andrew Duncan [a local psychiatric hospital] as an outpatient. What I was doing was punishing myself. I was trying to punish myself for what I had done. (First birth father)

I drifted further and further from my own family, rejecting them as they had done me. I lost my self-respect and this led to a lack of control, forethought and direction. Drugs, drink and promiscuity were the result. I became unable to trust adults and made myself thoroughly objectionable and argumentative. Eventually I became very depressed and tried to kill myself by taking an overdose. (Birth mother in Bouchier *et al*, 1991, pp 53–54)

I left my parents' house and got lost for a wee while. I drank a lot. Buried my head in the sand. Then it was a lot of bitterness and anger-ness and a bit like a bereavement. I lost all sense of direction and meaning to life, ran wild, lost my self-esteem. (Second birth father)

Since some birth fathers seemed to experience similar post-adoption reactions to those reported for birth mothers, what of the place of the adoption and the child in the men's subsequent lives? Are there other parallels between birth mothers and birth fathers? Exactly what did these birth fathers think of when they thought of the child?

The child in mind: a spectrum of thoughts, feelings and attitudes

Research on birth mothers has found evidence of a continuance of feelings of loss and, for some, feelings of enduring stress in the years that follow adoption (Baran *et al*, 1977; Deykin *et al* 1984; Winkler and van Keppel, 1984; Millen and Roll, 1985; Bouchier *et al*, 1991; Howe *et al*, 1992; Hughes and Logan, 1993).

Winkler and van Keppel (1984) surveyed 213 birth mothers who had relinquished a first child and found that the relinquished child 'has a continuing presence for the mother'. For a majority of those surveyed, relinquishment was 'the most stressful thing that they had experienced'. A vast sense of loss was reported and accompanied by illustrative comments such as 'part of me is dead' (p 52).

What does the existing literature tell us about the long-term experiences of birth fathers? Although extremely sparse, individual and anecdotal accounts would seem to indicate that some birth fathers may experience feelings of loss and retain a concern for their child (Pannor *et al*, 1971;

Concerned United Birthparents, 1983; Silber and Speedlin, 1983; Argent, 1988; Tugendhat, 1992; Wells, 1993; Clapton, 1996; Feast, 1994; Hilpern, 1998; NORCAP, 1998). One birth father quoted in Argent (1988, p 19) spoke of 'a mixture of guilt, curiosity, the certainty of something missing'.

There are only two previous studies focused on birth fathers – by Deykin *et al* (1988) in the USA and Cicchini (1993) in Australia. The findings of each were reviewed in an earlier paper (Clapton, 1997). In their postal survey Deykin *et al* dealt with matters such as attitudes to the adoption and participation (or not) in the process, as well as subsequent marital functioning, parenting and search activity. Cicchini's research served to redress a gap in the earlier Deykin *et al* study in that the psychological and emotional dimensions of the lives of birth fathers were given attention. The Australian study showed that thoughts of the child continued and were associated with a range of beliefs and charged emotions such as worry concerning the child's welfare and feelings of responsibility and affection for their son or daughter. Cicchini (1993, p 18) concludes:

> *The most significant finding is that the relinquishment experience does not end at the time of adoption, but has enduring effects throughout life . . . These effects emerge most clearly decades later in a desire to be reunited with the child and seek assurance that the child is alright.*

In the present study, for most men various triggers in later life led to a resurgence of feelings regarding the child. For some this occurred when receiving professional help. Less extremely and more typically, thoughts of the child were prompted – as for birth mothers – by key dates such as birthdays ('There's never a 7 March goes by without thoughts of him') and Christmas ('a bad time'). Other occurrences such as the sight of, and contact with, children of the same age as the child who was adopted also instigated feelings about their child. For the 21 men who went on to have other children, their subsequent experiences of pregnancy, the birth and childcare activities all served – from time to time – as prompts for the onset of thoughts of the adopted child. However, thinking about the child was not confined to specific external reminders: for some this occurred 'at quiet moments'.

Table 1
What do you feel when you think of the child?

Primary feeling	*Number of men*
Curiosity	14
Parenthood	10
Concern/worry	9
Responsibility	7
Loss	6
Love	4
Guilt	4
Regret	4
Connectedness	2

What was the nature of these thoughts of the child decades later? The men's reports were categorised on the basis of both explicit content and implicit meanings. For instance, those who referred directly to "a curiosity" were grouped in a category entitled "curiosity", and men who talked of "wondering about the child" were also included in the same group. The men who had had experience of contact were asked to think back to how they had thought of the child before their meeting. The reports of this group of ten men therefore had a retrospective character that was influenced by their predominantly positive experiences of contact. However, both groups – those with and those without contact – gave remarkably similar accounts. Most of the men expressed more than one set of feelings, but usually there was a primary one that dominated the response. The frequency of these is presented in Table 1.

Curiosity
Fourteen men (50 per cent of those who responded) referred to curiosity about the child. Typical statements were:

I'd just like to know what had happened to him, where he'd been, what he'd done. Just like to know, just like to know. Curiosity, simple curiosity.

When she was a teenager: Is she going out dancing? Is she married? And has children? How old is she now?

Concern or worry

Curiosity sometimes shaded into more concentrated interest that became concern or worry for nine of the men (33 per cent):

I wonder what sort of person she is and, as I say, one then starts to worry about if there are tremendous difficulties in her life, either caused by the adoption or just because of who she is. I suspect, although I don't know because I don't have any other children, I suspect it is a parental worry that I have or it is a worry about, I suppose, children in general – in a world full of drugs and muggings, etc. It's a concern but it is also an interest.

Is she alive, is she doing well? Well, I would steam in and help her. If she was a drug addict, or anything, if she was desperate, you'd help her.

In a similar manner to the way that curiosity begins to dovetail with worry, so too do worry or concern shade into feelings of responsibility:

I worry about how abandoned she feels. Is she alive even? We want her to know if ever she needed us, we'd be there for her.

Responsibility

Cicchini (1993) suggested that the sense of responsibility expressed by birth fathers in his study derived from a maturational process. He contended that over the period from their teenage years to the time of the interview, the birth fathers in his study had developed a sense of responsibility towards the child. This development, he suggests, is part of the process of moving into mature adulthood.

Seven of the men in the present study (23 per cent) described feelings that conveyed a sense of responsibility. Responsibility, obligation and duty were words that were used to describe how they felt about the welfare of the child. Two men spoke of a feeling of "duty". One man spoke of his "duty of care" in relation to the child – in his case to provide himself as a father to her, although he also felt he had not been able to fulfil such a duty.

Another man also spoke of his "duty":

It's built up. I think brought on by my eldest daughter going to college – rites of passage – made me sort of start thinking. It was always there.

I wouldn't say that I am doing it out of duty [registering on a Contact Register], but there is also a certain sense of duty. I'd love to know how she is, how she got on. I'd be frightened about it as well. But I very much want to be available for her.

Another said that when he thought of his child:
I still have all the parental feelings. They won't go away. It's a burden you can never put down.

This man's words convey a sense of having "shouldered" a (difficult) obligation at the point of having the child adopted.

The widespread belief that good fathers are those who provide (e.g. Warrin *et al*, 1999) is summed up by a birth father in the literature who asks: 'Who am I if I am not a protector and a providing father?' (quoted in Rosenberg, 1992, p 35). Such a belief coupled with a feeling of having defaulted on it would contribute to these birth fathers' enduring thoughts of responsibility. This would also be linked to feelings of guilt, discussed below.

Parenthood
An overlap between feelings of responsibility, duty or obligation occurs with those of feelings of parenthood. The majority of the studies of birth mothers have pointed to a continuing sense of parenthood (Howe *et al*, 1992; Hughes and Logan, 1993). In this study, ten men (36 per cent) expressed a similar set of feelings:
There's one missing in my family. I wonder what she's like. I think 'waste of potential'. I feel I have abandoned my charge. I regard her as my child. As one that's missing amongst my children.

I've got a 14-year-old in my mind's eye. At the end of the day, in one sense, you can only turn around and say 'she'll always be my little girl'. But I know she's 14, she'll be 15 in June. She's no longer the madam who's growing up. She'll have her own ways.

This man also expressed a belief that:
I can't turn round and say 'she's mine' because I've never met the girl.

Although technically, in one sense, she is mine. On the other hand she isn't mine.

An acknowledgement of the division between being a parent with experience of caring for a child and being a biological father with no knowledge of the child was made in four out of the ten accounts that referred to a feeling of parenthood:

I wonder if she's OK, if she's healthy, if her parents are good to her. It depends who I'm speaking to but I sometimes say 'I've got three'. I think of J as a second daughter.

Although S, even if she came back, I'll never be her father. I'm her father biologically.

Love

Two men expressed feelings of parenthood and also said that they felt love for their child. Two others expressed love without directly referring to any feelings of parenthood:

There is a sense in which, I don't know, whatever he's done or hasn't done; or what would happen if he'd turned out and been a murderer or rapist or you know, I would not love him any the less. I don't think I've ever stopped loving him. Or the thought of him.

The above man was one of a group of nine who did not biologically father another child after the adoption. Others in the group who were explicit in their reference to loving their son or daughter had had experiences of subsequent parenting. In their case they likened their love for the adopted child to that felt for the children that they had had experience of parenting.

Connectedness

Related to these feelings of parenthood and/or love, two men expressed a feeling of connectedness with the child:

Who is he? What's his personality like? I wonder about someone out there that I'm close to. I feel like I know him.

It must be partly love. I'd love to see him. What I did was a wrong thing

215

in one way. I thought we were making the right decisions whatever. It goes against the grain. You're giving up somebody you instinctually love, is part of you.

This sense of a continuing connection and intimacy with the child is echoed in the birth mother literature (Millen and Roll, 1985; Weinreb and Murphy, 1988).

Loss

The literature on birth mothers' experiences has shown a keen sense of loss (Inglis, 1984; Winkler and van Keppel, 1984; Millen and Roll, 1985; Howe *et al*, 1992). In this study six men (22 per cent) spoke of a sense of loss when they thought of the child:

I hope she's well, OK. Then a little bit of anxiety steps in. Helplessness, you want to reach out to something you don't know where it is. You want to reach out and probably say who you are.

I still feel that she's a part of me. It's like something from inside of me is missing. Part of my being in a way.

Loss was deeply felt by at least two of this group who spoke of it in physical terms:

It's like, I don't know, it's like a finger cut off 30 years ago. There's so much to be regretted because we lost this child for that length of time. That's an accurate assessment of the factors. That's what I feel.

There is not a day that goes by when I don't think of him. I feel as if there is something inside me that has been ripped out and I feel empty and nothing is going to fill that.

A similar feeling of physical loss is reported in the research on birth mothers (e.g. Roll *et al*, 1986).

However, an additional dimension to a sense of loss was reported by the men. This was the loss of missed opportunities to parent the child:

I feel that I've been robbed of his childhood. Seeing him grow up and all his teething, taking him to parks and all that sort of thing . . . football games.

This reference to a sense of loss as regards the activities of parenting may indicate a gender difference in birth parents. What appears not to have been explored in the birth mother research is whether the loss reported by birth mothers concerns any components other than that centred on the "lost" child. It may be that because fathering is defined by what a man does, birth fathers are more susceptible to feelings of missed activity with the child.

There were connections between expressions of loss and feelings of regret.

Regret

Four men reported that they, *inter alia*, felt a sense of regret about the adoption when they thought of the child. In the case of one man this was added to by a sense of loss:

> *I think of her as somebody I miss. Somebody that I've missed all these years. Miss the contact. Missed even seeing her as a baby and I think that was totally unfair. I don't feel that I'm her natural father, that I was responsible for her birth. Had I been present it wouldn't have happened. She would have a different sort of life.*

Guilt

Four men said that they felt guilt, typically:

> *I feel guilty about the rich family life she could have had. I feel like we abandoned her.*

This emotion is also present in the birth mother research (e.g. Hughes and Logan, 1993). In terms of the men's motivations for searching and wish for contact at the time of the interview, such feelings of guilt appear to translate into a need to put "their side of the story". Birth father motivations for contact will be discussed in a future paper.

Conclusion

The term "connectedness" directly used by two men seems to sum up the group of child-centred, emotionally charged thoughts that exist for many of these birth fathers. The fact that such a connectedness exists in the case of men who have never parented the child in question is a surprising finding, even more so for the (few) cases where the child had never been seen. This is a finding that suggests a rethink of conventional notions of fatherhood, in particular those ideas that indicate that men derive their feelings of parenthood from a process of active participation in social caring for the child.

Ten years ago Brinich (1990) remarked on the existence of 'a differentiation between fathers and mothers based upon the assumption that fathering follows the birth'. Brinich suggests that this may be a 'stereotypical view of the development of fatherhood' and goes on to call for its re-examination. She concludes that research with men who have fathered children who were then relinquished for adoption would 'yield much more than the vacuum that previous authors have suggested exists' (p 59).

The present study of birth father experiences indeed points to a sense of continuing connection felt by birth fathers in respect of their child. This even occurs in the absence of having ever seen the child or at most having had a brief contact or glimpse. This finding challenges a stereotypical view that fatherhood is defined by the action of active parenting. This and the similarities between the experiences of birth mothers and those of birth fathers are central findings.

Since many aspects of the thoughts and feelings of adoptive fathers (and their journey to fatherhood) remain virtually unknown, ideas about men in general and their roles in adoption are still largely based on speculation and perhaps stereotyping. The challenge for professionals concerned with adoption is to redress this.

In respect of birth fathers, enhanced insight regarding their experiences and life courses, and their potential feelings about the child – even when adoption has been agreed – should now stimulate a debate about the best means possible to ensure that birth fathers, like birth mothers before, can emerge from the shadows. This could include a greater involvement of fathers in adoption and permanence planning at both individual case and panel levels, targeted post-adoption support for men and, perhaps controversially, an obligation on practitioners not to automatically accept the statement "father unknown" as acceptable in the future. From the point of view of the adopted adult who in later life may decide to consult their adoption papers, it is often crushing to find out that all that is known about their birth father is – apparently – his first name. A greater focus on the birth father in adoption is in the direct interests of the adopted person who may gain birth family history that has hitherto not been seen as so essential as that relating to the birth mother. The "myth of one natural parent" is now no longer sustainable.

References

Anglim E (June 1965) 'The adopted child's heritage – two parents', *Child Welfare*, pp 339–43.

Argent H (1988) 'The way ahead', in Argent H (ed), *Keeping the Doors Open: A review of post-adoption services*, London: BAAF.

Baran A, Pannor R and Sorosky A (1977) 'The lingering pain of surrendering a child', *Psychology Today* 88, pp 58–60.

Bouchier P, Lambert L and Triseliotis J (1991) *Parting with a Child for Adoption: The mother's perspective*, London: BAAF.

Brinich P (1990), 'Adoption from the inside out: a psychoanalytic perspective', in Brodzinsky D and Schechter M (eds), *The Psychology of Adoption*, New York: Oxford University Press.

Cicchini M (1993) *Development of Responsibility: The experience of birth fathers in adoption*, Perth, Western Australia: Adoption Research and Counselling Service Inc.

Clapton G (writing as Colvin G) (1996) 'A cache of feelings buried in a time capsule', *The Scotsman*, 7 March.

Clapton G (1997) 'Birth fathers, the adoption process and fatherhood', *Adoption & Fostering* 21:1, pp 29–36.

Clapton G (2000) 'Perceptions of fatherhood: birth fathers and their adoption experiences', *Adoption & Fostering* 24:3, pp 69–70.

Clapton G (2002) *Birth Fathers: Loss and fatherhood in adoption*, London: Jessica Kingsley.

Concerned United Birthparents (1983) *CUB Newsletter*, January.

Department of Health (1999) *Supporting Families: A consultation document*, London: DH.

Department of Health (2000) *Adoption: A new approach*, London: DoH.

Deykin E, Campbell L and Patti P (1984) 'The post-adoption experience of surrendering parents', *American Journal of Orthopsychiatry* 54, pp 271–80.

Deykin E, Patti P and Ryan J (1988) 'Fathers of adopted children: a study of the impact of child surrender on birth fathers', *American Journal of Orthopsychiatry* 58, pp 240–48.

Family Policy Unit (1998) *Boys, Young Men and Fathers: A ministerial seminar*, London: The Home Office.

Feast J (1994) *Preparing for Reunion*, London: The Children's Society.

Hilpern K (1998) 'Founding fathers', *The Times Magazine*, 4 July.

Howe D, Sawbridge P and Hinings D (1992) *Half a Million Women: Mothers who lose their children by adoption*, London: Penguin.

Hughes B and Logan J (1993) *Birth Parents: The hidden dimension*, University of Manchester.

Inglis K (1984) *Living Mistakes: Mothers who consented to adoption*, Sydney: Allen & Unwin.

Mason M (1995) *Out of the Shadows: Birth fathers' stories*, Edina, Minnesota: O J Howard Publishing.

Millen L and Roll S (1985) 'Solomon's mothers: a special case of pathological bereavement', *The American Journal of Orthopsychiatry* 53, pp 411–18.

NORCAP (1998) 'Charlie', *Norcap News* 53, Spring.

Pannor R, Massarik F and Evans B (1971) *The Unmarried Father*, New York: Springer.

Performance and Innovation Unit (2000) *Prime Minister's Review of Adoption*, PIU Report, London: Cabinet Office.

Roll S, Millen L and Backland B (1986) 'Solomon's mothers: mourning mothers who relinquish their children for adoption', in Rando T (ed.), *Parental Loss of a Child*, Illinois: Research Press Co.

Rosenberg E (1992) *The Adoption Life Cycle*, New York: The Free Press.

Silber K and Speedlin P (1983) *Dear Birth Mother*, Texas: Corona.

Tugendhat J (1992) *The Adoption Triangle*, London: Bloomsbury.

Warrin J, Soloman Y, Lewis C and Langford W (1999) *Fathers, Work and Family Life*, London: Family Policy Studies Centre.

Weinreb M and Murphy C (1988) 'The birth mother: a feminist perspective for the helping professional', *Women and Therapy* 7:1, pp 23–6.

Wells S (1993) 'Post-traumatic stress in birth mothers', *Adoption & Fostering* 17:2, pp 30–2.

Winkler R and van Keppel M (1984) *Relinquishing Mothers in Adoption: Their long-term adjustment*, Melbourne: Institute for Family Studies (Monograph No. 3).

14 Intercountry adoption: global trade or global gift?

John Triseliotis

This article was first published in Adoption & Fostering *24:2, 2000.*

Introduction

This paper sets out to question the legitimacy of intercountry adoption because of the way a significant part of it is currently practised. My views on the subject are less about intercountry adoption as such, or about individuals who adopt from abroad, and more about political and social attitudes in both the sending and receiving countries which tolerate trading in children. In the course of the discussion three key issues will be raised:

- how the lack of legitimacy manifests itself;
- how intercountry adoption came to be in this position;
- suggested measures for achieving greater legitimacy.

How the absence of legitimacy manifests itself

Irrespective of what we believe as individuals, the practice of intercountry adoption cannot be considered in a legal or moral vacuum. The absence of legitimacy is manifested in five different ways:

1 a disregard for children's rights as set out in the UN Convention;
2 the absence of legality;
3 lack of choice for birth parents;
4 disregard of empirically based knowledge of what is known to be best for children;
5 the absence of an ethical base.

1 A disregard for children's rights as set out in the UN Convention
The UN Convention on the Rights of the Child is meant to grant dignity and respect to children as human beings. These rights are also meant to be international and have been accepted globally. When it comes to

adoption, Article 21 of the Convention on the Rights of the Child is unambiguous:

The primary aim of adoption is to provide the child who cannot be cared for by his or her own parents, with a permanent family. If that child cannot be placed in a foster or adoptive family and cannot in any suitable manner be cared for in the country of origin, intercountry adoption may be considered as an alternative means of child care.

State parties are expected to enact laws to reflect these rights, but international instruments such as these lack ways of enforcement. Furthermore, when laws are enacted it does not follow that they will always be enforced or respected. There is no shortage of examples of children's rights being frequently violated and intercountry adoption has contributed to this violation (see Asquith and Hill, 1994). Adoption is meant to be a service for children first, but part of it is practised on the premise that every adult, especially those who are wealthy, has the right to get a child from anywhere and almost by any means in order to be a parent. Just when it was thought that after three or so thousand years adoption was at last becoming a more child-centred activity, much of intercountry adoption has been shifting the emphasis back to the interests of the adults. In some respects intercountry adoption, and the trafficking in children that is a characteristic part of it, has set back the clock for the rights of children and has been a bad precedent for countries still struggling to develop child-centred legislation.

Studies in the USA have found that, on the whole, those who adopt from abroad consider themselves as having a right to do so and are annoyed at the need for investigations and the preparation of background reports. In their view, it is enough that their prosperity and social position guarantee the child a better life (Bartholet, 1993; Gailey, 1999). The USA is not alone in this. Broadly similar sentiments have been expressed in Britain (see extensive article by Matthew Engel, *Weekend Guardian*, 29 May 1999, pp 10–17).

Because children around the world are suffering, it suits the needs of some people in the industrialised countries "to rescue" a tiny number of them. We should have no illusions, though, that the proportion of children around the world exposed to deprivations, poverty and suffering is so huge, that intercountry adoption is not even a drop in an ocean of need. I recognise that this does not make those adopted any less needy or vulnerable. However, the proposition that intercountry adoption offers children from the Third World a better future may be true at the individual, but not at the wider level.

2 The absence of legality

A number of sending and receiving countries have entered bilateral and other similar agreements, by which adoptions in one country are recognised in the other. Such agreements are usually reached after each country is satisfied that the practices of the other are acceptable, but until recently, there has been no yardstick of what is acceptable. Otherwise, much of intercountry adoption has relied on piecemeal legislation which has failed to safeguard the children's rights in such areas as the suitability of the adopters, matching or trafficking.

What gradually helped to enhance the legitimacy of domestic adoption in most industrialised countries was mainly legality, which was increasingly based on what was empirically known to be best for children. Alongside this were the widespread welfare programmes which brought significant improvements in the social and welfare conditions of all citizens, including children, resulting also in the overall extension of choice for parents.

Even after these improvements, domestic adoption in industrialised countries still raises serious questions about the respective powers and roles of parents and the state, the relative rights of children and parents, and the procedures and criteria which should govern those situations when plans for children are disputed, such as freeing for adoption (see Lambert *et al*, 1990). Intercountry adoption gives rise to all the same questions plus the trafficking that goes on.

Efforts to put some order to what are widely agreed to be unacceptable practices are not infrequently thwarted by powerful interests. Politicians in some countries, with the aid of some of the media, have come to recognise that there are votes to be gained when they urge no or minimum regulation in adoption in general. The same media are incensed at the idea of trade in children, but equally so, if obstacles are seen to be put in the way of adults when pursuing either domestic or intercountry adoption. (Again, see *Weekend Guardian*, 29 May 1999, pp 10–17.)

It is only recently that the international community, through the Hague Convention, has tried to develop standards and regulations, in line with the 1989 UN Convention on the Rights of the Child. Maybe it is too early to expect results, but the agreement reached between countries in the early 1990s does not appear to have diminished the major abuses. Even in Britain, with its strong immigration controls, a judge was recently forced to confirm an intercountry adoption despite its illegality, because it was a *fait accompli* [(in *re C (a minor) (adoption: legality)*, reported in *The Times*, 2 June 1998, p 24]. (I will be returning later to the work of the Hague Convention.)

3 Lack of choice for birth parents

Domestic adoption in the industrialised world is now practised on the premise of choice for birth parents and freedom from compulsion, unless the courts have declared a child free for adoption against the wishes of parents. If economic and other external forms of compulsion are not allowed to undermine the basic rights of parents and children in the industrialised world, the same expectations should also be applied to the countries from which the children are brought to the West.

When it comes to the rearing of children, many parents in some Third World and Eastern European countries, faced with abject poverty and/or ill-health and with no basic state welfare provision as a fall-back, find themselves with very limited or no choices. In relation to adoption they often act under compulsion and are sometimes exploited by corrupt agents, professionals and administrators. Unsurprisingly, perhaps, the parents' actions can lead to a conflict of interest developing between themselves and their children, with the children requiring protection.

4 Disregard of empirically-based knowledge of what is known to be best for children

A number of agencies and individuals in both sending and receiving countries have tried and managed to achieve high standards in the practice of intercountry adoption. No doubt, many of them have the best interests of the children in mind and have made their own contribution to the development of new knowledge and skills in this area. Nevertheless, and because of the clandestine way in which a significant part of intercountry adoption is now being practised, empirically-based knowledge of what has been found to be good for children, their birth and adoptive parents, is often disregarded or not systematically applied in such areas as:

- the preparation of would-be adopters for the additional tasks required of them for parenting children often of a different ethnic, racial, cultural and religious background;
- the matching of adopters to children;
- the collection of genealogical and other background information;
- the deployment of post-adoption counselling and other services (see Triseliotis *et al*, 1997).

The failure to deploy systematically available knowledge and skills in all the above areas can undermine the children's potential for development, including their genealogical and ethnic identity. With the exception of only a few countries, a large part of intercountry adoption is in the hands of private or third parties and organisations not always involving the participation of trained child welfare staff. Even where accredited agencies take part in the arrangements, not infrequently these operate outside the mainstream child welfare services, including what remains of domestic adoption. Under this system children adopted from abroad do not always benefit from the knowledge and skills developed over the years.

It could also be claimed that because of the separation, in many countries on the continent of Europe, of intercountry adoption from domestic adoption and from the wider childcare field, it has led to the neglect of domestic children with special needs requiring new families (see Anderson, 1999, in respect of Sweden).

I am not suggesting by this that domestic and intercountry adoption are or should be in competition. Far from it. Different couples or individuals are usually interested in different children and the needs of children can be met by differently composed households. Legitimate ways of practising adoption, whether domestic or intercountry, are likely to benefit both groups of children.

5 The absence of an ethical base

The issues raised so far add to the overall absence of an ethical base in the practice of a significant part of intercountry adoption. Trading in children, kidnapping, fattening of children to be more saleable to fetch higher prices, lying to birth parents about the fate of their children or the production of spurious background reports on adopters, all add up to a catalogue of ignoble and unprincipled practices (see later for references). Furthermore, and possibly because intercountry adoption has become so widespread and is largely isolated from other child welfare services, its practices seem no longer to be questioned. We know that, on the whole, intercountry adoption works well, but the ends do not necessarily justify the means.

How did intercountry adoption come to this?

Intercountry adoption in the post-World War II period has experienced a number of phases in its development. Depending on the country, some or all of the following phases may be happening simultaneously:
1 compassion and humanitarianism;
2 the wish to create or expand one's family;
3 trading in children;
4 beginning international regulation.

1 Compassion and humanitarianism

The compassionate/humanitarian, altruistic response, or "the kindness of strangers", has always been present in the practice of all forms of adoption and substitute parenting (see Boswell, 1988). Within the ancient world, the stories of Moses and Oedipus fulfil the requirements of both intercountry and interstate adoption as a compassionate response to the fate of unwanted and exposed children. More recently, the humanitarian response has been continued in the aftermath of wars and natural disasters. Examples of this are to be found in some of the initial responses of American servicemen adopting children from Germany at the end of the last World War, the adoption of children orphaned during the Greek Civil War of the late 1940s and early 1950s, and the adoption of children "orphaned" or "deserted" as a consequence of the Korean and later Vietnam wars.

Most of the children who were adopted then also had the characteristics of children with special needs, that is being older and sometimes displaying many physical, cognitive and emotional deficits.

2 The wish to create or expand one's family

After about the middle of the 1970s and because of the dramatic decline in the number of domestic infants made available for adoption in most industrialised countries, those wishing to create a family or expand it, now turned their attention to intercountry adoption. As a result, acts of humanitarianism went side by side with this new type of adoption until the latter came to pre-dominate. Studies after the 1980s show a decisive shift in both the type of person adopting and the type of child being adopted intercountry. For example, the children were becoming much younger, mostly under two years old, and the adopters largely middle class, wishing to create or enlarge their family (Triseliotis *et al*, 1997, Chapter 9).

3 Trading in children

The third phase, which is currently a characteristic of a significant part of intercountry adoption and overlaps with 1 and 2 above, is that of global trade. No doubt children were sold before, but this practice took off in a big way after the early 1980s. Nobody knows exactly how many of the 35,000 or so children coming each year to industrialised countries to be adopted are bought. Article 35 of the UN Convention on the Rights of the Child expects state parties to take 'all appropriate national bilateral and multilateral measures to prevent the abduction of, the sale of, or traffic in children for any purpose or in any form'.

There is no shortage of evidence on the trade in children (see Ngabonziza, 1991; Triseliotis, 1993). The UK Bill on intercountry adoption, which has now become the Adoption (Intercountry Aspects) Act 1999, recognised what has been said above by stating that one of its purposes was 'to regulate adoption to prevent trafficking in children' (p 1).

The trafficking in children has also often been highlighted by the British press, as in this example:

South of the border (USA), down Mexico way, duty-free shoppers are picking up bargains they can't find elsewhere in the world – babies. The

*land of tequila and sombreros is now the centre of a cruel and in-
humane trade in children. Sometimes kidnapped, other times bartered
or traded like wheat, the babies come from all over southern America
into processing houses where they are fattened like cattle to appeal to
the rich gringo women who desire them.* (*The Scotsman*, 25 August
1998, p 11)

There are many other stories of sales, kidnapping, stealing, exploiting,
cruelty and the fattening and selling of children, before they are adopted
in the industrialised world. Nor can it be claimed that this is a problem
exclusive to Third World countries because there are also documented
stories describing the sale of children within a number of Western
countries, e.g. the USA and Italy. *The Times* newspaper revealed that in
Ukraine corrupt doctors and officials were involved in the illegal sale of
babies to Western Europe and North America by deceiving the children's
"impoverished mothers" that their newborn babies had died or would
have a better life being brought up by the state. Apparently some children
were sold for as much as 40,000 US dollars (*The Times*, 9 February 1996,
p 4).

Children from Russia now top the USA intercountry adoption statistics.
Though there has been some disillusionment recently with children from
Eastern Europe because of the intractable emotional problems some are
said to present, nevertheless they continue to attract higher prices because
of their white colour (Gailey, 1999). Again *The Times* newspaper recently
wrote that the sale of children from Russia, mainly for the USA market,
was "by no means rare" (28 May 1999, p 23). The legislation on intercountry adoption in Russia states that international adoption is only
possible in 'exceptional, urgent situations in the interests of the child's
health', but is so vague that it has left the way open 'to profiteering by
unregulated agencies' (Bowring, 1999, p 132).

The question could be asked whether the industrialised countries have
created the climate which made possible this trade in children. Apart from
the demand for babies to adopt, by the early 1980s new ideas and values
associated with the operation of a free, and largely unrestrained market,
became the cornestone of most industrial governments' economic policy.
The idea of trade and profit was suddenly becoming the hallmark of good

policy and practice in other areas, besides trade (see Elliot and Atkinson, 1998). The market, it was claimed, recognised no moral imperatives even in such matters as education, health, children or human relationships.

Davis (1995) referring to the United States describes vividly how adoption there had been developing fast into a service business, limited to childless couples "willing to pay hefty fees". According to the same source, not only had fees been rising but a number of 'for profit agencies' had emerged as it had become apparent that many people were prepared to pay a high price to adopt either an incountry or intercountry child. The idea of setting up independent for profit adoption agencies was also canvassed in Britain in the early 1990s but found no support.

Parents too, whether in the Third World or elsewhere where adoption is not properly regulated, have learnt to shop around for the best deal. Market forces have been turning middle agents, birth parents and adopters into the main stakeholders. In this process, the children's interests may or may not be protected. Speaking of Germany, Textor (1991) wrote that:

> . . . large amounts of money are sometimes paid to children's homes, birth parents or middlemen in exchange for the children. In some cases children are even stolen or registered immediately after birth as the biological children of a German couple. (p 112)

In the sphere of human relationships intercountry adoption has revealed and exposed the weaknesses of corporate industrialised governments and of the helplessness, and sometimes corruption, of some Third World countries unable to develop non-profit democratic regulation as a way of stopping the trade in children. It may sound an exaggeration to say that intercountry adoption reflects, in a small way, the globalisation of the market and its excesses. In systems terms, thinking that dominates a supra system, such as global economics, eventually influences smaller systems and institutions as well, including that of adoption. Aspects of intercountry adoption have become a microcosm of what goes on in other walks of life when the supremacy of the market remains unchallenged. It includes the loose controls, the predominance of the profit motive, the absence of choice for the weakest and its endemic inequalities. In the way inter-country adoption is practised now, it is mostly open to those who are better off, though I have been told that in Norway a state subsidy can be made available to the less well off.

4 Beginning international regulation

The final phase in the post-World War II period for intercountry adoption comes in the form of beginning regulation from the early 1990s onward, reflected mainly in the work of the Hague Convention on Intercountry Adoption (ICA). The work of the Convention will be discussed later but suffice it to say here that as we enter the new millennium, we find examples of adoptions being arranged and concluded based on international, mainly bilateral agreements, adoptions arranged by accredited or private agencies, and of a significant number based on trade.

Achieving legitimacy in intercountry adoption

In my view, intercountry adoption could achieve greater legitimacy by promoting:
- a rights approach to children;
- full international regulation;
- practising adoption as a gift.

A rights approach to children

The UN Convention on the Rights of the Child offers a useful framework within which intercountry adoption could be regulated and practised. It is no more than a framework aiming to guarantee only basic rights to children, but it is good enough. The Hague Convention tried to base its own Articles on intercountry adoption on the UN Convention on the Rights of the Child, but in the process of doing so, many compromises had to be made. It reiterated, though, a child's right to be reared first by his or her own parents and in his or her own country, and for other solutions to be sought only when that is not possible. However, it is up to countries who ratify the Convention to give expression to these articles through their domestic childcare legislation, and more important to observe it.

Full international regulation

Experience so far has shown that full international regulation is the only way to bring greater legitimacy to the practice of international adoption. Leaving it to individual countries, whether sending or receiving, to put their house in order will not happen. The Hague Convention on ICA which was set up in 1990 achieved a fair amount, mainly by initially bringing together over 60 countries who eventually signed their agreement to the Convention's Articles (29 May, 1993). By the autumn of 1999, 27 countries had ratified and nine had acceded to the Convention. (Accession is essentially ratification by non-member states.) Of all Hague Conventions, the 1993 one on ICA has attained more signatories to ratification than any other Convention. Now that the new Adoption Bill has become law, the British government will also ratify it.

It is recognised that there are many difficulties in trying to apply universal principles to diverse realities so as to bridge the laws of countries with competing images of childhood, varied systems and diversity in cultural traditions and values, rights and obligations. However, the evidence so far suggests that the main obstacle has not been this, but scepticism about children's rights and the adult-centred approach adopted by some participating countries at the Hague Convention. Because of these attitudes, the presently agreed articles of the Convention are and can be easily bypassed. As an example, the following two measures could, if agreed and applied, reduce significantly trafficking.

The first suggestion is the prohibition of all privately or independently arranged non-related adoptions, except those undertaken by recognised, approved and inspected agencies. The International Social Service (1996) has identified seven types of privately arranged adoptions, most of them unwelcome. Carstens and Julia (1995) also write that:

> *Trafficking and the sale of infants is more likely to occur when independent adoption agents are involved because there is opportunity for improper financial gain at each stage of the adoption process.*

The attempt, though, by the Hague Convention to ban all privately arranged adoptions was bitterly resisted by many countries, especially the USA where few of the 50 states regulate the profit status of individuals or organisations involved in adoptions.

Concerns have been expressed about a number of European countries, too, for allowing international adoptions to be arranged by non-accredited or approved agencies. Writing about France, Greenfield (1995) comments that most families there adopting from abroad seem to take the independent rather than the agency route. The newspaper *Le Monde* reported that 3,666 children were adopted in France from abroad in 1996, adding that there was 'little regulation of these adoptions with intermediaries making increasing amounts of money and few checks made on the children's background' (16 February 1998, p 7).

The second measure is to stop the many privately commissioned reports on adopters which are taken to the sending countries as proof of suitability. After obtaining the report, adoptive parents send their application or travel abroad without the involvement of an accredited agency. Even when a report is prepared by an accredited agency, it does not guarantee that no purchase will take place (Selman, 1993). It is claimed that in the USA, assuming you have the money, you can bypass even the minimum requirements for a suitability study. Apparently, when would-be adopters offer to double the fees, some agencies are happy to prepare the report over the telephone without face-to-face interviews or a home visit (Gailey, 1999). An article in the *Guardian* quotes a family from Montana whose assessment was based solely on a social worker coming round one morning "for coffee and carrot cake". Unsurprisingly, perhaps, the author of the article is critical about the detailed social and medical reports required in Britain (Matthew Engel, the *Guardian*, 16 February 1998, p 7).

The questions of who finds the child, who does the matching and who makes the final arrangements are currently a murky area. It is not so much the individuals involved who are at fault, but the absence of suitable structures to provide confidence that the best interests of those involved, including the children, will be safeguarded. Though Britain banned third party domestic adoptions over 20 years ago, it is only recently that it has proceeded to extend the law to intercountry adoption. The 1999 Act also put beyond all legal doubt that the preparation of privately commissioned reports for purposes of adoption is a criminal offence. Norway no longer permits private adoptions. New laws have also been put in place in sending countries such as Romania, India and Sri Lanka to curb the worst excesses of intercountry adoption. The right climate seems to be developing to lend much greater support to the work of the Hague Convention, mainly to tighten controls and put teeth into its articles. To call for stricter international regulation may sound totalitarian. Donzelot (1980), writing on the policing of families, outlined what he called the positive aspects of 'social control' which need not be oppressive. Even the privatisation of social welfare, far from being a free for all, is going side by side with increased powers of inspection.

As late as the summer of 1998, that is before the collapse of the markets in Asia and later in Russia, for a government to try to regulate the implementation of global trade decisions was seen as being out of touch with the real world or just "plain daft". Within 18 months or so, things have been changing. Nobody now, apparently, believes any longer that markets work best if businesses are simply left to their own devices (Kaletsky, *The Times*, 22 April 1999, p 24). Soros (1998), who made his millions through the operation of a free market, has also been calling for "tough global controls". President Clinton, too, speaking on television on 20 April 1999, said that international financial markets need to be regulated by international agencies. If the financial markets need regulation, why not also intercountry adoption?

Proper regulation is not only in the best interests of children and adopters, but also in the interest of those countries which currently play or are trying to play by the rules. Once the public knows that there is a legitimate and more dignified way of adopting, they are more likely to accept restrictions. For intercountry adoption to shed its badly tarnished image of a global market in babies, and to gain legitimacy, it urgently needs to demonstrate that in any arrangement:

- The child is in genuine need of a new family.
- Adoption by a family abroad is in the children's best interests.
- The process follows closely standards of good practice set by accredited agencies.
- The laws of the sending and receiving countries strictly adhere to the Hague Convention on ICA.
- Adoption is freely entered upon by all parties.
- The process involves no profit, including disguised inflated fees and expenses.

- The arrangements are covered by a comprehensive range of after care services in the receiving country.

Prospective adopters too, require protection from the possible excesses of those undertaking suitability studies and need to be given access to independent tribunals to safeguard their rights.

Adoption as a gift and an act of altruism

Finally, and what may sound utopian, is the proposition that both domestic and intercountry adoption should eventually be practised within the context of the gift relationship and with openness and contact being part of this arrangement. In the words of Titmuss (1970), a gift relationship implies freedom of choice and an act of altruism without obvious immediate returns. Besides blood donation in the UK, possibly the nearest other example of total altruism and freedom of choice is the donation of organs, such as kidneys.

Apparently the Romans, who were great on families, and looked upon childlessness as a great calamity, would 'lend one another their daughter, sister and even sometimes their wives', as a way of ensuring that children were produced. It is claimed, in fact, that by about 200 AD the practice of adoption had been abandoned in favour of this form of "surrogacy" (Dupont, 1989). We cannot, however, declare this to be the ultimate gift because historians have not told us what the women felt or thought about it.

The scientists who originally invented the Internet did not intend it to be used as a trade tool but to exchange information. Though this "icon of modern technology" was originally invented for military purposes, it was later mainly used by academics and even amateurs as a cheap and sometimes free method of distributing information, exchanging ideas and discoveries and communicating with colleagues. It was proving to be a "gift" to humanity that was helping to strengthen international social relationships (Levi, 1997). However, "lurking" behind this new technology is the free market which has taken it over. It has even been used to advertise children for sale (Gailey, 1999).

I will leave it to social anthropologists to debate the various shades of the notion of gift and especially the difference between the gift as part of a "circular" form of exchange and a gift given solely for its intrinsic value or for the relationships it creates. A gift, whether as part of an exchange system or as an act of total altruism, has its place in the way adoption could develop, thus greatly enhancing its legitimacy. A gift relationship, in many cultures, implies an obligation to give and to exchange and circulate the gift idea, but not necessarily to the same person. Furthermore, the compulsion to return the gift is only a moral one.

As an idea, giving on a non-commercial basis to the stranger or the unknown, may sound like a panacea in an imperfect world. However, in any such arrangement we would still need to make certain that the interests of the children come first. In the same way that it is not right to sell children, neither is it right for them to be used as means to promote global humanism. Obviously we would still need to know how the parents of the children and the adopters conceptualise intercountry adoption; in other words, whether donors and receivers use a "moral vocabulary" to explain their actions, visualising it as the forerunner of an emerging global gift relationship, a commitment to global evolutionary humanism, or a more pragmatic one, such as economic considerations or simply the wish to parent a child.

The question could equally be asked of 'why we should expect the poorer people in the poorer countries to be motivated by lofty ideals' or 'have regard for the needs of affluent total strangers, often of a different race, culture, religion and ethnicity'? No doubt there are many other practical and moral questions to be considered. For example, does "donation" reduce the element of compulsion? Like the gift relationship, should some form of repayment or exchange be expected and in what form? Should any returns have to be on an individual basis or to the group or country as a whole? Ideally, reciprocity should not be directed to the individual who offers the gift but to that country's children as a whole. Funds could be earmarked for use solely for identifiable children's programmes in the sending countries via regulated, accredited, and monitored non-governmental international agencies. Such bodies might also come to exercise positive influence on governmental child welfare policies through their:

- control of resources which they can dispense accordingly;

- direct contact with policy-making politicians;
- rigorous monitoring and evaluation of the projects;
- publication of annual reports.

There is of course, no reason why individual families should not exchange gifts and continue to do so, provided that the initial matching and other arrangements have been done independently and without the possibility of trade and pay entering into the arrangements.

Conclusion

This article has questioned the legitimacy of some of the worst practices surrounding intercountry adoption and particularly the evils of its commercialisation. The initial humanitarian response to international calamities and the evils of war has gradually been supplanted in ways not altogether welcome. In some respects, the way intercountry adoption is often being practised now has set back the clock for children's rights and the idea of adoption being a child-centred activity.

Globalisation may have weakened the arguments against intercountry adoption, but it has strengthened the anti-trafficking agreements and the need for strong regulation. While accepting that most forms of regulation, especially international ones, are of an evolutionary character, nevertheless the Hague Convention on ICA seems to have had little impact, so far, in stemming the trafficking in children. This is because its Articles are insufficient or weak or both. The Convention requires much more support to enable it to exercise pressure on recalcitrant governments to put their house in order.

Finally, the idea was put forward in this paper, for all forms of adoption to be based on the gift relationship and to be practised more openly than now. This is not a novel idea, but neither has it been systematically promoted. A fitting conclusion, perhaps, to adoption being practised within such a relationship is Hyde's (1999) wider comment:

> . . . *a bond precedes or is created by donation and it is absent, suspended or severed in commodity exchange. . . . We do not deal in commodities when we wish to initiate or preserve ties of affection. . . Because of the bonding power of gifts and the detached nature of*

commodity exchange, gifts have become associated with community and with being obliged to others, while commodities are associated with alienation and freedom. (pp 62 & 66–67)

Note

A previous version of this article was published in the proceedings of the conference entitled *Mine-Yours – Ours and Theirs: Adoption, changing kinship and family pattern*, edited by Rygvold A, Dalen M and Saetersdal B (Department of Special Needs Education, University of Oslo, 1999).

References

Adoption (Intercountry Aspects) Act, 1999 (1999) London: House of Commons.

Anderson G (1999) 'Children in permanent foster care in Sweden', *Child & Family Social Work* 4:3, pp 175–86.

Asquith S and Hill M (eds) (1994) *Justice for Children*, London: Martinus Nijhof.

Bartholet E (1993) 'Adoption among nations', in *Family Bonds: Adoption and the politics of parenting*, Boston: Houghton Mifflin.

Boswell J (1988) *The Kindness of Strangers*, London: Penguin.

Bowring B (1999) 'Children of Russia: victims of crisis, beneficiaries or international law', *Child & Family Law Quarterly* 11:2, pp 125–35.

Carstens C and Julia M (1995) 'Legal, policy and practice issues in intercountry adoption in the United States', *Adoption & Fostering* 19:4, pp 26–33.

Davis D F (1995) 'Capitalising on adoption', *Adoption & Fostering* 19:2, pp 25–30.

Donzelot J (1980) *Policing the Family*, London: Hutchinson.

Dupont F (1989) *Daily Life in Ancient Rome*, Oxford: Blackwell.

Elliot R and Atkinson D (1998) *The Age of Insecurity*, London: Verso.

Gailey C (1999) Paper presented at the International Conference on Intercountry Adoption, Oslo, 6–9 May.

Greenfield J (1995) 'Intercountry adoption: a comparison between France and England', *Adoption & Fostering* 19:2, pp 31–36.

Hyde L (1999) *The Gift*, London: Vintage.

International Social Service (1996) *Intercountry Adoption: Developing good practice*, Geneva: ISS.

Lambert L, Buist M, Triseliotis J and Hill M (1990) *Freeing Children for Adoption*, London: BAAF.

Levi P (1997) *Collective Intelligence*, New York: Plenum.

Ngabonziza D (1991) 'Moral and political issues facing relinquishing countries', *Adoption & Fostering* 15:4, pp 75–80.

Selman P (1993) 'Services for intercountry adoption in the UK: some lessons from Europe', *Adoption & Fostering* 17:3, pp 14–19.

Soros G (1998) *Capitalism in Crisis*, London: Little Brown.

Textor R M (1991) 'International adoption in West Germany', in Altstein H and Simon R (eds), *Intercountry Adoption*, London: Praeger.

Titmuss, R (1970) *The Gift Relationship*, London: Penguin.

Triseliotis J (1993) 'Intercountry adoption: in whose best interests?', in Humphrey M and Humphrey H (eds), *Intercountry Adoption*, London:Tavistock/ Routledge.

Triseliotis J, Shireman J and Hundleby M (1997) *Adoption: Theory, policy and practice*, London: Cassell.

Section IV
Post-adoption services and issues

As noted by **Clark and McWilliam (1999)**, post-placement services are one of the main current priorities of adoption agencies, prompted partly by the new requirements introduced by the 1995 Act **(Plumtree, 1995)**. These may be needed by different parties – the child, adopters, birth parents or other members of either the adoptive or birth family. They are required at different stages. For instance, immediately post placement, the child may need help in adjusting to the change and settling in with a new family. Later in childhood, assistance may be required with long-term or previously dormant issues related to pre-adoption experiences in the birth family or when looked after. In adulthood, counselling and assistance may be wanted with respect to identity issues and birth family information or contacts. Adoptive families may want material help and specialist input, as well as or instead of more general advice and support.

When adoption (by strangers) typically involved healthy infants, adopters rarely wanted any external help after the adoption and indeed welcomed the freedom to become like other parents. This is still often the case, but with the increasing numbers of older children placed since the 1980s it has become recognised that many adopters need or want access to support. **Phillips (1988)** interviewed many adopters who had adopted school-aged children. Most of the families identified persistent behaviour difficulties, such as lying, aggression and destructiveness. As required by law, families received regular visits in the post-placement phase (before the adoption), but usually these stopped abruptly once the adoption order was granted. Most did not want further visits, but indicated they would have welcomed some form of group support. They might have used other kinds of service (e.g. advice lines, babysitting), but few were aware they existed or where to find them. Many other suggestions were made, such as a newsletter or help with holidays. Informality and flexibility were important features of the service they wanted.

As part of its commitment to permanency planning and partnership with adopters, Lothian Region helped set up an Adopters Support Group to provide some of the help outlined above. A questionnaire survey of group members was undertaken to identify adjustment experiences and support needs **(Hill et al, 1988)**. Over three-quarters of the adopted children had joined the family when already aged over five years. Most of the parents reported that the children had formed a good attachment, but a minority still experienced coldness or indifference. Many took satisfaction from seeing the child's progress or happiness, or receiving the child's love. However, one in five reported frequent worries about the future and nearly two-fifths said they felt despair sometimes or most of the time. The child's behaviour difficulties were often worse than expected or apparently not foreseen at the point of placement. Most of the parents felt well supported, by social workers, other adopters, friends, relatives or a combination of these. The main additional help wanted comprised practical help (e.g. respite care, holidays) or specialist assessment/therapy. Good information about the child and monetary assistance were also seen as crucial for certain families.

Support services have developed considerably since these two articles were written, although they are more easily accessed in larger urban areas than elsewhere.

A different form of post-adoption service is relevant to adult adopters who seek information about their birth families and possibly contact too. Young people can obtain a copy of their original birth certificate and court records from Register House in Edinburgh (Triseliotis, 1980). In the 1980s some agencies set up counselling and contact services (Arton and Clark, 1996). The latter include contact registers, whereby either a birth parent or an adoptee can register and, when both wish it, arrange to meet. **Lambert et al (1992)** conducted a study of adopted people who used the Adoption Counselling Centre in Edinburgh, which held a Birth Link Register. As other studies have found, when adopted adults made enquiries about their past and families, this was usually prompted by a wish to find out more about the reasons for being adopted and the original circumstances of their birth families, while some wanted to know or meet the family in their current situation. Some were able to gain information themselves, but sought out counselling when they encountered difficulties or wanted help preparing for a reunion. Staff helped by providing information about how to use the Register. They also gave emotional support in dealing with obstacles in locating birth relatives, anticipating reunion or reacting to contact with the birth family.

Another trend that accelerated in the 1990s was openness in adoption. This refers to a range of ways in which adoption is no longer necessarily closed off from the birth family throughout childhood. Openness can entail contact between any member of the birth family and adoptive family at any stage. Contacts vary in timing, nature and intensity. The main forms are indirect communication (letters, photos or presents sent via an agency) and face-to-face contact. Contacts may be one-off or continuing, with varied frequency (Paterson and Hill, 1994; Grotevant and McRoy, 1998). There is a growing body of knowledge about openness in England and North America (Hill and Shaw, 1998; Triseliotis et al,1997; Macaskill, 2002; Neil, 2002), but few writings available on Scottish practice.

One exception is the article by **Stone (1994)**. This describes an increasingly common arrangement whereby adopters and birth parents meet before the adoption. This can then lead to post-adoption contact, which is often mediated by the adoption agency. Strathclyde Region introduced a policy that adoptive applicants should be willing to meet birth parents who wanted this. This was intended to help adopters communicate with the child more effectively and positively about the birth parents, while the birth parents would gain from contributing to the child's future. This practice mainly applied to children placed under the age of two years. Feedback from adopters revealed that most had been apprehensive about the meetings, but nearly all found it a good experience. Many believed it was crucial to have a social worker present as facilitator. About half the couples went on to exchange information, posting direct, using the social work department as a post-box or with foster carers as intermediaries (cf. Rajan and Lister, 1998). Only a minority admitted to finding it difficult to know what to say and most were positive about this indirect from of ongoing contact. At the time, Strathclyde did not favour face-to-face contact. This still occurs in only a minority of adoptions. US research by McRoy (1991) and English research by Neil (2002) shows how agency policy has a big influence on the nature and extent of openness.

Arton and Clark (1996) described arrangements to manage ongoing open adoption, based on their experience in several authorities in Central Scotland. They emphasised the importance of clear information-giving and communication by the agency from the outset, thereby helping birth parents and adopters to foresee benefits, difficulties and practicalities. Also much time is needed to support contact, especially when this is face-to-face. Adopters pointed out benefits from openness, such as the child's greater and more realistic understanding of their origins.

15 Post-adoption services: the views of adopters

Rena Phillips

This article was first published in Adoption & Fostering *12:4, 1988.*

My work with adopters has brought home to me the need for post-adoption services. These are at present patchy and under-developed. But interest in this area is growing and some new initiatives are being tried out. It seemed therefore the right time to find out what adopters had to say about the provision of such services.

A study of 19 families was carried out in two social work departments in Scotland. Its aims were to:

1 look at the problems adoptive families experience with their children after an adoption order has been granted;

2 establish the level of post-adoption support families receive from social workers;

3 seek the families' views on different types of support from social workers, an adopters' group and a post-adoption centre;

4 obtain from families suggestions for improving post-adoption services.

Method

There was no intention to compare the organisation of post-adoption support of the two departments involved in the study, but rather to get a wider picture of the post-adoption scene. A set of criteria was established for the selection of families so that as much uniformity as possible could be maintained. Most were two-parent families with only one child placed for adoption in each. The children had been in placement between two-and-a-half and five years. The length of time since the adoption order was granted varied from two to four years.

The age of children at placement varied from seven months to 13 years and two had mental and physical disabilities. The average age for placement in one department was 4.4 and in the other 10.2 (reflecting the latter's policy of only placing school-aged children for adoption). The total average age at placement was 7.3 years. The average age of the children at the time of the study was 11.2 years.

The interviews with adopters involved the use of vignettes and a questionnaire. The vignettes were short stories based on the experiences of a real adoptive family. They were used in order to make the topic less threatening to the families. The questionnaire was semi-structured. Topics which were of particular interest were indicated and there was some order to the way questions were asked, but adopters were encouraged to take the initiative, and points of particular significance to them emerged freely. The majority of adopters prolonged the discussion in their enthusiasm to share their views on the children, the stress they experienced, and the support they received.

Findings

Behavioural problems

The term "post-placement" here means after a child had been placed for adoption, and the term "post-adoption" after an adoption order had been granted. The time taken from placement to the granting of the order varied from one to four years.

Difficulties in the post-placement phase were compared with those in the post-adoption phase. Three-quarters of the families experienced post-placement behavioural difficulties. By the post-adoption stage only two families were problem free. Three had experienced a disruption, and two saw themselves as having to cope with serious problems.

The most common difficulties recalled were lying, aggressive behaviour, attention seeking, school problems and destructiveness. There were idiosyncratic patterns of behaviour such as constantly losing things, giving things away and hiding in curtains. There were also severe problems such as sexual interference with girls and solvent and drug abuse.

Overall the findings confirm those of Macaskill (1985) and Yates (1985) regarding the wide range of problems experienced by adoptive families, and their long-term nature. As one family in the study put it 'an adoption order is a moment in time – for some children problems become better, for others worse'. Although the age of children at placement was older in one department, this did not seem to affect the range of problems. This highlights the fact that difficulties are experienced with pre-school age children and not just older ones.

These findings need to be put into context. Despite the duration of problems, improvements had been made since placement, and in some cases problems were described as less severe or frequent. On the whole parents seemed very aware of the damaging experiences their children had been through. For example, one family whose child was now 15 accepted his continuing fear of being abandoned by them, although he had been there since the age of ten. On the other hand, where there had been a reduction in the behaviour difficulties exhibited, the families were realistic as to the continuation of problems. One adoptive mother advocated that families should be told by social workers 'not to expect anything'.

Support by social workers

The support offered to the families by their social workers in the post-placement phase was compared with the support offered in the post-adoption phase. This was based on the assumption that the quality of the relationships with their social workers and support offered in the post-placement phase would shape the families' expectations with regard to a post-adoption service. Such support was measured in terms of frequency and purpose of visits, financial and practical help given, and information supplied about the child's background.

Visits

A visit by a social worker is taken to mean the family's social worker. In the majority of cases the child's social worker was only involved for a brief period after placement. Most families were quite happy with this arrangement, as the child's social worker was an unwelcome reminder, particularly to the older children, of their past history.

Social workers are under a statutory duty to visit until an adoption order is granted, and this happened in all cases. For half of the families this was on a regular basis and, with the exception of a few, the visits continued until the adoption order was granted. The level of visiting was generally considered to be adequate. The sharing of problems was seen as the most helpful aspect of the contact. Families appreciated being listened to and being given realistic feedback: 'We wanted to check that we were on the right track.'

Once the adoption order was granted, however, social work visits stopped abruptly. In only three cases did visits continue after the adoption order, due to continuing difficulties with the child. Generally, adopters had low expectations of post-adoption support. Some understood that it was up to them to take the initiative in contacting their social worker if help was needed. Others were unclear what to do in such a situation.

The majority of families in fact did not want visits to continue after the adoption order. This did not seem connected with the quality of the relationship formed with the social worker in the post-placement phase. Only one family who did not want visits related this to their negative feelings towards their social worker. The reason most often put forward against such an arrangement was that is would be difficult or upset the adopted child: 'it gives the child the feeling he is bad'. Other reasons given were the formality of such visits, the desire to be independent, and to live as a normal family.

Financial/practical help
The general impression gained was that financial help was not a major consideration. Nearly half of the families obtained financial help post-placement, in the form of either fostering allowances and grants for clothing and/or bedding. The rest did not expect or want such assistance. Two families had asked but were turned down. After the adoption order, two families with children with disabilities received adoption allowances, and one family obtained a bedding and clothing allowance. Two of the families, though, expressed strong views about the lack of financial help. In one family with five adopted children, adoption allowances were not in force when their adoptions were granted. They are now attempting through their local adopters' group to get retrospective allowances. In the other family, the adoptive mother had to give up her job in order to adopt, and their request for allowances had been turned down.

The level of practical help was low. Most of the families expressed surprise that help such as babysitting or respite care could be on offer. One family with a disabled child was using respite care. In a second family, where a disruption had occurred, and another adoptive child was in placement, a Community Service Volunteer came to babysit.

Families had very little knowledge of support services provided through other sources. Only four of the families had been informed by their social worker of the self-help group for adopters, Parent to Parent Information on Adoption Services (PPIAS), and the rest were unaware of its existence. A telephone advice line is provided for adopters by Barnardo's in Glasgow (Lindsay and McGarry, 1984), but only one family had heard of such a service, and this through a chance acquaintance. Again, only one family knew of the post-adoption support offered by the Adoption Counselling Centre run by Family Care in Edinburgh.

Information provided

It is a statutory duty to provide adoptive families with written background information on the adopted child. It is also considered good practice to write a letter to the child about his/her past and to make up a life-story book. Nearly half of the families had only been given verbal information, and there was no letter for the child. In five of these cases the adoption order had been granted after the statutory requirements for written information came into force. Seven of the children did not have a life-story book. In some cases only persistent "pushing" resulted in written information being provided. At the time of the research four families were still without such written information. This caused frustration and dissatisfaction as it made the task of answering questions or telling their children about the past more difficult: 'I was in knots about what the child was telling me, and what I had picked up myself verbally.'

The study confirms other findings which show that for quite a large number of families, "telling" children of their background is problematical (Goodacre, 1966; Triseliotis, 1973; Raynor, 1980; Haimes and Timms, 1985). Such research dealt with adoptions carried out many years ago. Despite recent advances in adoption practice, the evidence here suggests that this is an area where families need more help, not just in the post-placement phase but also in the post-adoption phase, and there is room for improvement in practice (Brodzinsky, 1984).

Most of the children knew they were adopted, except for two with disabilities who were considered by their parents unable to understand the concept of adoption. Seven families had not told their children (now aged between four and 15) of their background. Four families felt they had done so only superficially (with children aged 12 to 16). Families spoke openly about delaying this and not knowing how to handle the subject. In some cases they were waiting for the initiative to come from the child, and silence was interpreted as lack of interest.

Adopters' groups

Only half of the families were in favour of this kind of support. They were very positive about the benefits – their overall response can best be summed up as 'you don't feel you are on your own'. In terms of running such a group, the model most favoured was social workers and adoptive families working together. The support of a group did not lessen the need for a social worker who was seen as providing specialist advice and being used for crisis intervention. In one department there was a well-developed adopters' group (O'Hara, 1986) and the parenting skills course on offer, as well as the newsletter published by this group, was found to be particularly useful.

Those not belonging to a group felt that the adopted child was their sole responsibility and that attendance would "identify" their child as adopted. For some there were practical difficulties with babysitting or distance.

Nearly half of the families had contact with other adopters outside the adopters' group setting with whom to share similar problems or just to "talk", and this was seen as very helpful.

Post-adoption centre

Families were invited to project themselves into the situation of using such a resource. They are a recent innovation, run by voluntary bodies and are open to anyone who has been involved in the adoption process. At present there are only two in England (Sawbridge, 1986; Traverse, 1986). There is also an Adoption Counselling Centre in Scotland, but as previously mentioned families were unaware of its existence.

Sixteen families responded positively to the idea of such support, and three were noncommittal. Positive points identified included: informality, experts under one roof, a Samaritan line in a crisis, independence. This independence was also seen as a possible drawback, as workers have no previous knowledge of the family.

Families were asked about the use they would make of a post-adoption centre. The main issue to emerge regarded the child's background. The emphasis was on the adoptee as an adolescent coming to terms with their adoption. Areas highlighted were: both adopters and adoptees finding out more about past history; how to "tell" about adoption; help if the adoptee wanted to make contact with the natural family; and general information to young people about adoption. Next, in order of priority, was help to deal with teenage problems, becoming independent, sexual problems, drug abuse and unemployment.

These findings support the information so far available about the work of the Adoption Counselling Centre in Scotland (Family Care, 1987) and the Post-Adoption Centre in London (Howe, 1988; Sawbridge, 1988). Adoptive families are making use of such a resource on a variety of issues, including the question of explaining adoption.

Three-quarters of the families said they would use such a centre themselves, as well as seeing it as a resource for their adopted children. A quarter of the families could see their natural children and other relatives using it, while half were undecided.

General attitudes to post-adoption support
Three-quarters of the families responded positively to support being available to every family after the adoption order had been granted. They felt their problems were different from other families: 'You can't talk to friends who are natural parents, they don't understand.' Thirteen families expressed the need for a variety of post-adoption support services.

Families were presented with the model of support as practised by the voluntary agency, Parents for Children. They employ a post-adoption worker who, among a range of support activities, keeps in touch with every family through twice-a-year telephone contact until the child is 18, or beyond if necessary. Visits are made if required. As discussed previously, families were not in favour of visits by social workers in the post-adoption phase. Three-quarters of them, however, responded favourably to this model of support because it was offered on informal rather than formal lines. Families also highlighted the fact that the initiative would come from the social worker which would make it easier for them to ask for help. Adopters were not unrealistic about the demand this would place on overburdened agencies. But they felt that social workers had a definite role to play in this area, and they were reluctant to let go of the good relationships they had established with them.

Adopters' suggestions for post-adoption services

1 local library or resource centre to obtain books on adoption;
2 regular newsletter from the adoption agency as a way of keeping in touch;
3 leaflet by adoption agencies regarding post-adoption services on offer, with particular emphasis on what to expect from specialist services;
4 leaflet for relatives of the adopted family to explain what adoption is about;
5 post-adoption services advertised in the *Yellow Pages*;
6 a "service manual" about adoption problems;
7 employment of adoptive parents to support other adoptive parents;
8 group meetings on "parentcraft" which would include parents with natural children;
9 videos of their natural families for adopted children;
10 post-adoption support group meetings for adopted children;
11 specialist residential units for adopted children when adoptions reach breaking point;
12 money for holidays for children, as respite for families;
13 helping adopted siblings, placed separately, to keep in touch;
14 positive discrimination for jobs for adopted children;
15 advice on how to legally "undo" a disrupted adoption.

Implications for adoption practice

As this study demonstrates, given the opportunity, adoptive families have much to say which is relevant to practice. The clear message is that they see the need to come back from time to time over the years to various sources of help – agency staff, adopters' groups, a post-adoption centre.

To be acceptable such a service needs to be provided along informal lines, with the initiative coming from the adoption agency.

Section 1 of the Adoption (Scotland) Act 1978 provides the legislative basis for a comprehensive post-adoption service. But research and practice experience suggest that this is at present open to wide interpretation. Agencies will need to provide clear policy statements and guidelines regarding services on offer after legal adoption.

The question of funding needs to be addressed. The support model suggested here of twice-a-year telephone contact is demanding in terms of staff time. There is scope for experiment; employing a post-adoption worker or an experienced adopter to act alongside a social worker as counsellor to other adopters is being tried in some agencies. Some of the suggestions made by the families also carry obvious resource implications. But in some areas it is more a case of improving existing practice, providing families with written background details, finding more effective ways of helping them to "tell" about the past, and informing them about existing support services run by other bodies.

The innovative response of some voluntary agencies to post-adoption services raises the issue of whether they necessarily need to be provided direct by local authorities. Could the voluntary agencies be grant-aided by local authorities to provide such support? Or could the task be shared between them, as advocated by the families in this study? Such questions suggest the need for the two sides to start talking to one another, and for further research to be done to assist the social work profession in re-thinking its post-adoption responsibilities.

References

Brodzinsky D (1984) 'New perspectives on adoption revelation', *Adoption & Fostering* 8:2, pp 27–32.

Family Care (1987) *Adoption Counselling Centre: Family Care Report, 1987*.

Goodacre I (1966) *Adoption Policy and Practice*, London: Allen & Unwin.

Haimes E and Timms N (1985) *Adoption, Identity and Social Policy*, Aldershot: Gower.

Howe D (1988) 'Survey of initial referrals to the Post-Adoption Centre', *Adoption & Fostering* 12:1, pp 12–13.

O'Hara G (1986) 'Developing post-placement support services', *Adoption & Fostering* 10:4, pp 38–42.

Lindsay M and McGarry K (1984) *Scottish Adoption Advice Service – Adoption counselling – a talking point*, Edinburgh: Barnardo's Scottish Division.

Macaskill C (1985) 'Who should support after adoption', *Adoption & Fostering* 9:1, pp 45–49.

Raynor L (1980) *The Adopted Child Comes of Age*, London: Allen & Unwin.

Sawbridge P (1986) 'Adoption Support Centre', *Adoption & Fostering* 10:2, pp 4–5.

Sawbridge P (1988) 'The Post-Adoption Centre – What are the users teaching us?', *Adoption & Fostering* 12:1, pp 5–12.

Traverse E (1986) 'Norwich "Adoption Help" Centre', *Adoption & Fostering* 10:4, pp 6–7.

Triseliotis J (1973) *In Search of Origins*, London: Routledge & Kegan Paul.

Yates P (1985) 'Post-placement support for adoptive families of hard-to-place children', Unpublished M.Sc., Edinburgh University.

16 Adoptive parenting: plus and minus

Malcolm Hill, Sandra Hutton and Shona Easton

This article was first published in Adoption & Fostering *12:2, 1988.*

Being a parent is not easy. In the modern nuclear family most of the strains and responsibilities as well as the joys and rewards of bringing up children are concentrated on parents (especially mothers), rather than shared more widely among relatives and others. For many people of course the satisfactions outweigh the demands, but we have plenty of evidence that strain and depression are also common consequences of parenthood (Brown and Harris, 1978; Hoffman and Manis, 1978). About one in five children will experience the divorce of their parents by the age of 16 (Haskey, 1983; Osborn *et al*, 1984).

It should not surprise us, therefore, if those who assume the permanent care of children not born to them should encounter a similar range of pleasure and problems. They also have to negotiate the issue of acknowledging biological and perhaps social difference. When it comes to the placement of children with special needs it has become widely recognised that there are also extra difficulties to be encountered as a legacy of their previously unsatisfactory or disrupted care histories, or as a consequence of current disability. Hence the concept of "parenting plus" has evolved to depict those demands which are additional to "ordinary" parenthood. Yet for any family it may be hard to know whether a problem faced is normal for most families, is related to the way the child came to them or is something special to their circumstances. Knowledge about the extent and intensity of difficulties found in other families may be important in judging what it is feasible or reasonable to cope with.

Over the last ten years or so, it has become accepted that substitute parenting of children with special needs often requires much greater preparation and assistance than birth parenthood or infant adoption. From practice developments and a few research studies (Yates, 1985; Macaskill, 1985a, 1985b; Wedge and Thoburn, 1986) we now have a fair idea of the kinds of help needed not just before and after placement but also sometimes post adoption. A variety of sources and types of support is needed – from social networks, other adopters, social work agencies and other professionals. Some prefer to confide in their own parents, sisters or brothers, others in close friends, yet others in social workers. Different kinds of practical, social and supportive/counselling help are required because some families have multiple needs and also because what suits one person may not be available or appropriate for another. For instance, Macaskill (1985b) mentions relief care, discussions with other adopters, special leisure activities, medical and educational understanding and befriending of the children by volunteers. Ideally such help should be close at hand, accessible and well timed. Normally social work help should acknowledge the parental role of adopters and eschew direct work with the child except at their request (Thoburn *et al*, 1986). Sometimes counselling the whole family group together may be appropriate (Hartman, 1984).

Macaskill concluded from her evaluation of Parents For Children that voluntary agencies are in the best position to offer professional support, but it is probably fairer to say that it is the placing agency, whether voluntary or local authority, which has the greatest commitment to furnish the time and resources. O'Hara (1986) has described how Lothian Region set out to establish a comprehensive system of post-placement support, based on the community social work principles of co-operation between a social work agency on the one hand and natural and mutual-aid networks on the other. The Region has supported the development of an independent self-help group, Lothian Adopters Group (LAG). Adoptive placements of non-disabled pre-school children from Lothian are normally dealt with by a voluntary agency, the Scottish Adoption Association, but all other new parents are routinely referred to LAG by the homefinders. Between them, LAG and the social work department offer, among other things, access to support meetings, training groups, social work support, counsel-ling services and babysitting help (Hutton, 1988). In this article, we shall report on a survey carried out to assess the needs and opinions of some of the families who have experienced that system of services in its early evolving stage.

The study

This survey was a co-operative venture between the social work section at Edinburgh University, LAG and Lothian social work department. Members of LAG were invited to complete a written questionnaire about their experiences as parents. Fifty questionnaires were returned, which represents three-fifths of the membership, although a higher proportion of active members. We do not know how representative our sample was of new parents of school-age and disabled children in general. It is likely to have included more of those experiencing difficulties since people who see their situation as straightforward may feel no need to join a support group or complete a questionnaire. Moreover, Lothian has placed for adoption an above-average proportion of older children in recent years (Hill *et al*, 1985).

The characteristics of the children did indeed suggest that few had come to the families as uncomplicated infants. In the total sample of 50 families there were 83 "placed" children, i.e. those who had been placed for adoption or, less commonly, fostering. Over three-quarters of the children had been of school age when placed. Roughly one in three had been aged 11 or more when they joined the family. Eight of the children had a mental and/or physical disability. Most of the children had been placed directly for adoption, but there were a small number of children (12) fostered on a long-term or permanent basis. Just over half the children had been with their new families for three years or more. Five families had included seven children whose placements had disrupted. Lothian Region has calculated a total disruption rate of 11 per cent for all its children aged over two or more with disabilities placed for adoption in the last five years (O'Hara, 1987).

One-third of the families included birth children, leaving two in three who had been childless before taking adoptive or foster children. There were four single parents in the sample.

The impact of placement

The onset of parenthood through childbirth has been depicted as a crisis or, more recently and more fairly, as a "critical transition" (Rossi, 1968; LaRossa and LaRossa, 1981). When an older child comes to create or

257

extend a family, the adjustment called for in all parties is likely to be all the greater. According to family stress theory (McCubbin *et al*, 1983; Walker, 1985), how this readjustment is negotiated will depend on a number of factors, such as:

1 what the event means to those involved, i.e. for the childless it is the exciting beginning of parenthood but for those with children already it involves an extension and modification of parenting;
2 the severity of the event – eg the extent of the child's unmet needs resulting from previous experiences; the child's behaviour and its (mis-) match with parental expectations;
3 the coping and control strategies used by the family members, including adjustments of rules, roles and boundaries;
4 the personal and social resources and supports of the family.

In relation to the first two points above, we asked about the quality of the children's attachments to their new parents and about behaviour problems exhibited. Most of the parents thought that their children had attached well to them. Typical comments were: 'total attachment to us'; 'very happy and contented'; 'a pleasure to live with'. However some felt neutral or detached. Just under one in three (excluding the disruptions) regarded the attachment as less than they had hoped for. They mentioned 'coldness', 'indifference' or 'total rejection of our affection'.

Eighteen families were in the position to compare their relationships with older-placed children and their children born to them or adopted in infancy. Some saw no difference between placed and existing children but most had an easier and closer relationship to the latter. Distinguishing features of the placed children comprised fewer emotional returns, greater demands and more need for outside help. Most parents thought their basic values and approach had not altered, but some noted the greater emotional strain and difficulty in achieving obedience from the placed children.

Nonetheless there were many gains from having the children. Although five families could not state any satisfaction, the rest mentioned their pleasure in such things as:

- the child's progress   23
- the child's love   10
- becoming a complete family   9
- the child's nature   8
- seeing the child's happiness   7

Similarly, from fixed choice questions the two most frequently chosen benefits from placements were "seeing your new child blossom" and "seeing your child's confidence grow". While many did acknowledge more personal satisfactions such as "being needed" or "feeling of completeness", it was vicarious pleasure for the child which came top of the list.

Although the majority of families were positive or very positive about their placements, a significant proportion had experienced major worries (see Table 1).

It is disquieting that one-third of the families had experienced substantial anxiety or depression in relation to the placements.

More than 50 per cent of the sample had experienced the following types of behaviour from one of their placed children:

- attention-seeking;
- poor concentration;
- lying;
- reluctance to accept responsibility for own actions;
- poor peer group relations;
- mood swings;
- aggression;
- uncaring about own belongings;
- self-centredness;
- under-achievement at school;
- poor conscience;
- lack of initiative.

Table 1
Levels of anxiety

	Not/ occasionally	Sometimes	Most of the time
Worried about the future	30	9	11
Lengthy despair	32	12	6
Worried about effects on existing children	36	9	5
Wished had never begun	36	11	3
Feeling could not go on	40	6	4
Fearing marriage will end	46	3	1

In spite of quite detailed preparation for the children in most cases, nearly three-quarters said that some behaviour was more difficult than expected. The most common of these were lying, communication difficulties, coldness/rejection and stealing. These are all qualities or actions which prevent or undermine closeness and trust. Although many of the children had been with the family for two years or more, well over half of the behaviour difficulties were reported to be ongoing. About one-third of the families thought there were exceptional monetary costs resulting from the child's behaviour or disability. The most common reason for this (seven families) was the child's destructiveness. Other factors were exceptional wear and tear, bedwetting, soiling, extra tuition and paying for relief care.

Also of interest is the fact that many of the problems were said not to have been predicted. Some more common or obvious ones had mostly been expected (e.g. bedwetting, under-achievement at school, attention-seeking). However, three-quarters of families who reported experience of forgetfulness (26), lack of emotion (19), indifference (16), giving things away (14) and hoarding (9) said this had *not* been foreseen.

In order to obtain a measure of the changing impact of placement, we asked parents to rate their level of stress on a scale from 0–7 before placement and at two-yearly intervals thereafter. One-quarter of the respondents (12) reported no stress at all. At the other extreme, 13 of the 50 families indicated that they had encountered major stress, as indicated by a score of 6–7 at some point. Most of the parents indicated consider-ably higher stress levels after two years compared with pre-placement.

Macaskill (1985a) noted the disillusionment of some families when it has become apparent after two to three years that problems have not been overcome. This was borne out by subjective stress levels of families here:

Table 2
Stress rating

	0–2	3–5	6–7	
Two years on*	23	17	9	(49 families)
Four years on	4	11	7	(22 families)
Six years on	3	1	4	(S families)

(*or now, if placement under two years)

The most common types of stress experienced were dealing with the child's behaviour, parental anxiety and exhaustion, and splits or disagreements within the marriage and between children. Here are a range of comments:

 . . . *tested our marriage to the limit.*

 . . . *split us and created loneliness and isolation.*

 . . . *has come close to destroying our marriage more than once.*

and

 . . . *strengthened our marriage and has given us a new outlook on life.*

 . . . *brought us together.*

Most parents recorded moderate levels of stress caused by the placement for children already in the family. It is hard to know whether the jealousy and arguments were greater than is usual among brothers and sisters (Dunn, 1984). For several the strain seemed to be considerable, producing anxiety, headaches, poor sleep or intense dislike of the new child.

Use of personal, social and formal resources

We asked families what had helped them and what further help they would have liked. There was a fair degree of consensus about the personal qualities which helped them to survive difficulties:

- sense of humour   14 families
- patience/calm   14 families
- perseverance/determination   11 families
- marital support   8 families

As regards coping mechanisms, we invited people to say what advice they would give to others embarking on the same enterprise. Some specified particular ways of dealing with the children, such as 'set ground rules early so the children know where they stand'. Other frequently expressed guidance may be paraphrased as follows:

- Be realistic in your expectations and how you assess what you are doing.
- Be united and open with your partner.
- Make use of available external help.
- Be well informed and well prepared prior to placement.

Several had come to see that they should not keep blaming themselves:

> It is no reflection on your own abilities and capacities if you have difficulties.

> [Making use of] outside help is not a sign of failure or weakness in parenting adopted children.

> Remember that natural parents have problems too.

External help had been important too. The main ones were:

Table 3
External support

	Number of families (Total = 50)
Social workers	26
Other adopters	20
Breaks from children	20
Friends	19
Relatives	16

Clearly both social work and network support were important, as was practical relief from full-time care of the children. The majority of families said the help obtained from kin, friends and neighbours was both important and adequate before and after placement. Only two families had little assistance from any members of their social network throughout. Likewise most appeared satisfied with the help provided by social workers, but one-third believed that their social worker had underestimated the difficulties they faced with the children. A similar number thought that the information they had received about the children was inadequate in preparing them for placement.

Four-fifths of the sample had received financial help in relation to the placements. Usually this had consisted of an initial lump sum. About one in ten (six families) were receiving an adoption allowance. This included *none* of those who had experienced the greatest stress.

Opinions about post-placement support

Evidently these parents were, by and large, well supported both formally and informally. In response to an open invitation to comment, one in four wanted further help from public services. Top of the list were respite/relief care, more information about the child, counselling/psychiatric help and financial aid. Many were positive about LAG and how 'talking with other adopters relieves the pressure', but five wanted better contacts. A few would have welcomed opportunities to meet with people in a similar situation (eg with a same-age child or other single adopters).

Only four families regarded access to the social work department as unimportant. Most felt valued and fairly equal in their relationship with the department, but quite a few thought that too much was expected of them. A small number saw themselves as left to sink or swim in dangerous waters. For example, while 31 out of 50 agreed with a statement that the department saw them as 'a valued resource for the child', seven concurred that its perception was 'you knew what you were taking on, so don't complain'. Several gave glowing accounts of the help given by home-finders. A few did complain about not being believed by social workers or not being able to change an incompatible worker. The most common suggestions for what departments could do to enhance parenting were:

- provide more information about the child;
- give pre- and post-placement training;
- offer back-up, support, counselling;
- arrange groups with other adopters.

When specifically asked if they would make use of particular services, the replies were as follows:

Table 4
Services needed

	Number of families (Total = 50)
Practical help	
Respite care	15
Babysitter	14
Holidays	11
Befriender scheme	9
Home help	9
Outings with a volunteer	8
Assessment/therapy	
Psychiatric assessment of child	19
Regular measured assessment of child's progress	16
Child guidance	14
Sexual counselling for child	11
Group experience for child	9
Speech therapy	8

In total more than half the families wanted access to relief, assessment or therapeutic services, some of which are provided outside social work departments.

Many special needs children have learning or behaviour difficulties at school on account of either their limited intellectual capacity or their emotional deprivation. Most LAG members had found their children's schools helpful, but some had met with indifference or critical attitudes. It may be hard for teachers to get the balance right, since a few parents wanted them to make use of information about the child to understand their special needs, while others wanted their children treated like anyone else. At any rate, in a minority of cases parents would have liked a more sympathetic attitude or better feedback about their children.

For a long time the idea of payment in relation to adoption has met with widespread hostility and suspicion because of its presumed tarnishing of people's motivations and sense of full responsibility (Hill and Triseliotis, 1986). Yet as we have seen, payment of initial lump sums is now commonplace for non-infant adoptions. Moreover, many people in the survey thought adopters should be offered more financial assistance. Over half thought allowances should be offered to all adopters, although one or two evidently confused ongoing allowances with initial payments. Most of the remainder wanted allowances offered to families where finance is critical.

When it came to themselves, only three respondents wanted no monetary help at all. The rest wanted:

Table 5
Support for financial help

	Number of families
Initial lump sum	23
Adoption allowance	23
Periodic access to funds	12
Fostering allowance	5

Quite often attitudes about financial help had changed since placement. Usually this resulted from realising the extent of extra costs (eg of a sibling group, for special activities for deprived children) but occasionally was a response to unemployment or other financial difficulties. Remarks included the following:

Before placement we were very reluctant to accept any financial help but now, knowing how destructive our child is, we wish we had more financial help.

I had to give up good paid employment due to the disruptive behaviour of the child.

Emotional handicap means paying for substitute child care, friends not willing or not appropriate.

We had to cater to both their natural age and their emotional age.

Conclusions

We have presented the findings of a survey about the impact of placements on adopters and permanent foster parents, many of whom have taken into their homes older children with substantial difficulties. The majority were well satisfied with how things had gone and with the support received. A sizeable number of carers and siblings (and presumably placed children too) had experienced considerable stress, anxiety or exhaustion. For some of these the effort was worth it. As one couple put it, three years of 'continual hard work' were 'starting to pay dividends'. For a small but significant number whose placements had disrupted or whose early problems were persisting, the conflict, tensions or lack of response from the children continued to cause major emotional strains on the parents and/or existing children. For them, this was not simply parenting *plus* abnormal demands, but also *minus* the normal rewards and satisfactions which come from children's affection, responsiveness and progress. Consequently a few felt bitter towards social workers about what they had been let in for.

It is not adequate to judge the successful outcomes of placements according to whether they survive or not, nor by the child's reactions alone, important though that is. Account needs to be taken, too, of the costs to ordinary families in the community, which is part of the un-doubted success story of finding permanent family homes for some of our most vulnerable children. They need assistance partly, of course, to meet the needs of the child. They may also be due help which compensates for and recognises the personal sacrifices and adjustments they make. In many instances we have seen that existing informal and formal supports were used and valued to an extent which may not be true in less well-provided areas. Even so, there was scope for access to a wider range of respite, leisure, assessment and therapeutic services. Moreover adequate and well-timed provision of two basic commodities – information and money – could have made life for some families more tolerable and thereby enhanced their parental satisfactions and capacities, with ultimate dividends for the children.

References

Brown G and Harris T (1978) *The Social Origins of Depression*, London: Tavistock.

Dunn J (1984) *Sisters and Brothers*, Glasgow: Fontana.

Hartman A (1984) *Working with Adoptive Families Beyond Placement*, New York: Child Welfare League of America.

Haskey J (1983) 'Children of divorcing couples', *Population Trends* 31, pp 20–26.

Hill M and Triseliotis J (1986) *Adoption Allowances in Scotland: The first five years*, Edinburgh: Scottish Office Central Research Unit Paper.

Hill M, Triseliotis J and Buist M (1985) *For Love or Money?*, Edinburgh Department of Social Administration: Final Report to Social Work Services Group.

Hoffman L W and Manis J D (1978) 'Influences of children on marital interaction and parental satisfactions and dissatisfactions', in Lerner R M and Spanier G B (eds) *A Dynamic Interactional View of Child and Family Development*, New York: Academic Press.

Hutton S (1988) 'An independent adopters support group', in Triseliotis J (ed) *Groupwork in Adoption and Foster Care*, London: Batsford.

LaRossa R and LaRossa M M (1981) *Transition to Parenthood*, Beverley Hills: Sage.

Macaskill C (1985a) 'Post-adoption support: is it essential?', *Adoption & Fostering* 9:1, pp 45–49.

Macaskill C (1985b) 'Who should support after the adoption?', *Adoption & Fostering* 9:2, pp 21–25.

McCubbin H I, Sussman M B and Patterson J M (1983) *Social Stress and the Family*, New York: Haworth Press.

O'Hara G (1986) 'Developing post-placement services in Lothian', *Adoption & Fostering* 10:4, pp 38–42.

O'Hara G (1987) Personal communication.

Osborn A F, Butler N R and Morris A C (1984) *The Social Life of Britain's Five-year-olds*, London: Routledge & Kegan Paul.

Rossi A (1968) 'Transitions to parenthood', *Journal of Marriage and the Family*, pp 26–40.

Thoburn J, Murdoch A and O'Brien A (1986) *Permanence in Child Care*, Oxford: Blackwell.

Walker A J (1985) 'Reconceptualising family stress', *Journal of Marriage and the Family* 47:4, pp 827–37.

Wedge P and Thoburn J (1986) *Finding Families for 'Hard-to-place' Children*, London: BAAF.

Yates P (1985) *Post-placement Support for Adoptive Families of Hard-to-place Children*, Edinburgh University: Dissertation for MSc.

17 Using contact registers in adoption searches

Lydia Lambert, Moira Borland, Malcolm Hill and John Triseliotis

This article was first published in Adoption & Fostering *16:1, 1992.*

Moving towards openness

Since May 1991 it has been possible for birth parents or relatives and people who were adopted in England and Wales to get in touch with each other through the Adoption Contact Register maintained by the Registrar General. There are various conditions attached to the process and a fee is prescribed, but it marks an important official step towards greater openness in adoption. Nevertheless, as this article will show, there are certain pitfalls in using contact registers. In particular, they should be seen as a back-up to other more active methods of resuming contact and not relied upon as the main avenue to reunion.

For many years adoption workers have been informally enabling adopted people and their birth relatives to re-establish contact in certain carefully vetted situations, and NORCAP has maintained a register and provided counselling on request. In Scotland the Adoption Counselling Centre based at Family Care in Edinburgh holds the national Birth Link Register which was set up in the 1980s in response to a growing number of requests from birth parents for information about their children. Unlike the new Adoption Contact Register, where the Registrar General simply transmits the name and address of a relative to an adopted person who has also registered, the Birth Link Register offers a more personal service to both parties although they are, of course, free to make their own arrangements subsequently if they wish. The notes accompanying the registration form explain that:

> *If a birth parent or a relative and the adopted person have registered and both parties wish for contact, a counsellor from the Adoption Counselling Centre will get in touch with each person and work out*

with them the best way to begin the reunion process. Identifying information will not be exchanged until both parties are ready.

The Birth Link Register can also be used by birth parents to record a wish for "no contact", and in these cases the information will be conveyed to the adopted person and counselling will be available. However, birth parents are advised that there can be no guarantee that an adopted person will not make direct contact by other means. Birth parents who do not want to be contacted can provide some explanation for this in a section of the form for 'other relevant information'. The section invites people to include their 'present circumstances, medical information, attitude of family to this registration. Birth parents may wish to include their reasons for placing the child for adoption'. Such information can also greatly assist the introductory stages of reunions that are desired. Although, at present, the Register is only used by adoptees and their parents or relatives, the possibility is being explored of extending it to pass information between birth and adoptive parents of children who are currently being placed.

A study of adopted adults exploring their origins

While some adoption agencies have tried to ensure that full background details are passed on to the adoptive parents, the Adoption Counselling Centre is made aware constantly of how little information has been given to many members of the adoption triangle or circle through the enquiries it received. Nearly half of these come from adopted people who are exploring their origins and are often also wanting to contact their birth parents. In order to find out more about these enquiries so that future services could be targeted in the best way, a short research project was funded by the Social Work Services Group and conducted at the University of Edinburgh during 1990 (Triseliotis, 1991). The study concentrated on the views of 25 adopted people selected from those who had contacted the Adoption Counselling Centre between April and June 1989.

There were seven men and 18 women and their ages ranged from 17 to 48. The majority were in paid employment, married, with children and had good health. Nineteen people were adopted before their first birthday and all were placed in two-parent families. Just over half said they had been told about their adoption before the age of five or had 'always known'. Four learnt between the ages of five and nine, and seven were aged ten or older. Two-thirds said they did not know enough and few had been shown relevant documents, usually because their adopters had not been given any to keep. Younger people knew about their right to contact the General Register Office for Scotland at 17 for their original birth certificate, but only one older person had been told about this right although it has existed since adoption was legalised in Scotland in 1930. The general picture surrounding disclosure and the sharing of background information is somewhat more encouraging than that found by Triseliotis (1973) almost 20 years ago. It is not as good as that found by Craig (in press) when the adoptive parents were specially prepared to handle these issues.

Many of the adopted people said they had contemplated making a search for a long time before they took any action. For example, one woman in her twenties said:

Since I was about 15 I've been wanting to do this. It's one of these things you just say you're going to do and then you ask yourself, 'Should I or not just leave it?' One day I just thought I was going to do it. It was just constantly on my mind. I knew that if I didn't do something it would always be on my mind. If it was still going to be there in a few years time I was still going to be thinking, 'Should I or should I not?'

Curiosity and a desire to find out who they were and why they were adopted were frequent reasons for starting their enquiries, but these were often delayed until after the death of their adoptive parents for fear of hurting them. When they did begin to acquire information its impact could be overwhelming and time was needed to assimilate it before proceeding further. A similar reaction was noted from applicants to the Post Adoption Centre in London by Howe and Hinings (1989).

Seeking professional help when things get difficult

Two-thirds of those interviewed said they had already made attempts to trace their origins before making contact with the Adoption Counselling Centre and often had found out about the Centre during this process, or through the media. Many had obtained their original birth certificate; some had also gained access to the court papers about their adoption, which they are entitled to see in Scotland; others had been in contact with social work departments. It would appear that, as it is not compulsory in Scotland to receive counselling before seeing their birth records, adopted people often preferred to "go it alone" and make their own enquiries, at least in the early stages. They seemed more likely to seek professional help when things got difficult or in preparation for an actual reunion. Three-quarters of the enquirers were seeking contact with a birth parent but most of them were also looking for further information as well. The expertise of the Centre's staff in knowing where to find the appropriate records was rated as one of the most helpful aspects of the service.

Table 1
Current outcome of search

Outcome	No.	%
Still enquiring	7	28
Stopped for now	4	16
Met birth parent(s)	6	24
Other contact with birth parent	4	16
No contact – dead, refused	4	16
Total	25	100

During the 12–15 months after getting in touch with the Adoption Counselling Centre six people had traced and met the birth parent(s) they were seeking and a further four had achieved some contact with them or with relatives (Table 1). A reunion proved impossible for four people because the birth parents had died or had refused a meeting. Another four said they had come to a halt in their search, although one of them would probably resume the quest as some further information had just come through. The remaining seven, five of whom were men, were still pursuing their enquiries.

Only one of the people who had succeeded in meeting a birth parent was directly linked with them through the Register. In this case, 'it was just really a matter of them [ACC] writing a letter to her and she'd get back in contact with them. That all happened, even in that short space of time it was all quite quick', and then the Centre helped to arrange the reunion. Another person who registered on the Birth Link Register actually found her birth mother by other means 'in exactly a fortnight' through a series of coincidences which led to her being told, 'there's one very anxious woman waiting for you to phone'. She continued, '. . . there weren't any problems – the hurdles that could have been there disappeared'. She later discovered that her birth mother had been trying to find her for many years, but had not known about the Register. One of the unsuccessful searchers took several initiatives at the same time, including registering, but discovered from another source that her birth mother had died the previous year.

The other five people who had put their names on the Birth Link Register had not completed their searches at the time of our interview with them. Two were people who said they had come to a halt and one of them expressed some of the misery of constantly reaching 'blank ends' in the following words:

I think I thought it [the search] would be easier than it was. I think it's sort of constant not getting anywhere – you don't expect to get there right away, even if you had a little bit more to go on. But there hasn't been any encouragement. Everything I've tried, there has been nothing. It puts you off, you say 'Is it worth it?'

The remaining three were pursuing their enquiries with varying degrees of alacrity. One of them confessed that he was only 'slowly interested' in the search and had not made much of an effort, while another man had been pursuing several lines of enquiry with frustrating results. The third person was still at the beginning of her search and said she had registered in order to 'see if I get any useful information off that; see if she'd want to be contacted and just take it step by step. Just wait.'

For someone like this last respondent, who is prepared to wait, a contact register provides a useful but rather passive method of signalling a willingness to make contact if this is also desired by the other party. The result depends on both sides taking this step and also, crucially, on them both knowing about the Register's existence. Family Care has printed several leaflets about the Birth Link Register and tries to distribute them as widely as possible through social work departments and voluntary agencies. Every adopted person who contacts the General Register Office for Scotland has to be informed about the availability of counselling services and receives one of the leaflets which mentions the Adoption Counselling Centre's service, including the Birth Link Register. Arrangements have been made in England and Wales for the Registrar General to inform adopted applicants about the Adoption Contact Register through a revised version of the leaflet about 'Access to birth records' (ACR 100) and a new leaflet on the Register for adopted people and their relatives (ACR 110).

Reaching birth parents

Although this publicity is reaching a large proportion of those adopted people who are most actively seeking contact with their families of origin, there are considerable problems with informing birth parents about the Register. This is especially true for the parents of people who are now adults. The majority of those who parted with a child for adoption in former years are unaware of this means of resuming contact. Some discover the relevant leaflets if they call in to agencies that display them, but the media has provided the main source of dissemination. Family Care has taken advantage of opportunities to present information about the Birth Link Register and other services on TV, radio and in the press. However, it does so in the knowledge that every burst of publicity will increase the demands on an already over-stretched team of counsellors. While the registration process itself has been streamlined, many enquirers also seek advice or counselling and the work involved in actually arranging a reunion can be considerable.

Birth mothers are just as likely as some of the adopted people described earlier to find that making a registration brings no more than a glimmer of hope that contact will be re-established. As the process is at present only activated when the adopted child also registers, many birth mothers continue to wait and wonder how this child has fared (Bouchier *et al*, 1991). Although the prospect of allowing birth mothers a reciprocal right to initiate the contact was acceptable to some, there were others who felt ambivalent or thought that the situation should remain as at present.

However, there was general agreement that if more information was available to all the parties while the adopted child was growing up, there would be less need for people to search for each other or to wait forlornly.

Thus, at the same time as promoting the use of the Birth Link Register, staff at the Adoption Counselling Centre together with other adoption workers are actively seeking to address the issues which surround the exchange of information and continuity or resumption of contact. As other studies have shown (Lambert *et al*, 1990), many adoptive parents are fearful of maintaining contact with birth parents while the child is growing up, particularly where there has been abuse or neglect in the past. Although there is now more understanding of the need to integrate unhappy past experiences along with the benefits of a more stable new environment, it is still very important to adopters to be able to exercise full parental responsibility and care. However, most adopters have appreciated the practice changes which have led agencies to provide fuller details about the child's background and the reasons for the adoption and to emphasise the importance of sharing these appropriately with the child (Triseliotis, 1991). As well as increasing their confidence and security, these changes appear to have decreased the need to search for information from outside sources. They have also made some families more aware of the value of updating information and consequently more willing to exchange this. Some prefer to do this through their adoption agency but the possibility of extending the Birth Link Register for this purpose, as mentioned earlier, is also being discussed.

However good the information provided by adoptive parents or public agencies, some adopted people will still wish to go further and contact their birth parents. Our study confirmed other research in showing that such meetings have been helpful to both sides and led to a variety of new relationships, rarely affecting the bonds with adoptive parents except in a positive way. Although contact could be established with surprising ease in the most successful cases, it usually depended on an active pursuit of names, addresses and telephone numbers. When contact registers become better known, the chances of finding that the other party has already registered will undoubtedly improve but seem likely to remain haphazard. Many searchers will probably continue to try other methods of contact as well, and to need advice and support while making their enquiries.

Postscript

*The Scottish Register held by Family Care in Edinburgh received 1,385 enquiries from across Scotland in 1999 (*Birthlink Bulletin, *Summer 2000, Family Care, Edinburgh). Apparently less than ten per cent of birth parents registering were fathers.*

Though the introduction of the Register provided a move forward, dissatisfaction still remained because it was seen as too constricting a device. Furthermore, adoption workers were uncertain of the limits of their power to arrange for possible meetings. Arguments were now being advanced that short of changing the 1976 Children Act, adoption agencies, as part of their intermediary role should be given wider discretion to be more proactive on behalf of birth parents and other relatives who sought contact. This pressure resulted in a new document prepared by The Children's Society on behalf of the Department of Health. The new document, which appears to have been adopted by the Department of Health, makes it easier for birth parents and relatives who seek contact with an adopted person to do so. The examples given as guidance to agencies suggest that counsellors can now be far more proactive than they were before (Intermediary Services for Birth Relatives: Practice guidelines, 2000).

References

Bouchier P, Lambert L and Triseliotis J (1991) *Parting with a Child for Adoption*, London: BAAF.

Craig M (in press) *The Disclosure of Adoption and of Genealogical Information.*

Howe D and Hinings D (1989) *The Post Adoption Centre – First three years: adopted people*, Norwich: University of East Anglia.

Lambert L, Buist M, Triseliotis J and Hill M (1990) *Freeing Children for Adoption*, London: BAAF.

Triseliotis J (1973) *In Search of Origins*, London: Routledge & Kegan Paul.

Triseliotis J (1991) *Adoption Services in Scotland*, Edinburgh: The Scottish Office, CRU Paper.

18 Contact between adopters and birth parents: the Strathclyde experience

Stephanie Stone

This article was first published in Adoption & Fostering *18:2, 1994.*

Part of Strathclyde Region's criteria for couples who wish to adopt children aged under two years is that they should be willing to meet with birth parents if this is requested by the agency or the birth parent(s). Stephanie Stone reports on the impact this has had upon adopters.

In 1986 Strathclyde Regional Council restructured its baby adoption service, and since that time the Centralised Baby Adoption Service (CBAS) has dealt with all children under two years requiring adoptive placements within the Region. This allowed the department to review existing adoption practice and ensure consistent practice. The CBAS also monitors all adoption applications for children of this age range and the CBAS Adoption Panel recommends the acceptance, or otherwise, of all prospective adopters, matchings and applications for freeing. As the largest local authority in the UK, it is probable that the CBAS also deals with the largest number of adoption placements of children in this age group in a single year.

The social work department is committed to an "open" approach in adoption, and the sharing of as much information as possible between adoptive families and birth parents. It remains cautious, however, about "open adoption", in terms of ongoing access between birth parents and their adopted children, and has only made one placement where twice-yearly visits between the parties was agreed.

When the new service was created a number of eligibility criteria were established which enquirers had to meet before their application would be accepted. One of these criteria stated that, 'Applicants must agree to meet with birth parents if requested to do so by either the birth parents or the social work department.' It was envisaged that this would assist adopters in "telling" and passing positive messages about the birth parent to the child. It was hoped that birth parents would also benefit from this meeting and feel that they had been involved in the planning for their child's future.

In the initial years of the service this policy caused considerable anxiety among both social workers and adopters who had always viewed adoption in a traditional "closed" mould. Birth parents, too, were resistant to the idea of meeting the prospective adopters and change came gradually.

Assessing the impact

In 1992, 69 children aged from birth to two years were placed through the service. In February 1993 a questionnaire was sent to each family (66 placements) to try to ascertain the impact of this policy on adopters. Two of the families were no longer at the same address and could not be contacted, and of the 64 remaining, 35 families responded. These families commented on 40 placements as some had second placements and also commented on these. Families could choose whether or not they wished to remain anonymous.

Anxiety

In response to the question, 'Before your child was identified were you anxious about the prospect of meeting birth parents?', 23 couples said that they were anxious. However, once couples knew the details of their particular child, ten couples who were previously anxious became less so, while only one couple stated that they became more anxious, and this was because of their stated fear that the birth mother would not like them.

The age of the children ranged from two children placed at two weeks old, to two children of 24 months. The mean age was eight-and-a-half months. Out of the 40 placements, the adopters met with birth parents on 17 occasions. They met in a variety of places, including social work offices and cafés. Two couples met with their child's parent in the birth parent's own home and one couple invited the birth parents to their home. One couple, at the birth parent's request, met her at the court hearing before she would give her final agreement to the adoption.

Of the 15 couples who met the birth parents, all except one couple wrote of their nervousness, anxiety or apprehension prior to the meeting. Thirteen couples, however, were all very positive about the meeting, were glad it had taken place, and recommended it to other "would-be" adopters. One couple described themselves as "elated" after they met the birth mother, but this meeting was unusual. The child had been in placement over a year and was adopted. The mother had declined the opportunity to meet the adopters prior to the placement but had requested an exchange of information which took place around the child's first birthday. Following on from this, the mother had asked if the couple would be prepared to meet her. They were delighted to do so and felt very much as ease. The one family which was not able to see a positive outcome from their meeting had adopted a "special needs" child whose brain damage had been caused by physical abuse inflicted by the parent.

Much of the adopters' nervousness arose not from anxiety about facing the reality of meeting one's (adopted) child's birth parents, but from a fear that the birth parent would find them 'too old', or disappointing in some way.

I felt guilty for a while about taking this woman's child. I felt I had to be an almost perfect mother. This soon passed.

Preparation

Ten couples reported that they had been well prepared for the meeting by their social workers and the five who had felt inadequately prepared all felt that the individual circumstances surrounding the meeting had made this an impossible task but felt that their social workers had supported them. Some felt that they had not been prepared for the level of emotion generated on both sides.

Of the 19 couples who had not met the birth parents, only four said they were disappointed by this – the rest expressed some relief!

Sixteen out of the 35 couples exchanged information with the birth parents on a regular basis through a variety of means. Some used the social work department as a "post box" service, others sent their letters direct, some used the previous foster parent. Five of the families had exchanged information on a "one-off" basis. When asked if they found it difficult to write to the birth parents, three couples said that they did find it hard to find the right words to say and one family expressed the view that they might find it harder as the years went by. Eighteen couples expressed no difficulty at all.

Post-adoption support
Seventeen couples attended post-adoption support groups, and of those who didn't four couples expressed a wish to be invited to such a group. The others were 'happy without'.

Common themes

Four recurrent themes emerged from the survey. Firstly, although in general the couples were apprehensive about the prospect of meeting with birth parents, those that did meet viewed it very positively and were glad they had done so, even where their emotions had been very high. Those couples who did not get the opportunity to meet were in the main relieved not to have been put through the experience. However, their views should be contrasted with the positive response of those who did meet in spite of their reported initial apprehension. Only time will tell if they will come to regret this missed opportunity.

Secondly, it was very important to all the adopters that they had the support of their social worker at the meeting as a "facilitator". In most of the meetings two social workers were present – the social worker for the birth parent and the social worker for the family. They managed the meeting in terms of time, and assisted both parties if conversation became stilted or emotions ran too high to remember what they wanted to ask. They prepared each party by suggesting that they brought along photos and a small list of questions.

Thirdly, in general terms the adopters who are exchanging information are doing so willingly and welcome the feedback they get at the present time.

Finally, those couples who had joined post-adoption support groups found them enjoyable. Those couples who had not had the opportunity to do so were in the main quite wary, and felt that they were self-sufficient. Some adopters may, of course, prefer individual counselling which should always be available.

Strathclyde's experience would suggest that this approach enables the parties to make most use of the opportunities available to them, as social workers become more experienced and positive about adopters and birth parents meeting.

Although birth parents have not been contacted directly, feedback from their social workers suggests that meeting with the adopters is a positive experience for them too. The social worker has been encouraged to take along a camera and where possible take a picture of the adopters and birth parents together, so that each can retain a memento of the occasion. One family have this picture displayed in pride of place in their living room for all visitors to see. The birth parents tend to share the adopters' anxiety before the meeting and the main concern also seems to be, 'Will they like me?', and 'What will they tell my child about me in years to come?'

It is the department's intention to routinely review practice in the light of consumer experience and a questionnaire has recently been sent to the adopters of children placed in 1993. Although it has not yet been possible to study the results in detail, some information is available. Thirty-six questionnaires were returned from a total of 61 sent out. These questionnaires commented on 46 placements as some families had one and two previous children placed for adoption. Nineteen families had met with their children's birth parents. In general the feelings were similar to those reported above, although three families expressed feelings of guilt that their happiness had been gained through the birth parent's pain and loss. A number expressed feelings of sadness for the birth parent and empathy for the situation she found herself in. Only one couple expressed anger towards the birth parent. Concerns had been raised about this couple's ability to handle their first adopted child's birth history. However, they had convinced the department that they had successfully begun to tell their son of his adopted status. Twenty-three families have agreed to exchange information and/or photos with the birth family through the department.

Although only a snapshot of our adoption practice, it is hoped that social workers will take heart from the views and attitudes expressed by our adopters, and realise that the days of closed and secretive adoption are well and truly in the past.

Postscript

The Centalised Baby Adoption Service of Strathclyde Regional Council became defunct with local authority re-organisation in 1996. However, post-Strathclyde ten of the original 12 authorities continued to work together in a no-cost consortium recruiting, assessing and preparing families for children in the 0–2 age range. It is still part of the criteria that prospective adopters have to agree to meet with birth parents if requested to do so. The degree of anxiety associated with this has diminished over the years partly because experienced adopters are able to relay their very positive experiences in the preparation stages. However, some birth parents remain reluctant although some request meetings or post-box contact at a later stage, and this is usually met with a positive response. Some adopters speak of their very considerable disappointment if the birth parents are not willing to meet. Those that do so continue to comment on how much this meeting has meant to them and how it has facilitated telling their children about their birth parents.

Section V
Perspectives on foster care

A national survey of foster care in Scotland was carried out by Triseliotis *et al* (2000). This showed that foster carers are in most respects very similar to the range of other families in Scotland in their characteristics and lifestyles (e.g. as regards occupations, housing, education). They are, however, more likely to be stable couples (79 per cent). About one in ten were separated or divorced, six per cent were widowed and four per cent had never married. Most foster families have children of their own, though often these are older or grown up when they start fostering.

As would be expected, most of the carers in the survey had child-centred motivations for taking up fostering. Some got on well with birth parents and were very sympathetic towards them, but a significant minority found contact with birth parents the most difficult aspect of their fostering role. In general, the foster carers were positive about the support they received from agency staff, especially their link workers, but were more negative about the wider agency (e.g. with respect to rates of pay, delays in payment, few resources).

One of the factors that prompted the survey just described was apparently widespread concern about the supply of foster carers. As noted in the introduction to this book, the proportion of looked after children who were fostered grew significantly during the 1990s. Although the growth in foster placements was smaller in absolute terms, this trend meant that a greater variety of foster carers was needed to care for those who formerly would have been placed in residential care as they were older or presented more difficulties than usual. By the mid-1990s it was also thought that fewer people were coming forward to foster, partly, it was believed, because there were more opportunities for women outside the home and more were wanting to do paid work.[1] For similar reasons and also the

---

[1] Paid work outside the home is of course compatible with being a foster carer, but members of the public may well not have known this, while others might find it difficult to meet the needs of some children unless at least one carer is at home most of the time. While small numbers of male foster carers are the primary home-based parent (Walker *et al*, 2002), traditionally it is women who have tended to take on this role.

growing demands and complexity of the role, more foster carers were said to be leaving the service. Two articles shed some light on what was actually happening. They indicated that the situation was probably not as bad as many believed, but there were definite causes for concern.

Ramsay (1996) reported on recruitment and retention of foster carers in Fife. This authority was one of the first to pay all its foster carers a professional fee as well as an allowance. American experience had indicated that payment (together with training and support) reduced the turnover of foster carers. The Fife payment policy was not only influenced by the wish to retain carers, but also by recognition that the distinction between paid special community carers and unpaid "traditional" carers could not be sustained, since the demands placed on the latter by the children and the agency were often similar to those on the former (cf. Kirton, 2001).

Against this background, a questionnaire survey was carried out to assess the council's fostering resources. As previous studies had found, most of the carers were aged between 30 and 55 years. In one-fifth of the cases, two partners were working. Ninety-three per cent of households had a car and 75 per cent a pet. This last figure, though high, was lower than other studies had found.

Two-thirds said the fee had become an integral part of the household income and nearly as many (59 per cent) said they could not continue to foster if the fee were withdrawn. The carers were also asked about support they received from social workers, which as in many areas came from both the fostering link worker and the child's social worker. Since the link worker's prime duty is towards the foster home, it was perhaps not surprising that the link workers were more popular, with two-thirds rated as satisfactory all the time compared with just over one-third of the child's workers. Nevertheless, the majority were pleased with their child's worker all or most of the time. These findings correspond with patterns in England (Sellick, 1992; Sinclair *et al*, 2001) and other parts of Scotland (Triseliotis *et al*, 2000).

The questionnaire included some specific questions on recruitment and retention. One-third of the sample expressed a long-term interest in fostering, while two-thirds indicated that they had been prompted to apply by an external stimulus, although doubtless many had previously wondered about doing something like it. The two main "triggers" were newspapers (articles and adverts) and friends or relatives. Three-quarters said they intended to continue fostering for at least five years, indicating considerable commitment and stability. The main changes that carers wanted in the service were to have more frequent visits by the child's social worker and to be involved in case planning. Ramsay concluded that the fee, combined with generally well-received support, was helping to secure foster carers with a long-term commitment to fostering.

In their national survey, **Triseliotis** *et al* **(1998)** also found that annual losses of foster carers were lower than expected – around nine per cent. Furthermore, about half of those who ceased to foster had looked after foster children for six years or more – a considerable contribution. This does not mean there is no shortage, however, since there was also evidence that agencies had little choice when placing a child in foster care (Triseliotis *et al*, 2000). The survey included people who had ceased to foster, giving the opportunity to compare their characteristics to see if they differed in some way that might help predict losses to the service. There were no evident differences on most key items compared, such as age at recruitment, length of experience, motivation to foster or household composition. Those who ceased to foster were more likely to say they had difficulties with parental contact and to be doing a type of fostering they had not wished (e.g. older children). These dissatisfactions might well have been remedied or used as indications of inappropriateness for the agency's needs.

Some foster carers had ceased to foster for reasons unconnected to their experience of fostering, at least on the surface. For instance, some had become ill or moved, while some had adopted their foster child. However, in over half the cases the answers given to explain why they had stopped fostering related to dissatisfactions with the role and/or support given. Often the reasons for giving up were very similar to experiences of continuing foster carers, such as stress, the child's behaviour and the parents' actions. Perhaps their threshold for coping was lower, but equally they might have persisted if given more preparation and support, as some of their comments indicated. Those who gave up for service-related reasons also usually recorded less good relationships with social workers than continuing foster carers and wished they had been given more help (e.g. in the form of short breaks). Interestingly, the agencies often appeared unaware that foster carers had stopped as a result of grievances, since they had recorded mainly pragmatic reasons for ceasing to foster.

Foster carers are less likely to give up if they feel well prepared for the tasks they undertake. For a considerable time now, it has been recognised that carers should not only be assessed for their suitability before starting to foster, but should be equipped with relevant knowledge and skills. Fostering is not the straightforward care of children that anyone with good will can do. Even experienced parents can struggle with elements of the role, such as helping children recover from abuse, handling sexualised or aggressive behaviour and relating to "difficult" birth parents in a positive way. Initial preparation or training is now offered routinely to foster carers and in many areas supplementary or specialist short courses are available too.

Gilchrist and Hoggan (1996) described an innovative approach to training, which included birth parents. It was hoped that this would help foster carers understand and empathise with their feelings and difficulties. The staff realised that it would be daunting for most birth parents, so it was planned that the parents' social workers would attend the training session to provide support. The programme was carefully planned to promote discussion and to give attention to positives as well as negatives in parents' lives. The birth parents shared their strong apprehensions about meeting foster carers and made a number of practical suggestions about how social workers and carers could make that process easier. Pleas were also made to simplify the language and agendas of review meetings.

Staff and carers valued hearing about the details of birth parents' emotions and wishes. Just as important, the parents themselves were pleased and proud to have been given a positive role in the training process. Gilchrist and Hoggan also noted that this development illustrated that innovations can occur in the public as well as the voluntary sector. Key ingredients were adequate resources, autonomy and ready access to decision-makers.

Other accounts of preparation for fostering and adoption in England and elsewhere are available (Triseliotis *et al*, 1995b; Argent and Kerrane, 1997) and these often provide feedback from participants. However, positive experiences of training do not necessarily make a difference to the actual performance of those taking part, so it is helpful, though difficult, to obtain systematic evaluations of the impact of training. **Minnis and Divine (2001)** wrote about a rare example of an attempt to assess whether training could help foster carers reduce children's problems. Unusually in research in this field, the study took the form of a randomised controlled trial. This meant that foster families were randomly allocated to one of two groups, the first receiving standard preparation and the second attending an additional dedicated three-day course. As a result of the random process, the range of previous experience and competence in both groups should have been very similar, so that any differences ought to be due to the extra training.

The training was based, firstly, on understanding the origins of foster children's unusual feelings and behaviour in their personal history of trauma and, secondly, on open communication. The approach was inter-active and individualised. The foster carers liked it and found it helpful. They reported that the course improved their relationship with the child and their caring abilities (Minnis *et al*, 1999).

However, attendance at both routine and extra training was low, with only about half those invited actually attending. Moreover, the evidence about impact on the children did not support the claims of the carers. Small improvements were detected, but there were not statistically signifi-cant gains compared with those who only attended the routing training. It is possible that the research measures were not sensitive enough to detect changes, but the more likely implication is that training was insufficient in scale to have much effect on the capacity of carers to address the "massive needs" of these children.

In addition to assessing the training, the study provided details showing (like previous research) that children looked after away from home have very high rates of challenging behaviour and mental health difficulties. Over nine in ten had been abused or neglected, with the very high figure of three-quarters having been sexually abused. Attachment disorders and low self-esteem were also common. Despite this, 40 per cent of the children were progressing well. During the training, foster carers de-scribed the wide-ranging and often unpredictable situations in which children communicated about their experiences of loss and abuse.

Although fostering is a family-based service for children, the position of foster carers' own children – now often referred to as "sons and daughters" – was long neglected. A small flurry of articles on this topic appeared within a short period in the early 1990s (Ames Reed, 1996; Pugh, 1996), as well as a video-tape (National Children's Support Group, 1990). These highlighted that the sons and daughters of foster carers were usually very involved with their fostered "siblings". They made important contributions, for example by listening, giving advice, acting as role models or simply providing enjoyable company. They were also much affected emotionally by the past and current difficulties and in some cases abuse experienced by the fostered children. Yet social workers usually paid little attention either to the needs of carers' sons and daughters or to their role in supporting the child and placement. This is an important omission for at least two reasons. Firstly, foster carers' sons and daughters are children too and entitled to have their interests considered. Secondly, the adverse impact on their own children is one of the main reasons why foster carers cease to foster (Triseliotis *et al*, 2000), so that sensitivity to their needs and providing appropriate responses could reduce placement breakdowns.

One article on this theme was based on Scottish research in Tayside. Here **Part (1993)** obtained the views of 75 children of foster carers in 43 families by means of self-completion questionnaires. Four-fifths of those who took part said they liked fostering, whereas one-fifth disliked it or were uncertain whether it was a good thing. Although the great majority were positive about fostering, many of these described aspects that were difficult or upsetting. The most common complaints were about coping with the foster child's difficult behaviour, resentment at the attention given, lack of privacy and the need to share. For the most part, these drawbacks were outweighed by the benefits of fostering. The most common gains were companionship, the pleasures of young children and the satisfactions of helping and broadened horizons.

Part described the circumstances and views of the small number of young people who actively disliked fostering. Interestingly each had at least one brother or sister who was positive or mixed about fostering, so that responses within the same family tended to be varied.

Overall it appeared that fostering was a positive experience for most of the family members involved. However, it could often be problematic, especially when the fostered children were in their teens. Part concluded that more attention should be given to the views and needs of young people – 'to help families continue through and after the difficult times' (p 353).

19 Recruiting and retaining foster carers: implications of a professional service in Fife

Donald Ramsay

This article was first published in Adoption & Fostering *20:1, 1996.*

The development of foster care began in Scotland in the mid-nineteenth century (Triseliotis *et al*, 1995), although different forms of boarding-out existed as far back as the seventeenth century and beyond (Reeves, 1980). Its original aim was to provide substitute parents for children requiring public care. Some maintenance allowances were paid for looking after children but there was an historical view which persisted well into the following century that self-sacrifice was an 'essential ingredient of the mother–child relationship', and that 'payment for the work cut at the roots of [that] relationship' (Care of Children Committee 1946, cited by Smith, 1988).

The traditional role of foster carer was to act as substitute parent, so very often contact between the child and the birth family was discouraged in an attempt to strengthen the fostering relationship. Short-term care and reunification came to be seen as complementary goals only after the 1948 Children Act (Triseliotis *et al*, 1995). Different skills were required as the role developed from foster parent to foster carer, e.g. working with birth families and contributing to case planning. The speed and scope of these changes were increased by the philosophical and economic movement away from residential care towards community-based care in the 1980s: specialist foster carers or community carers were recruited to care for children with particular disadvantages who were previously thought to require children's home or other residential care.

As a consequence of this change in direction children entered foster care with a wider variety of needs, and made additional demands on foster carers (Bullock, 1990). Bullock argued that if foster carers were wanted to take disturbed or disabled young people they would have to be partners rather than agents of social workers. Indeed, Bebbington and Miles (1990) wrote that many carers were leaving fostering because they felt undervalued and unsupported. Triseliotis *et al* (1995) cite a US study which found the attrition rate of foster carers reduced when they were better paid, better supported and better trained by the agency (Chamberlain *et al*, 1982).

Nonetheless, attitudes towards the financial reward of foster carers still vary across the country, both among agencies (National Foster Carers' Association, 1990) and among carers (Smith, 1988). The National Foster Carers' Association (NFCA) reported wide differences in allowances paid by authorities – over and above whether or not a financial reward element was included; this despite NFCA campaigns for increased standard allowances, predicated on the greater demands on foster carers to attend reviews and operate as quasi-professionals. Foster carers themselves, however, have shown ambivalence about payment; on the one hand not wanting to see themselves or be seen as mercenary, but also not wanting their commitment to be taken for granted or exploited.

In Fife, two types of foster carer existed during the 1980s: "traditional" foster carers/parents and "community carers". The "traditional" foster carers/parents received maintenance allowances based on the age of the child and any particular needs which caused extra expense. They were recruited, trained and supported by local field-workers. Community carers, on the other hand, were paid a professional fee plus maintenance allowances; they were contracted to take teenagers for up to two years. Initially, community carers were recruited, trained and supported by specialist social workers from the Adolescent Placement Scheme whose remit was to offer childcare placements as an alternative to residential care.

While older children often presented different types of care needs from younger children, it was convincingly argued that carers looking after younger children expended just as much energy as those looking after teenagers. Furthermore, all foster carers were expected to take part in child-in-care reviews, so there was no differentiation between the "professional" tasks expected of them. Consequently it was decided to rationalise the financial and professional support for carers by making conditions for all foster carers the same. Following departmental re-organisation in 1990, all carers were paid one professional fee per household as well as age-related allowances for each child. Professional support is now concentrated in two teams of specialist foster care social workers, amalgamating the area-based homemakers and the Adolescent Placement Scheme staff. Each foster carer household is allocated a link social worker from one of two foster care teams.

The White Paper 'Scotland's Children' (Cmnd 2286, HMSO, 1993) suggested that local authorities obtain a comprehensive picture of fostering resources in their area. Prompted by this, the foster care teams in Fife requested a survey from the social work department's research station. Its three aims were:

- to obtain an overall picture of fostering resources, complementing the information on individual files;
- to obtain a general picture of the rewards and difficulties foster carers experienced;
- to discover what made people interested in fostering, in order to guide future recruitment.

Ninety-two structured questionnaires were sent out and 72 were completed, a return rate of 78.3 per cent. Anonymity was offered to the foster carers to encourage candour in their replies and a high response rate. While these two objectives appear to have been met, it was not possible to identify any non-response bias accurately, although foster care social workers thought long-term carers of children from their own extended families were least likely to have replied.

Foster carer population

Sixty-three of the foster homes covered by the survey were provided by a married couple, the other nine by sole female carers. The lone carers were either divorced or widowed, i.e. none was never married.

The majority of carers were in their 40s (42 per cent) which is close to the finding of Dando and Minty (1987) who found the mean ages of female and male foster carers were 44 years and 47.5 years, respectively; and the 80 per cent of foster mothers in the study by Bebbington and Miles (1990) who were between 31 and 55 years old.

Twenty-three of the 126 married carers had been married previously and 40 per cent of those had children from their previous marriage. This figure comes very close to the 1987 figure obtained by Bebbington and Miles.

In two of the dual-carer foster homes both partners were unemployed; in the others at least one partner was in employment. In 13 homes one carer was employed full-time and the other was either self-employed or employed part-time, similar to the findings of Dando and Minty (1987).

Ninety-two per cent of homes had three or more bedrooms (compared with 90 per cent in Bebbington and Miles' study). Ninety-three per cent of foster homes had use of at least one private car, which is not a requirement of foster caring but confers a degree of mobility which helps them, among other things, to attend child-in-care reviews, meetings, etc.

Forty-six per cent of foster homes had a smoker in the household. This figure is similar to the proportion of smokers in the general population (Scottish Abstract of Statistics, 1993). It is not clear from the data whether the smokers are the foster carers themselves or other members of their family; this distinction may be relevant in respect of the role models foster carers and their own families present for children, although the risks of passive smoking apply whatever the age of the smoker.

Dando and Minty found 90 per cent of foster households had at least one pet – often two or three. The figure was slightly lower in Fife, 75 per cent of homes having at least one pet.

Foster carers in Fife therefore share many of the characteristics of foster carers in other recent surveys, irrespective of the service having been fully professional for five years. Where they may differ from carers in other authorities is in the role they are given in childcare provision. Fife greatly reduced its residential provision for children between 1980 and 1988, leaving only one social-work run residential establishment whose primary aim was assessment. Children received into the physical care of the department are, typically, placed with emergency foster carers. Then, if they require further care, they are matched with longer-term carers.

Support to carers

The survey was also used to gauge the value foster carers attached to the financial and professional support they received; and it was particularly important to assess the role of the professional fee. Rather than ask a direct self-report question about dependency on the fee, carers were asked whether they thought the fee had become part of foster carers' household budgets in general. They were then asked whether their own continued service as foster carers was dependent on receiving a fee.

Almost two-thirds of carers said they thought the professional fee had become an integral part of the household budget, and one-third said they thought it had 'possibly' become an integral part of household budgets 'for some carers'. Only 5.6 of carers said the fee was 'not usually' part of the household budget.

Over half of carers (59 per cent) said they would not be able to continue fostering if only maintenance rates were paid and the professional fee were withdrawn (though that was expressly not presented as a future proposal). Carers most likely to continue without a fee were those who had already fostered for more than ten years (55 per cent of this group).

It appears, therefore, that the professional fee has become a widely accepted, and indeed necessary, part of foster carer conditions of service. The spirit of voluntarism has not been eroded since, as Smith (1988) points out, 'a fair wage would far exceed current payments'. There is no evidence from the Fife survey that payment of a fee has been effective in attracting 'carers from previously under-represented groups, e.g. black people, low income, unemployed' (Rhodes, 1993). On the other hand, a professional fee has enabled carers, primarily women, to resist the lures and opportunities of the labour market, either by not seeking paid employment or taking part-time employment instead of working full time.

Besides its financial support to carers, the social work department also provides professional and group support. Preparation and training groups are run for people applying to foster; and foster carer support groups are run for all approved foster carers. Additional courses have been run for carers on relevant subjects, for example sexual abuse and HIV/AIDS. Each foster home has a link social worker, normally the worker who carried out their assessment. The link worker's main tasks are to ensure the carers' training and practical needs are met; to offer ongoing support and guidance; and to ensure placement contracts are drawn up which meet the needs of both child and carer.

A clear majority (69 per cent) of carers said they were satisfied with the support from their link worker "all of the time" and a further 29 per cent said they were satisfied "most of the time". Carers with more than ten years' experience were slightly more likely to say "most of the time" than "all of the time" while less experienced carers were most likely to say "all of the time" (see Table 1). This may mean that experienced carers are less reliant on their link worker and are more able to evaluate critically the support they provide; it may also mean that link social workers do not feel they have to give the same degree of support to the most experienced foster carers. Nonetheless, these figures represent a very high degree of satisfaction with professional support from the link social workers.

The same questions were asked of carers about support from the social workers of children currently placed with them. Although one of the link social worker's tasks is to effect liaison between the foster carer and the child's social worker, a lower degree of satisfaction was anticipated with support from the latter since lack of awareness of carers' needs, missed appointments and a too-hectic schedule are commonly thought to characterise the field-worker's lot. Encouragingly, over two-thirds of carers said they were either satisfied with the support from their foster child's social worker "all of the time" or "most of the time", and only 5.6 per cent said they were satisfied with their current child's social worker "none of the time".

As with support from link workers, the carers who were least likely to be satisfied with their child's social worker "all of the time" were those who had been fostering more than a decade, perhaps drawing on their years of experience to assess the support they were receiving. That said, two-thirds of the most experienced carers said they found the support from the child's social worker satisfactory most or all of the time.

Table 1

Comparison of satisfaction with support from 1) "link" workers and 2) foster children's social workers

	All of the time	Most of the time	Some of the time	None of the time
1) Satisfaction with support from 'link worker'	66.6%	27.8%	1.4%	0
2) Satisfaction with support from child's social worker	35.2%	32.4%	23.9%	5.6%

NB Total percentages are less than 100 per cent because of two missing cases.

Recruitment

It is likely that people are attracted to fostering by a combination of general factors, e.g. knowledge of foster carers, childhood experience, a desire to contribute. It is worth noting, however, the things which foster carers identified as the trigger for applying to the social work department since this has implications for future recruitment. Twenty-five per cent were prompted to apply having seen an article or advert in a newspaper; 11 per cent said they were attracted to fostering by a television programme or advertisement; 25 per cent said their interest was prompted by a friend or relative who was fostering; and 33 per cent did not identify a particular event which triggered their interest but said it had been long term.

Advertising cost is a major consideration in recruitment so adverts in the local press have provided the mainstay of recruitment campaigns. However, the local press had a relatively low circulation among foster carers, with only 16.5 per cent buying a local paper. Indeed only six foster homes whose interest was prompted by a press advert bought a local paper. The national press and television are seen to be too expensive and inappropriate media for local recruitment, although national campaigns have also stimulated interest in fostering at local level. (Data are not available on the number of applications received from different forms of recruitment; nor are the numbers known of people who sustain their interest and who are subsequently approved.)

Given that one-quarter of foster carers were motivated to apply from an acquaintance with friends or relatives who fostered already, the reward and recognition carers receive from the fostering agency is likely to be an important influence on the image of fostering acquired. As Reeves (1980) points out, foster carers are less likely to recruit others if they feel the fostering agency's organisation is poor. Conversely, foster carers are more likely to attract new recruits if they feel valued by the agency and find the work rewarding.

Retention of foster carers

High levels of satisfaction with social work support are important in retaining the services of foster carers. In turn, stability in the foster care population offers greater continuity of care for children and adds to the sum of fostering skills in the area. Three-quarters of carers in the survey said they intended to continue fostering for more than five years. Sixteen per cent said they would continue for three to five years, and less than six per cent intended to give up within three years. All but one of those who anticipated giving up within three years were aged over 50, indicating that changes in personal circumstances were more influential than the degree of satisfaction with social work support in determining turnover of foster carers. Changes in life-stage and preferred lifestyle aside, these figures suggest a low turnover of carers can be expected.

Local foster carer groups provide a valuable conduit for suggestions for improving the service, as well as providing mutual support and a forum for training. These groups notwithstanding, suggestions for improvement of the service were also invited in the survey. Many suggestions not only serve as reminders of good social work practice, they are also indicative of the contribution foster carers wish to make and the role they seek as partners of the social work department.

The most frequent plea from carers was for more frequent visits from the children's social workers and an increased involvement in case planning. A small number of carers asked for better information on the background and lifestyle of children prior to placement; and three carers also wished for follow-up information on children's progress after moving on from their placement. One recent suggestion, echoed in two of the completed questionnaires, was for an itemised payslip detailing the composition of the allowances being paid for children in care. Another suggestion was for identification cards for foster carers to use when taking children to hospitals, schools, etc. Work has already been undertaken to implement these suggestions.

Conclusions

Foster carers in Fife share many of the socio-demographic characteristics of foster carers in general. They exhibit considerable stability and satisfaction with their role despite changes in the nature of their task, particularly in the last ten years.

The evidence from the Fife survey clearly indicates that an element of financial reward, and the support infrastructure which link social workers and foster carer groups provide, play an important part in attracting and retaining a stable number of foster carers. The professional fee reduces the need for people to find alternative paid employment and allows them a degree of financial freedom to put into practice their wish to contribute to the care of children.

Foster care teams provide valued professional support to carers which acknowledges their role in child care and enhances the quality of the care they provide. As local authorities reorganise in 1996 and develop new structures with which to deliver services, a clear opportunity arises to ensure that adequate support systems for foster care services are established.

References

Bebbington A and Miles J (1990) 'Supply of foster families for children in care', *British Journal of Social Work* 20, pp 283–307.

Bullock R (1990) 'Implications of recent child care research findings for foster care', *Adoption & Fostering* 14:3, pp 43–45.

Dando I and Minty B (1987) 'What makes good foster parents?', *British Journal of Social Work* 17:4, pp 383–400.

National Foster Carers' Association (1990) *Foster Care Finance: Advice and information on the cost of caring for a child*, London: NFCA.

Reeves C S (1980) Chapter in Triseliotis J (ed.) *New Developments in Foster Care*, London: Routledge & Kegan Paul.

Rhodes P (1993) 'Charitable vocation or "proper job"? The role of payment in foster care', *Adoption & Fostering* 17:1, pp 8–13.

Smith B (1988) 'Something you do for love: a question of money and foster care', *Adoption & Fostering* 12:4, pp 34–38.

Triseliotis J, Sellick C and Short R (1995) *Foster Care: Theory and practice*, London: BAAF/Batsford.

20 Foster carers who cease to foster

John Triseliotis, Moira Borland and Malcolm Hill

This article was first published in Adoption & Fostering *22:2, 1998.*

Introduction

In recent years concern has often been expressed that there is a looming crisis in fostering as a result of difficulties in recruitment and retaining carers (see National Foster Care Association, 1997). Issues of supply and demand have often featured prominently in fostering literature over the last 50 or so years, but specific information has been lacking. In particular little is known about who ceases to foster and why. The only published research known to us on the matter is what came to be known as the "Portsmouth study", carried out some 20 years ago (Jones, 1975), and Gregg's (1993) study, also based on samples drawn from a single agency in England. In addition, Pasztor and Wynne (1995) provide a summary of US studies on the subject. The dearth of studies in this area is illustrated by the fact that Berridge's (1997) excellent review of foster care research for the Department of Health makes reference to only one study which was part of more extensive research carried out within a single English authority (Cliffe and Berridge, 1991).

We report on this issue from a much larger study which was prompted mainly by concerns about the supply and demand of foster carers in Scotland. The study was set up in 1996 with the twin aims first, of establishing who the carers are and second, identifying the policies, structure and organisation of the fostering services in 32 local authorities and one voluntary agency. The two parts of the study were designed to complement each other. The key aims were:

1 To examine the characteristics, motives and social circumstances of those who foster and seek explanations concerning the retention and loss of foster carers; describe the experience of fostering, including contact issues between parents and children; and evaluate post-placement support and general experiences of the fostering service.

2 To identify the policies, organisation and structures of the new social work departments for fostering, including the agencies' fostering needs, recruitment approaches, the preparation, assessment and training of carers, continued placement support to children and carers, the assessment of children and the matching processes followed, financial arrangements and monitoring mechanisms.

Phase 1 of the study, which was carried out in 1996, identified the characteristics and lifestyles of active and former carers and, more important, how they perceived the operation of the fostering services in 16 Scottish local authorities and in one voluntary agency. This article reports findings from this phase, but with the main focus on the former carers and why they gave up fostering. Where appropriate, data are contrasted with similar information from active or continuing carers. Knowing the former carers' views of why they ceased to foster, though only one of a number of aspects that have to be taken into account, nevertheless provides valuable feedback for agencies in developing their fostering services. The perspective of the agencies was pursued during the second phase of the study which took place in the summer period of 1997.

Sampling methods

Identifying exact figures of who ceased to foster and why was far from straightforward. Not all of the sampled authorities had accurate lists of those who ceased or, if they had, the lists did not always give the reasons why these had stopped fostering. Furthermore, modern systems of information technology had hardly been used to keep up-to-date information on issues of supply and demand, foster carer availability, preferences and so on. The implications for policy making, planning and monitoring arising from the absence of such basic information are obvious.

After a rather complex and laborious process, including tapping the memories of staff, we were able to piece together what we think is a reliable picture of those who ceased to foster in 1994 and 1995 and why. We are confident that in relation to two-thirds of the agencies featuring in the study we were able to obtain fully accurate information. With the remaining one-third we may be over- or under-estimating losses by about one per cent.

Methods of data collection

Information on carers who ceased to foster was obtained in three ways:

1 *Postal questionnaires* Of 216 former carers identified by the 17 agencies, postal questionnaires were sent out to 201 of them. (No questionnaires were sent to 15 carers who had been de-registered following mainly allegations of abuse.) Of the questionnaires sent out 97 (or 49 per cent) were returned. (One arrived too late to be included in the analysis.) The response rate was less satisfactory than the 74 per cent obtained from continuing carers.

2 *Agency records* Information was also obtained from staff and agency records on why the 216 carers gave up fostering. Eventually a picture was compiled on 149 (or 69 per cent) of the original 216 who withdrew or who were asked to withdraw. Data from this exercise were invaluable in helping to check with the replies received from carers through the postal survey.

3 *Personal interviews* Personal interviews were also held with 27 former foster carers who ceased to foster. These were randomly selected after excluding those who left fostering because of retirement. The interviews provided in-depth material which helped again to act as a check on the statistical data and on information obtained from staff and records. This form of triangulation has helped to provide a more accurate and consistent picture of why these carers gave up fostering.

The proportion who gave up fostering

During the two-year period preceding the start of the study, the 17 agencies had incurred a total loss of 216 carers. Between them the same agencies had 1,184 active foster carers, so the annual loss was around nine per cent. Translated into national figures for Scotland this would result in an annual loss of around 160 foster carers in relation to a total of about 1,900 fostering households. As was to be expected, there were variations between agencies. The lowest loss of four per cent was experienced by the only voluntary agency featuring in the sample, which had

51 active carers on its books. The highest loss of 13 per cent was incurred by a middle-sized agency with almost 100 active foster carers.

Our figures are similar to those reported from a recent survey carried out by the National Foster Care Association (NFCA) of English local authorities. The agencies in that study who answered the question on losses reported an overall eight per cent loss, with a quarter of these experiencing more than ten per cent (Waterhouse, 1997). No explanation was given about the nature of the losses. In contrast, the Portsmouth study, though poorly documented as far as actual numbers were concerned, identified an annual loss of around 27 per cent (Jones, 1975). Some American studies suggest up to 50 per cent losses within the first year of fostering (Pasztor and Wynne, 1995). With no previous Scottish studies to compare with, we cannot say whether these findings represent an improvement or not.

Background characteristics

The study contrasted a number of personal and background characteristics shared by former and continuing carers such as marital status, number of own children, religion, housing, ethnicity, health, educational qualifications, employment and social class. No significant differences were found between those who ceased to foster because of dissatisfaction with some key aspect of the operation of the fostering service and the active ones, except that those who ceased were more likely to:
- have poorer health at the time of giving up (female carers);
- have somewhat larger families and more own dependent children;
- be active worshippers (female);
- hold non-manual occupations (female);
- have larger houses.

Unlike Jones (1975), this study found no significant differences between age at recruitment and ceasing to foster.

Motivation to foster

When it came to their stated motivation to foster, no discernible differences could be identified between former and continuing carers. The same concerns and interests had attracted both the former as well as the continuing carers. Even certain differences found between female and male carers that were identified in the active group persisted within the group who ceased.

Overall, and except for those who enter fostering with a view to adoption or because it suits their family's circumstances at a particular point and time, looking for the carers' motives as a key reason for ceasing to foster does not appear to be a productive line of enquiry. It is possible that better methods of preparation and selection in the last decade or so have led to greater uniformity in the type of person who comes into fostering now.

The foster children

The study also contrasted the number and type of children fostered at any one time by continuing and former carers, the ages of the children, sibling groups, children with mental or physical disabilities fostered, type of fostering undertaken (including community care schemes for adolescents), difficulties presented by the children, breaks and holidays taken. No significant differences were again found except that former carers were more likely to:

- be fostering under-five-year-olds;
- have had fewer breaks;
- say they were not undertaking the kind of fostering they preferred;
- have had more difficulties with parents over contact.

Why carers ceased to foster

We now turn to the more vital question of why these former carers gave up fostering. Table 1 presents side by side the primary explanations offered by the surveyed former foster carers and those stated by fostering staff/ social work records.

While the main reasons for which foster carers cease to foster are diverse, there are also a number of consistent patterns which can be grouped into two broad categories: (1) internal factors connected with the fostering services; and (2) external factors.

1 Internal factors connected with the operation of the fostering services included:

- outright dissatisfaction with the operation of the fostering services;
- the children's behaviours;
- impact of fostering on own family/no privacy;
- burn-out/stress/no respite;
- allegations;
- biological parents' behaviours.

The above areas of dissatisfaction amounted to 57 per cent of all the responses. If we were to add those who said they had left because of ill-health resulting from the stress of fostering, then around three-fifths of carers left because of some aspect connected with the operation of the fostering services. These reasons did not always have to do with the behaviour or attitudes of social workers or the agency. A large part of it was related to the general implications arising from caring for some very

Table 1

Why carers ceased to foster based on the views of former carers and fostering workers/records

Explanations	Former f/carers' primary reason		Fostering staff's primary reason	
	N	%	N	%
Dissatisfaction with the service	25	26	3	2
Retirement or illness	18	19	32	22
Adopted the foster child	17	18	19	13
Children's behaviour	16	17	8	5
Needing to work, move, no space	14	15	30	20
Impact on own family, no privacy	12	12	13	9
Stress, no respite	10	10	6	4
Allegations	5	5	17	11
At own request or had enough	–	–	12	8
Biological parents' behaviours	4	4	–	–
End of unique placement	2	2	4	3
Other (bereavement, no placements)	5	5	5	3
Total	128*		149	

* The percentages are based on multiple responses and do not add up to 100.

problematic children. There was no evidence to suggest that those who ceased were fostering more problematic children compared to the rest. Hardly any black, Asian or mixed-race children featured in the study. The Portsmouth study too found that about half the responses of those who ceased were in some way connected with the operation of the fostering services (Jones, 1975), albeit withdrawals were much higher in that study.

On this basis the fostering services in Scotland can expect to have an annual loss of around six per cent (between 80 and 100 carers) who leave because of dissatisfaction with fostering, including the children's problems and for having had no placement. In contrast, Gregg (1993), based on his study of the carers of a single agency in England, claims that for foster carers ceasing to foster is 'a natural process'. Furthermore, though the social work support they received could have been improved, it was generally appreciated and found to be helpful. Inevitably studies based on single agencies simply show what is happening in that agency and findings cannot be generalised.

2   External factors included:
   • the adoption of the foster child;
   • illness/retirement;
   • no space or needing to work;
   • moving house.

Retirement and illness featured in almost a fifth of the responses offered (eight retired and four withdrew because of illness). With one exception, the 17 carers (or 18 per cent) who withdrew after adopting the foster child were some of the most satisfied with the fostering services. Other key explanations offered by carers included moving house, the need to work or no space. A few had been fostering for the sole reason of fostering only one child known to them. Once this was completed they withdrew.

Levels of congruence found between former carers and fostering workers/records

Though there were a number of similarities in the explanations offered by former carers and social workers of why carers ceased to foster, there were also notable differences. Fostering workers significantly underestimated the proportion of carers who withdrew because of dissatisfaction with the fostering services, the foster children's behaviours, stress and parental interference. They "exaggerated" the numbers of those who left because of moving house and/or the need to work, illness or retirement and "own request" (see Table 1).

The most glaring difference between the two groups was the much higher proportion of carers to fostering workers, who said they had left fostering because of outright dissatisfaction with the operation of the fostering services (26 per cent to two per cent). It could be argued that those who returned the postal questionnaire or spoke to us were not a true representation of all those who ceased to foster and that the fostering workers' views were more representative. We tried to check this by comparing the levels of congruence (where we had the names) between the views expressed by social workers and those of former foster carers. Where foster carers gave as their main reason for withdrawing the 'lack of social work support', the 'attitudes and behaviour of social workers' or 'the activities of the social work department', fostering workers tended to say the carers had withdrawn 'at their own request', 'own decision' or that 'they had had enough', or 'because of work commitments'.

It seems that in part carers' real reasons for ceasing to foster were not conveyed to fostering staff or adequately recorded. In other instances social work records used generalised explanations like 'own request' and 'own decision' which obscured the problem.

We can also make some comparisons between the explanations offered by the former carers who gave up because of factors associated with fostering, and those offered by continuing ones when describing times they felt like giving up. There were many similarities between the two. Both spoke about children's problems, chronic lack of social work support and related issues concerning the operation of the fostering service, including stress and effect on own family. On the basis of these findings, the difference between the two groups was one of degree rather than of substance. Eventually the pressure or a crisis become too much for some individuals, tilting the balance towards withdrawal.

Working relationships with the fostering services

Next we contrasted the perceptions of former foster carers with those of active ones on the quality of relationships with the children's social workers, link workers and the agency as a whole. The ratings of satisfaction offered by the former carers were, as expected, below those of continuing ones. The same applied when it came to the levels of support and whether expectations had been met or not.

However, it was thought that to obtain a truer picture all those carers who gave up for external reasons should be left out of the analysis, which should concentrate instead on the 50 carers who left because of definite dissatisfaction with some key aspect of the operation of the fostering services. These form the basis for the next section.

The overall picture that emerges from Table 2 is that just over half the former carers rated their relationship with the social workers and the agency as "good", or "very good", but the rating for "very good" was notably lower. As we say in the main report, carers were very discriminating between "very good" and "good". Somewhat more favourable ratings were given to relationships with the link workers. However, compared to continuing carers, former carers rated all three types of relationships significantly lower. Perhaps it was to be expected that, as far as relationships were concerned, former carers would feel more disillusioned compared to continuing ones.

Much of the dissatisfaction of the former carers with the children's social workers centred around the latter's failure to visit often enough or provide sufficient background information on the child, being unresponsive to requests for help and support when the children were being difficult, being unappreciative of their efforts and not being available when needed. Typical comments included: 'no support from child's social worker'; 'could have done with more support'; 'lack of commitment from certain social workers'; or "poor matching".

Worse in the eyes of the carers were telephone calls or other messages never being returned or being told the social worker was always somewhere else and unable to come to the phone: 'calls to child's social workers not being returned'; 'no say in what happens'; or 'being left to cope on our own'.

Table 2

Contrasting the rating of relationships between continuing and former carers who left because of dissatisfaction with some aspect of the fostering service

Relationship level	Relationship with social workers		Relationship with link worker		Relationship with agency	
	Cont.	Former	Cont.	Former	Cont.	Former
Level	%	%	%	%	%	%
Very good	46	31	68	40	37	18
Good	32	22	22	31	45	36
Neither good nor bad	13	14	8	20	13	26
Poor	6	18	1	7	4	12
Very poor	3	14	1	2	1	8
Total	100	99	100	100	100	100

Table 3

Levels of support as perceived by continuing and former carers

Level	Continuing %	Former %
Very good	37	12
Good	35	20
Neutral	18	40
Poor	7	16
Very poor	3	10
Total	100	98

There were a variety of other comments suggesting that as carers they had very little say in what happened to the children and there was little recognition of them as members of a working team or as partners.

Support

Another comparison made between the two groups of former and continuing carers was in the amount of support received.

The pattern found with relationships was repeated here but more strongly. Significantly fewer former than continuing carers described the level of support as "very good" or "good". Correspondingly, more former carers described support as neutral ("half and half") or as "very poor" to "poor". Former carers repeated some of the comments made earlier, especially infrequent visits, unavailability and unresponsiveness to requests for help. Nevertheless many were satisfied with the support contact but still gave up.

When asked to say whether their overall expectations of fostering had been met, only 29 per cent of those who gave up because of dissatisfaction with the fostering services said that they had. This contrasted with just over half of active carers who said their expectations were fulfilled. Their main explanation for the apparent disappointment was of fostering turning out to be much harder than they had expected and the lack of support from the fostering services.

Fostering experience

We also compared former and current carers' characteristics, and views on the service, in relation to their length of service. Carers who ceased to

Table 4

The number of years former carers had fostered compared with continuing carers

No. of Years	Former carers		Continuing carers	
	N	%	N	%
0–5	45	48	418	52
6–10	25	26	179	22
11–20	23	24	170	21
21–30	2	2	34	4
30+	–	–	5	1
Total	95*	100	806	100

*One missing

foster had an average of 7.5 years of fostering experience compared to 7.0 years of continuing ones. Even taking account of only those who ceased because of dissatisfaction with some aspect of the work of the fostering services, their fostering experience still amounted to an average of 7.3 years. It cannot be said, therefore, that those who withdraw do so only after a short period of caring. Just under half had fostered for less than five years, but over a quarter had fostered for more than ten years (see Table 4). In fact only nine per cent had fostered for less than a year compared to 40 per cent found by Jones (1975). However, almost all those who gave up before the first year was over were the ones who were dissatisfied with the fostering service.

The large percentage of carers leaving after a year prompted Jones (1975) to write that 'there is little to be gained from higher recruitment of foster parents if large numbers of recruits cease to foster only after a short period as an active foster parent' (p 41). There is no answer, perhaps, to the question of how long carers should be expected to foster before they give up. Would the perception of themselves as doing a professional job or having a career make any difference, or does the demanding nature of the job impose its own time-limits? As we say in the main publication, carers on the whole do not see themselves as making a career out of fostering.

Factors that triggered the final decision

Apart from those who retired or stopped fostering because of other external factors, the decision by the rest of the carers to cease fostering was not usually taken lightly. In the view of many, the situation had been building up over a period of time, but the final decision was usually triggered by some recent event such as action or inaction by the social work services, the behaviour of the placed child, deterioration of health, the need for a break or the end of a placement. Typical comments illustrating the precipitating factor included: 'disillusionment with the social work department'; 'trying to argue with social workers for better matching'; 'lack of support'; 'child's bad behaviour increased', 'the end of placement seemed a good time' or 'we could not take any more; our health and our family's life were affected'.

While the majority said that once they decided to stop nothing would have made them change their minds, there were a few who indicated that changes in attitudes within the social work services might have stopped them from giving up. Typical comments included: "with more support"; 'if the social work department's attitudes were different'; and 'changes in the social work department'.

Some of the above comments were repeated when asked what, if anything, might bring them back to fostering. A number mentioned changes in the operation of the fostering services, more space in their house, better health, better pay and better conditions of service or after their adopted child settled down. The total numbers of possible returnees, assuming their grievances were attended to, did not amount, however, to more than ten per cent of all those who ceased to foster.

Summary

The annual loss of foster carers for all reasons found among 17 agencies in Scotland was around nine per cent. There were variations between agencies but these were not usually high, suggesting a uniform practice across the country. The annual losses sustained for reasons relating to the operation of the fostering services amounted to almost six per cent or between 80 to 100 carers lost annually across the whole of Scotland. In England, with over 20,000 carers, this percentage would amount to around 1,000 carers lost each year. The losses are much lower than those found in the Portsmouth study some 20 years ago (Jones, 1975). Former carers fostered for an average of 7.5 years which may not seem low, though some agencies in the sample demonstrated that they could keep their carers longer.

There was no evidence that the majority of foster carers gave up easily. The reasons why they withdrew were diverse, but almost three-fifths were related to some aspect connected with the operation of the fostering services and the rest to external factors. Background characteristics and declared motivation were in most respects similar to those of active carers. The eventual decision to cease fostering by those who are dissatisfied is a culmination of four main interacting factors:

- a past history of unresponsiveness and unavailability of social work support;

- the child being more difficult than expected;
- unresponsiveness to requests for help and support during the most recent crisis;
- impact on own family.

The lower than expected losses should not lead to complacency. Many of the dissatisfactions expressed by those who ceased to foster were also shared by a significant proportion of continuing foster carers and require urgent attention. They include infrequent social work visits, unavailability of social workers, the stand-by service covered by staff who are not knowledgeable about fostering, absence of partnership, lack of information on the children's background, the children being more difficult than expected, stress arising from the fostering task and low pay. Meanwhile, fostering staff may have to establish more accurately and also properly record the main reasons for which carers give up.

Note
More details covering the first phase of the study on continuing and former carers appear in the publication *Fostering Good Relations: A study of foster care and foster carers in Scotland, Part I*, available from the Scottish Office Central Research Unit, 21 South Gyle Crescent, Edinburgh EH12 9EB.

The study was financed by the Social Work Services Group of the Scottish Office and co-ordinated by the Central Research Unit.

References

Berridge D (1997) *Foster Care: A research review*, London: The Stationery Office.

Cliffe D and Berridge D (1991) *Closing Children's Homes*, London: National Children's Bureau.

Gregg P (1993) *Why do Foster Parents Cease to Foster? A study of the perceptions of foster parents*, M. Phil. Thesis submitted to the University of Southampton.

Jones E (1975) 'A study of those who cease to foster', *British Journal of Social Work* 5:1, pp 31–41.

National Foster Care Association (1997) *Foster Care in Crisis*, London: NFCA.

Pasztor E M and Wynne S F (1995) *Foster Parent Retention and Recruitment: The state of the art in practice and policy*, Washington DC: Child Welfare League of America.

Waterhouse S (1997) *The Organisation of Fostering Services*, London: NFCA.

21 Involving birth parents in foster carer training

Anne Gilchrist and Pauline Hoggan

This article was first published in Adoption & Fostering *20:1, 1996.*

Lothian Region social work department has run a large foster care service since its establishment in 1975. In mid-1995 there were 330 foster families contracted by the social work department, caring for around 520 children and young people at any time. Since the early 1980s, the Department has had a growing commitment to promoting a high standard of care for children and concern for their birth families by providing effective training and ongoing support to substitute family carers, e.g. by payment of monthly fees as well as boarding-out allowances, by having specialist local staff teams dedicated to carer support and recruitment, and by the provision of planned training programmes and events.

For many years, prospective foster carers have been required to participate in a series of basic group preparation sessions before their approval as carers. Although workers have drawn on a number of sources for the style and content of these sessions, including their own ideas, much material has been drawn in recent years from the National Foster Care Association (NFCA) training packs, particularly *The Challenge of Foster Care*. Following the basic seven-session programme, staff in the carers' local district resource team offer regular support group sessions as well as topic-based training. For example, one district has commissioned the Barnardo's Skylight Project, which offers a post-sexual abuse support service for children and young people in care, to deliver a series of four-day sessions for foster carers on safe caring practice and helping abused children.

This article describes and discusses a recent initiative by one district resource team to involve birth parents in ongoing training for approved foster carers. The objective was to enhance the existing carers' sensitivity to birth parents' feelings and difficulties, and their ability to empathise with them.

Preparation

The resource team staff broached the idea of involving birth parents in a training session with their colleagues in the local practice teams which work directly with children and families. Workers within the teams responded positively to the idea and were able to obtain the involvement of five birth parents with children who were currently or previously in the care of the department. It was agreed that the parents' workers should attend the training session with them, particularly as this was a pilot venture and it was difficult to predict the level of protectiveness vis-à-vis independence which would be needed and wanted by the individual parents. In pre-discussion with the workers certain issues affecting particular parents were identified, thus enabling some of the possible implications of these issues to be explored at the training session. Among the issues were:

- alcohol dependency;
- lack of self-confidence;
- recurring severe depression;
- feelings of failure as a parent;
- feelings of being judged negatively.

The birth parents' experiences with carers ranged from very positive, through mixed to very negative – sometimes all these feelings being around for one person! The birth parents included men and women, all of whom had had experience of being a single parent. Care was taken to avoid involving birth parents and carers who already knew each other.

In the light of the sensitivity of the above issues, the workers attempted to structure the session in a way that minimised the vulnerability of the parents, for example by using small groups and ensuring that each parent's worker, who had a clear remit to support that person, remained alongside them throughout all the discussions. It was recognised that there was a risk of discussion focusing on negative experiences and perceptions in a way that might feel disabling, or even destructive. The workers provided a framework for the parents during their preparation session and during the introductory part of the evening by focusing on "what was" or "would have been" helpful when your child was in care, rather than "what was awful" about it. Workers from the resource team had the role of leading the small group discussions and part of their remit was to maintain this constructive framework. It was acknowledged that one of the drawbacks of this particular session was the unusually large number of social work staff present (ten).

Programme

The event was held one evening during the middle of the week. The venue was a comfortable community room adjacent to a social work department office.

7.30 pm: *Introduction* highlighting the importance of carers' sensitivity to feelings and issues which might be around for parents at different stages of the placement. These stages could be:
- when the decision is taken to place the child in care;
- the actual move;
- the first visit after the move;
- subsequent face-to-face contact;
- participation in reviews;
- when the child goes home or moves to another placement.

7.50 pm: *Small group discussion* about how these different stages were experienced and the feelings around. Each group consisted of a birth parent, the parent's worker, carers and a resource team worker. The latter was responsible for encouraging group discussion, promoting participation and sustaining a constructive framework, as well as providing feedback to the larger group at the end of the session.

8.40 pm: *Coffee and social chat.*

9 pm: *Drawing the threads together*, based on feedback from the small groups (five in all, with 25 carers).

Feedback

The initial stage of placement

The discussions highlighted parents' feelings of anxiety, "uptightness" and the fantasies they had about the consequences of their child being in care. As Triseliotis *et al* comment, 'Parents may have all sorts of misconceptions about fostering and varying degrees of guilt, anxiety and suspicion about foster parents looking after their child' (Triseliotis *et al*, 1995, p 170). They spoke of the helpfulness of introductory visits and meetings and the vital importance of being involved in the planning. The importance of good communication between all parties (carer, social worker and parent) was emphasised, for instance the importance of returning phone calls to give straightforward practical information about times of meetings. It was clearly much easier for parents when they felt comfortable with a carer and their setting. Attention was drawn to the feelings parents have of fear, guilt, jealousy and lack of self-respect. One parent spoke of how difficult it was, in the face of her huge feelings of failure and inadequacy, to have to meet carers for the first time in their own comfortable, well-run home. She thought it might have been easier if the initial meeting had taken place in a more neutral setting, such as the social work office. However, subsequent discussion with workers suggested that the carer's home was felt by other parents to be a more relaxed venue.

First and subsequent visits and contacts

Again attention was drawn to how "judged and threatened" parents can feel and the value of feeling welcomed by carers. This can be helped by focusing on the child, i.e. talking about how they are doing and what has been happening in his or her day-to-day life. One practical issue which emerged was that, because our department always has an initial 72-hour review, it often coincides with the birth parent's first visit. The business-like focus necessitated by the review and the presence of other staff such as the senior social worker makes it more difficult for the carers to provide a relaxed and welcoming ambience for parents. This points to the importance of workers making greater efforts to ensure that the parent's first visit to the carer's home happens before the 72-hour review and/or that review meetings do not take place in the carer's home, if for some reason it is inappropriate for a visit to take place so soon.

The role of good communication between carers, parents and social workers in promoting a positive visiting pattern was stressed, as was the need to be "upfront" in sharing information. The lack of a phone on the part of either party (usually the parent) makes it more difficult to sustain regular informal communication. The importance of being given detailed information about what the child was doing was emphasised, as was the need to be given sufficient time and space to do something with the child independently. The difficulties inherent in supervised access arrangements were noted, but time (and probably the public nature of a group setting) did not allow for this topic to be explored in any depth.

Birth parents valued a welcoming approach on the part of carers, which gave reassurance about their role as parents and about their child's attachment to them. One parent referred to the courteous approach of her child's carer, who not only provided coffee but also home baking, 'as if I was somebody important'. Parents also appreciated their opinion being sought in relation to the child, for example about their ways of dressing, expectations about them and their behaviour at school. One parent valued the straight approach of a carer who could clearly explain to her why arrangements for weekend visits needed to be made so that the carer and child would be at home when the parent came, and to ensure space and privacy for the visit.

Another learning point related to a parent feeling that a flexible, open-ended invitation to visit was insincere and that it was important for carers and workers to check out with parents their preferences. Some parents might find it easier to have specific times and set arrangements for visiting and other contact. Another parent explained the difficulty of having her children placed geographically near her home, despite this being against her explicit wishes. This was very uncomfortable for her and, she felt, made it much more difficult to sustain helpful boundaries between the two homes. It also made the situation much more visible to the local community, which she experienced as humiliating. The importance of checking out lifestyle patterns for the child and new carers was highlighted. This included such matters as eating habits and mealtimes, bedtimes and style of family communication, so that some kind of continuity or bridging could be consciously built in for the child's benefit.

The observations and feeling expressed by the parents reflect and re-affirm much of the good practice guidance offered in recent years in the literature published by British Agencies for Adoption and Fostering (BAAF), particularly in *Contact: Managing visits to children looked after away from home* (Hess and Proch, 1993) and *Foster Care: Theory and practice* (Triseliotis *et al*, 1995).

Participation in reviews

All five parents had attended reviews and saw this as an important entitlement. They commented on the frequent use of jargon by pro-fessional staff. Another complaint related to overloaded discussions where too many issues were addressed. Both carers and parents spoke of having no say as to what was to be discussed. Some parents were unhappy that certain issues were addressed in the presence of their children – not always appropriately, they felt.

The role of the chairperson of childcare reviews and child protection case conferences has recently been highlighted in updated departmental training and guidance, and chairs are now expected to make time before meetings to discuss the process and content of the meeting with parents and children.

Moving back home

There was considerable awareness of how difficult and confusing this process can be for the child, attention being drawn to the need for conscious and detailed work with them at this stage. Comment was made about the range of feelings experienced by parents, for instance apprehen-siveness as well as eagerness for the child's return, and the usefulness of maintaining contact between carers, parents and the child in order to provide continuity of relationships for the child.

Outcome of the session

While much that was shared and referred to was reasonably familiar to carers and staff, they all recognised the value of highlighting again and in more explicit detail the extremely painful and difficult feelings of parents.

The parents' workers underlined the importance of continually reminding themselves of the rawness of such pain, in order to ensure that our sensitivity to it, as workers and carers, is not dulled.

Perhaps most significant of all was that all the parents commented on how positive they had found the experience of taking part in the training. There were a number of different strands to this:

- a sense of being accepted and perceived as having a contribution to make;
- a greater sense of partnership or parity with carers and professionals, an offshoot of which was the "demystifying" of what carers had to offer;
- a sense of relief and comfort from knowing that carers, too, feel anxious and vulnerable.

The workers also expressed the view that the session had been positive and enjoyable for them.

The importance of aspiring to this sense of mutual learning and respect is reflected in many studies which include consumer feedback, such as June Thoburn's recent findings on parents' experiences of child protection investigations.

All family members stressed the importance of being cared about as people. They could understand that the professionals had a job to do . . . but strongly objected to workers . . . who did not appear to listen, did not show warmth and concern, and just did things by the book. (Thoburn, 1994, p 66)

The workers' experience of this event has been shared with the other district resource teams and similar events could become standard post-approval training. While it is possible that, with increased confidence in the process, training organisers might be able to have less intensive involvement by such a high number of staff, it is essential to heed the lesson from this experience, about the benefits of careful planning, debriefing and attention to detail in achieving a successful outcome.

Conclusion

The event we have described took place in the context of the radical shift in perception there has been since the establishment of social work as a profession which was dominated by a culture in which decision-making by and about clients was made in secret by so-called experts with little, if any, commitment to encouraging the participation of non-professionals. Over the last 15 years, there have been substantial moves towards involving substitute family carers in practice development; for example, since the early 1980s our agency has routinely deployed (and paid sessional fees to) experienced foster carers and adopters to contribute to training. The move towards more openness in adoption means that, in many areas, it is now more common than not for birth parents to meet with prospective adopters before their child's placement. In the child protection context, several years ago many professionals would never have envisaged that social work managers, medical consultants and police officers would have found it acceptable – and indeed desirable in the interests of effective decision-making – to have parents participating throughout a child protection case conference. However, the outcome of the introduction of such practice consistently shows benefits for the quality of the service, particularly if professionals tackle potential difficulties in a constructive manner and if policy implementation is not flagrantly tokenistic. For instance, little purpose is served in setting up events such as case reviews at which parents may be physically present but not genuinely enabled to participate, thereby making it likely that the real decision-making will still take place elsewhere.

Another aspect of our local and national context is the change in Scotland this year to mainly smaller local authorities, combined with pressure to move towards private or voluntary sector provision of services traditionally provided directly by the public sector, such as the large mainstream fostering services. This training event provided a good example of specialist staff with dedicated time, working within a local authority, being able to carry out innovative work and benefiting from their ease of access to decision-makers and to the relevant resources (in this case, family social workers and the birth parents). If there is a move towards non-public sector agencies providing more of these services, it is essential that they have the kind of close professional relationships and credibility with key staff responsible for work with children and families, so that practice development such as this can be initiated from a point at which the child and family are the centre.

On the other hand, it is important not to be tempted to see public sector delivery of service as being automatically the most effective or best value for money. Although the staff in this resource team had relatively straightforward access to the resources they required, the event was by no means cheap. In order to carry it out effectively, it required a higher than normal number of resource team staff to work in an evening running a group, and there were also expenses to cover the birth families workers' time and for the parents themselves, in addition to the preparation and de-briefing time required to ensure that the event could be meaningful for all concerned. As David Berridge (1994, p 138) has observed, 'Foster care is only cheap if it's done on the cheap.'

References

Berridge D (1994) 'Foster and residential care reassessed', *Children & Society* 8:2, pp 132–50.

Hess P and Proch K (1993) *Contact: Managing visits to children looked after away from home*, London: BAAF.

Thoburn J (1994) *Child Placement: Principles and practice*, Aldershot: Wildwood House/Gower.

Thoburn J, Lewis A and Shemmings D (1995) *Paternalism or Partnership? Family involvement in the child protection process*, London: HMSO.

Triseliotis J, Sellick C and Short R (1995) *Foster Care: Theory and practice*, London: Basford/BAAF.

22 The effect of foster carer training on the emotional and behavioural functioning of looked after children

Helen Minnis and Clare Devine

This article was first published in Adoption & Fostering *25:1, 2001.*

Introduction

The Foster Carers' Training Project attempted to answer two main questions:
- What emotional and behavioural problems do children have in foster care?
- Can training help foster carers to reduce children's problems?

The study consisted of a randomised controlled trial in which 121 foster families, with 182 children from 17 Scottish local authorities, were randomly allocated into two groups. Any family could take part if they were looking after children aged five to 16 who were likely to be in placement for a further year. The "intervention" group was invited to attend three full days of extra training and the "control" group received standard services alone. Before the training, immediately afterwards and nine months later foster carers, teachers and children were asked to complete questionnaires. We were particularly interested in the children's general mental health, their self-esteem and symptoms of attachment disorders. Background information was obtained about the children (physical or learning disability, past abuse, placement history, parental access) and their birth families (mental health, substance misuse, criminal record) by means of a standard telephone interview with social workers, who consulted case files.

The training

The training was based on a Save the Children Manual, *Communicating with Children: Helping children in distress*, by child psychiatrist Naomi Richman (Richman, 1993). Originally designed for people caring for children who had been affected by war and other disasters, its focus is to help carers understand the behaviour and feelings of children and to be open to their communication about themselves. Our use of this manual was based on the assumption that many children in foster care have experienced disasters and wars, albeit private ones. With this in mind, it was felt that the contents of the manual could be equally relevant to this group. The aim of the training was to help foster carers develop their skills in communication and increase their confidence in understanding and coping with their foster children's feelings and behaviour.

The training was piloted with eight carers and the final format has been described previously (Minnis *et al*, 1999). Based on principles of adult learning, it was consultative in style, with discussion and dialogue being the main vehicles for learning, recognising that carers brought their own knowledge and skills about caring for children (Knowles, 1984). Carers talked about themselves, their foster children and their communications. This led to sharing among the group so that there was peer training, with the trainer acting as facilitator rather than expert teacher. During introductions, the children were described and, although not physically present in the room, they were the focus of much of the work. It was the trainer's task to recognise each child's uniqueness, enabling participants to make links between the learning about communication with children in general and the specifics of the particular child they were looking after. The material discussed during the training was of two kinds: firstly, information based on the manual and some of trainers' own material was presented on flipcharts; secondly, examples of communications and behaviours presented by the children/young people looked after by participants provided live case material for discussion. There was no role play, much to the participants' relief.

Empirical findings

Of those families offered entry to the study, 42 per cent agreed to take part and these families were found to be similar, in their level of deprivation and rate of placement breakdown, to those who did not take part.

What problems did the children have?
Almost all (93 per cent) of the children were known to have been abused or neglected according to information given to us by children's social workers (see Table 1). Over 70 per cent had been in care before, eight per cent in more than five previous placements. Nearly 30 per cent were described as having a learning disability, although 87 per cent of these were "mild". Twenty-two per cent had no contact with birth parents, but we have no information on the reasons for this.

To examine the children's mental health, we used a screening instrument called the Strengths and Difficulties Scale (Goodman, 1997; Goodman *et al*, 1998) which has questionnaires for carers, teachers and children. This gives an overall score with a cut-off point above which children are likely to have problems of clinical significance. It also has various subscales measuring hyperactivity, emotional problems (anxiety and depression), conduct problems and problems with peer relations. According to both foster carers and teachers, over 60 per cent of the children in the study had some degree of mental health problems. Around 50 per cent had problems with hyperactivity, 60 per cent had conduct problems and 50 per cent had problems with peer relations. Foster carers thought that 45 per cent of children had emotional problems, but teachers

Table 1
Previous experience of abuse

Type of abuse	Percentage experiencing this in the past
Physical abuse	40%
Sexual abuse	77%
Emotional abuse	75%
Neglect	75%
Any type of abuse or neglect	93%

thought only 12 per cent did, a figure which is nearer to the level of problems found in the general population. This is particularly interesting as it has been noted in another recent study that the number of children suffering from major depression can be grossly underestimated by others (McCann *et al*, 1996).

We developed a questionnaire for the study to measure attachment disorders, called the Reactive Attachment Disorder (RAD) scale. As it had not previously been used in children of this age, we recruited a comparison group of 251 children from Glasgow schools. This comparison group was considerably more deprived than the general population but, despite this, the looked after children had significantly higher scores for attachment disorders than the "school" children (see Figure 1). Similarly, using the Modified Rosenberg Scale (MRS) (Warr and Jackson, 1985), the looked after children were shown to have significantly lower self-esteem scores than the "school" children.

There were some interesting associations between past and current problems. In all of these analyses, the child's gender and age were taken into account. There was a significant association between attachment disorders and sexual abuse ($p = 0.02$). While, at face value, one might assume that sexual abuse leads to attachment disorders, it is possible that children with attachment disorders might be more vulnerable to sexual abuse. The characteristic features of an attachment disorder include disinhibited behaviour and indiscriminate friendliness (World Health Organisation, 1992), both of which could put children at risk of abuse.

As some other studies have found (Gean *et al*, 1985; Cantos *et al*, 1996), mental health problems in general were significantly associated with the number of previous placements the child had been in ($p = 0.04$). Current mental health problems were also associated with past sexual abuse ($p<0.001$) and emotional abuse ($p = 0.001$). A surprising finding, in view of the fact that we only had information on 42 birth fathers, was that there was a significant association between current mental health problems and the birth father having a criminal record ($p=0.03$). This is an area which needs further study before conclusions can be drawn as to the reasons for this association.

Figure 1

The statistical association between fostered and school children on the RAD scale

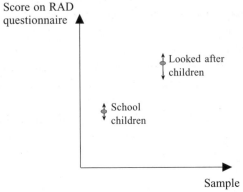

Note: The error bars do not overlap, therefore the difference is statistically significant.

Children's progress nine months after the training

Before examining the effect of the training programme, we looked at the progress of the whole sample after nine months. Approximately 13 per cent of placements had broken down over this period, a rate which compares well with other studies (Berridge and Cleaver, 1987; Strathclyde Regional Council Social Work Department, 1991). In this study, 'placement breakdown' was defined as any placement which ended in a manner not in accordance with social work plans.

We assessed the link between behaviour and foster carers' previous experience. Figure 2 shows the association between the placement breakdown and the numbers of children the carers had previously looked after. In this figure, the "odds ratio" is the number of times more likely a placement is to break down compared to the chances of breakdown if only one to five children had been looked after previously. For example, if a family had looked after between 31 and 60 children previously, the placement was ten times as likely to break down compared to a family who had looked after five children or less. Those foster carers who had already looked after more than 30 children were much more likely to

Figure 2
The odds ratio of placement breakdown *vs* the number of previous children looked after

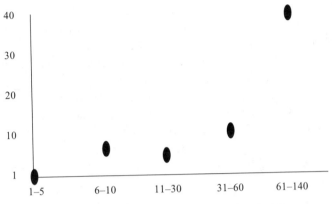

Number of children previously placed with carers

experience breakdown of the current placement, something already noted in previous Scottish research (Strathclyde Regional Council Social Work Department, 1988). The reasons for this are not clear. As participants in the study suggested at feedback meetings, perhaps more experienced carers are being expected to look after more disturbed children with less support. Perhaps they are experiencing burn-out. This phenomenon of loss of interest in and energy for work has been noted among the "caring professions" (Starrin *et al*, 1990). Unlike foster carers, though, most of these professionals have regular holidays and do not have responsibility for their clients 24 hours a day.

The level of deprivation of the immediate neighbourhood each foster family was living in was measured using Carstairs scores, a composite measure of unemployment, car ownership and social class based on small post-code areas. We found that carers from more deprived social backgrounds had a lower rate of breakdown of placement (p = 0.03). This is not something which has been shown before. Dando and Minty (1987), however, found that foster mothers who said they had had unhappy experiences in childhood were seen by social workers as being good foster carers, perhaps due to an ability to identify with the children in their care.

Most children placed with foster carers come from very deprived backgrounds and perhaps the foster carer's ability to identify with the child extends to material circumstances and cultural attitudes. In the USA, Barth *et al* found that an increased rate of breakdown of adoptive placements was related to a higher educational level in the adoptive mother (Barth *et al*, 1988). This might be associated with more educated parents having expectations which are at odds with the adoptee's potential, leading to interpersonal stress and hence breakdown.

A very positive finding was that, regardless of whether families received extra training, the self-esteem of the children in foster care improved significantly over the nine months of the study (p = 0.03). It is impossible to be certain about the reasons for this, but it suggests that foster carers are able to provide an environment in which children can flourish.

The effects of the training

The participants of the pilot study thought that the training improved their relationship with the child and improved their ability to care for the children they looked after (Minnis *et al*, 1999). However, they did not think the training was likely to reduce children's problems because of all the other influences on their lives. A major aim of the main study was to see whether these impressions were borne out by the empirical research. During the course of the research project, foster carers had attended an average of six hours of training offered by the local authority. Forty-eight per cent had attended none at all. Of those invited to take part in our training programme, only 52 per cent attended. This level of attendance seems to be typical of training offered within current fostering services.

Those carers in the main study who did attend the extra training on offer were very positive about it. Like the carers in the pilot study, they enjoyed it, felt they had learned a lot and believed that it helped them to be better foster carers. However, in contrast with those in the pilot study, they felt it did have an effect on the children. They thought the child was better behaved and that they had a better relationship. When we looked at the questionnaire results, however, the predictions of those in the pilot study group were borne out. There were apparent improvements in mental health (five per cent reduction in symptom scores), attachment disorders

Figure 3
Changes following the training at nine-month follow-up

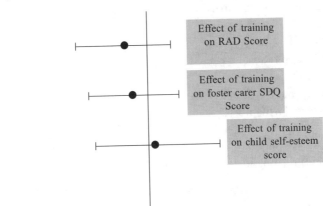

Change in questionnaire scores with training

(eight per cent reduction in symptom scores) and self-esteem (two per cent reduction in symptom scores) in those who were invited to attend the training compared to the control group.* However, the findings were not statistically significant and Figure 3 shows that while the mean scores on each scale changed in the hoped-for direction, the margins of error are such that confidence cannot be placed in the results.

Themes from the training

Although this was a quantitative study, rich information about the children and their foster carers emerged from the training. This illuminates the empirical findings.

---

* Those who were invited to the training but did not attend were similar to those who did, except that they had looked after more children and the children they were looking after had lower questionnaire scores for mental health problems at baseline (these differences did not reach statistical significance). Their non-attendance might be explained by these carers deciding they did not need training.

The children

The participants described a range of behaviours in the children, similar to those previously identified by Richman (1993):

- social withdrawal;
- apathy;
- poor concentration;
- restlessness;
- aggression and destructiveness;
- sadness and irritability;
- fear;
- difficulty in play;
- problems relating to other children;
- stealing;
- lies;
- difficulties in relating to adults;
- lacking of trust;
- 'testing out' behaviour;
- clinging.

These are typical emotional and behavioural symptoms of children who have experienced trauma and/or have attachment difficulties (Howe and Fearnley, 1999). Many children also had problems at school, both behavioural and in relation to learning, and some had been excluded. There were also children with pre-existing physical problems such as epilepsy, physical disabilities or developmental delays. Sometimes children's problems were expressed as physical symptoms, for instance:

- disturbed sleep;
- eating problems;
- aches and pains;
- dizziness and fainting spells;
- bed wetting;
- soiling.

Children's communication

Some of the themes in children's verbal communication were about profound issues, whereas others related to day-to-day events. Foster carers acknowledged, in the course of the training, that all could be important to the child. Some communicated feelings of being unloved and alone. For example, a newly placed six-year-old, during her first car journey with the carer driving, said 'Do you like me? I'm a bad girl; no one likes me'. The carer, stunned, was unable to answer and was relieved to get home. This was never discussed again, but the carer reflected during the training that this experience impacted on her relationship and subsequent communications with the child.

Children sometimes expressed confusion about who they were and where they belonged. For example, some wanted to use the foster carer's name or asked about where they would be for the following Christmas, birthday or holiday. When there was a lack of planning or drift, this created uncertainty and made it difficult for carers to give clear answers. Some children wanted to talk about past and current family experiences and relationships. Those in contact with birth families communicated about this in both words and behaviour. Carers often had difficulty responding appropriately and did not always know what to pass on to social workers.

Children's experience of death was an important theme and magical thinking could complicate matters. A five-year-old thought she had caused the death of the male carer in her previous foster home. This only emerged when she was reluctant to sit on her current carer's knee. When asked about this, she explained that because she had sat on her previous carer's knee, he had a sore knee and had died, and she had caused his death. Another child thought she had caused her grandmother's death because 'she was old and sick and had to look after me'.

Not infrequently, carers had to deal with disclosures of abuse. A foster carer spoke of disclosure from a nine-year-old boy when she was bathing him. She spoke of her shock but also of her awareness of the need to stay calm and to listen for his sake. Foster carers also had to deal with questions from children about both ordinary sexual development and sexual identity, discussing the facts of life and providing guidance about behaviour, rules and boundaries. One carer described a young boy who wanted to wear lipstick and earrings. She accepted this as it seemed important to him.

These communications by children were often presented when carers were least prepared, for example, in public or in the midst of busy household activity. Because of this, carers said at times they did not listen or 'listened but did not hear'. They recognised the need to have time to talk with individual children and some had family times when issues were discussed. The use of "third things" as described by Clare Winnicott, eg animals, letters and the telephone, were important vehicles for communication. For vulnerable traumatised children even the smallest change in routine was important and carers had to explain in detail to some children the reason for any alterations. This was highlighted by carers' attendance at this training programme and the need to make childcare arrangements clear to the child. For insecure children who had experienced many separations there was the concern that their carer might not return.

In discussion, foster carers identified various blocks to communication. Firstly, blocks occurred in the children themselves. Many had low self-esteem, had experienced rejection, felt unloved, did not expect to be cared for and felt to blame for their situation. There were difficulties in communicating with a child who was distressed and angry or withdrawn, and in managing the behaviour of those who were out of control. Secondly, the carers' own feelings about their past and childhood could get in the way. On the other hand, insight and understanding of their own childhood helped them to understand and empathise with the children. Thirdly, there was an affect on carers of knowing the facts of a child's life, either through disclosure or through the information provided by social workers. Despite this impact they were aware of the need to know, the need for them to deal with associated feelings and receive appropriate help with this. Not being kept informed about the child's past, present family issues and future plans could produce major blocks to communication. Conversely, clear consistent exchange with social workers was said to help carers in their communications with children and young people. For example, a carer described a social worker's life-story work with a young boy whose mother had died and who was silent and withdrawn. At the end of each session the social worker spent time with the carer, while the boy was still present, to keep the carer in touch with the child's feelings and with current issues. This in turn helped the carer respond to the youngster on a day-to-day basis.

Foster carer responses

Communication with children at all levels was clearly an integral part of the role of participating foster carers. Some were already skilled verbal communicators and observers of the nuances of children's behaviour. For example, upon waking two newly-placed siblings, a foster carer found that both had soiled their beds and were clearly very anxious about her response. With acceptance she reassured the children: 'Come on my wee darlings into a nice warm bath and I will clean you up.' One foster father spoke enthusiastically about the enjoyment he got from talking with the teenagers he fostered. He described them as 'little apprentices of life' and felt that these conversations were among the most significant elements he had to offer.

Support

Carers were clear that at times they needed support and advice in understanding and making sense of a distressed and distressing child's behaviour and communications. They looked for help from a range of sources: family and friends, link social workers, the child's social worker, teachers or GPs. They sometimes felt the need for more specialist input from psychologists or psychiatrists. This request was not always heard or responded to. For instance, some specialists were not prepared to provide a service until the child was in a permanent situation. In seeking support, the kind of qualities carers sought in those they approached, both for themselves and for the children they looked after, were trustworthiness, honesty, preparedness to listen, empathy and taking them seriously. Where there was good, open, close and continuing communication between social workers and carers, they felt supported and helped in their care of the child. Where this did not happen, carers were left unsupported and struggling at times. This lack of support included material things such as transport or house extensions.

Learning from the training

Participants identified several key learning points from the training:
- Each child is unique.
- Everything, verbal and non-verbal, is communication.

- Children need to be listened to.
- Carers need to be listened to.
- Carers are in a key position to identify the needs/special needs of children.
- Looked after children have a range of difficulties and may need specialist help.

Discussion and implications for practice

The main aim of the study was to examine the effect of training on the emotional and behavioural functioning of looked after children. As a randomised controlled trial, the proportion of families who took part and the numbers involved were high enough to lend validity to the results regarding the outcome of training. A useful secondary outcome of the research was the interesting information gained about the characteristics of children and their families. However, the aim of the study was not to conduct a survey of foster families, and a response-rate of 42 per cent would not be seen as adequate to give a representative portrayal of this population, so these results should be viewed as preliminary.

An underlying assumption of the study is that better communication between foster carers and the children they look after will engender secure attachments between carers and children which will improve the emotional and behavioural functioning of these children, who may not have experienced secure attachments before. There is already good evidence that secure attachments between biological parents and infants, mediated through sensitive care-giving and reciprocal communication (Main *et al*, 1985; Reddy *et al*, 1997), have a positive effect on the psychosocial development of children (Crowell and Feldman, 1988; Goldberg, 1991; Lyons-Ruth, 1996; Warren *et al*, 1997). Research has also shown that an adult's ability to process his or her past attachment-related experiences has a direct relationship with the security of attachment with the child (Main *et al*, 1985). This research has, on the whole, taken place in normal populations. We do not yet know what facilitates children's new attachments when there has been severe, chronic disruption of relationships. Recent research in Nicaragua has shown that "foster mothers" in group care situations were more likely to communicate with children they looked after about difficult issues if they themselves had a secure adult attachment style. This suggests that adults who have come to terms with their own pasts are more able to help children in doing this (Reder and Lucey, 1995). We do not yet know for certain whether this improved communication is beneficial for the child's psychosocial development. Although there is a considerable literature on attachment and looked after children (Howe and Fearnley, 1999), there has been little actual research. This study aimed to test whether helping foster carers to understand and communicate with children would impact on the emotional and behavioural functioning of the children they were looking after.

It is clear that the impressions of the foster carers who participated in training, about their children, closely mirrored the findings of the empirical study. This is further evidence that foster carers are an important source of information about looked after children and their needs. The implications of certain empirical findings warrant further discussion. The finding that nearly all of the children in the sample were *known* to have experienced neglect and/or abuse in the past suggests that the population of children in foster care is even more vulnerable than had been previously realised. This sample was largely drawn from children in 'mainstream' foster care, not considered to have special needs. The findings demonstrate that this is not the case. The vulnerability of the children is further emphasised by the fact that over 60 per cent fulfil the criteria for being 'psychiatric cases'. In other words, if a population screening were taking place for mental health problems, 60 per cent of these children would be recommended for more complete psychiatric assessment with the assumption that the vast majority would, in fact, be displaying psychiatric symptoms. There are various important implications from these findings. Many children going into foster care do not receive a psychiatric screening at any time and, as has been found previously, this can lead to significant and even life-threatening mental illness being missed (McCann *et al*, 1996). The implementation of the Looking After Children materials could be a major step towards avoiding this, but only if forms are completed on every child, using information from someone who knows the child well, and appropriate action is taken on information gathered. Only a co-ordinated multidisciplinary response is likely to address the particular needs of this group (Dimigen *et al*, 1999).

The picture of the children's well-being was not entirely negative and the almost universal incidence of previous maltreatment leads to the question of why almost 40 per cent of these children are apparently doing well. This could, of course, be due to the fact that the instruments we used were not sensitive enough to detect problems which this minority of children have. Assuming, however, that our instruments were adequate, there could be various reasons. Current knowledge about the factors which promote resilience is being increasingly used in practice (Daniel *et al*, 1999). Perhaps these are children who, despite their disturbed background, found attachment figures who provided positive role models for them. Perhaps they have benefited from a positive, stable experience within a foster family or from excellent social work practice which has facilitated a resolution of past traumas. This group is a fertile potential source of answers to some crucial questions about what protects children in adversity, with obvious practical implications for social work practice.

The research revealed findings that were not part of the main research questions, but which merit discussion. For example, the findings about a higher proportion of placement breakdown for more experienced carers sound a cautionary note. It is easy to assume that families who have already looked after many children are continuing to do so successfully but this may not be the case. There is previous evidence that social workers are less likely to write negative impressions about foster families in case files than they are to write positive impressions (Strathclyde Regional Council Social Work Department, 1991). Therefore, it is easy to imagine that information about characteristics of certain foster families which may have led to a series of placement breakdowns may not have been passed on to new workers. A new worker would then have no choice but to place further children, based solely on the positive information about potential carers found in the case file. Additionally, it is possible that experienced carers might be expected to look after increasingly difficult children with decreasing amounts of support once their reputation as competent carers is established. All of these possibilities argue for close scrutiny of each placement on its merits and for continuing post-placement support for even the most competent carers.

The finding that carers living in more socially deprived areas are less likely to experience placement breakdown suggests that empathy with a child's background may count for more than material circumstances. It sounds another cautionary note to those on fostering panels to take a fresh look at the potential effects of carers' social background. The finding that the children's self-esteem improved over nine months is a very positive piece of evidence for the beneficial effects of foster care.

With regard to the impact of the training on children's emotional and behavioural functioning, the data revealed no clear-cut results. It is important to note that there were positive effects on all the measured areas of the children's functioning which may have yielded "significant" results had the sample size been larger. Despite this, such positive effects were fairly small which suggests that the training, while a positive experience for foster families, was insufficient to address the massive needs of these children. In view of the level of mental health problems and the prevalence of past abuse and neglect, this group of children as a whole should be considered a "special needs" population.

Participants thought that the training improved foster carers' relationships with the children they were looking after and helped their ability to care for them, but it did not significantly reduce the children's problems. The research has suggested that foster care itself may be helping to improve children's self-esteem, which is likely to have effects on their later functioning.

A three-day training programme within existing services is clearly not enough to make a useful impact on the massive emotional and behavioural problems of children in foster care in Scotland. There is good evidence that children with such problems benefit from "specialist" schemes (Chamberlain *et al*, 1992), but, as is clear from this and other studies, more than half of children in "ordinary" foster care are suffering from emotional and behavioural problems. Some "specialist schemes" now place all teenagers requiring accommodation by the local authority. As Shaw and Hipgrave (1988) mention in their survey of specialist services in the UK, 'During a discussion of the "hard-to-place" teenager, [we posed the question] what would an "easy-to-place" teenager look like?' As 93 per cent of the children in the current sample have been abused or neglected, this question could probably apply to the younger children too. The term "specialist scheme" covers a wide range of services, but the successful projects evaluated by Chamberlain's group included:

weekly group sessions lasting two hours; three to five hours of family contact with project workers each week; individual meetings with foster carers and project staff at least weekly; telephone contact with project staff three times per week; individual work with young people on a weekly basis; and a significantly improved fostering allowance. Recently researchers in the USA have suggested that we need to go beyond even "specialist" foster care into "professional" foster care, in which carers are paid a substantial annual salary in addition to good training and support (Testa and Rolock, 1999). Clearly, to institute such a radical reorganisation of services for all children would require a major effort of political will and a massive injection of finance, but perhaps this is what these very vulnerable children need and deserve. The cost of such a service must be offset against the probable lifetime savings to the health and penal services, not to mention the potential avoidance of family breakdown and future generations of children in care.

Conclusion

Around 60 per cent of the children in this sample of children in foster care were suffering from emotional and behavioural problems, associated with past emotional and sexual abuse. Despite this, there was a significant improvement in the self-esteem of the children during the course of the study. A three-day training programme which focused on communication was well received by participants who perceived a benefit in terms of their ability to care and their relationship with the child, but the training did not have a significant impact on the emotional and behavioural functioning of the children. A great deal of research is still needed about the complex relationship between adult attachment styles, the development of new attachments in looked after children, the child's psychosocial development and the role of communication in facilitating this. The understanding of these issues would contribute considerably to the planning and development of appropriate services for looked after children.

From this and other studies, it is clear that the level of problems experienced by children in foster care in the UK warrants urgent action. This study has, at the very least, provided some direct evidence that three days of training within the normal structure of services is insufficient to improve the emotional and behavioural functioning of children in foster care. We would like to use these results to advocate for much more intensive services for children in "mainstream" foster care. These services will need to be subjected to rigorous scientific scrutiny to ensure that we are providing the best for these very vulnerable children.

References

Barth R, Berry M, Yoshikami R, Goodfield R K and Carson M L (1988) 'Predicting adoption disruption', *Social Work* 33:2, pp 227–33.

Berridge D and Cleaver H (1987) *Foster Home Breakdown* (first edition), Oxford: Blackwell.

Cantos A L, Gries L T and Slis V (1996) 'Correlates of therapy referral in foster children', *Child Abuse & Neglect* 20:10, pp 921–31.

Chamberlain P, Moreland S and Reid K (1992) 'Enhanced services and stipends for foster parents: effects on retention rates and outcomes for children', *Child Welfare* 71:5, pp 387–401.

Crowell J and Feldman S (1988) 'Mother's internal models of relationships and children's behavioural and developmental status: a study of mother–child interaction', *Child Development* 59:5, pp 1273–85.

Dando I and Minty B (1987) 'What makes a good foster parent?', *British Journal of Social Work* 17:4, pp 383–400.

Daniel B, Wassell S and Gilligan R (1999) ' "It's just common sense, isn't it?": exploring ways of putting theory of resilience into action', *Adoption & Fostering* 23:3, pp 6–15.

Dimigen G, Del Priore C, Butler S, Evans S, Ferguson L and Swan M (1999) 'Psychiatric disorder among children at time of entering local authority care: questionnaire survey', *British Medical Journal* 319: 7211, p 675.

Gean M P, Gillmore J L and Dowler J K (1985) 'Infants and toddlers in supervised custody: a pilot study of visitation', *Journal of the American Academy of Child Psychiatry* 24:5, pp 608–12.

Goldberg S (1991) 'Recent developments in attachment theory and research', *Canadian Journal of Psychiatry* 36, pp 393–400.

Goodman R (1997) 'The Strengths and Difficulties Questionnaire: a research note', *Journal of Child Psychology & Psychiatry* 38, pp 581–86.

Goodman R, Meltzer H and Bailey V (1998) 'The Strengths and Difficulties Questionnaire: a pilot study on the validity of the self-report version', *European Psychiatry* 7:5, pp 125–30.

Howe D and Fearnley S (1999) 'Disorders of attachment and attachment therapy', *Adoption & Fostering* 23:2, pp 19–30.

Knowles M (1984) *The Adult Learner: A neglected species*, Texas: Gulf.

Lyons-Ruth K (1996) 'Attachment patterns among children with aggressive behaviour problems: the role of disorganised early attachment patterns', *Journal of Consulting & Clinical Psychology* 64:1, pp 64–73.

Main M, Kaplan N and Cassidy J (1985) 'Security in infancy, childhood and adulthood: a move to the level of representation', in Bretherton I and Waters E (eds), *Monographs of the Society for Research in Child Development*, 50 edn, 1–2.

McCann J B, James A, Wilson S and Dunn G (1996) 'Prevalence of psychiatric disorders in young people in the care system', *British Medical Journal* 313:7071, pp 1529–30.

Minnis H, Devine C and Pelosi A (1999) 'Foster carers speak about training', *Adoption & Fostering* 23:2, pp 42–7.

Minnis H, Pelosi A, Knapp M and Dunn J (in press) 'Mental health and foster carer training', *Archives of Disease in Childhood*.

Reddy V, Hay D, Murray L and Trevarthen C (1997) 'Communication in infancy: mutual regulation of affect and attention', in Bremner G and Slater A (eds), *Infant Development: Recent advances*, Hove: Psychology Press/Erlbaum.

Reder P and Lucey C (1995) 'Significant issues in the assessment of parenting', in Reder P and Lucey C (eds), *Assessment of Parenting: Psychiatric and psychological contributions*, London: Routledge.

Richman N (1993) *Communicating with Children: Helping children in distress*, London: Save the Children.

Shaw M and Hipgrave T (1988) 'Specialist fostering: a research study', *Adoption & Fostering* 13:3, pp 17–21.

Starrin B, Larsson G and Styrborn S (1990) 'A review and critique of psychological approaches to the burn-out phenomenon', *Scandinavian Journal of Caring Sciences* 4:2, pp 83–91.

Strathclyde Regional Council Social Work Department (1988) *Fostering and Adoption Disruption Research Project: Temporary placements*, Glasgow: Strathclyde Regional Council.

Strathclyde Regional Council Social Work Department (1991) 'Fostering and adoption disruption research in Strathclyde Region: the permanent placements', in Anonymous, *Adoption and Fostering: The outcome of permanent family placements in two Scottish local authorities*, Edinburgh: Scottish Office.

Testa M F and Rolock N (1999) 'Professional foster care: a future worth pursuing?', *Child Welfare* 78:1, pp 108–24.

Warr P and Jackson P (1985) 'Factors influencing the psychological impact of prolonged unemployment and of re-employment', *Psychological Medicine* 15:4, pp 795–807.

Warren S, Huston L, Egeland B and Sroufe A (1997) 'Child and adolescent anxiety disorders and early attachment', *Journal of the American Academy of Child & Adolescent Psychiatry* 36:5, pp 637–44.

World Health Organisation (1992) *The ICD-10 Classification of Mental and Behavioural Disorders: Clinical descriptions and diagnostic guidelines*, Geneva: WHO.

23 Fostering as seen by the carers' children

Diana Part

This article was first published in Adoption & Fostering *17:1, 1993.*

There is little in social work or foster care literature that looks at the part the carers' birth children can and do play in families that foster. They live with the fostered children, frequently share their bedrooms with them, can become close and grieve when they leave, or can dislike and resent them.

The evidence so far

The only reference given to the children of the foster carers in the practical handbook *Foster Care: A guide to practice* (Social Work Services Group, 1976) was that they 'can sometimes be included in the discussions'.

Prosser (1978) investigated Wilkes's 1974 American study which examined 'the impact of fostering on the foster family'. This study found that minor upsets in the family's own children were common following the introduction of foster children to their home. Although these were generally transitory, unless such behaviour was understood, and adjustments made in family functioning, the children could develop or display more maladaptive behaviour. Resentful feelings could be generated if the foster child's stay was longer than anticipated. Wilkes also found that hesitancy and discrepancies in the treatment of the fostered and the birth children's behaviour could lead to trouble. The children as well as the adults of the family needed to understand what was likely to happen when a foster child came.

Brown (1988) looked at support groups for foster families and how foster parents talked about the impact of foster children on their own children. She found that new carers wanted to hear and discuss more about the effects on families. The meetings she attended were all orientated to the foster children and not towards the families' birth children. This demonstrated the practice found in much of the literature - that the foster carers' children were only discussed in regard to the fostered children, and the children themselves were not seen as a separate and important part of the dynamic.

The more recent Department of Health publication *Patterns and Outcomes in Child Placement* (1991), did call for more attention to be given to the needs and feelings of birth children. It referred to Thoburn's follow-up studies of older child adoptions and to an unpublished pilot study by Von Arnim (1988) which looked at the effect on children aged between eight and 12 years whose parents fostered adolescents. Both studies showed that children gained a great deal but also paid a price, especially at certain stages of their development. Both felt that the birth children's problems could cause a fostered child's placement to fail.

The video *Children who Foster* (Natural Children's Support Group, 1990) was made by and for children who foster. This followed recognition in one social services department, after a letter from two of the children of their carers, that the children of carers have an important role to play. It was realised that they need to know a certain amount about the children who are living with them, both to help and protect themselves and the children, particularly if the children have or might have been abused.

The video showed a group of perceptive young people, aware both of their own feelings of displacement and of the needs of the children who came to their homes. There was an absence of the judgemental attitudes that mid-teenagers can display, but a feeling of being overwhelmed by the problems the children brought with them.

In my recent study, children of foster carers in a Scottish region were asked by questionnaire what they felt about being part of a foster family. This was part of a larger piece of research by postal questionnaire in which all temporary carers in the region were asked to participate. A separate section was enclosed as a loose sheet for each of the children of the carers to complete if they wished.

They were asked their age, if they were a girl or a boy, if they liked their family being a foster family and what were the best and worst things about having a foster child or children in their home. They were invited to write a letter or draw a picture if they wished. Seventy-five children from 43 foster families replied, a response rate of 78 per cent of families with children living at home. The children ranged in age from three to 24 years.

The children who responded

Eighty per cent (60) of the children liked fostering. Only 5 per cent (four) were clear that they did not like their family being a foster family, and 15 per cent (11) were uncertain or said they "sometimes" liked it. So a fifth were not certain that fostering was a good thing.

A problem for some of the parents was access visits being held in their homes. This did not appear to affect their children – most of the children who were unsure about fostering did not have birth parents coming to their home for access visits. Five children did, but it did not seem to impinge on them in the same way as it affected their parents. None of the children, whether they liked fostering or not, mentioned birth parents in their homes as one of the worst things about fostering.

Many replies about the worst aspects of fostering showed that although the majority liked fostering, it was often difficult and upsetting for them.

The best about fostering

The children were asked what 'the best things about having a foster child or children in our home are'. This enabled them to choose what they felt was the best about fostering for them and not have to select from a list. Their replies fell into three main categories:
- companionship;
- looking after babies and young children;
- the challenge of helping.

Companionship

For 43 per cent of the children the best thing about having a foster child in their home was the company:

There is someone to play games with and read to, and I can be the teacher when we play schoolies. (Girl, aged 7)

They are always funny, and they make me laugh. I like having lots of brothers and sisters because they keep me company. (Girl, only child, aged 13)

It is like having a younger brother or sister. I like being with younger children. I feel sorry for them and I want to help them as much as I can. (Girl aged 14)

These replies were mainly from children in families which fostered young children. Few recorded company as the best thing about fostering if they were fostering teenagers.

Looking after babies/young children

A quarter (24 per cent) of the children chose "looking after babies/young children" as the best thing about fostering for them:

Being able to give them the things that they appreciate because they have never had them before, where other kids their age would take for granted. (Girl aged 17)

The best thing is when we get babies because I like playing with them. (Boy aged 12)

The challenge

Fifteen per cent of the children said that the best thing about fostering was the challenge and the need to help. These tended to be from the older boys:

You realise how lucky you are to live in a caring family, and you get to show the kids another side to life. (Boy, aged 20)

It's good to know that you are giving a child who has had problems at home or with their family a good home and a caring family. (Girl, aged 17)

I believe I am more socially aware than children who do not foster. Partially through the experiences of fostering I believe I have matured and become more responsible. (Boy, aged 15)

There were several other responses which could not be categorised: a 14-year-old-girl wrote that 'everything' was good about fostering (while her brother was not happy as he had to share a room with the fostered child). A 15-year-old girl who 'sometimes' liked her family being a foster family said that the best thing for her was that it 'keeps Mum at home but still working and earning'.

Fifteen per cent of the children did not record anything for the "best things", but did write about the bad times. It is interesting to speculate whether some children, knowing that their parents could read their replies when they were handed back, were conscious of their parents' opinions and feelings and wrote accordingly. One mother wrote on her children's behalf that although neither of them had recorded any "best things" they both enjoyed having children in the home.

The worst about fostering

The worst things about being a foster family fell into three main categories:
- difficult and annoying behaviour, and stealing;
- the attention given to the foster children;
- the lack of privacy.

Difficult behaviour
For a quarter (24 per cent) of the children the worst thing about having foster children in the house was their difficult behaviour:

When they're narky, when they're selfish, when they moan a lot. (Girl, aged 11)

She constantly stole from us when we felt we were trying so hard to get her to like us and for us to like and accept her. (Male, aged 21)

They always talk and are loud all of the time. I can't have a decent conversation with any of them because they are all under ten . . . they annoy me when I'm in a hurry to go out. (Girl, aged 15)

Attention given to the foster child

Closely following, and related to the difficult behaviour, was the attention received by the foster children, which 20 per cent felt to be the worst aspect:

I think that the foster child gets too much pocket money. I don't have as many designer clothes as them. I don't like their friends coming to the house as I don't always get mine in. (Boy, aged 10)

Foster child gets too much attention mostly when they are bad. Also they get away with things that I would never be allowed to do. They get things too easy from the social workers. I don't get someone to come and take me out for tea, or ten-pin bowling paid for by the social worker. (Girl, aged 15)

Some of the children are a real pressure to look after, e.g. disruptive, badly behaved. Sometimes, partly due to fostering I believe my youngest brother does not get the same amount of attention as myself and my other brother received at his age due to having the foster child. (Boy, aged 15)

Lack of privacy and sharing

Twenty-three per cent of the young people regretted the lack of privacy and having to share with the fostered children:

You don't have the same privacy. (Girl, aged 19)

Privacy – trying to keep them out of my room and leave my things alone. (Boy, aged 15)

Associated with the lack of privacy was the difficulty of sharing a room, and sharing the foster child with their parents:

The only thing I would like is to have my own room and I know my sister would like this as well. (Girl, aged 15)

Sometimes I would like to get out by myself with my mum because the others go out with their mums/social workers. (Girl, aged 13)

Sometimes I wish that it was just our own family together again with no-one else. (Girl, aged 12)

Five per cent of the children said that the foster children crying was the worst thing about fostering for them:

They cry all the time. (Girl, aged 8)

Five per cent of the children said that the foster children leaving was the worst for them:

When they go away it makes me upset. (Girl, aged 14)

When we are fostering someone that I like they have to go to somebody else. (Girl, aged 10)

Three per cent of the young people said that:

The babysitting is sometimes a pain in the neck and also the constant chatter and noise when watching something on TV etc. But that's part of being in a foster family and the pros balance with the cons. (Girl, aged 17)

Seventeen per cent of the children said there was nothing that was the worst thing for them.

It was apparent that some found it difficult when the foster child seemed to get a great deal of attention. This was mainly with reference to fostered teenagers and their behaviour both in the home and outside. Some of the replies which spoke of practical issues may have veiled less tangible feelings of resentment and displacement which are not so easy to put into words. Only a couple of children stated that they wanted more of their parents' time. One was a child who had been fostered and then adopted by a family who continued fostering. There was a thread of wistfulness that life was never as it had been before fostering.

One of the positives that was apparent was the altruism and under-standing that some of the children showed. This confirmed the feelings presented in the *Children who Foster* video. The sample examined in this study, whilst not without some angry and resentful youngsters unsym-pathetic to the difficulties of the fostered young people, also showed a high level of understanding and tolerance.

The young people who did not like fostering

There were four young people, two girls and two boys, who stated that they did not like their families being foster families. The parents were asked what they felt the effect of fostering on their children had been. One said the effect had been good, two said they thought it had sometimes been bad, and one felt fostering had a bad effect on their teenage daughter and their other children.

Case A

The first, a teenage girl, had brothers and sisters who 'mostly' enjoyed fostering. A harrowing few months following a placement breakdown had led all of them to comment:

She stole constantly from us . . .

She sometimes called me names and it made me cry.

It put a strain on the whole family which resulted in us being angry and easily annoyed with each other. What I could do in my own home was limited by the presence of the foster child and also my private possessions were at risk. I could not trust her. . .

All but the one girl gave positive comments as well, however, about the experience:

The challenge of trying to integrate a person into family life who isn't used to coping within a family situation.

It gives you a sense of being able to help people worse off than you.

Playing board games with her was good.

This placement had turned into a nightmare for all concerned; the father said that he couldn't wait to get the fostered teenager out and commented elsewhere in the questionnaire: 'I found the experience physically, emotionally and almost spiritually draining.' Three of five children of that family recorded that they liked being part of a foster family, however. This demonstrates how children's experiences can be different from that of their parents. In stressful situations children can still have positive experiences, perhaps by being sheltered by their parents.

Case B

The second child who did not like being part of a foster family was an 11-year-old girl in a family that fostered teenagers. Her older sister 'sometimes' liked fostering. The girls were able to see beyond the immediate circumstances:

> It is good to learn that other kids don't get loved or cared for in the same way as we do.

> I get extra pocket money for putting up with them.

There were aspects of being a foster family they were not happy with involving their parents, the foster children, and social workers, including:

> I don't usually get on with them which isn't much fun having someone in your home that you don't like.

> I don't like when my mum and dad argue about them.

> Some of the children don't deserve to have kind, loving families because they just kick them in the teeth when they try to help.

> The social workers stay so long that by the time they leave our tea is overcooked. If they came on time maybe they wouldn't leave so late.

Case C

The third person disagreed with his sister who liked 'everything' about fostering, whereas he, a 17-year-old, did 'not really' like fostering. He recorded no best things, but 'sharing a room', which he felt was the worst facet of fostering, may well explain much of the difference in attitude between the siblings.

Case D

The final young person who did not like fostering was a 16-year-old boy. The preceding families all fostered teenagers. His family fostered babies and young children. His 14-year-old sister liked being part of a foster family and commented:

You get satisfaction when you see the child/children happy and see how you have given them a good start in life.

However, her brother did 'not really' like fostering as it gave:

A lot of extra work for Mum.

Conclusions

The overall impression is that most children and young people enjoy, or at most tolerate, being part of a foster family. It can give them a greater appreciation of their own family, and an awareness of the difficulties that some of their peers have to live with. Several commented on the greater maturity they thought they had because of the experiences the family had with fostering. They can undoubtedly gain a great deal.

Fostering is not without difficulties for the birth children of the foster families, however, and they can pay a price. Some of the children had to share bedrooms and missed their privacy. Possessions were tampered with, if not broken or stolen.

The conclusion seems to be that fostering is difficult, that fostered children can be annoying and intrusive, and that the nuclear family is never the same again. Despite this almost all the children of the foster carers said that they enjoyed being part of a family that fostered. Their views are important and should be heeded – to help families continue through and after the difficult times.

Postscript

The Children Act (Scotland) 1995 introduced new terminology which was not in use when this paper was written and is therefore not reflected here. Whether "fostered" or "accommodated" and having "access" or "contact" with the families of the children and young people, however, the issues remain the same. Living and sharing lives with other people's children is often hard, marks out the carers' children as different from their peers and changes the dynamics in their family. Social workers are still seen as being late, disrupting their routine and making it too easy for the accommodated young people while not considering the family of the carers.

References

Social Work Services Group (1976) *Foster Care – A guide to practice*, London: HMSO.

Prosser H (1978) *Perspectives on Foster Care*, Windsor: NFER Publishing Company.

Brown J (1988) 'Foster parent support group in a rural area', in Triseliotis J (ed) *Groupwork in Adoption and Foster Care*, London: Batsford/BAAF.

Department of Health (1991) *Patterns and Outcomes in Child Placement*, London: HMSO.

Natural Children's Support Group (1990) *Children who Foster*, Leeds: Vera Publications.

Section VI
Placement outcomes

A natural question has been asked recurrently about foster and adoptive placements: How do they work out? For a long time, the answer was given almost entirely in terms of one dimension, namely did they last? Many research studies provided data on breakdowns (also referred to as disruptions), usually in relation to longer-term fostering and adoption. These tended to show that breakdown rates in fostering were high (sometimes over 50 per cent), while those in adoption were much lower (often under ten per cent) (Berridge and Cleaver, 1987; Berry and Barth, 1990; Triseliotis *et al*, 1995b, 1997). This difference was not surprising, since for many years adopters brought up healthy infants, while foster carers cared for older children with problematic histories. However, the performance of short-term fostering was generally good (Rowe *et al*, 1989; Stone, 1995).

In relation to both fostering and adoption, it was consistently found that two main factors affected the chances of continuity or breakdown (Triseliotis *et al*, 1995b; Triseliotis *et al*, 1997; Howe *et al*, 2001; Rushton, personal communication):

- the age of child at placement;
- the level of emotional-behavioural difficulties.

This confirmed practice experience and indeed common sense that children with a longer experience of poor or inconsistent care and entrenched behaviour problems are more challenging to manage, love and stick with, while young children tend to be more resilient and easier to commit to (though there are of course exceptions). Higher age at placement is usually also connected with longer periods in foster or residential care.

Beyond the age of nine to ten, the chances of success can be as low as 50/50. (This does not apply to teenagers being adopted by foster carers with whom they have lived for some years.) The reasons for this are many. Older children have a number of features which require more adjustment on both their part and the adopters. These include:

- personal history;
- family loyalty;
- developed personalities;
- habits, rituals, etc.;
- established networks;
- sense of self.

On top of this, they have usually had longer exposure to adverse circumstances, such as starting life in poverty, unresponsive, rejecting or abusive parenting, family tensions and conflicts, separations, and changes of main carers. This means that their ways of relating to others are often very demanding or emotionally distant (Quinton *et al*, 1998; Schofield *et al*, 2000).

Rowe *et al* (1989) pointed out that "breakdown" is an ambiguous and crude indicator of placement success or failure. They used a wider range of more detailed questions to assess whether placements had lasted as long as planned or as needed and whether the children had benefited or not. Besides these placement-related outcomes, the children's development can be assessed. The Looking After Children programme identified seven key dimensions (Parker *et al*, 1991; Ward, 1995):

- health;
- emotional and behavioural development;
- education;
- family and social relations;
- identity;
- self-care;
- social presentation.

Measures of progress on these features are now used alongside placement considerations to assess children's progress (Hill *et al*, 1996). The seven dimensions are also widely used in practice, thanks to the widespread use of the Looking After Children materials, devised to assist record-keeping information sharing, communication, planning and decision-making (Jackson, 1998; Ward, 1998). Adapted versions were developed for use in Scotland (Wheelaghan and Hill, 2000).

Another factor affecting success rates is the timing of the assessment.

Studies vary greatly in the length of time after which they assess outcomes.

The journal has included few articles from Scotland about outcomes, which reflects the rarity of substantial longitudinal studies carried out here. Two articles provided details on the progress of permanent family placements made by Lothian Region in the mid-1980s as a major part of its commitment to permanency planning (see **McKay, 1980**, in Section I). According to **O'Hara and Hoggan (1988)** about three to four per cent of children admitted to care were found to have no meaningful contact or attachment to their birth families, so that a permanent substitute family was sought, usually via adoption. A specialist team was set up to recruit, prepare, assess and support families taking on older children and those with special needs.

O'Hara and Hoggan provided statistics for 335 children aged over two placed for adoption (86 per cent) or permanent fostering (14 per cent) between 1882 and 1987. The overall breakdown rate was 11 per cent. This is a lower figure than reported for comparable groups of children elsewhere (Rushton, personal communication). It is also noteworthy that almost a third of the children who experienced breakdowns moved on to their permanent families and only a few were placed in residential care.

The authors outlined the key features they saw as necessary for an effective service. These included clear and consistent policies, a specialist team, access to psychological and educational support, practical help including the availability of adoption allowances, and a partnership approach to families.

A more comprehensive study of the outcomes of Lothian placements was described by **Borland et al (1991)**. The authors reviewed the literature to date and pointed out some of the complexities and pitfalls in ascertaining accurate disruption figures. In Lothian nearly all the children placed in permanent families before they were 11 had been placed for adoption, whereas permanent fostering was more common for those placed in their teens. However, putting the age difference to one side, the two groups had similar rates of severe difficulties.

The overall disruption rate (determined as placement ending before or without adoption) was 20 per cent. Like an earlier study of Strathclyde placements, it was found that children with learning disabilities usually had stable placements. Children with severe difficulties were most likely to have their placement end. The most common problems precipitating a breakdown were aggression, running away, stealing and lying. Those in continuing placements were more likely to have birth family contacts, suggesting a comparatively less troubled family attachment history. Childless couples were more successful with younger children, but experienced parents did better with older children. Families with continuing placements were, on average, less stressed, more open in their communication and flexible in their expectations. The intensive social work support following placement was much valued by the families.

In 2001, Barnardo's published a short report on the outcomes for their Family Placement Service in Scotland. The average age at placement for fostering, mainly on a permanent basis, was eight years. In other words these were high risk cases. Nevertheless the disruption rate was only 12 per cent. Of 42 adoptive placements made, only two broke down. Nine of the 17 children whose placements disrupted were successfully re-placed with another project family (Barnardo's, 2001).

24 Permanent substitute family care in Lothian: placement outcome

Gerry O'Hara and Pauline Hoggan

This article was first published in Adoption & Fostering *12:3, 1988.*

Jane Rowe (1987) has pointed out how complex assessing placement outcomes and interpreting breakdown rates can be. She also reminds us that generally foster care is under researched, although the Berridge and Cleaver (1987) study is a major contribution in this area. Placement outcome in special needs adoption and permanent fostering is also under researched but will be considerably helped by Jane Rowe's recent study in six local authorities and by June Thoburn's (1986) evaluation of The Child Wants A Home adoption agency. There are also useful contributions from different agencies such as Parents for Children (Reich and Lewis, 1986), Barnardo's (Kerrane *et al*, 1980), Triseliotis and Russell's study of adoption and residential care outcome (1984) and the Adoption Resource Exchange placement study (Wolkind and Kozaruk, 1986).

However, most of the outcome studies into permanent placements are American and a good deal of evaluation in the UK needs to be done if we are to continue with confidence what has amounted to a permanent family placement revolution since the 1970s. The purpose of this article is to begin to assess the outcome of placements, intended to be permanent, made in Lothian Region (excluding under-twos) by means of adoption or fostering, during the period September 1982 to September 1987. Lothian Region has a well publicised permanency planning policy (McKay, 1980) which whenever possible involves maintaining children in their own homes, or at least returning them to their families, should they be received into care, as quickly as possible. If the return home cannot be achieved adoption is the preferred option, unless:

1 Parents are committed to and involved with the child, and the child would benefit from the relationship continuing.

2 The child is aged approximately ten or older and does not wish to have a relationship with his or her parents legally severed.
3 The foster parents are not willing to adopt, but the child would suffer if removed from their custody and placed for adoption.

In other words, children with meaningful links to their parents need to be returned home, or have a relationship which acknowledges these attachments, and only relatively young children with no meaningful contact or attachment to their family of origin are placed for adoption. This in fact amounts to a very small proportion of the total number of children who are received into care (i.e. less than four per cent) but tends to involve children who may well be described as among the most disturbed in the community. A recent survey in Lothian of 15 children placed by one adoption panel indicates that all but one had been subjected to some form of physical or sexual abuse.

Permanency planning

Maluccio *et al* (1986) described permanency planning as

> ... *the systematic process of carrying out, within a brief time-limited period, a set of goal directed activities designed to help children live in families or, for continuity of relationships, with nurturing parents or caretakers and the opportunity to establish life time relationships.*

Permanency planning, as the Short Committee (1984) noted, has become almost 'synonymous with adoption'. Margaret McKay (1980), who introduced permanency planning in the UK, saw it as an approach to the delivery of services to children in placement or at risk of being taken into care. The three strands of prevention, restoration and permanent alternative care make up the constituent parts of permanency planning but arguably too much emphasis has been placed on the third strand. In this context, given that less than four per cent of the total number of children who are received into care in any one year remain permanently in care, it would seem that the identification in Lothian of permanency planning with adoption is one dimensional. Much of the debate about permanency planning happened in the late 1970s when there were large numbers of children who had grown old in the care system and who had no meaningful attachments with their families. In fact, as Triseliotis (1986) points out, the children identified by Rowe and Lambert in their 1973 study have grown up and left the care system and the scene is now much changed. Children placed permanently now are much more likely to have:

1 spent less time in care than in the past;
2 experienced repeated failed rehabilitation efforts;
3 been known to have been abused, either physically or sexually;
4 had very stormy and turbulent backgrounds with many different adults;
5 brothers or sisters who will need to be placed with them;
6 be in the main under ten years of age;
7 been actively worked with in relation to their family history, feelings and attitudes.

Additionally there are a small number of severely or profoundly mentally handicapped children who require permanent care, which may or may not also involve contact with their family of origin.

There are a number of agencies in the United States who have set up permanency projects which work with children in their own homes, away from their own homes with a view to restoration, and in permanent alternative substitute families. The evidence suggests that children can do very well indeed in permanent new families (see Barth and Berry, 1987).

Any outcome study of permanent placements should consider the possible alternative outcomes if different plans had been followed.

The service in Lothian

A specialist team was set up in September 1982 to recruit, prepare, assess and support families adopting or fostering children who were older and had special needs. In foster placements the intention was to achieve permanent placements.

Preparation in groups for both applicants and children to be placed has been available throughout the period of the evaluation as has organised post-placement support and approved adoption allowances. The involvement of consumers in all aspects of the service is a fundamental and guiding principle. Many of these programmes have been described in various publications (O'Hara, 1986, 1988; Hoggan, 1988 and Hutton, 1988). The placements are made and sustained by a combination of specialist workers from the central homefinding team and area team social workers. Since 1985 the authors have been overall unit manager and team leader respectively and during the period 1982–85 were team leader and team member. Six of the original seven-member team therefore still manage, organise and deliver the service.

The evaluation

We decided to identify every breakdown from the placements made during the period September 1982 to September 1987. Breakdowns were defined as any placement which ceased before the child reached the age of 16 years, regardless of the circumstances, other than in four cases where children returned to their birth family on a planned basis, after short stays in new families.

We have highlighted those placements made:
- directly for adoption;
- placed on a fostering basis with the intention of permanency;
- adopted after a period of fostering.

We have excluded placements of babies or children under two which are made on behalf of the region by The Scottish Adoption Association. Every placement was formally made by one of Lothian's five adoption panels.

Comments

These statistics do not reflect the capacity of commitment, endurance, courage and imagination which families need to parent children who have suffered in early childhood. Two further studies in Lothian by Yates (1985) and Hill et al (1988) outline the need for support outside existing family and friendship networks which should be practical and financial, emotional and at times highly specialist. The Hill study suggests that some families have had to make enormous adjustments in their expectations and have been disappointed by the experience, and although Yates found that families could see the positive changes in children the cost was higher than they had expected. They worried a great deal about the future.

STATISTICS

No. of children placed for adoption or fostering intended to be permanent in the period September 1982–87		335
No. of placements disrupted/broke down		39
Percentage breakdown rate		11.3%
Disruption rate of children who were ten and over at the time of placement		21.7%
Disruption rate of children who were nine and under at the time of placement		4.6%
Adoption or fostering Total no. placed		335
Placed for adoption	290 (86%)	
Placed for permanent fostering	45 (14%)	335
New adoptive placements or claims by existing carers No. placed for adoption		290
No. claimed for adoption by existing carers	28 (9.6%)	
No. of new placements	262 (90.4%)	290
Approved adoption allowances No. placed for adoption		290
No. of approved adoptional allowances paid		85 (29%)
Children with disabilities No. of children with severe/profound mental disability		39
No. of breakdowns (i.e. two aged ten +: one aged nine)		3 (7.7%)
Outcome of failed placements Total no. broken down/disrupted		39
No. placed in teenage fostering scheme	18	
No. replaced in permanent placements	11	
No. in temporary foster care	6	
No. in residential care	3	
No. in supported accommodation	1	39

Thoburn *et al* (1986) identified similar themes. Children were doing remarkably well relative to their past experiences, but at a high cost to families and consequently demanding of support services.

Our own experience echoes these research findings and we see the following components as essential for a permanent substitute family placement service in a large local authority:

1 an approach which promotes clarity about the legal, policy, procedural, practice and knowledge frameworks in relation to planning for children in care;

2 specialist workers leading the service, but in partnership with area team non-specialist placement workers;

3 professional leadership from specialist managers;

4 constant evaluation of policy outcome and appraisal of practice "sacred cows";

5 consumer feedback and participation in all aspects of the service, including preparation and assessment work, adoption panel decision making and post-adoption and post-placement support services;

6 realistic preparation programmes which are clear about the educative/ preparation/ training components, but do not deny the responsibility of the agency to assess and evaluate capacities in partnership with applicants;

7 parent-focused support services;

8 approved adoption allowances for all families who take children with special needs;

9 informed help from specialist social workers, teachers and educational psychologists who have an understanding of special needs adoption and fostering and from health personnel with a similar understanding;

10 an open-door approach to support so that families can choose for themselves when they need it and an open-door system when families request direct work to be done with the child in placement;

11 a service to families after disruption.

These elements are not ranked according to any priority.

These initial findings from the Lothian experience require much more scrutiny. At the very least they need to be considered alongside the findings of Yates (1985) and Hill *et al* (1988) but we hope they will prove useful to other agencies who are looking critically at their permanency planning policies. There are plans to look specifically at the 39 placements which have failed, but the real test in relation to outcome will be to monitor these children's progress over the next ten years or more.

References

Barth R P and Berry M (1987) *Outcomes of Child Welfare: Services under permanency planning*, Chicago: University of Chicago.

Berridge and Cleaver (1987) *Fostering Breakdown*, Oxford: Basil Blackwell.

Hill M, Hutton S and Easton S (1988) 'Adoptive parenting – plus and minus', *Adoption & Fostering* 12:2, pp 17–23.

Hoggan P (1988) 'Preparing children for family placement through the use of small groups', in Triseliotis J (ed), *Groupwork in Adoption and Fostering*, London: Batsford/BAAF.

Hutton S (1988) 'An adopters' support group', in Triseliotis J (ed), *Groupwork in Adoption and Fostering*, London: Batsford/BAAF.

Kerrane A, Hunter A and Lane M (1980) *Adopting Older and Handicapped Children: A consumers' view of the preparation, assessment, placement and post-placement support services*, Barnardo's Social Work Paper 14.

Maluccio A, Fein E and Olmstead K (1986) *Permanency Planning for Children*, London: Tavistock Publications.

McKay M (1980) 'Planning for permanent placement', *Adoption & Fostering* 99:1, pp 19–20.

O'Hara G (1986) 'Post-placement support services in Lothian', *Adoption & Fostering* 10:4, pp 38–42.

O'Hara G (1988) 'Preparing families in groups', in Triseliotis J (ed), *Groupwork in Adoption and Fostering*, London: Batsford/BAAF.

Reich D and Lewis J (1986) 'Placements by Parents for Children', in Wedge P and Thoburn J (eds), *Finding Families for 'Hard-to-Place' Children*, London: BAAF.

Rowe J and Lambert L (1973) *Children who Wait*, London: ABAFA (now BAAF).

Rowe J (1987) 'Fostering outcomes: interpreting breakdown rates', *Adoption & Fostering* 11:1, pp 32–34.

Short Committee (1984) *Social Services Committee Report on Children in Care*, London: HMSO.

Thoburn J, Murdoch A and O'Brien A (1986) *Permanency in Child Care*, Oxford: Basil Blackwell.

Triseliotis J and Russell J (1984) *Hard to Place: The outcome of adoption and residential care*, London: Heinemann.

Triseliotis J (1986) 'Older children in care', in Wedge P and Thoburn J (eds), *Finding Families for 'Hard-to-Place Children'*, London: BAAF.

Wolkind S and Kozaruk A (1980) ' "Hard to place?" children with medical and developmental problems', in Wedge P and Thoburn J (eds), *Finding Families for 'Hard-to-Place' Children*, London: BAAF.

Yates P (1985) 'Post-placement support', MSc Research, University of Edinburgh, unpublished.

25 Placement outcomes for children with special needs

Moira Borland, Gerry O'Hara and John Triseliotis

This article was first published in Adoption & Fostering *15:2, 1991.*

This article describes the outcomes of placements of "special needs" children by one local authority, in its attempts to achieve permanence in their lives, either through adoption or long-term fostering. The article also examines the factors that appeared to contribute to disruption or stability and contrasts them where possible with factors identified in other comparable studies. We recognise that outcome studies present many methodological problems, some of which will be referred to later. In recent years also, the distinction between adoption and permanent foster care has become blurred because of the similarities in many of the children's circumstances and characteristics. For example, children classified as "special needs" may find themselves either placed for adoption or permanent foster care. This may depend on the wishes of carers, those of the children involved or because of the need to maintain important links between children and their birth families. Thoburn *et al* (1986) demonstrate how, with older children, some families put on ice their original adoption intentions and choose to continue on a fostering basis.

The placements covered by the study were made between September 1982 and the end of 1985. A minimum of three years elapsed between the last placement and the start of the study, though some placements had reached their fifth year. A total of 40 (or 20 per cent) placements out of 194 made during the study period had subsequently disrupted and those formed the sample of disrupted placements. Because of resource constraints, a sample of 60 was identified from the remaining 154 ongoing placements. The sample was stratified to ensure a sizeable number of children aged ten and over to include children with learning difficulties. The subsequent analysis took account of the sampling variations.

Information on the children and families was obtained from

records primarily from the BAAF Form E and Form F completed prior to placement. Minutes of linking and co-ordination meetings gave information on reasons for matching and early developments in the placements, and in the case of the disrupted placements, the minutes of disruption meetings provided an assessment of what had precipitated the breakdown. Other reports often supplemented those primary sources of information. Social workers were also asked to assess certain family attitudes in the majority of the ongoing cases and in about half of the disrupted ones. Information on the social work service input prior to and during the placement was obtained primarily from questionnaires completed by the social workers who supported the placement, but in a few cases this information was obtained from the records. A degree of inconsistency was therefore inherent in this aspect of the data collection process. The assessment of how the ongoing placements had progressed was made from information supplied by social workers and parents through questionnaires. Social workers responded in 95 per cent of the cases and parents in 58 per cent. Only a few parents responded in respect of disrupted placements. Most of the data was analysed by computer using an SCSS programme. The quantitative material obtained from parents and social workers on the progress of the placements was analysed manually. Most of the analysis involved comparing the characteristics of the children and families whose placements disrupted with those whose placements continued, and identifying which characteristics predominated in each group.

Other studies

The mid-1970s witnessed the start of a movement, almost a crusade, whose main objective was to secure new families for what became known as "special needs" children. The families of origin had either dropped out of the picture or were unwilling to resume their care. The term "special needs" came to cover older children, those with disabilities, emotional or learning difficulties, sibling groups or combinations of these conditions. Previously these children had been thought "unadoptable".

The move to place children with "special needs" was largely dictated by the increasing scarcity of babies for adoption and by emerging studies showing that many children were drifting within the care system without clear plans for their future (Rowe and Lambert, 1973). A further impetus came from studies demonstrating that children require continuity of care and stability in their lives, preferably within a family environment in order to develop "properly" (Pringle, 1975). Other studies were highlighting how vulnerable young people are after leaving care (Triseliotis, 1980; Triseliotis and Russell, 1984; Stein and Carey, 1986). Possibly the biggest encouragement though came from new studies, suggesting, unlike earlier ones, the reversibility of early negative emotional experiences, providing stable and caring conditions could subsequently be obtained (Kadushin, 1971; Clarke and Clarke, 1976; Tizard, 1977; Triseliotis and Russell, 1984; Quinton and Rutter, 1988).

A spate of studies which have been monitoring and evaluating the permanency movement began to emerge in the 1980s, most of them US and some British. At the initial stage, most of these covered very small numbers and were descriptive or anecdotal in nature. More detailed studies are now emerging using bigger samples. While providing some-what contradictory results in some areas, the studies also demonstrate a number of consistencies. The inconsistencies are, in some part, inevitable because different researchers have studied children of different ages or within different periods of time following placement. Additional difficul-ties include the fact that some studies have based their judgements solely on records, while others have relied on reports by adoptive parents and very few indeed have talked to children. Furthermore, the baselines of the children were not always established and outcome criteria of what is a "disruption" or "success" vary between studies. Some studies, such as this one, have excluded, for some purposes, long-term foster carers adopting their foster children to avoid distorting the findings. Thoburn (1990) claims that the apparently higher levels of successful placements suggested by US studies is not unconnected with the fact that they have included foster carers adopting their long-term foster children (see for example, Berry and Barth, 1990). Similarly, while some studies have concentrated on disruptions before and after adoption, others focused on what happened following the granting of the adoption order. It is not surprising, therefore, as Rowe (1987) also warns us, that comparisons of outcome studies should be made with great caution. Neither can it be assumed that disruptions are always harmful to the child, or that the continuation of a placement is always beneficial.

One consistent finding is that disruptions for children placed when under the age of ten are below ten per cent, but for those aged ten and over they vary from between 15 and 50 per cent. Where increased age and increased disturbance go together the disruption rates can be expected to be higher. For example, Tremetiere (1984) reviewed around 2,500 adoptions from 1979 to 1983 and found that six- to ten-year-old children had a disruption rate of 9.7 per cent and 12- to 18-year-olds 13.5 per cent. Boyne *et al* (1984) identified a 23.2 per cent disruption rate among 219 "special needs" children with disruption rates of nine, 15, 25 and 47 per cent for age groups 0–5, 6–8, 9–11 and 12–17 respectively. Kagan and Reid (1986) reported around 50 per cent adoption disruption of "emotionally disturbed" teenagers. Barth and Berry reported a disruption rate of only 22 per cent for those adopted aged 12 to 14 and 26 per cent for those aged 15 to 17, but these results are biased because they included foster parent adoption. This study, however, is not specific about the period that elapsed between placement and the study taking place. A somewhat surprising finding in the latter study was that transracially placed children disrupted at the rate of only 11 per cent compared to 28 per cent for same-race placements. The Oregon Project's policy of "aggressive adoption" resulted in 64 adoptions and only two disruptions in the months following the end of the project (and two or more years after the placement 75 per cent of the children remained in placement [Lahti, 1982]). Nelson (1985) also found that seven (28 per cent) out of 25 children placed when eight years of age and over disrupted within a year of the adoption order. In another study Nelson (1985) noted that almost none of the 257 already adopted children had disrupted and three-quarters of the families said they had an "excellent" or a "good" adoption. For only a few families had the adoption proved to be a negative experience. Satisfaction with adoption included the acceptance by adoptive parents that some children were so damaged that they would never overcome all their emotional problems. Festinger (1985) reported equally low disruptions. Thoburn and Rowe's (1988) large survey of voluntary agencies in Britain covered 1,165 children placed by agencies between 1979 and 1984. Overall breakdowns were 21 per cent but the rate for 10- to 12-year-olds rose to 30 per cent, and for those aged 13 or more to 48 per cent, which was similar to Kagan and Reid's (1986) findings. The recently completed Strathclyde Permanency Study (1990) identified 43 per cent disruptions over a period of three years. In line with other studies, most disruptions happened during the first 12 months. Most of the placements were made with permanent fostering in mind. Children aged 12 and over were significantly more vulnerable to disruption. Low breakdown rates are reported by Macaskill (1985) on the adoption of children with learning difficulties, by Wolkind and Kozaruk (1986) who studied 108 children with medical difficulties and by Thoburn et al (1986) and Rushton et al (1988).

The relevant literature is generally concerned with identifying the significance of adoption disruptions in terms of associations with the child's characteristics, those of the adoptive family and with the nature of agency practice. Besides the association found between disruption and increasing age and disturbance in the child, boys were also found to be more likely to disrupt (Nelson 1985). That a history of serious child abuse also reduces placement stability was found by Kagan and Reid (1986), Boneh (1979), Partridge et al (1986) and Zwimper (1983), but not by the Strathclyde Permanency Study (1990). The significance of all these characteristics was confirmed by Partridge et al (1986) who also identified that particular behaviours such as soiling bed clothes, stealing, serious eating disorders and being unable to receive or give warmth were particularly difficult for adoptive parents, which is consistent with Nelson's (1985) finding that the ability of the child to form an attachment to the adoptive family was important. Thoburn et al (1986) equally found that this was likely to be more difficult for boys over 12 who had been in care for more than six years, having had multiple carers and not "good enough" attachment to a previous carer. The contribution of previous multiple placements to disruption was also found by Partridge et al (1986) and Boneh (1979) and Festinger (1986). Physically abused children were also found by Martin and Beezley (1977) to be more likely to have had 'three or more home changes'. Thoburn et al (1986) also identified that children who had accepted that they could not return to their birth parents and who definitely wanted a new family would more readily make an attachment. This is consistent with Berridge and Cleaver's (1987) finding that children with strong family allegiance found the quasi-adoptive nature of long-term fostering difficult and with Borgman's (1980) conclusion that children placed against the wishes of their birth parents were more vulnerable to disruption.

Whether placing siblings together leads to placement vulnerability or stability is not yet clear from the literature. While Boneh (1979) and Kadushin and Seidl (1971) associated sibling group placements with disruption, more recent studies such as Kagan and Reid (1983) found an association with stability, and so does the Strathclyde Permanency Study (1990). Barth *et al* (1986) claim that attachment between a child and birth siblings was associated with stability and, although placements of sibling groups tended to be more difficult, they did not find they were more prone to disrupt. Berridge and Cleaver (1987) also conclude that preserving sibling relationships promotes stability and that the importance of these relationships to children in care has been undervalued. Boyne *et al* (1984), while supporting the association between placing siblings together and placement stability, also add that increased size of the sibling group makes disruptions more likely. Their somewhat contradictory findings about the decision to split or not to split siblings could suggest that other factors, such as a child's behaviour and individual needs, may be more important than the fact of being a member of a sibling group (Wedge and Mantle, 1990). Research findings vary on the degree of significance they attach to factors related to the family as opposed to the child. Jacka (1973), writing about baby adoptions, for example, and Berridge and Cleaver (1987) found that factors relating to the placement rather than the child contributed significantly to disruption. Partridge *et al* (1986), however, referring to special needs children concluded that disruption was associated with child factors more than with family or agency variables.

Cohen (1984) comments on a lack of flexibility in family rules and roles as contributing to disruption and Simon and Sherwen (1983) refer to an inability to expect and accept the child's behavioural and emotional difficulties along with an excessive need to meet the child's needs as associated with breakdown. A recent study by Westhues and Cohen (1990) places a great deal of emphasis on "positive" family functioning, including the adoptive father playing a key role by being 'actively involved in parenting, and able to nurture and support the mother in her role'.

Fitzgerald (1983) remarked that social workers described many parents in his sample of disrupted placements as 'lacking in warmth' and many of them also had significant unresolved conflicts in their past. Zwimper (1983) added that families with too many sources of stress and inadequate resources were likely to fail in adoption, but no guidance is offered of how to recognise these in advance. Several studies have linked instability in the placement with the adoptive family having biological children, particularly if a biological child is aged within five years of the adoptive child. Trasler (1960) and Parker (1966) drew attention to this and so did Berridge and Cleaver (1987). Wedge and Mantle's (1990) recent study has confirmed this association. Barth et al (1986), however, found that families with biological siblings were not more prone to disrupt and that the number of children in the family was not significant.

When it comes to agency factors a number of studies place increasing importance on "good" preparation and post-placement support. Careful preparation of the adopters, both in terms of knowledge of the individual child's past and of what behaviour to expect from the child, was found to be associated with adoption stability by Cohen (1984) and Lahti (1982), while Nelson (1985) found insufficient training or information about the child was associated with disruption, a point indirectly made by Berridge and Cleaver (1987) and the Strathclyde Permanency Study (1990). Several studies have advocated the use of groups in preparing and assessing adopters. Macaskill (1985) claims that learning in groups had a long-lasting impact on adopters, and Gill (1978) and Tremetiere (1979) found that groups for adopters were helpful in conveying general information about adopting an older child and in providing informal networks. Jarret and Copher (1980) also suggest that groups can be used to assess the motivation of adopters. O'Hara (1988) found groupwork helpful in conveying information and in enabling couples to assess and develop their potential capacity as adoptive parents. (For more details on group preparation and support see Triseliotis, 1988.)

Kagan and Reid (1986) emphasised the need for careful preparation and for post-adoption services to families to help them cope with the experiences of grief, loss, detachment and anger which an older child is likely to exhibit within the adoptive family. Crowley (1982), too, indicates the need for post-placement support based on her finding that the influence of pre-placement training can lessen with time, while Yates (1985) concluded that post-placement support was "essential" and enabled many placements to survive. Barth *et al* (1986) also advocate sustaining post-placement support over a longer period rather than concentrating input in the initial period, pointing out that the average time for disruption is at 18 months.

The importance of providing adequate financial assistance was emphasised by Barth *et al* (1986) and Nelson (1985), who concluded that such provision can make life for families more tolerable. The valuable role of adoption allowances in securing permanence was confirmed by Hill *et al* (1989). Informal sources of support, including extended family and other adopters, were found to be important for adopting families (Tremetiere, 1979; Coyle and Lyle, 1983; Nelson, 1985). In addition Macaskill (1985) and Yates (1985) claimed that, though informal networks were beneficial, the specialist skills of the placing agency were most helpful when a crisis occurred, so that informal support could supplement, but not replace, a professional post-adoption support service.

Many of the children in Fitzgerald's (1983) sample had not been carefully enough assessed, which resulted in their specific needs not being identified. Barth *et al* (1986) suggest that the use of a standardised Child Behaviour Checklist would be helpful for assessment and matching purposes and for providing adopters with an accurate and detailed picture of the child. Lack of attachment is the most frequently quoted reason for placement disruption, but there is little guidance in the professional literature on how social workers can more accurately predict a child's capacity to attach him or herself to carers. Such knowledge could contribute towards better preparation and matching of child and adopters.

Finally, and considering the special needs of the children involved, it could be claimed that successful results achieved so far are considerable and that disruptions, though distressing for all concerned, are still within acceptable levels. Recent British studies outlined above suggest that successful placements average between 75 and 80 per cent, but wide variations exist depending on age. Perhaps practitioners do not take as many risks now in placing older children as they did at the start of the 'permanency' movement.

The present study

Disruptions*

Our findings confirm those of other studies, referred to earlier, that age is a significant factor contributing to disruptions. The overall disruption rate found among all placements made (Table 1) was only 20.6 per cent, but this escalated with increasing age. It started with a rate of about six per cent for children placed when under the age of nine and then rose dramatically to over a third for those placed in adolescence, but not as high as that found by Thoburn and Rowe (1988).

Like the Strathclyde Permanency Study, almost half of the disruptions occurred in the first year. Seven out of ten disrupted placements had ended by the end of the second year with the overall mean time being 18 months. Somewhat more boys (22 per cent) than girls (18 per cent) disrupted but age at placement, rather than sex, was the decisive factor.

Though the majority of the children in the ongoing sample were adopted (55 per cent), for the remainder the placement had been made on the basis of permanent fostering. The major difference between those children who were adopted and the rest was age. Only one of the children placed before the age of 11 had not been adopted, while adoption was the choice for less than half of those who were over 11 at placement. A similar observation was made by Thoburn *et al* (1986). On the other hand, the children who were adopted were not any less difficult than the rest. An equal proportion (25 per cent) of both groups were considered to have severe difficulties, though since the adopted children were younger their problems often proved less entrenched. Fostering was not only associated with older age but also with ongoing contact with their birth family.

---

*The term disruption as used here refers to termination of placements which happened before or after legislation through adoption.

Children with severe learning difficulties

The experiences of the children with severe learning difficulties were considered separately. Of the 14 children in this sub-sample only one disrupted. This child, whose placement disrupted within six weeks, was placed some distance away which meant supportive services could not be provided, and limited contact with the child's social worker. The Strathclyde Permanency Study also found high levels of placement stability among children with learning difficulties. The children's level of disability varied as did their background experiences prior to this placement. As well as having learning difficulties, six of the children were also physically disabled. Their ages at placement ranged from two to 14 years, with five of them being over ten. The children had experienced a variety of placements and long-stay hospital care was common for them. An average of five years had been spent in care prior to this placement. The child's disability was a major reason for admission to care.

In a majority of the new families at least one parent had previous experience of caring for children with learning difficulties which lends support to similar findings from other studies. Despite the considerable demands of the children, parents were very satisfied with the placements and found caring for the children rewarding. Evidence of the child's emotional development was the greatest reward. The child's dependency needs seemed to help promote attachment between child and parents. The level of social work input was high with good supportive services being considered by social workers to be a main source of strength in the placement. Respite care was identified as particularly crucial. A major concern for many parents was who would care for their children when they were no longer able to do so.

Child variables

Overall the children whose placements disrupted displayed more behaviour problems and were assessed by social workers as being *generally* more difficult than those whose placements continued. Aggressive and destructive behaviour prior to placement made disruption more likely, and this association was particularly strong among children aged 2–10, with 62 per cent of those whose placements disrupted compared with 27

Table 1

Disruption rates by age for the total number of children placed during the period 1982–85

Group	2–5	6–8	9–10	11–14	15+	Total
Total placed	36	43	28	79	8	194
Disputed	2	3	6	29	40	
Disruption rate	5.6%	7%	21.4%	36.6%	0%	20.6%

per cent of those who continued in placement displaying this type of behaviour. Among those aged 11+ a higher proportion of children whose placements disrupted than children whose placements continued were assessed by social workers as having severe difficulties (43 per cent compared with 22 per cent). Though they were assessed as being more difficult, older children did not display more emotional or behavioural problems than the younger ones. What the findings suggest is that carers seem more able to cope with similar behaviour in younger than in older children. The responses from the parents also indicated that during placement younger children's behavioural problems were more likely to improve. It does seem, therefore, that more caution is required in the placement of older children who also display emotional and behaviour problems.

The most common types of behaviour which precipitated disruption were aggression, running away, stealing and lying. Though some of these problems appeared in the ongoing group, "running away" was not mentioned. Particularly testing was behaviour which was perceived by the parents as rejection by the child. Correspondingly the most frequently mentioned strength of the ongoing placements was the emerging attachment between the child and the family. "Attachment" was less often mentioned as a strength in the continuing placements of those placed when over the age of ten. A kind of mutuality, though, was established between child and carers and the carers' commitment and willingness to accept the child facilitated this. Many parents also found the lack of communication from the children very difficult to cope with. Despite the problems and the eventual outcome, the behaviour problems of most children reduced in frequency and severity during the placement and many had developed in confidence and self-esteem.

For those aged 11 and over who had been in care for over five years, foster care rather than residential care seemed to reduce the likelihood of the child's difficulties being severe. Wolkind and Kozaruk (1986), too, found that children adopted from residential homes displayed significantly more problems than those adopted from foster homes. Nonetheless older children who had been predominantly in foster care were more likely to experience disruption while the opposite was true for those placed before 11 years old. The suggestion is that foster families seem to prepare young children well to move on to adoption, but older children may find it more difficult to move from one family to another. Increased numbers of receptions into care and increased moves between foster homes augmented the children's vulnerability to disruption.

Contact with a member of the birth family was more likely to be maintained in placements which continued than in those which disrupted, which was also found by Wedge and Mantle's (1990) study. Some contact with a birth parent had occurred in 18 per cent of ongoing and six per cent of disrupted placements while 49 per cent of children in ongoing placements, compared to 31 per cent of those whose placements disrupted, had contact with at least one member of the birth family during placement. Three-quarters of the children who retained contact were aged ten and over at placement and among this age group 72 per cent of the ongoing group, compared with 37 per cent of the disrupted group, kept in touch with a family member during placement. Several placements which were arranged in other parts of the country disrupted for what appeared to be the children's inability to cope with being totally cut off from their family network of people and surroundings. Placement of siblings together was associated with stability in the placement and the benefits were particularly clear for those placed after being in care for two years or less, a finding supported by Berridge and Cleaver (1987) and the Strathclyde Permanency Study (1990), but not by Wedge and Mantle's (1990) study which attaches more importance to the siblings' individual characteristics.

Substitute family variables

The adoptive/foster parents in the ongoing group were on average older than those whose placements disrupted, but the difference between the two groups were largely cancelled out when those who were previously fostering the child were removed. Unlike some previous studies which linked successful fostering with foster mothers being aged 40 and over, the absence of any connection here may reflect a recent change in recruitment, better preparation of families and increased post-placement support. On the other hand, we found that parents in the ongoing group had been married to each other for longer and were less likely to have had a previous marriage than those whose placements disrupted.

Childless couples seemed more successful in parenting children aged ten and under, but part of their success may have been due to the fact that more children with few difficulties were placed with them and that they were more likely to take sibling groups. Childless couples were, however, also more successful than experienced parents, with more difficult children in this age group. The intervening variable for the lower success rates with young children among experienced parents may have been the presence of their own children near the age of the placed child, but our data were not sufficient to substantiate this or not. On the other hand, childless couples had difficulty in parenting children aged 11 and over even when the latter presented relatively few problems. Families having other adopted or fostered children already as part of the family were associated with increased rate of disruption for those under 11 and with increased chance of success for those who were older. What we may be seeing here is the presence of young children interacting with children of a similar age, which many studies have identified as carrying a high disruption risk.

Sources of stress within the substitute family were more often concerned with relationship rather than practical problems and disrupted placements exhibited more such difficulties. Among parents in successful placements there was greater acknowledgement of some fears about the child's past experience and this was true irrespective of the age of the child placed. This finding confirms impressionistic views and other similar feedback obtained in the past from adoptive parents (Button, 1988; Hill *et al*, 1989).

A higher proportion of successful families were described as "open" in their emotional responses, rather than "restrained" compared to the disrupted group. Note also similar findings by Zwimper (1983). There also seemed to be a close relationship between the making and observing of firm and clear rules and placement stability for children aged two to ten, while both flexibility and "firmness" in rule-making appeared to contribute towards stability for those aged over ten.

Failure of the child or the parents to attach is often quoted as a reason for disruption and factors relating to both the children and families can lead to attachment being achieved or not. Attachment seemed to be achieved earlier when the child was not over the age of ten and was less problematic. A clear desire to make a new family also promoted attachment and this applied to older as well as younger children. Families were able to form attachments when they were committed and ready to persevere, demonstrating acceptance frequently in the face of rejection. Willingness to adjust their expectations or recognise and accept that their children had acquired "handicaps" which might endure also helped families sustain placements.

Agency and childcare practice variables

It may be a surprising finding, but disruptions in this study had not occurred because of a lack of social work support. In fact, disrupted placements had received more frequent post-placement visits and used more services such as day and respite care compared to non-disrupted ones. Increasing difficulties also prompted more visits and back-up services but did not succeed in preventing disruptions. Once a deterioration begins to occur, increased support then seems unable to stem it. Possibly the "risk" has to be assessed from the start and built into the placement.

What families most valued from social workers was their support and it was important that this was readily available and attuned to what the family wanted. Families who adopted a problem-solving approach appreciated the opportunity to talk over ways of tackling problems, and others valued reassurance that they were on the right track and were not to blame for lack of progress. Some parents were also supported by friends, family and other adopters but when there were serious difficulties, their social worker's experience of similar situations was valued, an observation made also by Macaskill (1985) and Yates (1985). The ongoing placements were more generously provided for in terms of allowances. Social workers and parents identified adoption allowances, respite care, babysitting services and holiday breaks as additional support which would have been helpful but was not always available.

The style of service offered differed to some extent according to whether or not the child had been adopted. For example, it was possible during stable periods to withdraw service from adopters, whereas routine visiting and reviewing of the placement continued in respect of those who were fostered. All placements in the study were supported either by a social worker from the homefinding (specialist) team, by an area team worker or by a social worker from another agency. Placements made on behalf of the authority by a range of voluntary agencies disrupted at the rate of 38 per cent compared to the authority's disruption rate of 17 per cent. The differences cannot be completely explained by greater difficulties presented by children referred to voluntary agencies.

Identifying the effectiveness of different types of worker is problematic because of the influence of other factors. For example, experienced social workers in area teams can become specialist in a particular area of work and specialist teams are usually expected to work with the more difficult placements, making "success" more difficult to achieve. In this particular authority, the situation was further complicated by the fact that there was an element of joint working between area team and the homefinding staff in virtually every case, particularly at the preparation stage. This method of working seems to have to some extent overcome the problems usually associated with specialisation, which Rowe *et al* (1990) described as lack of knowledge of local needs, tension with area team staff and the specialist's exclusive use of knowledge. In this case, the centrally-based team had opportunities to develop expertise and to share it with others while at the same time ensuring a degree of uniformity of standards in child placement practice.

After having taken these variables into account, certain differences still emerged. Homefinding staff were particularly successful with difficult children. Their knowledge and expertise, as well as their position in the organisation, seems to have combined to increase their effectiveness. Area team staff had few disruptions but a larger proportion of the placements they supervised were longstanding ones which moved towards permanent arrangements and therefore the most stable. In our view it may not be the organisation of the service itself that matters, but the up-to-date knowledge and expertise possessed and used by the staff involved in this type of work, which is also indirectly supported by Berridge and Cleaver (1987), the Strathclyde Permanency Study (1990) and by other studies which refer to the application of such knowledge in the preparation and post-placement support of families and children.

Beyond 16

The aim of permanency planning is to provide children with an opportunity to form life-time relationships (Triseliotis and Russell, 1984; Thoburn, 1990). The kind of relationships a young person sustains with his new family in adult life will therefore be an important indication of the long-term success of this policy.

Of the 25 children aged 16 and over at the time of the study, 18 were either still living at home or elsewhere but keeping in contact with the family. Overall, five of the children had lost all contact with the family, two of them returning to live with their birth parents. A higher proportion of children beyond the age of 16 who had been adopted, compared with those fostered, continued to live with their new family but of those who left home, the young people who had been fostered were equally likely to keep in touch with their new family as those who had been adopted. For those who moved away from home but kept in touch (six) this was part of the normal process of moving towards independence with their family's support. With the exception of those who were not in touch with their children, the parents expressed satisfaction with the young person's present situation.

Most of the parents anticipated a good future for the children and where problems remained the parents believed they would be able to help the child to cope with them. The outlook was best for those placed before they were 11, but was reasonably hopeful for almost three-quarters of them all. The majority of the placements went a long way in providing opportunities for life-time relationships without depriving older children of continued relationships with members of their biological family.

Summary

Almost 80 per cent of the permanent placements studied here achieved stability by the end of the three-year period covered by the study. The disruption rate of around 20 per cent found is one of the lowest identified by recent studies in Britain. The study could not assess the merits or otherwise of preparation, training and post-placement support because of the almost comprehensive service made available to all children and families included in the study. We can only speculate, therefore, that without this the rate of disruptions would have been higher. More instructive is the fact, confirmed also by other studies, that disruptions increase particularly with an increase in age and then by the degree of difficulties displayed by the child. Children with learning difficulties and those staying on with their foster parents experienced almost no disruptions. Keeping siblings together seemed to aid stability, and contact for older children with members of their birth families did not appear to threaten the stability of the placement.

Childless couples were more successful in parenting young children, but experienced parents were more successful in parenting older children who were disturbed. The presence of biological children posed a serious threat to the stability of the placements of children under ten. Overstressed families experienced more disruptions compared with those whose stresses were not so manifest. A realistic view from the start of possible difficulties and what it takes to parent a "special needs" child, along with the ability to adjust expectations to take account of the child's rate of progress, seem to reduce the risk of disruptions. Commitment and a willingness to persevere were other characteristics that stood out in the ongoing group. Families in the ongoing group, compared with those whose placements disrupted, were more generously provided for in terms of financial support. This enabled them to make personal choices in the selection of support systems. Especially in times of crisis, the social workers' encouragement and expertise were highly valued by the families.

It is apparent from this and other studies, that parenting dimensions vary. Who can successfully parent a child and which children can be successfully parented by carers is still not very clear. Parenting children with "special needs" presents a different challenge from that of caring for children presenting no difficulties. The evidence, however, suggests that the placement of "special needs" children with new families as part of a policy to achieve permanence in these children's lives works well, particularly for those under the age of ten and almost irrespective of disability. Older children, too, can benefit from such arrangements but the risks are considerable. More accurate assessment, better planning, greater thought, preparation and post-placement support seem to be required before a lower disruption rate is achieved. Such placements require agencies to enter into unobtrusive partnerships with new families, making available their expertise and a range of supportive packages without taking control away from them.

Postscript

Rereading this article after ten years, I was struck by the persistence of some of the core issues. In particular I was keenly aware of the links between the work reported here and a recent evaluation, carried out by colleagues and myself, of a foster care project offering an alternative to secure care, the Community Alternative Placement Scheme (CAPS).[1] The links were all the more remarkable since, on the face of it, the newer project was at the opposite end of the permanency spectrum from the work in Lothian.

It was originally envisaged that CAPS placements would last six months, while carers are paid at a level which equates to a full salary and view fostering as their job. However, in practice it turned out that most young people needed at least a couple of years to address their serious

---

[1] Walker M, Hill M and Triseliotis J (forthcoming), *Testing the Limits of Foster Care: An Evaluation of foster care as an alternative to secure accommodation*, London: BAAF.

difficulties, with best outcomes being achieved by young people who found in their carers a life-long friend. As with the children placed in Lothian, the relationship with the carers was crucial. Though within CAPS the term "attachment" was seldom used, carers and social workers talked about young people "engaging" with the carers. Some young people talked about learning to trust and in time believing that they could be valued for themselves. It was also part of the caring task to foster resilience (a concept which is noticeably missing from the earlier article), an essential component of which was reliable support and encouragement from a consistent individual who cared. Carers sought to achieve a balance between encouraging change and conveying acceptance, a challenge similarly faced by the adopters in Lothian.

Links in terms of service delivery were also striking. Some of the youngest children placed with CAPS (age 9–10) needed life-long families, but services geared to permanency had not been able to attract people able or willing to manage the high demands the children posed and were expected to pose throughout their childhood. It seemed that these young people could only be offered stability when their care was undertaken as a job and, for a few, CAPS came to provide this. Stability had certainly eluded many of the 15–16-years-olds placed within the scheme. Some of them represented the failure of permanency planning, having experienced a series of foster and residential placements. In light of this, their placement with CAPS illustrated enduring faith that, even at this late stage, a good experience of family life would enhance young people's future life chances. Both studies showed that these high expectations are more likely to be realised if placements are well resourced, not only in terms of social work support, but also financially and through ready access to other services, notably education.

No doubt other articles in this volume will also serve as a reminder that children and young people's needs remain in some respects constant, even though we may expect to cater for them differently depending on their age, position in the care system and how their needs (and deeds) are framed in the wider social and policy context.

Moira Walker

References

Barth R P, Berry M, Goodfield R and Carson M L (1986) *Older Child Adoption and Disruption*, Chicago: University of Chicago.

Berridge D and Cleaver H (1987) *Foster Care Breakdown*, Oxford: Blackwell.

Berry M and Barth R P (1990) 'A study of disruptive adoptive placements of adolescents', *Child Welfare* 69:3, pp 209–25.

Boneh C (1979) *Disruptions in Adoptive Placements*, Boston: Massachusetts Department of Social Welfare.

Borgman R (1980) 'Antecedents and consequences of parental rights termination for abused and neglected children,' *Child Welfare* 59, pp 391–404.

Boyne J, Denby L, Kettering J R and Wheeler W (1984) *The Shadow of Success: Research report*, Westfield: Spaulding for Children.

Clarke A M and Clarke A D B (1976) *Early Experience: Myth and evidence*, London: Open Books.

Cohen J (1984) 'Adoption breakdown with older children in adoption', in Sachder P (ed) *Current Issues and Trends*, Toronto: Butterworth.

Coyle N and Lyle I (1983) 'The risks in adoption,' *Residential Group Care and Treatment* 2, pp 17–28.

Crowley M (1982) *Preparation for Foster Care Practice*, Monograph: University of East Anglia, Norwich.

Donley K (1983) 'Adoption disruptions before and after legislation,' Paper given at 'Think Tank' Symposium, Cornell University, New York.

Farmer E and Parker R (1989) 'A study of children home on trial in four local authorities', Bristol: Bristol University, Department of Social Administration.

Festinger T (1985) *Necessary Risk*, New York: Child Welfare League of America.

Gill M (1978) 'Adoption of older children: the problems faced,' *Social Casework* 59, pp 272–78.

Hill M, Lambert L and Triseliotis J (1989) *Achieving Adoption with Love and Money*, London: National Children's Bureau.

Hutton S (1988) 'An independent Adopter Support Group,' in Triseliotis J (ed) *Groupwork in Adoptions and Foster Care*, London: Batsford.

Jacka A A (1973) *Adoption in Brief*, Slough: National Foundation for Educational Research.

Jarret J M and Copher M V (1980) 'Five couples look at adopting,' *Children Today* 9:4.

Kadushin A (1971) *Adopting Older Children* (second edition), New York: Columbia University Press.

Kadushin A and Seidl F (1971) 'Adoption failure', *Social Work*, 6 July, pp 32–37.

Kagan M R and Reid J W (1986) 'Critical factors in the adoption of emotionally disturbed youths', *Child Welfare* 1, pp 63–73.

Lahti J (1982) 'A follow-up study of foster children in permanent placement,' *Social Service Review* 56, pp 556–71.

Macaskill C (1985) *Against the Odds*, London: BAAF.

Martin H P and Beezley P (1977) 'Behavioural observations on abused children,' *Dev. Med. Child. Newrol* 19.

Nelson K A (1985) *On the Frontier of Adoption*, New York: Child Welfare League of America.

O'Hara G (1988) 'Preparing families in groups', in Triseliotis J (ed) *Groupwork in Adoption and Foster Care*, London: Batsford.

Parker R (1966) *Decision in Child Care*, London: Allen & Unwin.

Partridge S, Homby H and McDonald T (1986) *Legacies of Loss: Visions of gain an inside look at adoption disruption*, Maine: University of South Maine.

Pringle K (1975) *The Needs of Children*, London: Hutchinson.

Quinton D and Rutter M (1988) *Parenting Breakdown: The making and breaking of inter-generational links*, Aldershot: Avebury.

Rowe J and Lambert L (1973) *Children who Wait*, London: National Children's Bureau.

Rowe J (1987) 'Fostering outcomes: interpreting breakdown rates,' *Adoption & Fostering* 11:1, pp 32–34.

Rowe J, Hundleby M and Garnett L (1990) *Child Care Now*, London: BAAF.

Rushton A, Treseder J and Quinton D (1988) *New Parents for Older Children*, London: BAAF.

Simon D W and Sherwen L N (1983) *Mothers and their Adopted Children: The bonding process*, New York: Tiresias Press.

Stein L M and Carey K (1986) *Leaving Care*, Oxford: Blackwell.

Thoburn J and Rowe J (1988) 'Research: a snapshot of permanent family placement', *Adoption & Fostering* 12:3, pp 29–34.

Thoburn J (1990) *Success and Failure in Permanent Family Placement*, Aldershot: Avebury.

Tizard B (1977) *Adoption: A Second Chance*, London: Open Books.

Trasler G (1960) *In Place of Parents*, London: Routledge & Kegan Paul.

Tremetiere B T (1979) 'Adoption of children with special needs: the client-centred approach', *Child Welfare* 79, pp 681–5.

Tremetiere B T (1984) *Disruption: A break in commitment*, Trasler Lutheran Services.

Triseliotis J (ed) (1980) *New Developments in Foster Care and Adoption*, London: Routledge & Kegan Paul.

Triseliotis J and Russell J (1984) *Hard to Place*, London: Gower.

Triseliotis J (ed) (1988) *Groupwork in Adoption and Foster Care*, London: Batsford.

Wedge P and Mantle G (1990) 'Sibling groups and social work', Norwich: University of East Anglia.

Westhues A and Cohen J S (1990) 'Preventing disruption of special needs children', *Child Welfare* 69:2, pp 141–55.

Wolkind S and Kozaruk A (1986) 'Hard to place? Children with medical and developmental problems', in Wedge P and Thoburn J (eds) *Finding Families for 'Hard-to-place' Children*, London: BAAF.

Yates P (1985) 'Post-placement support for adoptive families of "hard-to-place" children', University of Edinburgh, M.Sc. Dissertation.

Zwimper D M (1983) 'Indicators of adoption breakdown', *Social Casework* 64.

Section VII
Assessment and meeting children's needs

While the input of social workers to step-parent adoptions has usually been late and the influence minimal, for other adoptions they are required to undertake a comprehensive assessment, which has then informed the agency decision whether or not to approve. This can raise great anxieties among prospective adopters, with the future nature of their family and their own self-image and self-esteem at stake.

In the past, the model of assessment tended to be one of the expert social worker in judgement on the adopters (Ryburn, 1992), but in recent years the approach has shifted to a more equal and participative one, with a recognition that at the end of the day there is still a need for a decision to be made about suitability as adopters.

Clark *et al* **(1998)** described an empowerment approach they developed to be more consistent with the principle of working in partnership. A central aim is to enable prospective adopters to assess themselves in the light of information they are given about the needs and demands of the children available for adoption. Corresponding practice with foster carers is also now to combine information and preparation with a considerable degree of self-assessment as regards to general suitability and also the types of children carers believe they are able to look after.

While some practitioners had previously encouraged adopters to make significant contributions to the assessment and report, this new model went further, since all the forms were completed by the applicants except for the social work assessment section and the applicants presented their own assessment to the adoption panel. Group work was an essential component of the approach, providing opportunities for trust-building, mutual support and learning. Feedback from a small numbers of adopters, workers and adoption panel members was generally very favourable, but also drew attention to a few features that required alteration.

The Children (Scotland) Act 1995 requires local authorities, adoption agencies and the courts to take into consideration children's religious, racial, linguistic and cultural background when making decisions about them. This applies to all children, so that for example social workers and carers should respond to the needs of a child whose parents are Irish or Polish Catholics by considering that child's religious identity and linguistic heritage. However, this section of the Act and its equivalent in the Children Act 1989 of England and Wales have been most discussed with respect to children of black and minority ethnic background. In Scotland, the most common minority ethnic backgrounds are Pakistani and Indian (often referred to as Asian or South Asian) and Chinese. Many fostered children are of mixed parentage (Barn *et al*, 1997; Triseliotis *et al*, 2000).

It has become generally accepted that it is preferable for children of minority ethnic background who require substitute care to be placed in families of similar background (Scottish Office, 1997). This means that there should be a suitable pool of foster carers and adopters available, though it does not mean that all minority ethnic carers should only care for a child of the same background.

Singh (1997) argued that the needs of black children arising from their heritage had been largely ignored by adoption and fostering agencies in Scotland. He noted how "colour-blind" approaches to child placement in the 1980s had contributed to the neglect of children's needs to understand, identify with and belong to the community into which they were born. This was particularly important for minority ethnic children who also need support, empathy and role models to deal with racism in its various forms (see also Rhodes, 1992; Barn, 2001). Partly as a result, Barnardo's set up the Khandan Initiative in Edinburgh as part of its family placement scheme.

Appointed as a worker for the Initiative, Singh described an integrated model for assessing Asian families. An essential pre-requisite for white workers is to question and set aside myths and prejudices (e.g. about so-called "arranged" marriages), as well as recognise the strengths of families. What the Americans have termed cultural competence entails assessing relationships according to their own meanings, not those of the majority culture (O'Hagan, 2001). Singh noted how common Asian values about low-key or deferential self-presentation in public could easily be negatively misinterpreted. He pointed out the usually minimal attention

given to religion by white social workers compared with the great importance of this to most Asian families. He urged that religion be a central
and positive part of assessment. The individualism of Western social work
also contrasts with the close (extended) family orientation of Asian
families.

The focus by practice and research for a long time on children as
individuals, meant that two crucial facts were overlooked: the great
majority of looked after children have at least one sister or brother,
and many are placed with siblings. When researchers examined sibling
relationships in relation to foster care, the main emphasis was on whether
or not having a sibling present affected the likelihood of placement
disruption. The results were on the whole inconclusive (see e.g. **Borland
et al, 1991**; Wedge and Mantle, 1991). More recently greater attention
has been given to the meaning of sibling relationships (Mullender, 1999).

Kosonen (1994) stated that psychological research on siblings in
general had shifted from a statistical concern with outcomes (for instance,
as affected by family size or position in the family) to assessing the
processes of sibling relationships. She noted that research had shown
children who have difficult or disrupted relationships with parents are
more likely than usual to have problematic relations with their siblings.
For instance, children with insecure attachments to their parents tend to
display more conflict with each other. Parental conflict and stress is also
likely to affect sibling relationships negatively. In other words, children
in unloving or conflicted families tend to transfer features of their parents'
attitudes and behaviour to each other. However, Kosonen also cited
evidence that in some circumstances siblings can compensate for ill-
treatment by parents and that adults who have been looked after tend to
report the experience as having been eased through sharing it with a
sibling. Kosonen drew the implications that social workers should expect
difficulties in the sibling relationship, but seek to promote the positives
rather than put the children through yet another separation.

Kosonen described the important concept of "non-shared environment". This term was coined to counter the common assumption that
siblings have more or less the same nurturing environment because they
normally grow up in the same household cared for by the same adults. In
fact, the household environment is significantly different, since brothers

and sisters experience the same events at different ages and stages, the context is affected by each other and there are different interactions with the outside world. This helps account for the fact that on many non-physical characteristics, siblings are often very different from each other. Another factor is that some individuals set out to differentiate themselves, partly in order to avoid invidious comparisons (Bryant, 1982; Scarr, 1992).

Subsequently, Kosonen (2002) went on to complete her own study of siblings in foster care. She showed how fostered children usually have more complex sibling relationships that their peers, with high numbers of step- and half-siblings and a considerable likelihood of having siblings they have lost touch with. Foster children's views of their brothers and sisters were found to be varied and often ambivalent, as is the case more generally, but most valued the relationships and expected them to be very important for them in future. She concluded that, despite the adverse factors that children in care often face, it is important for professionals to recognise and optimise their sibling relationships.

It has long been known that children who are separated from their birth parents on a 24-hour basis for long periods and/or have been ill-treated by them tend to have high levels of emotional and behavioural difficulties (Rutter, 1981; Wolkind, 1988). These difficulties have not always been characterised in terms of "mental health", but in the 1990s a number of psychiatrists and psychologists carried out studies showing that high proportions of looked after children had "psychiatric disorders" (McCann et al, 1996; Dimigen et al, 1999). It was also indicated that some conditions, notably depression, often went unrecognised, especially when a young person's unhappiness was masked by anti-social behaviour. **Minnis and Del Priore (2001)** discussed the evidence and the implications for child and adolescent mental health services (CAMHS). One study carried out in Glasgow showed that half the children who were looked after away from home had problems requiring psychological interventions. Older children and boys had higher rates. The most common problems differed by age – whining for under-fives, demanding attention for 5–12 year olds and concentration difficulties for those aged 13 plus. Multiple problems (co-morbidity) were common. The other study also showed high levels of difficulty and low levels of self-esteem. Foster carers were much more likely to identify emotional problems than teachers.

Minnis and Del Priore argue that many of the difficulties are related to attachment problems. The age differences suggest a progression from emotional and relating expression of these difficulties to behaviour problems.

Although the children had relatively high rates of contact with GPs and community paediatric clinics, only a small minority had seen child psychiatric services. This confirms a common concern among social workers and teachers that it is difficult to access psychiatric and psychological services. Minnis and Del Priore suggested that it may be difficult for GPs and teachers to recognise problems that are all too evident to carers, so they do not refer on for treatment. They believe the Looking After Children materials will help act as a screening tool to identify children requiring CAMHS help. Treatment can be difficult, since proven methods have been based on intact families. However, a dedicated service involving foster carers in Glasgow has produced promising results.

The findings of Minnis and Del Priore fit with conclusions drawn by others that careful assessment of children's needs must be carried out before placement. Ideally this should be done with interdisciplinary input (Douglas, 1996; Hindle, 2001).

26 **Empowering prospective adopters**

Irene Clark, Emma McWilliam and Rena Phillips

This article was first published in Adoption & Fostering *22:2, 1998.*

Introduction

This article discusses a change of practice in assessing prospective adopters, introduced by a statutory adoption agency in central Scotland. The innovation was influenced by service users' comments on previous practice. Through a post-adoption support service, feedback was obtained from adopters that the traditional home study was experienced as a passive and sometimes threatening process, over which they had little control.

As a result a new model was developed based on the concept of interactive learning, whereby prospective adopters bring to the process their life experiences, knowledge and skills to share with and learn from each other. It is an attempt to work in partnership, with a gradual transition of power from a position where the social worker uses their expertise to enable prospective adopters to assess themselves. The key elements of the new model are:

- Participants write the BAAF Form F themselves, take part in group work and carry out home work.
- Participants have, as their key worker, one of the two social workers who co-work in the group. The role of the key worker is to facilitate and provide feedback.
- Three to four private sessions are held with the key worker to help participants prepare their written work, raise more personal issues and look at matching issues. For couples, a private session takes place with each of them.
- An experienced adoption worker acts as a consultant to the key workers.

Background

Over the years there have been several accounts of methods of preparation and assessment, such as the investigative individual model based on a home study, the educative/preparation group model and the systemic assessment model, with the emphasis shifting from vetting to the preparation of applicants. Most agencies seem to combine the individual home study with preparation groups (Smith, 1984; Dubois, 1987; Triseliotis, 1988; Douglas, 1996).

Whatever model is employed, the assessment of prospective adopters has attracted a fair degree of criticism. In challenging 'the myth of assessment', Ryburn (1991) has written:

> Social work notions of assessment are based on the idea that there is an objective reality concerning those whom we assess, and that through a process of careful enquiry we can come to discover what this reality is. Such a belief in my opinion accords to recruitment and placement in adoption a scientific base that is very far removed from the 'hit and miss' process which I think it really is. (pp 20–21)

While the previous government's attack on politically correct adoption assessments was in many ways exaggerated, it raised important issues about a complex and challenging area of work. In a recent review of what works in family placements Sellick and Thoburn (1996) established that no outcome research studies have been conducted to evaluate different methods of assessment, either in terms of effectiveness in recruiting more families or in helping children. They conclude:

> In this area of practice unproven 'certainties' abound, and more work is urgently needed to seek out models of practice which are identified with positive service and child outcome results. (p 75)

There is evidence that prospective adopters find the traditional home study daunting (Laing, 1995). Selwyn (1991, 1994) has argued that the powerful and complicated role of workers assessing applicants has largely been ignored and that those who are rejected by agencies lack basic rights and need an effective complaints procedure. In the context of race discrimination Singh (1997) makes the important point that a valid assessment of black prospective adopters needs to steer away from negative myths 'which seriously undermine black people's needs to move towards a richer understanding of the unique and diverse nature and functioning of black families' (p 36). Other issues regarding empowerment are that decisions about what makes a good adoptive parent tend to be subjective, there are difficulties in the operation of adoption panels and concerns exist about the procedures which surround them (McKenna, 1989). There are signs of progress, with some agencies inviting applicants to attend adoption panels (Bingley-Miller and McNeish, 1993; Hender, 1994).

In our view, prospective adopters need to be encouraged and supported, with the power of assessment and evaluation handed back to them as much as possible. This is more likely to happen where the emphasis shifts from professional assessment by social workers to self-assessment by prospective adopters (Stevenson, 1991; MacFadyen, 1995). However, very little has been written about self-assessment by prospective adopters. A recent article in the journal *Adoption UK* describes the result of work carried out between some PPIAS co-ordinators and a new unitary authority to produce good practice guidelines on adoption, with a view to making these applicable to agencies in general. It is interesting to note that under the heading of assessment no mention is made of self-assessment, but the recommendation is made that 'applicants should be given the opportunity to read their Form F in privacy and to recommend amendments and additions where necessary.' (*Adoption UK*, 1997, p 10).

The assessment model

In seeking to develop a more empowering model, the following stages were developed and piloted:

Key stages of the model
- Enquiries from recruitment campaign for hard-to-place children are interviewed by two different social workers.
- Selected enquirers attend a two-day preparation course.
- Adoption team agree from which enquirers to accept an application. Departmental/police/health checks and medicals are satisfactorily concluded.

- Individual working agreements are drawn up with applicants by their key worker. A consultant is appointed.
- Weeks 1–4: Applicants participate in group sessions co-run by the two key workers, and complete sections of BAAF Form F and other related home work.
- Weeks 5–8: Interviews are conducted by a key worker with referees, couple applicants separately and single applicants' main support person. Verbal summary of progress is provided.
- Weeks 9–12: Further group and home work is carried out as before.
- Weeks 13–14: BAAF Form F is completed by applicants with the social worker's assessment section completed by their key worker. Agreement to sign and lodge papers is reached.
- Applicants present their assessment to the adoption panel with preparation and support from the two key workers.

At the pilot stage, the model of self-assessment was offered to those who at the preparation course seemed reasonably comfortable in a group situation and able to express their views and feelings adequately in writing. In subsequent groups there was less concern about writing ability, the content being far more important than the grammar. Participants were given a choice of taking part in a traditional home study combined with a preparation group or the model of self-assessment and group work. They had a right to leave the group at any stage, and the key worker had a right to request they leave the group should a problem arise which necessitated this. In either case, the understanding was that their assessment would then be completed using a home study, unless participants withdrew or were counselled out.

In the pilot of the self-assessment model there were three couples and two single women who had applied to adopt hard-to-place children. All were childless and first-time adopters. One couple withdrew halfway through the group.

Group dynamics

Participants were expected to show a transfer of learning from the group work to their written assessments. For example, they learned in the group about attachment theory and were then asked to examine how their own patterns of attachment would affect them as adoptive parents (Kaniuk, 1996). This can provide evidence of the participants' ability to think critically about what they are learning and their capacity for change. The content and process of the group work was adjusted as the participants progressed, in order to address issues that arose. For example, when they brought up problems around issues of how to deal with lying and stealing behaviour more time was devoted to this through discussion. Techniques such as sculpting were used if participants had difficulties in expressing themselves verbally.

Strong relationships were formed in the group due to the fact that participants were involved in such an intense shared experience. Usually at some point during the group work, the key workers went out of the room and participants were left to carry out an exercise as a group or in two sub-groups. Such opportunities generated a great deal of conversation about relevant experiences which then carried over when the key workers rejoined the group.

Participants gradually became more at ease with sharing personal information and more able to use the group to explore their own and others' issues. The key workers observed increased awareness and changes in attitudes following from this. Participants spontaneously offered support to each other by keeping in touch by phone, meeting outwith the preparation group, checking out information, sharing ideas about the work to be done at home, assisting each other in taking photos for an intro-ductory book and making short videos about themselves for use with the children to be placed with them. However, participants did not read each other's self-assessments, which were regarded as confidential.

Being part of the group helped participants to compare motivations, expectations and current circumstances. It was apparent that they made evaluations of each other and these could help group members acknow-ledge their strengths and weaknesses. For example, specific concerns arose in discussion between the key workers and the consultant about the timing of one couple's application. These issues were discussed with the couple by their key worker at the midway private session, which led them to withdraw. The key workers felt that the group had enabled them to realise that they should not proceed, a decision which they might not otherwise have accepted. The couple gave their key worker permission to outline the reasons for their withdrawal to the rest of the group. In doing so, the key workers realised that the group did not feel threatened by this event as they had identified for themselves that there were problems.

This model seems to be a powerful method which clearly and quickly brings to the attention of participants and the key workers any significant cause for concern about the former. On the other hand, earlier research on self-assessment suggested it was very difficult for the families taking part to say 'no' to each other, so this had to be done by a social worker (Stevenson, 1991). Yet it may well be easier to drop out of a group, especially at the midway break, than to request that a social worker stop visiting in your own home. A recent study which looked at whether preparation groups helped participants to decide whether or not to adopt, concluded interestingly that those who had decided they wanted to adopt before attending the group kept to their decision despite their experience in the group (MacFadyen, 1995). But among a comparison group of participants who withdrew after attending the group, it was found that the group seemed to help people to decide not to go ahead – 'thus, while not deterring the determined, the groups did not encourage the uncertain' (p 102).

Homework

After each group session participants were assigned homework which consisted of reading handouts and undertaking specific tasks. For example, they were asked to produce diagrams of 24-hour clocks showing their current time management and how this would change when a child was placed with them. "Traffic lights" was an exercise used to gauge participants' response to a range of children's emotional and behavioural problems. A response of red signalled non-acceptance, amber indicated a willingness to consider and work through implications and green meant acceptance. Discussion in the group gave participants the opportunity to compare their responses with others and sometimes to modify them.

Participants were given a copy to keep of the book *A Child's Journey through Placement* by Vera Fahlberg (1991) which they made use of and referred to as the sessions progressed. Being introduced to the language and concepts of adoption made participants feel valued, but some were not used to reading more academic works and found it hard going at times. However, the case material in the book was considered particularly helpful. Participants commented on how the life experiences of children placed for adoption illustrated in the book were mirrored in having to look at their own life experiences.

Participants were asked to work on sections of the BAAF Form F as homework after these had been discussed in the group work sessions. Where the participants were a couple, both were expected to contribute to the written work on the Form F. How couples decided to do this provided insight into their relationship – for example, who took the lead in organising the work. Some used computers and others wrote by hand, in which case the key worker arranged for their work to be typed up. As different parts of the form were completed, the key worker gave advice and suggestions about headings, gaps that needed to be filled in, examples they had used in the group work and ways of expanding on what they had learned from a particular experience. Participants were helped to incorporate responses to experiences such as mental illness or reactions to infertility treatment. The key workers saw their role in relation to the Form F as raising questions that an adoption panel might ask. The written contribution by the key worker to the Form F was in the section on the social worker's assessment. This took the form of a summary of the self-assessment process which identified strengths and weaknesses in relation to approval and matching.

The adoption panel

It seemed a natural extension of applicants acting as their own advocates for them to present their self-assessment at the adoption panel. This also served the purpose of giving panel members information additional to that included in Form F. As well as this Form, panel members received material on the content of each group session, the work outside the sessions which participants had completed, the story book compiled on themselves for use with the children to be placed, the key workers' transcripts of each session and the minutes of the consultancy sessions.

Participants were prepared by their key workers as regards the purpose and procedures of the panel. It was emphasised that panel members were not looking for "perfect" adopters. Participants and both key workers arrived together for the panel and were met by the chairperson outside. They had coffee with the panel and were given an explanation of the format before the full discussion took place. The role of the key workers was to be supportive of participants, often acting as a prompt to help them provide relevant examples. For the decision stage, the key workers stayed while participants left but remained in the building. The recommendation of the panel was then conveyed to them by the chairperson.

Consumer feedback

Semi-structured interviews were held with three couples and two single participants, about four months after their approval as adopters and before children were placed with them. As mentioned above, one couple withdrew halfway through the assessment, but it was felt important that their views should also be included.

The participants said their decision to take part in the process centred on the benefits of being with people in the same situation as themselves and the challenge of doing something interesting and different. All but one had taken part before in group programmes through their work situation. Some participants found it more difficult than others to feel part of the group at the beginning. There was consensus that more time should have been spent at the start for participants to get to know each other better in terms of their past histories and reasons for wanting to adopt. The need for more time to help group members relax, make acquaintance and thus participate more in the discussions was found in another study on preparation groups (MacFadyen, 1995).

Visits to the pub to "unwind" after the sessions became the norm, and increasingly participants formed support networks outwith the group, suggesting the need for building in more time for informal contact. After the first few sessions most participants were able to relax and be open with each other, and felt that overall the group was cohesive and worked well together. Among the difficulties reported were members raising issues which were very specific to themselves which took away time from other people, and initial reticence before realising that 'it does not matter if you say something stupid'. One of the single participants felt disadvantaged at not having her sister participate in the group work with her because she saw her sister as closely involved in the adoption plan and as 'the second parent who needed to be educated as well'. Participants thought that the group work should have continued into the matching stage, both to keep the participants informed about each other's progress and to offer support during the difficult stage of waiting for a placement.

There was unanimous agreement that the content of the group work was highly informative and helpful, that participants learned a great deal about child development and were given the opportunity to think seriously and deeply about adoption. There were some criticisms about the over negative picture presented of adoption and the "dwelling on problems". The methods employed such as role play and sculpting were described as enjoyable and good fun. The skills, professionalism and sense of humour of the key workers added to this positive learning experience. The volume of material to read was seen as unrealistic by some, but its usefulness and quality was very much appreciated, and participants thought they would dip into various handouts once they had children placed with them. The break of a month in the middle of the group session and midway meetings with the key worker was perceived by most participants as helpful, particularly in enabling people to reflect as to whether adoption was the right step to take.

This was in fact the point at which one couple decided to withdraw. They felt that without the learning about adoption that happened in the group 'we might not otherwise have pulled out'. They would have found it helpful to have had feedback on the effect on the group of their withdrawal. From the comments of the participants it seems that this did not have too disruptive an effect on the group.

None of the participants had previous experience of writing about themselves in the way required for the Form F. In some this triggered off strong emotions and memories. Responses ranged from it being experienced as therapeutic to having difficulties such as remembering childhood events, not knowing how to deal with "nasty experiences", having 'not an awful lot to say' and lack of writing experience. Finding time to do the writing was also problematic. Most participants were pleased with their efforts and generally felt they were able to share a great deal of themselves through the Form F, though one couple said they were conscious of what was "politically correct" to include. Comments ranged from 'It's my story and I am proud of it' and 'This is me, you have to be honest with yourself', to 'What you see is what you get.'

The private sessions with the key workers were described as helpful and necessary, giving the opportunity to clarify and elaborate points in the Form F and discuss personal issues. Interestingly, the contribution of the social workers to the Form F was seen as affirming and repeating what the participants had already written about themselves.

The attendance at the adoption panel was described as something of an anti-climax for participants. They had felt anxious at the prospect of coming before the panel and had expected to be in for a "grilling", so were surprised and somewhat disappointed at how short their appearance was. Some thought this was because of "the experimental nature" of the process. Also, as one participant said, 'It was all there in the writing', leaving little more to be said.

All the participants liked the fact that the process of being approved as adopters was much quicker than in a more conventional assessment. This contrasted with the frustration expressed at the longer time involved for a placement to happen. By the time of the interviews one couple and one single applicant had been linked with children, but the latter felt this was not right and was subsequently matched with another child. For the rest, waiting for this to happen was difficult to cope with:

We got the impression that there were children in the pipeline.

We expected more offers.

We've done our bit. Where are the children?

Participants were linked to a "waiters' group" for approved adopters waiting for a placement. Some found it helpful 'to meet people in the same boat', but others felt they 'were waiting with nothing to do'. Most of the support was obtained from the participants keeping in touch with each other on an informal basis, and this was expressed as the 'group coming into its own'.

Adoption panel feedback

Interviews were held with three adoption panel members (out of a possible six), who had sat on panels dealing with participants who took part in this new model of assessment. Two of those interviewed were new, both to the self-assessment model and prospective adopters attending adoption panels. The other panel member had some experience of the latter through the membership of another adoption panel in a voluntary adoption agency.

Panel members were very much in favour both of the introduction of self-assessments and of participants presenting the material themselves to the adoption panel. Positives highlighted were the provision of group support and group learning and a shift of responsibility from 'things being done to applicants' to 'taking a strong lead, with social workers in the back seat'. Panel members had no formal training to prepare them for prospective adopters attending the adoption panel. A paper had been written for the panel by the key workers involved with the new model of assessment. After minor adjustments there was agreement to proceed. Panel members were enthusiastic and positive about the experience, stressing the principle of empowerment and the practical benefit of helping panel members to do a more effective job:

It's a fairer process – people taking major decisions should show how they do it.

Adoption should be made an inclusive process as much as possible.

If a worker is raising concerns, we can see applicants addressing it themselves.

While panel members were clear that it was not their job to reassess participants, there was a dilemma as to whether to ask general questions or tackle more sensitive and contentious issues. Overall, the view was that both these areas needed to be addressed – 'You have to keep a balance between not putting people on the spot and not ducking issues.' The experience of taking part in the self-assessment was seen by panel members as helping participants to learn about themselves at the panel. The benefits to panel members of prospective adopters being present were expressed as livelier panels, sharpening practice, being clearer about what they wanted to ask, challenging the panel on what their role was and generally 'helping panels to grow'. Attendance by prospective adopters at adoption panels has now become standard procedure which was very welcomed. At times it was they, rather than panel members, who raised the contentious issues!

One panel member felt that the presence of a prospective adopter at the panel was crucial in moving him away from a negative to a positive view. In this instance the prospective adopter had written about herself in the third person and used "clichés" which was experienced as distancing. This raised questions in his mind as to 'where this person was emotionally'. In contrast, a strong presentation at the panel positively changed the picture for him. In other cases, panel members were reassured, participants were fleshed out and a three-dimensional picture was obtained.

While some applicants were better than others at writing, panel members said that the quality of the Form F was superior to those written by social workers. It was more interesting and informative, the style and content revealed a lot and there was no jargon –'it spoke from the heart'. Interestingly though, the adoption panel members still wanted to have the synopsis from the key workers in order to reaffirm what the prospective adopters had written about themselves in the Form F. This may suggest that the strength of the model is in having the key worker assess how prospective adopters assess themselves. On the negative side it could point to anxieties about the redefinition of the professional role to one of a skilled facilitator.

Feedback from the consultant

When the adoption panel originally agreed to the piloting of this model of assessment they recommended that a consultant be used. Immediately after each group work session the key workers taped a record of what had happened. The transcript was sent to the consultant who then met with the key workers to discuss their observations. Participants knew about the consultant's role and were given feedback on areas of concern and issues that needed further exploration by the key worker.

The consultant observed that the new model helped integrate the theoretical and the personal in a more direct way. This was thought to enable participants to move closer to the reality of older child adoption and focus better on how it would affect them. Another perceived advantage was having two workers throughout, who could lend support to each other and enable them to check out each other's perceptions.

As regards disadvantages of the model, the use of personal experiences in the group work and filling in sections of the Form F might have been too personally and publicly intrusive at an early stage, although participants seemed to cope well with this. The intensity of weekly groups and also having to do formal "personal" homework between sessions raised the question of whether there was enough time for participants to 'internalise the processes or did it instead take on a "task-centred" focus which substituted for allowing the "internalising" work to take place?'. While the consultant was reassured by the key workers that the participants appeared to manage this, she felt that an important task for any workers using this model would be to monitor the process and to slow the pace or make changes if necessary.

Key workers' views

Achieving four to five self-assessments using the new model was more work over a concentrated period of time for the two key workers than undertaking two or three home studies each. No extra resources were made available, there was no reduction in their workload and it was difficult to get a suitable venue for the group meetings in a central location. As a compensation they were working in a highly motivating and supportive situation, with a co-worker and a consultant. A further advantage was 'not formulating opinions about suitability on their own – it's two views not one view'. The support of the consultant was seen by the key workers as 'luxury' and 'heaven'. It helped to dispel anxieties, to talk and think about the work and to be flexible about changes of direction in the groups. This was found to be a challenging approach in which workers are far more exposed than in the conventional model. The balance of power is not so weighted towards the assessing social worker and efforts are made to demystify the process and explain jargon. Participants put pressure on their key worker to keep to agreed timescales and were annoyed when on two occasions there was a significant delay between submitting the papers to the adoption panel and obtaining a date for hearing the application.

As the process is more speedy in this form of assessment, the waiting for a match between families and children becomes more frustrating. One key worker was surprised at how assertive participants became after their approval as regards matching, as they appeared more able to turn down children for good reasons. While the key workers felt that in some respect they were 'losing power' it is important to remember that real power to recommend participants as adopters was still in their hands and those of the adoption panel.

Conclusion

We have described an innovative model of self-assessment by adopters combined with group and homework tasks. Participants were enthusiastic about this model. They reported that they had found the experience made a positive contribution to their lives, and boosted their self-confidence and competency in skills such as communication and assertiveness. After approval, strong ties have continued between group members who have supported each other through the matching process and introduced their adopted children to one another. Six children have been placed with the families from the first group – three singleton placements and one sibling group.

We believe this model produces more meaningful assessments which illustrate the qualities of the participants, evidence their understanding of the adoption task and demonstrate their capacity to learn. Self-assessments showed whether applicants could narrate their own history openly, express anger, consistency and coherence. The model of assessment provides demanding but achievable goals which test out their motivation and ability to see tasks through to completion. When participants were approved it was felt that there was a real measure of the strengths of the resource they were offering.

This model has yet to be tested out in a situation where there is conflict about approval or matching issues between the prospective adopters' self-assessment and the key workers' contribution to the Form F. It is also possible that in this model prospective adopters could more easily deceive the agency about risk factors in their background, but no model of assessment has guarantees attached to it. It could be argued that the components of this model have additional safeguards: the professional judgement of two workers supported by a consultant, sharing life experiences with other prospective adopters in a group situation, and presenting their self-assessment to the adoption panel.

The model needs further refinement but in essence it represents a significant step forward. It can be used with a wider range of participants than first envisaged, and in a subsequent group there were three childless couples and one couple with a young primary school aged child of their own. Future groups could include second-time around prospective adopters who could make a significant contribution from their experience. As discussed earlier, one single prospective adopter would have preferred to have their closest support person attend the group with them. This also raises issues about how to involve the children of prospective adopters in groups, their contribution to the self-assessment and attendance at adoption panels.

We would like to continue to develop the practice of self-assessments but consider it vital to do so in close collaboration with the adoption panel, and for panel members to be offered preparation and training for making decisions in relation to this model of assessment.

Postscript

Concern was expressed in a BAAF Research Symposium when we presented our findings, that under this model of assessment paedophiles could more readily achieve approval as prospective adopters. This is an extreme example of more general concerns that have been expressed about the perceived loss of power by assessing social workers. However, we would argue that this model has more checks and balances than the traditional home study, even when the latter is combined with training sessions.

This is a resource-intensive model of assessment, requiring two experienced social workers and a consultant, to operate within a specified timescale. This model has not been used since local government reorganisation led to the establishment of three smaller authorities and the dispersal of specialist adoption workers. Even within resourcing teams, there is tension between the demands of the adoption and fostering services. Fostering, because it is required to meet more immediate needs, tends to take precedence.

Increasing emphasis is being placed on "partnership" in all forms of social work assessments. In the current climate of criticisms of the role of the social worker in undertaking adoption assessments, would this model of assessment not encourage more people to come forward as adopters and to feel empowered by the process?

References

Adoption UK 82, Daventry: Parent to Parent Information on Adoption Services (PPIAS), August 1997.

Bingly-Miller L and McNeish D (1993) 'Paramountcy or partnership? Applicants attending adoption panel', *Adoption & Fostering* 17:4, pp 15–22.

Douglas C (1996) 'A model assessment and matching', in Phillips R and McWilliam E (eds), *After Adoption – Working with adoptive families*, London: BAAF.

Dubois D (1987) 'Preparing applicants in Wandsworth', *Adoption & Fostering* 11:2, pp 35–37.

Fahlberg V (1991) *A Child's Journey through Placement*, London: BAAF.

Hender P (1994) 'Applicants attending local authority adoption panels', *Adoption & Fostering* 18:1, pp 45–48.

Horne J (1981) 'Group work with adopters', *Adoption & Fostering* 106:4, pp 21–25.

MacFadyen S (1995) 'Preparing or deterring? Consumer feedback on preparation groups for prospective adoptive parents in Barnardo's Family Placement Project, Edinburgh', in Fuller R and Petch A, *Practitioner Research – The reflexive social worker*, Buckingham: Open University Press.

McKenna M (1989) 'What makes a good adoptive parent?', MSc dissertation, University of Stirling.

Ryburn M (1991) 'The myth of assessment', *Adoption & Fostering* 15:1, pp 21–27.

Selwyn J (1991) 'Applying to adopt: the experience of rejection?', *Adoption & Fostering* 15:3, pp 227–29.

Selwyn J (1994) 'Spies, informers and double agents – adoption assessments and role ambiguity', *Adoption & Fostering* 18:4, pp 43–7.

Sellick C and Thoburn J (1996) *What Works in Family Placement?*, Ilford: Barnardo's.

Singh S (1997) 'Assessing Asian families in Scotland – a discussion', *Adoption & Fostering* 21:3, pp 35–9.

Smith C (1984) *Adoption and Fostering: Why and how*, London: Macmillan.

Stevenson P (1991) 'A model of self-assessment for prospective adopters', *Adoption & Fostering* 15:3, pp 30–4.

Triseliotis J (1988) 'Introduction to the preparation and selection of adoptive and foster parents', in Triseliotis J (ed), *Group Work in Adoption and Foster Care*, London: Batsford.

27 Assessing Asian families in Scotland: a discussion

Satnam Singh

This article was first published in Adoption & Fostering *21:3, 1997.*

Introduction

A holistic assessment of the needs of children requiring substitute families is paramount not only for a successful placement, by which I mean a placement that does not disrupt, but also for ensuring the psychological well-being of the child.

In Scotland an important aspect of the child's needs has been largely ignored or underplayed by adoption and fostering agencies. I am referring to the identity needs of black[1] children arising from the child's heritage.[2]

As early as 1979, identity formation and identity maintenance were seen as significant tasks for all children in substitute care. In the words of Germaine (1979):

> *The child who must be placed in substitute care at any age, and regardless of the reason, is torn from the biological and symbolic context of his identity. No matter how nurturing the substitute care, the child's ongoing task will always be to reweave the jagged tear in the fabric of his identity to make himself whole again.*

For black children, however, the denial or whitewash [*sic*] of the child's heritage has resulted in black children being placed transracially into white substitute families. Consequently the task of reweaving the fabric of their identity is made all the more difficult.

---

[1] By black I mean all people who share the common experience of racism, and this includes people from all ethnic minorities.

[2] By heritage I mean the child's racial, cultural, religious, social and linguistic background.

The "colour-blind" approach to social work which precipitated many of these transracial placements of black children owes much to the prevalent ideology of the late 1970s and early 1980s, when it was believed that black children who identified more closely with white people were actually assimilating successfully and, as such, this was seen as a sign of psychological well-being. This assimilationist philosophy was derived from a "cultural deficit" model of social work which viewed black people as lacking, abnormal or deviant. In a critique of this view Rhodes (1992) made explicit the assumptions which were so pervasive throughout the above period:

> ... Black people's lifestyles, family patterns and child-rearing practices are deemed inappropriate to life in the modern, advanced Western society. Social workers' role is to preserve the integrity of British cultural values and to facilitate assimilation.

These melting pot theories also propagated a belief that racism, prejudice and discrimination amounted to a normal and logical reaction to such shortcomings and would necessarily decline once black people fully assimilated into the dominant culture.

Since the 1980s, however, there has been a gradual but significant shift in this thinking due to the influence and struggle of an increasing number of black professionals. This epistemological shift can be traced back to the Association of Black Social Workers and Allied Professionals (ABSWAP), who in their submission to the House of Commons Select Committee in 1983 wrote that:

> Bonding without a sense of racial identity is pathological and is against the best interest of the black child.

Other writers and researchers were also finding evidence to contribute to this emerging ideology. A controversial 1983 study by Gill and Jackson found that transracially placed children only

> ... coped by denying their racial background and had not developed a sense of racial identity – they saw themselves as white in all but skin colour.

Maximé (1984), writing in the mid-1980s and drawing on her work with black children and adults in care, asserted that black children's misidentification or over-identification with white people was in fact pathological. In a letter to the *Caribbean Times* (18 March 1983), David Divine wrote passionately that this one-way trafficking of black children into white families was the modern-day equivalent of slavery. These children, he stated, are:

> . . . *lost to our communities . . . No community can afford hundreds of such casualties each year. No community can be so profligate with its most precious resources – its children.*

There is – and has been for some time – a clear imperative for action, both from academic sources and from the black communities themselves. This imperative is now further legitimated in Scotland by the requirements of the 1995 Children (Scotland) Act, to take account of a child's racial, cultural, religious and linguistic needs.

The Khandan Initiative

It was in response to these imperatives, coupled with a realisation that in Scotland the needs of black children were remaining unmet, that in 1996 Barnardo's Family Placement Services, an adoption and fostering agency based in Edinburgh, developed the Khandan Initiative. "Khandan" means "family" in Punjabi, Hindi and Urdu, and as such reflects very clearly the nature of the work. Put simply, the Khandan Initiative is trying to attract, recruit and support adoptive and foster carers from the Asian population in the central belt of Scotland.

The primary aim of the Initiative is to ensure that same-race placements are the placements of choice for all children referred to the project for placement in a substitute family. In order for this same-race commitment to become a reality, there are many areas of policy and practice that have changed and continue to change. In the rest of this paper I want to look critically at only one aspect of this process, that of the assessment of Asian families.

Towards an integrated model for the assessment of Asian families

Any discussion about work with black families must give regard to the context in which that work takes place. Dutt (1991) argues that for black people in Britain the context is always of racism. Racism is such an indelible part of our lives, it permeates everything we do and it effects every interaction and relationship we have.

It was in this context of racism that Nobles (1978) identified that the history of the study of black families is one which has focused primarily on three themes: poverty, pathology and victimisation. Clearly assessment of black families needs to steer away from these myths which seriously undermine black people and devalue their contribution. Valid assessment of black people needs to move towards a richer understanding of the unique and diverse nature and functioning of black families.

Nobles warned of the danger of "transubstantiation" through a process of "conceptual incarceration" when undertaking assessments of black families. He described transubstantiation as a process 'wherein one defines or interprets the behaviour and/or medium of one culture with the "meanings" appropriate to another culture'. For example, one aspect of a typical assessment of any family might be to try to establish the quality of the relationships within that family, particularly between the husband and wife. A typical worker might then try to assess this by trying to identify the "behaviours" of the family which relay the "meanings" that the worker is seeking. In a typical white family this might mean such things as holding hands, linking arms, cuddling and spending time in shared leisure activities. It would be fair to say that a typical Asian family would probably not display these behaviours. Being unable to identify the "behaviours" which carry the required "meanings" sought by the worker, the Asian family would then certainly fail the assessment.

Another example of possible misinterpretation could arise from the actual structure and process of the interview itself. In a traditional Asian family the gender roles are very clearly defined. This often results in the wife adopting a much more deferential role in public situations. The interviewer might then find that throughout the interview the wife says very little, perhaps even avoids eye contact, often sitting some distance away from her husband or occasionally with her head slightly down. This behaviour in a traditional interview would probably sit uncomfortably with most social workers. It appears to represent an unequal relationship, where the husband holds and wields the power in the family and where the wife is seen as weak and unassuming. The reality, however, would in most cases be very different with the wife having much more responsibility, autonomy and authority within the context of family, extended family and community. What is being observed is not a negative expression of the quality of the husband's relationship, but rather a manifestation of the values of the family's traditions and culture, in other words positive attributes.

The process of "conceptual incarceration" is not dissimilar to that of transubstantiation, and is described by Nobles as a process which 'inhibits people from asking the right questions'. Nobles argues that this so-called inhibition occurs as a result of workers having internalised the dominant culture. I would take Nobles's point a stage further and suggest that, even if the right questions are asked, there is a danger of the worker not having the cultural specificity to understand the answers received. For example, most assessment forms ask for information about religion. A recent review of a random selection of assessment forms within our own project showed that the information about religion was either missing, or was so sparse as to be of no value.

Religion may no longer play an important role in the dominant culture, but for many Asian families and communities it is still a significant factor in the ways in which their lives are ordered. A typical social worker may not give this area much significance throughout the assessment process, and thus be culturally inhibited from asking the right questions. Even if questions are asked about the family's religion, what will the social worker do with a response that the family is, for instance, Sikh, Hindu or Muslim? She or he is not likely to have the conceptual framework to interpret the information being received in any meaningful way. As Nobles puts it:

> One's ability to understand black reality is limited if the "interpretative framework" for the analysis of that reality is based on assumptions associated with a non-black reality.

An effective assessment of black families which is both reliable and valid requires a reorientation away from the traditional structures of assessment towards one which seeks to focus on each family's strengths. It is this position, that assessments should focus on a family's strengths, drawn from their social and cultural milieux, which will form the backcloth for the rest of this discussion. (For a useful discussion and checklist of the strengths of black families which provides a reliable tool around which to build an assessment see Small, 1989.)

Elements of assessment

The traditional assessment focuses on a wide variety of factors, usually including at the very least: childhood, education, health, relationships, work and family.

Each of these areas are also of significance in an assessment of Asian families. However, it is my assertion that a valid assessment of Asian families must at the very least take cognisance of four more specific factors:

- the experience of racism;
- marriage as an institution;
- religion and its impact on family functioning; and
- the balance between the family and the self.

The experience of racism

It is important to recognise the impact that the experience of racism has in the way the family functions, about the attitudes and values the family expresses, and the way family life is generally structured on a day-to-day basis. Without a recognition of the centrality of these experiences it is not possible to produce a valid assessment. Without a doubt, the experience of racism will be the single most common feature of every Asian family. This common experience will impinge on every aspect of life, on every member of the family and on every system and sub-system within that family.

For many individuals the experience of racism will be an inextricable part of their growing up, education, work and leisure throughout their lives in Britain. For others this experience will be amplified by the experiences of loss and change associated with the process of migration. It is important then to ensure that, as these experiences are so central to the existence of Asian people and families, they are not marginalised, side-lined or denied. Instead it is important to recognise the strength, stamina and capacity to flourish and develop in adversity as being positive attributes.

Marriage as an institution

It is probably true to say that the institution of marriage is still of fundamental importance to Asian families and communities, to the extent that its corollary of divorce, separation, adultery and infidelity all exist but are either repressed, denied or not spoken about. Such issues as same-sex relationships are strictly taboo.

The crucial point for an assessment is the recognition that although marriage is "universal", the actual structure, form and meaning vary dramatically across cultures. Most Asian marriages have in the past been arranged, as are many today. These simple words "arranged marriage" carry many racist connotations of young girls being forced against their will to marry older men. The truth of the matter is that "force" and "against their will" are social constructs imposing a reality that does not exist. Marriage within Asian communities, as anywhere else, is a complex social arrangement with subtleties inextricably rooted in culture and history. Marriage is seen not just as a union of two people, but a union of two families. For this union of families to be successful meticulous planning and preparation are required, much of it shrouded in ritual and custom. It is this planning that gives rise to the myth of "arranged".

Marriage is rarely the end product of a long romance, rather the beginning of one. Indeed, romance is rarely seen as a prerequisite for a successful marriage. In many cases marriages will have taken place abroad, or where one partner is from abroad. Marriages nearly always exist within the context of an extended family and, even where the extended family is fragmented across geographical space, its unity and sanctity remain paramount.

It is clear that in assessments of Asian families we need to be aware of the many extra dimensions to marriage, for it is this richness of marriage as an institution that provides the positive substance and material of assessment.

Religion and its impact on family functioning

Although in the West we live in an increasingly secular society, this contrasts sharply with the role of religion in Asian families for whom it provides many things. Against the backdrop of racism religion provides a mechanism for affirming and re-affirming identity, not only with other Asians but also with Asian culture and history

Religion can then be seen as providing meaning, security and continuity in the lives of most Asian families. It also shapes, informs and structures much of their daily lives, by providing rules of conduct, codes of ethics and moral frameworks for interpreting life events. Therefore any proper assessment of Asian families must consider the role of religion in the family's life and how it shapes or influences family functioning. Religion is a central concept to the assessment and should not be confined to a peripheral question to be ticked off on an assessment checklist.

Balance between family and self

The modern world has been described by Lasch (1977) as narcissistic, based as it is on the "cult of the individual". He describes the modern personality as shallow, self-centred and lacking emotion. The Asian family, in contrast, does not necessarily place so much importance on the individual. In many cases it is the family or community that is considered to be supreme. It is assumed that either the needs of the individual are one and the same as the needs of the family or group, or that the needs of the individual will be fulfilled when the needs of the family or group are met.

This shift in emphasis in the balance between self and others sits uncomfortably with social work values of promoting independence or empowerment. It is important that assessments take into account that individuals and families do function differently and that at times these may be based on different value systems. Cognisance needs to be given to the way this strong family orientation manifests in the daily functioning of the family and how it is expressed in the family's value system.

Conclusion

It is not possible to be conclusive about what should and should not form part of an assessment. As every worker knows, assessments are as individual as the families being assessed, and we need to be alert to this fact. I have, however, tried to bring together four key elements which must inform any valid assessment of Asian families. Only then can we be sure of identifying the real potential of Asian families in a way that is both relevant to their experiences and that focuses on their particular strengths in a much more meaningful way.

Postscript

Since the publication of this paper in 1997, the Khandan Initiative has assessed and approved a number of Asian families, and indeed made placements of children. The majority of these assessments and the post-placement support has been and will be provided to the Asian families by white workers, raising new challenges to our practice. It is useful to consider the perspective of white workers and a white colleague writes (Singh and McFadyen, 1997):

> *In the two previous assessments I had undertaken of black and Asian applicants I had found myself floundering. I was both paralysed by an acute awareness of the cultural bias in much of the process and content of a conventional fostering assessment and at the same time I was uncertain as to how to integrate different perspectives, values and norms into the usual criteria of a Form 'F'. The framework being proposed in this article has helped me with both dilemmas, and it has provided another and very significant guide to the assessment structure process. Focusing on these four (and there may be others) themes within each conventional area of the Form 'F' has opened up territory that might otherwise have remained unexplored or misunderstood on my part. It has also helped me to shift my own thinking and perspective as well as my intention, beyond what is over familiar and culturally biased and thus discriminatory.*

My experience of this assessment has been radically affected by sharing it with an Asian colleague. This joint work has challenged and encouraged my own learning and sensitisation. The value of such an opportunity should not be underestimated.

The Khandan Initiative continues to develop and over the last few years we have placed six black children into permanent same-race placements. In addition we have two black families approved for respite and fostering. In November 2001, the Khandan Initiative won the Community Care awards for innovative work within the children and families category.

References

ABSWAP (1983) 'Black children in care', Evidence to the House of Commons Social Services Committee.

Ahmed S (1981) 'Children in care: the racial dimension in social work assessment', in Cheetham I, Loney M, Mayor B and Prescott W, *Social and Community Work in a Multi-racial Society*, London: Harper & Row.

Cheetham J (1982) 'Problems of adoption for black children', in Cheetham J (ed), *Social Work and Ethnicity*, London: National Institute of Social Work.

Divine D (1983) 'Time for decision', The *Caribbean Times*, 18 March.

Dutt R (1991) 'Open adoption – a black perspective', *Adoption & Fostering* 15:4, p 111–15.

Gaber I and Aidridge J (eds) (1994) *In the Best Interests of the Child: Culture, identity and transracial adoption*, London: Free Association Books.

Germaine C B (1986) 'Social work practice: people and environment' (1979), in Maluccio A, Fein E and Olmstead K, *Permanency Planning for Children: Concepts and methods*, London: Tavistock.

Gill O and Jackson B (1983) *Adoption and Race: Black, Asian and mixed-race children in white families*, London: Batsford/BAAF.

HMSO (1995) The Children (Scotland) Act, London: HMSO.

Lasch C (1977) *Haven in a Heartless World: The family besieged*, New York: Basic Books.

Maximé J (1991) 'Some psychological models of black self-concept', in Ahmed S, Cheetham J and Small J (eds), *Social Work with Black Children and their Families*, London: Batsford/BAAF.

Maluccio A (1986) *Permanency Planning for Children: Concepts and methods*, London: Tavistock.

Nobles W (1978) 'Toward an empirical and theoretical framework for defining black families', *Journal of Marriage and the Family* 70, pp 679–88.

Rhodes P (1992) *Racial Matching in Fostering*, Aldershot: Avebury.

Small J (1989) 'Transracial placements: conflicts and contradictions', in Morgan S and Righton P (eds) *Child Care: Concerns and conflicts*, London: Hodder & Stoughton.

Small J (1991) 'Ethnic and racial adoption within the United Kingdom', *Adoption & Fostering* 15:4, pp 61–9.

28 Sibling relationships for children in the care system

Marjut Kosonen

This article was first published in Adoption & Fostering *18:3, 1994.*

Studies of children in foster and residential care confirm the importance of siblings. A review by Hegar (1988) of the literature on siblings and child placement concluded that 'sibling bonds are highly important to many foster children', and that 'brothers and sisters usually have a meaning for each other that unrelated children lack'. Studies exploring the experiences of adults who were brought up "in care" or who grew up adopted (Ferguson, 1966; Meier, 1966; Triseliotis, 1980; Triseliotis and Russell, 1984) confirm the long-term importance of brothers and sisters to children who grow up separated from their parents.

This article will look at the qualitative aspects of children's relationships with their siblings and identify a number of factors which are likely to make the development and maintenance of positive sibling relationships more problematic for children who are looked after in residential and foster care than is the case with children in general.

The outcome of research studies exploring the development of sibling relationships for children in general – and for particular groups of children such as children in divorced families, abused and neglected children, and children living in dysfunctional families – point to factors which make the nature and quality of sibling relationships potentially difficult for children in residential and foster care. These factors are emerging from an increasing number of studies, mainly in the field of developmental psychology.

Much more is now known about factors which influence the development of sibling relationships during childhood, yet little of this knowledge appears to have an impact on current social work practice. These factors are discussed in the light of research evidence drawn both from social work and psychology literature in Britain and North America.

Sibling research

Academic interest in children's sibling relationships is a fairly recent development. Research interest in the 1960s and 70s focused mainly on the effect of family structure variables such as age, gender, family size and the child's position in the family on sibling relationships (Bossard and Boll, 1956; Koch, 1960; Sutton-Smith and Rosenberg, 1970). The focus of study was on the individual.

During the following two decades there has been a shift in focus from the individual to the relationship (Dunn and Kendrick, 1982; Lamb and Sutton-Smith, 1982; Dunn, 1983; Furman and Buhrmester, 1985; Boer, 1990; Buhrmester and Furman, 1990). Research concerning children's sibling relationships during early and middle childhood periods focused primarily on sibling pairs living in intact two-parent, middle-class families. Sibling relationships, although marked by a degree of conflict, were generally found to be viewed positively by the children. Following this influential research into the development of sibling relationships for children in the general population, attention has also focused on particular groups of children and on the impact which family relationships and other early experiences have on the nature and quality of sibling relationships during childhood.

Factors influencing the development of sibling relationships

There has been an increasing interest in the complexity of sibling relationships and the many factors which influence the quality of children's relationships with their brothers and sisters. It is this more recent research which can be particularly significant for children in the care system. Several of these factors indicate that children with difficult or interrupted relationships with parents are more likely to have problematic relationships with their brothers and sisters.

These factors include:
- quality of parent–child relationships and early attachment;
- quality of parental relationship;
- emotional climate in the family, family stress and conflict;
- neglect and parental unavailability;

- impact of abuse on the abused and non-abused children;
- differential parental treatment;
- impact of non-shared environment;
- "high access" to siblings.

The significance of these factors is considered below in more detail.

Attachment to mother and parent–child relationship
The internal working model of relationships, based on the quality of the relationship with the child's early attachment figure, has been considered to influence the child's relationship with siblings and others (Sroufe and Fleeson, 1986). Research into young children's relationships with their siblings has found that children who are securely attached to their mother are more likely to react positively towards their younger siblings and comfort them, whereas insecurely attached children are likely to react negatively and show aggression towards their mothers and siblings (Bosso, 1985; Teti and Ablard, 1989; Volling, 1990, cit. in Vandell and Bailey, 1992). Volling found that children who had been insecurely attached to both mother and father displayed most frequent and intense sibling conflict. Dunn and McGuire (1992) suggest that the link between attachment status and sibling relationships is not straightforward and that more research in this area is needed.

Parental relationship
The quality of the relationship between parents has been found to be important in shaping sibling relationships. A number of recent research studies have found an association between parental disharmony or conflict, and poor sibling relationships (Hetherington, 1988; MacKinnon, 1989; Jenkins, 1992). Little evidence was found of supportive relationships developing between siblings in divorced families. Boys, in particular, were found to have problematic relationships with their siblings (MacKinnon, 1989). Researchers concluded that children tend to imitate their parents' hostile interactions, leading to increased conflict between siblings. However, it is important to bear in mind that children who were found to have hostile relationships with one sibling often had closer relationships with other siblings.

Emotional climate and family stress

The general emotional climate of the family, including parents' psychological state, has also been found to influence the quality of sibling relationships. In a poor family environment sibling relationships are also more likely to be negative than when the emotional climate in the family is positive (Brody and Stoneman, 1987).

Bank and Kahn (1982) suggest that even in a poor family environment sibling relationships are likely to be more positive if children's early emotional needs are met, the emotional climate was found to be better during the pre-school years and where one sibling is not favoured over others. Jenkins (1992) suggests that where children from disharmonious homes had a close and supportive relationship with a sibling, this affords some protection against the development of psychological disturbance when they are under stress.

Neglect and parental unavailability

When parents are not available, either physically or psychologically, the vacuum of parental attention may be filled by an older sibling taking care of the younger ones. In large families maternal unavailability has been found to promote interactive and prosocial behaviour between siblings (Bryant, 1992). Weisner and Gallimore (1977) in their review of studies into sibling caretaking, suggest that older siblings can have an important role in the socialisation process and that children do not suffer when cared for in part by older children as opposed to their parents. However, in some situations lack of parental care may lead to a failure to meet the child's needs, leading to increased conflict between siblings. Also, lack of parental care and attention may leave children inadequately supervised and at risk of abuse by siblings or others. Bank (1992) agrees that parental unavailability can increase bonding between siblings, but suggests this bonding is not always a positive emotion. Sibling bonding which develops particularly in traumatic conditions can be 'warm, clinging, fearful, ambivalent, violently negative or marked by disappointment'.

Impact of abuse

The impact of the trauma of abuse on all children in the family is significant. Both abused and non-abused children in the same family have been found to be negatively affected. Halperin (1983), in her study of children's perceptions of each other and their parents, found that children in abusing families perceived each other more negatively or ambivalently than those in the control families. Pfouts (1976) suggests that abused children may feel more hostility towards their siblings than vice versa. Boys were found to be hostile towards their brothers, particularly if they were compared with them (cit. in Halperin, 1983).

Parental favouritism

Children's perceptions of how their parents treat them and their siblings is considered to have an effect on the quality of their relationships with their siblings. It does not matter how fairly the parents think they treat their children, it is the children's perceptions which count. Vandell and Bailey (1992), in their review of the literature on sibling conflict, suggest that differential parental treatment increases sibling conflict, and has a negative effect on both the favoured and non-favoured child. Also, 'children, who experience a marked decline in the quality of their inter-action with their mother, reflect this in their relationship with their siblings'. Dunn and McGuire (1992) suggest that the link between differential maternal treatment of children and conflict and negative behaviour between siblings may be especially strong for families under stress.

Impact of non-shared environment

Despite living in the same family, children are subject to environmental influences, which are not shared with their siblings. These are called non-shared influences and are considered to be developmentally important (Dunn and Plomin, 1991). Such non-shared influences include parent–child relationship, sibling–sibling relationships, relationships with friends, relatives, teachers and other adults outside the family. The impact of potentially stressful changes in the child's life, such as separations from parents and siblings, illness, house moves, changes of school and parental unemployment, may have a different impact on each child – an effect which can have a cumulative effect over a period of time. Dunn and Plomin suggest that the non-shared influences are particularly important for the development of sibling relationships, as they are likely to make siblings different from each other.

427

"High access" to siblings

The amount of contact children have with their siblings is also considered to have an impact on the children's relationships with their siblings. Children who are closely spaced, or twins, inevitably spend a lot of time together, particularly during the pre-school years. "High access" to siblings occurs in situations when siblings are closely spaced and the same gender. "High access" siblings are likely to share more in terms of physical space, school, friends and similar interests. High access is likely to promote emotional intensity, leading to increased conflict between siblings.

Closely spaced siblings have been found to experience more conflict in their relationships with their sibling than those more disparate in age (Buhrmester and Furman, 1990). Bank (1992) suggests that if there is "high access" and parents are frequently unavailable, sibling relationships are likely to be particularly intense.

This literature review has identified from the research into sibling relationships a number of factors which can have an influence on the development of sibling relationships for children who are looked after. These factors are not independent, they are likely to interact with each other. Dunn and McGuire (1992), in their review of literature on sibling and peer relationships in childhood, stress the importance of recognising the possibility of mutual influence, and not assuming causal direction from the findings of the current research. They suggest that research evidence is not straightforward. Links between the factors identified as having an influence on sibling relationships should be treated as correlational rather than causal.

Much more needs to be known about the dynamics between the factors which influence sibling relationships and which combinations of particular factors are likely to have the most crucial impact on children's relationships with their brothers and sisters, and in what way.

For many children in residential and foster care, sibling relationships undoubtedly provide a sense of kinship and family identity, and support and comfort while they are living separately from their parents. However, children in care also possess many of the background features which characterise children with problematic sibling relationships. Many of the children come to be looked after because of abuse, from homes marked by parental conflict and family stress. Such children are likely to express ambivalence and conflict in their relationships with their siblings. It is not therefore surprising that sibling conflict is often cited as a reason for not placing siblings together.

Another commonly found reason for placing siblings separately is an assumption that the child's individual needs are considered too pressing. The child is considered to have emotional and behavioural problems requiring undivided parental attention. Rarely is there an acknowledgement that these particularly vulnerable children are likely to have the most difficulties in developing and maintaining positive and supportive relationships with their brothers and sisters. Yet studies of adults who have been brought up in care or adopted tell us that they were the children most likely to need the continuity of supportive sibling relationships.

Conclusions

A review of the literature concerning the development of sibling relationships during early and middle childhood points to the emergence of factors which are likely to hinder the development and maintenance of strong and supportive sibling bonds for children in the care system. Many children in care possess the same background features which characterise children with problematic sibling relationships. Family relationships, quality of parenting and children's early experiences have an influence on the nature of relationships children develop with their brothers and sisters. Some children in care may be closely bonded to their siblings, although this bonding is not always a positive emotion. Others may express hostility or ambivalence towards their siblings. All sibling relationships are likely to have both positive and negative features. Although the negative features are common and may relate to more generalised relationship difficulties with peers and others, they do not need to be inevitable.

Children's relationships with their brothers and sisters require much closer attention from social workers, their managers, fostering and adoption panel members, those making decisions within the judicial system and, most importantly of all, from substitute carers. Decisions about the placement of children with their siblings or separately should be made after a careful assessment of the quality of the relationship has been undertaken. The assessment should take into account the key factors which have been identified as having an influence on children's relationships with their siblings.

Much more needs to be known about the complexity of sibling relationships for children separated from their families. Children's own views and perceptions about the meaning of sibling relationships should be explored.

Proactive ways of working with siblings should be developed by social work practitioners and carers. The focus of this work could be the children's shared and separate experiences in their families of origin, and a sense of identity and knowledge about their birth family. Attempts should be made to counteract the potentially negative early influences and to help children to foster positive aspects in their relationships with their siblings. Sibling bonds formed during childhood are likely to be an investment for the future, ensuring opportunities for the development of life-long relationships.

Postscript

In 1994, I urged social workers to learn more about the quality of children's sibling relationships from a body of literature, located primarily within developmental psychology. This literature seemed to stand apart from social work in that there were few exchanges of ideas between the two fields of study. The reviewed literature supports the notion that the quality of children's sibling relationships is likely to reflect their early relational experiences and quality of parenting. These are particularly likely to affect the "intensity of the emotional tone", relationships between siblings being more hostile (characterised by high level of hostility and low warmth) in families where both parent–child and parental relationships are negative (McGuire et al, 1996). Researchers, working from the perspective of developmental psychology, were focusing on relationship aspects, looking for ways of categorising the key qualities that characterise sibling relationships for children in general, and those in special populations. The review concludes with a suggestion that looked after children share similar family background features that characterise children with difficult sibling relationships; therefore, it is not surprising that sibling conflict is a commonly cited cause for placement difficulties.

The aim of this article was to draw social workers' attention to this previously less well-known field of research. This of course presents only a partial picture. Sibling relationships are multifaceted and complex, and not easily understood by the use of any single approach. During the 1990s there was an increasing interest in children's family relationships in general, representing a broader range of theoretical perspectives and supporting a more complex and differentiated view of children's sibling relationships. While there is evidence to suggest that children's family processes and environments affect the way siblings interact with one another, there are other important consideration to be born in mind.

Sibling relationships are characterised by their enormous diversity *(Boer, 1990). The way siblings interact and negotiate their relationships also depends on family constellation, i.e. age, birth order, age difference, gender and family size. Birth order and age difference between siblings are considered to determine the power balance between siblings. Studies of sibling interaction and behaviour suggest that there are some* relationship processes *that are particularly salient for children in middle childhood. Siblings can provide considerable emotional and practical support to one another. They can develop strategies to deal with competition and potential rivalry, yet in many sibling relationships conflict manifests itself in arguments, physical aggression and fighting, and for some children, in sibling abuse. Some children's ability to survive their adverse circumstances reflects their* resilience. *It is important to remember that children are not passive recipients of their family and environmental processes; they interact with, and influence the course of their relationships by their own choices and responses. Regrettably, children's views on their siblings, and their contribution to the nature and quality of relationships are not generally reflected in the research literature.*

Siblings are individuals' life-long key family and kin, and a source of shared knowledge of one's biological and social roots. It is through siblingship that a network of kin, i.e. aunts and uncles, nephews and nieces, are acquired. When making any decisions about children's welfare which can potentially lead to the severance of sibling ties, social workers should consider children's right to siblings in the long term as their key family and kin. Decisions which are based solely on the quality of the current relationship *between siblings may lead to separation of siblings when relationships are poor, and deprive individuals of the potential sibling support in adulthood and old age.*

In conclusion, it is no longer fair to say that siblings are absent in social work literature. There has been a real growth of interest in looked after children's siblings, representing a broad range of perspectives. By 1999, 24 papers were published in an excellent anthology of writing, We are Family: Sibling relationships in placement and beyond, *edited by Audrey Mullender (1999). This brought together the most recent research on sibling placements and relationships, first-hand personal and professional accounts, and experiences of siblings in adulthood. The needs of particular groups, such as black siblings and sexually abused and abusing siblings were considered. Although many of the studies are small scale, they address current concerns in the context of British social work policy and practice. The book is a real "must" for social work students and practitioners. Another welcome addition to social work literature is Rushton* et al's *(2001) study of siblings in late permanent placements. This follows a sample of 133 children in 72 new families for a year in placement. The book presents a wealth of information on the complexity of placing children, with or without siblings in permanent care, that no child care worker should do without.*

References

Bank S (1992) 'Remembering and reinterpreting sibling bonds', in Boer F and Dunn J (eds), *Children's Sibling Relationships: Developmental and clinical issues*, Hillsdale, NJ: Lawrence Erlbaum.

Bank S and Kahn M D (1982) *The Sibling Bond*, New York: Basic Books.

Boer F (1990) *Sibling Relationships in Middle Childhood*, Leiden: DSWO Press, University of Leiden.

Brody G H and Stoneman Z (1987) 'Sibling conflict: contributions of the siblings themselves, the parent–sibling relationship and the broader family system', in Schachter F F and Stone R K (eds), *Practical Concerns about Siblings*, New York: The Haworth Press.

Bryant B K (1992) 'Sibling caretaking: providing emotional support during middle childhood', in Boer F and Dunn J (eds), *Children's Sibling Relationships: Developmental and clinical issues*, Hillsdale NJ: Lawrence Erlbaum.

Buhrmester D and Furman W (1990) 'Perceptions of sibling relationships during middle childhood and adolescence', *Child Development* 61, pp 1387–398.

Dunn J (1983) 'Sibling relationships in early childhood', *Child Development* 54, pp 787–811.

Dunn J and Kendrick C (1982) *Siblings: Love envy and understanding*, Cambridge, Mass.: Harvard University Press.

Dunn J and McGuire S (1992) 'Sibling and peer relationships in childhood', *Journal of Child Psychology and Psychiatry* 33:1, pp 67–105.

Dunn J and Plomin R (1991) 'Why are siblings so different? The significance of differences in sibling experiences within the family', *Family Process* 30, pp 271–83.

Ferguson T (1966) *Children in Care and After*, Oxford: Oxford University Press.

Furman W and Buhrmester D (1985) 'Children's perceptions of the qualities of sibling relationships', *Child Development*, 56, pp 488–61.

Halperin S M (1983) 'Family perceptions of abused children and their siblings', *Child Abuse & Neglect* 7, pp 107–15.

Hegar R L (1988) 'Sibling relationships and separations: implications for child placement', *Social Service Review*, September, p 446–67.

Hetherington E M (1988) 'Parents, children and siblings: six years after divorce', in Hinde R and Stevenson-Hinde J (eds), *Relationships within Families: Mutual influences*, Oxford: Clarendon Press.

Jenkins J (1992) 'Sibling relationships in disharmonious homes: potential difficulties and protective effects', in Boer F and Dunn J (eds) *Children's Sibling Relationships: Developmental and clinical issues*, Hillsdale NJ: Lawrence Erlbaum.

Koch H L (1960) 'The relation of certain formal attributes of siblings to attitudes held towards each other and towards their parents', *Monograph of the Society for Research in Child Development* 25:4, serial no. 78.

Lamb M E and Sutton-Smith B (1982) *Sibling Relationships: Their nature and significance across the lifespan*, Hillsdale, NJ: Lawrence Erlbaum.

McGuire S, McHale, S M and Updegraff K (1996) 'Children's perceptions of the sibling relationship in middle childhood: connections within and between family relationships', *Personal Relationships* 3, pp 229–39.

MacKinnon C A (1989) 'An observational investigation of sibling interaction in married and divorced families', *Developmental Psychology* 25:1, pp 36–44.

Meier E G (1966) 'Adults who were foster children', *Children* 13:1, pp 16–22.

Mullender A (ed.) (1999) *We are Family: Sibling relationships in placement and beyond*, London: BAAF.

Rushton A, Dance C, Quinton D and Mayes D (2001) *Siblings in Late Permanent Placement*, London: BAAF.

Sroufe L A and Fleeson J (1986) 'Attachment and construction of relationships', in Hartup W W and Rubin Z (eds), *Relationships and Development*, Hillsdale, NJ: Erlbaum.

Sutton-Smith B and Rosenberg B (1970) *The Sibling*, New York: Holt, Rinehart & Winston.

Triseliotis J (1980) 'Growing up in foster care and after', in Triseliotis J (ed.), *New Developments in Foster Care and Adoption*, London: Routledge & Kegan Paul.

Triseliotis J and Russell J (1984) *Hard to Place: The outcome of adoption and residential care*, London: Heinemann.

Vandell D L and Bailey M D (1992) 'Conflicts between siblings', in Shantz C U and Hartup W W, *Conflict in Child and Adolescent Development*, Cambridge: Cambridge University Press.

Weisner T S and Gallimore R (1977) 'My brother's keeper: child and sibling caretaking', *Current Anthropology* 18:2, pp 169–90.

29 Mental health services for looked after children: implications from two studies

Helen Minnis and Christina Del Priore

This article was first published in Adoption & Fostering *25:4, 2001.*

Introduction

Serious concerns have recently been voiced in a number of reports about the high level of emotional and behavioural problems experienced by children in residential and foster care (McCann *et al*, 1996; Quinton *et al*, 1998; Dimigen *et al*, 1999; Minnis *et al*, 2001). McCann *et al* found that 96 per cent of children in residential care and 57 per cent in foster care had psychiatric disorders and that potentially life-threatening yet treatable conditions such as major depressions were being under-diagnosed (McCann *et al*, 1996). Evidence suggests that neglect and abuse are common precipitants for entry into care (Lawder *et al*, 1986; Benedict *et al*, 1996), and levels of disturbance found after entry into care may reflect experience both before and after accommodation. It is generally agreed that looked after and accommodated children are among the most vulnerable in society and many require psychological help. There has been insufficient attempt to study how mental health services might best contribute to this population in the UK. This may be due to the fact that not much is known about the particular needs of these children.

There is good evidence that, for children with severe psychopathology, specialist fostering schemes are beneficial (Chamberlain *et al*, 1992; Clark *et al*, 1994). The successful specialist schemes which were evaluated offered two-hour group sessions, three to five hours of face-to-face contact plus frequent telephone communication with staff each week, therapy for the child and family where appropriate and a significantly improved fostering allowance. Recently researchers in the USA have suggested that we need to go beyond "specialist" foster care into "professional" foster care in which carers are paid a substantial annual salary in addition to receiving good training and support (Testa and Rolock, 1999). These schemes are expensive and only cater for the most severely disturbed young people. There is still no good evidence for what will help the many children in "mainstream" foster or residential care who have significant mental health problems.

This paper describes two studies which have recently been completed in Scotland and which, in different ways, contribute to this issue. The Survey of Children Entering a Looked After and Accommodated Episode in Greater Glasgow Health Board (known as "the Glasgow study") was a cross-sectional survey examining the mental health of children entering a first episode of foster or residential care (Dimigen *et al*, 1999). The Foster Carers' Training Project (known as "the Central Belt study") was a randomised controlled trial of a training programme for foster carers and the cross-sectional data only will be discussed here (Minnis *et al*, 2001). The two studies, despite being planned and funded independently, fortuitously provided complementary data on the mental health of Scottish looked after children, and gave pointers towards the kinds of services which may be most appropriate for this most vulnerable of groups.

Aims and methods of the two studies

The Glasgow study

This study aimed to gain information on the frequency and severity of mental health problems in children entering local authority care, with a view to planning a psychological service and an early intervention programme to help these children. The methodology is described in detail elsewhere (Dimigen *et al*, 1999), but in short, a survey was carried out in Glasgow between August 1996 and June 1997, targeting children between the ages of nought and 18 years, who attended for medical assessment within six weeks of admission into care. During the study period 234 children attended the health assessment and 140 of their carers were asked to complete questionnaires. Information was obtained on 123 of these children (a response rate of 88 per cent). Fifty-five per cent of them were boys and 45 per cent girls; 65 per cent of the children were in foster care, 35 per cent in residential care. The children were subdivided into three age groups: nought to four years, five to 12 years, and 13 to 18 years of age. Children's emotional and behavioural functioning was assessed using the Devereux Scale and the Pre-school Behaviour Checklist. The questionnaires were handed out to the children's carers at the six-week health assessment and returned by post to the Department of Clinical Psychology.

The Central Belt study
This was a randomised controlled trial of a training programme for foster carers. It involved 121 families, with 182 children, from 17 Scottish local authorities and is described in full elsewhere (Minnis and Devine, 2001; Minnis *et al*, 2001). Children's emotional and behavioural problems were assessed using the Strengths and Difficulties Questionnaire (SDQ) (Goodman *et al*, 1998), completed by foster carers, teachers and children. Children also completed the Modified Rosenberg Self-esteem Scale (MRS) (Warr and Jackson, 1985). In order to probe the "costs to society" of foster care, the Costs of Foster Care Questionnaire was developed for the study which asks about contact with social workers, doctors, psychologists, the criminal justice system, other foster carers and school.

Investigation of attachment disorder symptoms
In addition to looking at child mental health in the traditional sense, the Central Belt study also set out to explore attachment disorder symptoms (Howe and Fearnley, 1999). The Inhibited Type of attachment disorder describes children who have usually suffered abuse or neglect and who display symptoms such as frozen watchfulness, aggressiveness and unpredictability in their social relationships, and who find it difficult to accept affection or comfort. The Disinhibited Type of attachment disorder describes children who are over friendly, attention-seeking and indiscriminate in their social relationships (American Psychiatric Association, 1992). This latter kind of behaviour is common in children who have been brought up in institutions (Hodges and Tizard, 1989) and may indicate that a child has not had the opportunity to form any primary attachment relationship. Children with both types of attachment disorder have in common a history of grossly distorted early attachments. In addition, new carers can find it very difficult to forge fresh attachments with them. Attachment disorders have only recently been officially recognised by psychiatrists, but practitioners working with very deprived and institu-

tionalised children have long been aware of these difficulties (Goldfarb, 1945; Tizard and Hodges, 1978) and the field of social work has been at the forefront in highlighting the nature of these children's difficulties (Howe and Fearnley, 1999). A 17-item questionnaire for attachment disorders was developed for the study. Because it had not previously been used in a study of this type, it was validated by also testing it in a group of 253 children from local Glasgow schools who, like the looked after group, tended to come from quite deprived backgrounds.

In discussing the two studies, it became clear that behaviours assessed by the Devereux 'Critical Pathology Composite' were also relevant to children with attachment disorders. Behaviours making up this subscale describe 'the child being out of contact with reality so that his or her interpretation of ordinary situations is grossly distorted and daily functioning is substantially impaired'. While disorders such as psychosis or autism could result in such a distortion of reality, severe early attachment difficulties can also lead to difficulties which would be coded on this subscale, as will be seen in later case examples.

Results

The Glasgow study

About half of the total group of children had considerable emotional and behavioural problems which needed attention from professionals, using the criteria suggested by the authors of the Devereux Scale of Mental Disorders and of the Pre-School Behaviour Checklist. Older children were more affected than younger children, and boys were more affected than girls (see Graph 1). Generally, there were more children with problems in residential care than in foster care.

Schoolchildren and adolescents displayed a range of difficulties including behaviour problems, emotional problems and 'critical pathology'. The greater prevalence of problems in children in residential care was especially evident in their conduct (62 per cent), mood (62 per cent) and attention span (56 per cent). The higher level of pathology in boys was particularly evident in the fostered children. Sixty-five per cent of the fostered boys had problems compared to 36 per cent of the fostered girls. Foster carers complained that boys more often than girls got into fights, damaged property, disobeyed orders, cheated or swore. They also felt that these boys got more easily excited than foster girls, were more restless and had trouble in concentrating on a task. More fostered boys than fostered girls avoided social contact, refused to talk or did not appear happy. Depressed mood was particularly common among children in residential units, many of them tending to refuse going to school or to avoid participating in other children's activities. This was observed among older and younger children alike and the percentage increased with age.

Specific problems among looked after infants and pre-school children
The most frequent problems among the infants and pre-schoolers were excessive whining, over-sensitivity and bossiness towards other children (see Graph 2). In addition, over ten per cent of the children had not completely mastered bladder and/or bowel control at an age when they would have been expected to do so, and ten per cent needed speech therapy.

Graph 1
Percentage of children by age and gender requiring psychological interventions

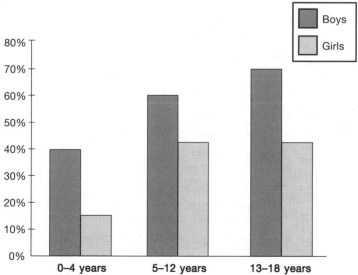

Although the majority of infants and nursery children seemed to have settled well in their foster families, a small minority had considerable problems.

Most common problems among five to 12-year-old children
Frequently or very frequently occurring problems among the five to12-year-old children are recorded in Table 1. We have highlighted (with an asterisk) behaviours which might be most pertinent to children with attachment disorders. The most common problems were related to social relationships, emotional control and settling down to do things. Attention-seeking behaviours and quarrels were prevalent in over half of the children. Non-compliance, lack of concentration ability and dishonesty were observed in over one-third.

Most common problems among 13 to 18-year-old children
Problems experienced frequently or very frequently by the adolescents are reported in Table 2. Again we have highlighted behaviours which

Graph 2
Major problems in infants and pre-schoolers in care

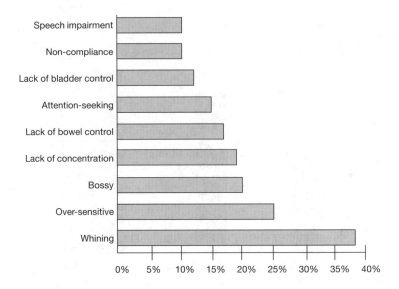

might be most pertinent to children with attachment disorders. The most common problems concerned inability to concentrate, refusal to go to school, social inadequacy and emotional instability.

Multiple behavioural difficulties

Many of the children did not only exhibit one problem, but multiple behavioural difficulties (comorbidity). Table 3 shows the percentage of children experiencing elevated levels of external, internal and/or critical pathology, the greyer shading in the table the higher the degree of comorbidity. The highest degree of comorbidity was observed in the fostered boys, whereas the lowest level was in the fostered girls.

The Central Belt study

The results of this study have been described in detail elsewhere (Minnis and Devine, 2001), and so only salient points will be mentioned here, but the overall findings were very much in accordance with the Glasgow study.

According to social workers, nearly all participating children (93 per cent) had a definite history of abuse or neglect. Over 60 per cent of children had abnormal or borderline scores on the Strengths and Difficulties Questionnaire indicating a very high level of difficulty similar to adolescents in both the Glasgow study and previous studies (McCann et al, 1996). According to both foster carers and teachers, around 50 per cent of children had symptoms of hyperactivity, 60 per cent displayed conduct problems and 50 per cent had problems with peer relations. The findings for anxiety and depression were less clear cut. Forty-five per cent of foster carers thought the child they were looking after showed signs of anxiety or depression, whereas only 12 per cent of teachers did (a similar result to that which would be expected in studies of the general population). The reasons for this are not clear. It may be that foster carers are over-sensitive to such problems, but this seems unlikely, particularly as children's ratings of themselves were more similar to foster carers' than teachers' ratings. Perhaps teachers are not detecting these children's emotional problems within the classroom situation. This would fit in with previous findings that major depression may be missed in looked after children (McCann et al, 1996). It may also be that the problems

Table 1

Most common problems exhibited by five to 12-year-old children

Prevalence	Description
55%	Demands attention from adults*
52%	Annoys others*
49%	Talks too much*
45%	Becomes easily upset or angry when frustrated*
44%	Acts impatient
44%	Resists or refuses to do what is asked of him/her
44%	Gets easily distracted
42%	Blames others for his/her own actions
41%	Becomes easily over-excited
40%	Acts without thinking (impulsively)
40%	Has difficulty following rules
38%	Initiates or picks fights
38%	Becomes easily upset
37%	Argues with adults*
36%	Says that others were picking on him/her
36%	Becomes disruptive or gets in trouble while he/she is playing
36%	Tells lies
34%	Becomes irritable
34%	Fidgets or appears restless
33%	Has difficulties playing or working quietly
31%	Suddenly changes mood*
31%	Appears angry
30%	Acts bossy or dominates others

* The items marked with an asterisk may be symptoms of attachment disorder

experienced by this group of children are particularly likely to be expressed in one-to-one relationships. This is clearly an area which needs more research.

When questionnaire findings were compared between the Central Belt looked after children and the children from local schools, these children had a significantly lower mean score on the attachment disorders questionnaire, despite the high level of deprivation in the school sample. The self-esteem of the looked after children was also compared with the school comparison group. Again, children from local schools had significantly higher self-esteem than the looked after children (see Figure 1, p 446).

Table 2

Most common problems among 13 to 18-year-old children

Prevalence	Description
59%	Appears easily distracted
53%	Skips classes, misses work
53%	Gets taken advantage of by others
47%	Becomes easily upset or angry when frustrated*
47%	Insists on doing things his/her own way
47%	Becomes irritable
47%	Avoids discussing problems
47%	Becomes easily upset*
42%	Acts sneaky or deceptive in what he/she does
42%	Has trouble concentrating
42%	Argues with adults*
41%	Appears bossed or dominated by peers
41%	Demands attention from adults*
36%	Refuses to go to school or work
36%	Appears overly high in mood
36%	Fails to control his/her anger
36%	Has difficulties in paying attention
36%	Acts impatient
36%	Becomes easily over-excited
36%	Fidgets or appears restless
36%	Acts loud and boisterous
36%	Appears unconcerned about how others feel towards him/her*
36%	Acts without thinking
35%	Appears easily annoyed with others
35%	Appears over-concerned or anxious about the future
30%	Has difficulties in making or keeping friends*
30%	Has shown no interest in more than one activity
30%	Worries a lot about past behaviour
30%	Appears unaware of how others feel towards him/her*
30%	Clings to adults*
30%	Appears unemotional or without feelings*
30%	Remains alone or isolated*
30%	Mumbles or makes unusual noises
30%	Fails to show sorrow or regret for wrong things he/she has done
30%	Refuses to do what is asked of him/her
30%	Tells lies

*The items marked with an asterisk may be symptoms of attachment disorder

Table 3
Comorbidity by gender and (foster/residential) status

	Boys		Girls	
	Foster	Residential	Foster	Residential
No elevated level of psychopathology	26%	33%	56%	33%
Elevated level of externalising symptomatology (problems of attention and conduct, or delinquency)	9%	0%	8%	11%
Elevated level of internalising symptomatology (anxiety and depression)	0%	8%	0%	6%
Elevated level of critical psychopathology (autistic symptoms and acute problems, eg compulsive acts, self-injury, hallucinations, etc)	4%	0%	0%	0%
Elevated level of externalising and internalising symptomatology	9%	17%	4%	11%
Elevated level of externalising and critical psychopathology	9%	0%	4%	6%
Elevated level of internalising symptomatology and critical psychopathology	0%	4%	0%	0%
Elevated level of externalising and internalising symptomatology and critical psychopathology	43%	38%	28%	33%

When foster families were asked about their use of various health and social services for the child in question over the previous six months, not surprisingly nearly all families (93 per cent) had had contact with their social worker. We were initially surprised that not all families had seen a social worker, but a few of the children were in permanent placements with foster families. Over half of the children (55 per cent) had seen their GP in the past six months. This figure may have been inflated by routine medicals, but since very few of the children in the Central Belt study were in short-term placements or had only recently entered an episode of care, most of these visits were presumably due to genuine health concerns. For a group of supposedly healthy five to 16-year-old children, this rate of GP attendance seems high, and it may reflect attendance for emotional or behavioural problems. This may also explain the high rate of attendance at community paediatric clinics (32 per cent in six months). In contrast, only eight per cent of families had had contact with child psychiatry services in the previous six months, which seems like a low attendance rate in view of the high rate of emotional and behavioural problems exhibited by these children. More worryingly, there was a significant association between high questionnaire scores for hyperactivity and attendance at community paediatrics, but no such association with attendance at child psychiatry.

The future for children with severe attachment difficulties

The complex and multiple needs of this population require careful service planning. Previous research evidence shows that carefully tailored services for clearly identified groups of looked after children can have good cost-effective outcomes (Chamberlain and Weinrott, 1990). Child and adolescent psychiatry and psychology services have a range of therapies applicable for many of the emotional and behavioural problems displayed by the children in the two studies. However, such services have no well-researched interventions available for children with severe attachment problems. So what happens to such children if they do not receive appropriate intervention? The following case material, from both studies and from our clinical experience, may help to illustrate this.

Figure 1

Distributions of attachment disorder and self-esteem scores in school and fostered children

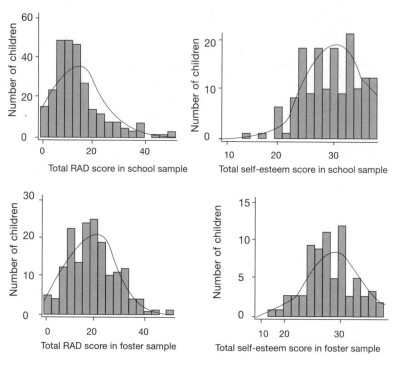

Pre-schoolers

Symptoms in this age group which could be viewed as signs of serious attachment difficulties were noted in the Glasgow study: for example, a child with excessively frequent temper tantrums, wandering around the nursery school looking unhappy and miserable and attaching herself to any strange adult, or a child constantly wanting food and seeking attention.

Middle childhood

Symptoms in an 11-year-old-girl in the Glasgow study illustrate how behavioural problems have become entrenched. This child lived in a residential unit and the unit manager filled in the Devereux. Her Total

Scale score was high even when compared to the other children in this study who scored within the "very elevated" range. She had severe problems in her interaction with others, was in great emotional distress and substantially impaired in her daily functioning. She expressed many anxieties and frequently showed depressed mood. Furthermore, she showed "autistic-like" behaviours, ie poor emotional attunement with detached manner, and also apathy and alienation. She frequently displayed gravely disturbed behaviours including torture of animals, self-injury and inappropriate sexual activities. She was described as being a very restless child, suffering from sleeping problems. Her attention span was short and she was unable to concentrate on a task for any length of time, frequently failing to complete it. Emotionally she was unstable, easily becoming over excited, angry, upset or jealous. She showed exaggerated fears of being hurt in physical activities and was upset by changes in her daily routine. Socially she was inept, constantly picking fights with other children, provoking, threatening or bossing them around. Her relation-ship to adults was also disturbed. She often demanded physical contact or attention, but disobeyed orders and did not keep to the rules of the home. (For more on this case, see Dimigen *et al*, 2000.)

Adulthood

Symptoms in an adult whose severe attachment difficulties had not been addressed are illustrated by the case of a 21-year-old woman who had been in almost permanent psychiatric inpatient care for the previous two years with what was described as a psychotic illness. She came into foster care aged 11 when she was hit over the head by her mother's stiletto heel after years of emotional abuse. By the age of 16, she had lived in 32 different foster and residential placements. Social work notes described her, in one residential placement, as 'sitting staring for hours, tense and frightened in this stare' – a vivid description of frozen watchfulness. She was unpredictable in her social responses and could be friendly one minute and unfriendly the next. She made and lost friends rapidly. The usual reason for placement breakdown was her unpredictable aggression. In other words, she was suffering from an attachment disorder. Her behaviour as a psychiatric inpatient was no different. A careful perusal of her psychiatric casenotes revealed little evidence for psychosis. Her "delusions" could be seen in the context of the magical thinking of someone functioning emotionally at an earlier developmental stage and her disturbed thoughts as a reflection of her lack of social boundaries. Understanding this young woman's difficulties as primarily an attachment disorder had some positive effects in that she was taken off her anti-psychotic medication and placed in a setting which provided the structure and routine she needed. Unfortunately, her unpredictable violence meant that she was eventually placed in a secure psychiatric facility (Minnis and Ramsay, 1996).

Implications for mental health services

Currently, there is a range of services available to looked after children and access may vary from region to region. Some social work departments or individual social workers offer individual and family work to looked after children and families, although our impression is that this is becoming rarer as there is more pressure on social workers to perform statutory duties. Voluntary bodies such as Barnardo's and NCH Action for Children may offer important services to looked after children including therapeutic work with children and families and specialised fostering services. It was clear from the Central Belt study that more looked after children than expected were in contact with GPs and community paediatricians, and it may be that these services are attempting to deal effectively with significant emotional and behavioural difficulties in looked after children without recourse to more specialised services. Our results seemed to suggest patchy involvement of clinical and educational psychology with wide geographical variations.

Child and adolescent mental health services (CAMHS) were used by looked after children considerably less than would be expected from the levels of difficulty found by both studies. Many CAMHS now work according to fairly strict referral criteria which may make it difficult for children who do not have an easily identifiable mental health problem to be seen. If, for example, a child is exhibiting clear symptoms of Attention Deficit Hyperactivity Disorder, depression or psychosis, the GP may successfully refer to CAMHS. If the child's problems are less clearly delineated, such a referral may not be made, or may not be accepted. This can prove to be a barrier to referral for children with problems in the realm of one-to-one social relationships of the kind which may not be noted by teachers or GPs, but which may cause serious difficulties in placement. For such children who are seen by CAMHS, traditional therapeutic techniques may prove unsuccessful and there is little, if any, scientific evidence demonstrating which interventions are likely to work best with this group. Many CAMHS workers and social workers now recognise the need for rapid service development for looked after children, but opinions are divided as to how this may be best achieved.

The children in the two studies were overwhelmingly white, which reflects the lower rates of minority ethnic looked after children in Scotland compared to the rest of the UK. There has been little written about CAMHS for minority ethnic children, although there are various ongoing studies including one in South Glasgow (Minnis et al, submitted), but we are not aware of any focusing on the mental health needs of minority ethnic looked after children. Nearly a third (28 per cent) of the children in the Central Belt study were described as having a learning disability. Education is known to protect the mental health of high-risk children (Rutter, 1985), yet many looked after adolescents attend school only intermittently and are at considerably higher risk of exclusion than others (Blyth and Milner, 1996; Fletcher-Campbell, 1997). Educational expectations have been found to be low and academic success limited in both residential and foster care (Cheung and Heath, 1994; Heath et al, 1994; Jackson, 1989, 2001) and school absence of children in residential care is particularly high (Sinclair and Gibbs, 1998).

When the two studies and the literature are considered, it becomes clear that mental health service planning must be made on the basis of highly articulated and targeted programmes. These should range from individualised psychological assessment of all children entering an episode of care through early intervention to ensure children stay on the appropriate developmental paths, corrective tertiary intervention aimed at mental health problems, to highly specialised intervention for children with serious attachment difficulties or disorders.

But how will young people gain access to such interventions? In order for children to be referred for services, their difficulties must first be recognised, yet those who work exclusively with looked after children may have particular difficulty in recognising problems warranting referral because they have become accustomed to working with disturbed children. One of the major aims of the Looked After Children (LAC) materials is to provide a basic screening of all children who are accommodated (Polnay and Ward, 2000). This should allow social workers to be alerted to significant difficulties in most children, provided that adequate training is given to workers in the interpretation of the information contained in the LAC forms. However, even optimal use of the LAC materials as a screening tool will fail to identify some children with significant problems. A major difficulty in this area has been the characterisation of attachment disorder behaviours. Children who display major problems which interfere with intimate relationships may not necessarily have obvious difficulties outwith intimate relationships and it is easy to miss attachment disorders in the clinical setting. Yet children who cannot form the emotional bonds essential for normal development are at grave risk. A fuller psychological assessment, with close reference to those who are living with the child, is more likely to identify children whose placements may be at risk of breakdown because of their failure to form secure relationships with new carers. A pilot study of an assessment service, which attempts to offer a detailed psychological perspective on individual looked after children, has recently been launched in Glasgow.

A particularly challenging area is that of adolescents in residential care, who may display highly disturbed and disturbing behaviour but who may refuse consent to interview by a psychiatrist or psychologist. It will be important to identify methods of screening in residential care which not only are palatable to the young people themselves, but also give accurate information. Young people in the Central Belt study appeared to enjoy completing the Strengths and Difficulties Questionnaire on laptop computers and, since then, with the help of Kate Robinson, a local artist, we have developed an illustrated version. This is currently being tested and preliminary results are encouraging.

Once a mental health problem has been identified, where should looked after children receive treatment? Child and adolescent psychiatry provides patchy provision for them (Kurtz et al, 1994) and there is a current debate about whether or not specialist mental health services should be developed for looked after children, or whether they are better served within existing services. The need for access to skilled psychological intervention is now recognised more widely, but service evaluations are still rare. Arcelus *et al* (1999), in an account of a mental health service for looked after children, found that more than two-thirds of referrals were for children with aggressive behaviour, but there was a striking absence of adult carers and informants present in the assessment. This presents a major treatment challenge because the therapies indicated for such difficulties usually involve parents/carers or families. Where children could be engaged in treatment, and when there was enough stability in the child's life for treatment to be supported, both psychodynamic and cognitive-behavioural therapeutic techniques appeared to enhance children's coping skills (Arcelus *et al*, 1999). An evaluation of a pilot mental health service specifically for looked after children (the LACES project) is currently taking place in Glasgow and early feedback is encouraging. Workers in this project have found that ongoing consultation with foster carers regarding a particular child seems especially promising.

Children with severe attachment difficulties or disorders remain a major challenge to child and adolescent mental health services and the therapies used routinely in clinics have not proved effective for such children. Intensive treatments for children with serious attachment difficulties, including innovative methods such as "holding therapy", are being used in some centres (Hughes, 1997; Howe and Fearnley, 1999). Formal trials need to be carried out before such therapies can be integrated into current services.

The extant literature gives a clear message that the only interventions which have been proven to improve the mental health of looked after children are highly co-ordinated programmes which focus on the foster family as the main agent of therapeutic change (Chamberlain *et al*, 1992). In the Chamberlain study foster carers were highly trained, supported and remunerated and this effected significant improvements in the emotional and behavioural functioning of the children they looked after. The Central Belt study set out to test whether a less intensive intervention with "mainstream" foster carers (three days of training based on communication with children) could effect significant change in looked after children. While there were promising reductions in questionnaire scores for mental health problems, attachment disorders and self-esteem, this modest intervention was clearly not enough to have a significant impact over and above the many other factors in the children's lives (Minnis *et al*, 2001).

Conclusions

A better understanding of the emotional and behavioural difficulties experienced by many looked after children is crucial if appropriate interventions are to be provided. The first step towards this is for every child entering an episode of care to have a comprehensive psychological assessment so their individual needs can be identified and met.

Those who plan services should be clearly advised that, in dealing with this population, services should not be amorphous and generalised. Instead they need careful articulation and several strands offered from different tiers of service and from various mental health professionals in terms of their core and differing skill contribution. Practitioners are understandably concerned that simply opening clinic doors to any looked after child who is referred could overwhelm existing services. Conversely, most are aware that more needs to be provided for this particularly vulnerable group of children. The literature suggests that foster carers need to be closely involved at every level of service delivery as they are likely to be crucial agents for change in the child. Radical service development is urgently needed, with the understanding that a wide range of services is required to deal with different levels of problem.

References

American Psychiatric Association (1992) *Diagnostic and Statistical Manual of Mental Disorders* (*4th edn*), Washington, DC: American Psychiatric Association.

Arcelus J, Bellerby T and Vostanis P (1999) 'A mental health service for young people in the care of the local authority', *Clinical Child Psychology & Psychiatry* 4, pp 233–45.

Benedict M I, Zuravin S, Somerfield M and Brandt D (1996) 'The reported health and functioning of children maltreated while in family foster care', *Child Abuse & Neglect* 20, pp 561–71.

Blyth E and Milner J (1996) *Exclusion from School*, London: Routledge.

Chamberlain P, Moreland S and Reid K (1992) 'Enhanced services and stipends for foster parents: effects on retention rates and outcomes for children', *Child Welfare* 71, pp 387–401.

Chamberlain P and Weinrott M (1990) 'Specialised foster care: treating seriously emotionally disturbed children', *Children Today* 19, pp 24–7.

Cheung Y and Heath A (1994) 'After care: the education and occupation of children who have been in care', *Oxford Review of Education* 20, pp 361–74.

Clark H B, Prange M E, Lee B, Boyd L A, McDonald B A and Stewart E S (1994) 'Improving adjustment outcomes for foster children with emotional and behavioral disorders: early findings from a controlled study on individualised services', *Journal of Emotional & Behavioral Disorders* 2, pp 207–18.

Dimigen G, Del Priore C and Butler S (2000) 'Mental health problems in children at start of an episode of being looked after by the local authority', Unpublished paper.

Dimigen G, Del Priore C, Butler S, Evans S, Ferguson L and Swan M (1999) 'The need for a mental health service for children at commencement of being looked after and accommodated by the local authority: questionnaire survey', *British Medical Journal* 319, p 675.

Fletcher-Campbell F (1997) *The Education of Children who are Looked After*, Slough: National Foundation for Educational Research.

Goldfarb W (1945) 'Effects of psychological deprivation in infancy and subsequent stimulation', *American Journal of Psychiatry* 102, pp 18–33.

Goodman R, Meltzer H and Bailey V (1998) 'The Strengths and Difficulties Questionnaire: a pilot study on the validity of the self-report version', *European Child & Adolescent Psychiatry* 7, pp 125–30.

Heath A F, Colton M J and Aldgate J (1994) 'Failure to escape: a longitudinal study of foster children's educational attainment', *British Journal of Social Work* 24, pp 241–60.

Hodges J and Tizard B (1989) 'Social and family relationships of ex-institutional adolescents', *Journal of Child Psychology & Psychiatry* 30, pp 77–97.

Howe D and Fearnley S (1999) 'Disorders of attachment and attachment therapy', *Adoption & Fostering* 23:2, pp 19–30.

Hughes D (1997) *Facilitating Developmental Attachment*, New Jersey: Jason Aronson.

Jackson S (1989) 'Residential care and education', *Children & Society* 4, pp 335–50.

Jackson S (2001) *Nobody Ever Told Us School Mattered*, London: BAAF.

Kurtz Z, Thornes R and Wolkind S (1994) *Services for the Mental Health of Children and Young People in England: A national review*, London: Department of Public Health.

Lawder E A, Poulin J E and Andrews R G (1986) 'A study of 185 foster children five years after placement', *Child Welfare* 65, pp 241–51.

McCann J B, James A, Wilson S and Dunn G (1996) 'Prevalence of psychiatric disorders in young people in the care system', *British Medical Journal* 313, pp 1529–30.

Minnis H and Devine C (2001) 'The effect of foster carer training on the emotional and behavioural functioning of looked after children', *Adoption & Fostering* 25:1, pp 44–54.

Minnis H, Kelly E, Bradby H, Ogilthorpe R, Raine W and Cockburn D (submitted) 'The use of child psychiatry by South Asian families in South Glasgow'.

Minnis H, Pelosi A, Knapp M and Dunn J (2001) 'Mental health and foster carer training', *Archives of Disease in Childhood* 84, pp 302–6.

Minnis H and Ramsay R (1996) 'Reactive attachment disorder: usefulness of a new clinical category', *Journal of Nervous & Mental Disease* 184, p 440.

Polnay L and Ward H (2000) 'Promoting the health of looked after children', *British Medical Journal* 320, pp 661–62.

Quinton D, Rushton A, Dance C and Mayes D (1998) *Joining New Families: A study of adoption and fostering in middle childhood*, Chichester: John Wiley & Sons.

Rutter M (1985) 'Resilience in the face of adversity: protective factors and resistance to psychiatric disorder', *British Journal of Psychiatry* 147, pp 589–611.

Sinclair I and Gibbs I (1998) *Children's Homes: A study in diversity*, Chichester: John Wiley & Sons.

Testa M F and Rolock N (1999) 'Professional foster care: a future worth pursuing?', *Child Welfare* 78, pp 108–24.

Tizard B and Hodges J (1978) 'The effect of early institutional rearing on the development of eight-year-old children', *Journal of Child Psychology & Psychiatry* 19, pp 99–118.

Warr P and Jackson P (1985) 'Factors influencing the psychological impact of prolonged unemployment and of re-employment', *Psychological Medicine* 15, pp 795–807.

Bibliography

Abrams L (2001) ' "Blood is thicker than water": family, fantasy and identity in the lives of Scottish foster children', in Lawrence J and Starkey P (eds), *Child Welfare and Social Action in the Nineteenth and Twentieth Centuries*, Liverpool: Liverpool University Press.

Ames Reed J (1996) 'Fostering children and young people with learning disabilities: the perspectives of birth children and carers', *Adoption & Fostering* 20:4, pp 36–4.

Andersson G (1991) 'To feel or not to feel Swedish – Is that the question?', *Adoption & Fostering* 15:4, pp 69–74.

Argent H and Kerrane A (1997) *Taking Extra Care: Respite, shared and permanent care for children with disabilities*, London: BAAF.

Arton K and Clark I (1996) 'Managing open adoption arrangements', in Phillips R and McWilliam E (eds), *After Adoption*, London: BAAF.

BAAF Scotland (2001a) *Adoption Procedure and Practice*, London: BAAF.

BAAF Scotland (2001b) *Achieving Permanence for Children in Scotland: The place of adoption*, Edinburgh: BAAF Scotland.

BAAF Scotland (2002) *Intercountry Adoption News* 1/2, Edinburgh: BAAF Scotland.

Barn R (ed) (1999) *Working with Black Children and Adolescents in Need*, London: BAAF.

Barn R (2001) *Black Youth on the Margins*, York: Joseph Rowntree Foundation.

Barn R, Sinclair R and Ferdinand D (1997) *Acting on Principle: An examination of race and ethnicity in social services provision for children and families*, London: BAAF.

Barnardo's (2001) *Outcomes for Children: Family placement services*, Edinburgh: Barnardo's Scotland.

Barth R P and Berry M (1987) 'Outcomes of welfare services under permanency planning', *Social Service Review* 61:1, pp 71–90.

Barth R P and Berry M (1988) *Adoption and Disruption*, New York: Aldine de Gruyter.

Beckett C, Bredenkamp D, Castle J and Groothues C (1999) 'The role of social workers in intercountry adoption: an analysis of the experience of adopters from Romania', *Adoption & Fostering* 23:4, pp 15–23.

Berridge D and Cleaver H (1987) *Foster Home Breakdown*, Oxford: Basil Blackwell.

Berry M and Barth R P (1990) 'A study of disrupted adoptive placements of adolescents', *Child Welfare* 69:3, pp 209–25.

Bouchier P, Lambert L and Triseliotis J (1991) *Parting with a Child for Adoption: The mother's perspective*, London: BAAF.

Bray S and Minty B (2001) 'Allegations against foster carers and the implications for local authority planning', *Adoption & Fostering* 25:1, pp 55–66.

Brown H C (2002) 'Fostering and adoption', in Adams A, Dominelli L and Payne M (eds), *Critical Practice in Social Work*, Basingstoke: Palgrave.

Bryant B K (1982) 'Sibling relationships in middle childhood', in Lamb M E and Sutton-Smith B (eds), *Sibling Relationships: Their nature and significance across the lifespan*, Hillsdale, NJ: Lawrence Erlbaum.

Canavan J and Dolan P *et al* (2000) *Family Support: Direction from diversity*, London: Jessica Kingsley.

Castle J, Beckett C, Groothues C and ERA Study Team (2000) 'Infant adoption in England: a longitudinal account of social and cognitive progress', *Adoption & Fostering* 24:3, pp 26–35.

Chakrabarti M, Thorne J, Brown J, Hill M, Khand I, Lindsay M and Hosie A (1998) *Valuing Diversity*, Edinburgh: Scottish Office.

Clarke A and Clarke A (2000) *Early Experience and the Life Path*, London: Jessica Kingsley.

Clyde Lord (1992) *Report of the Inquiry into the Removal of Children from Orkney*, Edinburgh: Scottish Office.

Colton M, Drury C and Williams M (1995) 'Children in need: definition, identification and support', *British Journal of Social Work* 25, pp 711–28.

Convention of Scottish Local Authorities (COSLA) (2000) *Foster Care*, Edinburgh: COSLA.

Cowperthwaite D J (1988) *The Emergence of the Scottish Children's Hearings System*, Southampton: Faculty of Law, University of Southampton.

Daniel B, Wassell S and Gilligan R (1999a) *Child Development for Child Care and Protection Workers*, London: Jessica Kingsley.

Daniel B, Wassell S and Gilligan R (1999b) ' "It's just common sense isn't it?" Exploring ways of putting the theory of resilience into action', *Adoption & Fostering* 23:3, pp 6–15.

Department of Health (1995) *Child Protection: Messages from research*, London: HMSO.

Dimigen G, Del Priore C, Butler S, Evans S, Ferguson L and Swan M (1999) 'Psychiatric disorder among children at the time of entering local authority care: questionnaire survey', *British Medical Journal* 319, p 675.

Douglas C (1996) 'A model of asessment and matching', in Phillips R and McWilliam E (eds), *After Adoption*, London: BAAF.

Dutt R and Sanyal A (1991) 'Openness in adoption or open adoption: a black perspective', *Adoption & Fostering* 15:4, pp 111–15.

Fahlberg V (1994) *A Child's Journey through Placement*, London: BAAF.

Ferguson T (1948) *The Dawn of Scottish Social Welfare*, London: Nelson & Sons.

Ferguson T (1958) *Scottish Social Welfare 1864–1914*, Edinburgh: Livingstone.

Fox Harding L (1982) *Perspectives in Child Care Policy*, London: Longman.

Fox Harding L (1996) *Family, State and Social Policy*, London: Macmillan.

Gilligan R (1997) 'Beyond permanence: the importance of resilience in child placement practice and planning', *Adoption & Fostering* 21:1, pp 1–20.

Gilligan R (2001) *Promoting Resilience: A resource guide on working with children in the care system*, London: BAAF.

Glasgow City Council (2001) *Annual Review of Children's Services Plan*, Glasgow: Glasgow City Council.

Grotevant H D and McRoy R (1998) *Openness in Adoption*, Thousand Oaks, CA: Sage.

Hallett C, Murray C, Jamieson J and Veitch B (1998) *Deciding in Children's Interests*, Edinburgh: Scottish Office Central Research Unit.

Hendrick H (1994) *Child Welfare: England 1872–1989*, London: Routledge.

Heywood J (1978) *Children in Care*, London: Routledge & Kegan Paul.

Hill M (ed) (1999) *Signposts in Fostering: Policy, practice and research issues*, London: BAAF.

Hill M, Lambert L and Triseliotis J (1989) *Achieving Adoption with Love and Money*, London: National Children's Bureau.

Hill M, Murray K and Rankin J (1991) 'The early history of Scottish child welfare', *Children & Society* 5, pp 182–95.

Hill M, Nutter R, Giltinan D, Hudson J and Galaway B (1993) 'A comparative survey of specialist fostering schemes in the UK and North America', *Adoption & Fostering* 17:2, pp 17–22.

Hill M, Triseliotis J, Borland M and Lambert L (1996) 'Fostering adolescents in Britain: outcomes and processes', *Community Alternatives* 8, pp 77–94.

Hill M, Triseliotis J, Borland M and Lambert L (1996) 'Outcomes of social work intervention with young people', in Hill M and Aldgate J (eds) *Child Welfare Services*, London: Jessica Kingsley.

Hill M, Tisdall E K M and Murray K (1998) 'Services for children and their families', in English J (ed.), *Social Services in Scotland*, Edinburgh: Mercat Press.

Hill M and Shaw M (eds) (1998) *Signposts in Adoption: Policy, practice and research issues*, London: BAAF.

Hindle D (2001) 'Rethinking the process of specialist assessments for looked after children', *Adoption & Fostering* 25:3, pp 29–38.

Hoksbergen R (1996) *Child Adoption*, London: Jessica Kingsley.

Holman B (1988) *Putting Families First*, London: Macmillan.

Holman B (1996) 'Fifty years ago: the Curtis and Clyde Reports', *Children & Society* 10:0, pp 197–209.

Holman B (2002) *The Unknown Fostering*, Lyme Regis: Russell House Publishing.

Howe D (1995) *Attachment Theory for Social Work Practice*, London: Macmillan.

Howe D (1998) *Patterns of Adoption*, Oxford: Blackwell Science.

Howe D (2001) 'Age at placement, adoption experience and adult adopted people's contact with their adoptive and birth mothers', *Attachment and Human Development* 3:2, pp 227–37.

Howe D, Shemmings D and Feast J (2001) 'Age at placement and adult adopted people's experience of being adopted', *Child & Family Social Work* 6:4, pp 337–50.

Jackson S (1998) 'Looking after children: a new approach or just an exercise in form filling? A response to Knight and Caveney', *British Journal of Social Work* 28:1, pp 45–56.

Kearney B and Mapstone E (1992) *Report of the Inquiry into Child Care Policies in Fife*, Edinburgh: HMSO.

Kearney B (2000) *Children's Hearings and the Sheriff Court*, Edinburgh: Butterworths.

Kirton D (2001) 'Love and money: payment, motivation and the fostering task', *Child & Family Social Work* 6:3, pp 199–208.

Kirton D (2001) 'Family budgets and public money: spending fostering payments', *Child & Family Social Work* 6:4, pp 305–14.

Kosonen (1999) ' "Core" and "kin" siblings: foster children's changing families', in Mullender A (ed.), *We are Family: Sibling relationships in placement and beyond*, London: BAAF.

Kosonen (2002) *Foster Children's Sibling Relationships in Middle Childhood*, PhD Thesis, Department of Social Policy and Social Work, Glasgow: University of Glasgow.

Lambert L, Buist M, Triseliotis J and Hill M (1990) *Freeing Children For Adoption*, London: BAAF.

Lamond R P (1892) *The Scottish Poor Laws*, Glasgow: Hodge.

Levitt I (1988) *Poverty and Welfare in Scotland 1890–1948*, Edinburgh: Edinburgh University Press.

Lloyd G, Stead J and Kendrick A (2001) *'Hanging on in There'*, London: National Children's Bureau.

Lockyer A and Stone F (eds) (1998) *Juvenile Justice in Scotland*, Edinburgh: T & T Clark.

Logan J and Hughes B (1995) 'The agenda for post-adoption services', *Adoption & Fostering* 19:1, pp 34–36.

Logan J (1996) 'Birth mothers and their mental health: uncharted territory', *British Journal of Social work* 26, pp 609–25.

Lowe N and Murch M, Borkowski M, Weaver A, Beckford V with Thomas C (1999) *Supporting Adoption: Reframing the approach*, London: BAAF.

Lowe N, Borkowski M, Copner R, Griew K and Murch M (1993) *Report of the Research into the Use and Practice of the Freeing for Adoption Provisions*, London: BAAF.

Lowe N and Murch M (2002) *The Plan for the Child: Adoption or long-term fostering*, London: BAAF.

Macaskill C (2002) *Safe Contact? Children in permanent placement and contact with their birth parents*, Lyme Regis: Russell House Publishing.

Martin F, Fox S and Murray K (eds) (1981) *Children out of Court*, Edinburgh: Scottish Academic Press.

Mason K and Selman P (1997) 'Birth parents' experiences of contested adoption', *Adoption & Fostering* 21:1, pp 21–8.

McCann J B, James A, Wilson S and Dunn G (1996) 'Prevalence of psychiatric disorders in young people in the care system', *British Medical Journal* 313, pp 1529–530.

McKay G A (1907) *Practice of the Scottish Poor Law*, Edinburgh: W Green & Son.

McNeill P (2000) *Adoption of Children in Scotland*, Edinburgh: W Green & Son.

McRoy R (1991) 'American experience and research on openness', *Adoption & Fostering* 15:4, pp 99–111.

Millham S, Bullock R, Hosie K and Little M (1989) *Access Disputes in Child Care*, Aldershot: Gower.

Minnis H, Devine C and Pelosi A (1999) 'Foster carers speak about training', *Adoption & Fostering* 23:2, pp 43–7.

Minnis H and Devine C (2001) 'The effect of foster carer training on the emotional and behavioural functioning of looked after children', *Adoption & Fostering* 25:1, pp 44–54.

Mullender A (ed) (1999) *We are Family: Sibling relationships in placement and beyond*, London: BAAF.

Murphy J (1992) *British Social Services: The Scottish dimension*, Edinburgh: Scottish Academic Press.

National Children's Support Group (1990) *Children who Foster*, Leeds: Vera Publications.

NCH Scotland (2002) *Factfile 2002*, Glasgow: NCH Scotland.

Neil E (2002) 'Contact after adoption: the role of agencies in making and supporting plans', *Adoption & Fostering* 26:1, pp 25–38.

O'Hagan K (2001) *Cultural Competence in the Caring Professions*, London: Jessica Kingsley.

Parker R, Ward H, Jackson S, Aldgate J and Wedge P (1991) *Assessing Outcomes in Child Care*, London: HMSO.

Paterson L and Hill M (1994) *Opening and Reopening Adoption: Views from adoptive families*, Edinburgh: Central Research Unit, The Scottish Office.

Phillips R and McWilliam E (eds) (1999) *After Adoption: Working with adoptive families*, London: BAAF.

Pitts J (2001) 'Recent developments in youth crime and youth justice in England and Wales', in Vorland B and Porteuous D (eds), *Working with Young People*, Lyme Regis: Russell House Publishing.

Pugh G (1996) 'Seen but not heard: addressing the needs of children who foster', *Adoption & Fostering* 20:1, pp 35–41.

Quinton D, Rushton A, Dance C and Mayes D (1998) *Joining New Families*, Chichester: John Wiley & Sons.

Rajan P and Lister L (1998) 'Nottinghamshire's letterbox contact service', *Adoption & Fostering* 22:1, pp 46–52.

Rhodes P (1992) *Racial Matching in Fostering*, Aldershot: Avebury.

Rose K and Savage A (1999) 'Safe caring', in Wheal A (ed), *The RHP Companion to Foster Care*, Lyme Regis: Russell House Publishing.

Rowe J, Hundleby M and Garnett L (1989) *Child Care Now*, London: BAAF.

Rutter M (1981) *Maternal Deprivation Reassessed*, Harmondsworth: Penguin.

Rutter M, O'Connor T, Beckett C, Castle J, Corft C, Dunn J, Groothues C and Keppner J (2000) 'Recovery and deficit following profound deprivation', in Selman P (ed), *Intercountry Adoption: Developments, trends and perspectives*, London: BAAF.

Ryburn M (1992) 'Contested adoption proceedings', *Adoption & Fostering* 16:4, pp 29–38.

Ryburn M (1994) *Open Adoption: Research, theory and practice*, Aldershot: Avebury.

Ryburn M (ed) (1994) *Contested Adoption: Research, law, policy and practice*, Aldershot: Arena.

Scarr S (1992) 'Developmental theories for the 1990s: the development of individual differences', *Child Development* 63, pp 1–19.

Schofield G, Beek M, Sargent K and Thoburn J (2000) *Growing Up in Foster Care*, London: BAAF.

Scottish Association for the Adoption of Children (1983) Unpublished report on the history of the Association.

Scottish Executive (2000) 'Adoption applications in Scotland', News release, Edinburgh: Scottish Office.

Scottish Executive (2001) *Information on Looked After Children*, Edinburgh: Government Statistical Service.

Scottish Executive (2001) *Children Looked After in the Year to 31 March 2000*, Statistical Bulletin, Edinburgh: Scottish Executive.

Scottish Executive (2002a) *Adoption Applications in Scotland – 2000*, Edinburgh: Scottish Executive Education Department. http://www.scotland.gov.uk

Scottish Executive (2002b) *National Care Standards: Adoption agencies*, Edinburgh: Scottish Executive.

Scottish Executive (2002c) *National Care Standards: Foster care and family placement services*, Edinburgh: Scottish Executive.

Scottish Office (1996) *Statistical Bulletin: Services for children*, Edinburgh: Scottish Office.

Scottish Office (1997) *The Children (Scotland) Act Regulations and Guidance*, Edinburgh: Scottish Office.

Scottish Office (1999) *Review of Children's Services Plans*, Edinburgh: Scottish Office.

Sellick C (1992) *Supporting Short-term Foster Carers*, Aldershot: Avebury.

Sellick C (1996) 'The role of social workers in supporting and developing the work of foster carers', *Adoption & Fostering* 20:2, pp 21–6.

Selman P (ed.) (2000) *Intercountry Adoption: Developments, trends and perspectives*, London: BAAF.

Selwyn J and Sturgess W (in press) 'Achieving permanency through adoption: following US footsteps', *Adoption & Fostering* 26:3.

Sinclair I, Wilson K and Gibbs I (2001) 'A life more ordinary: what children want from foster placements', *Adoption & Fostering* 25:4, pp 17–26.

Skinner A and McCoy K (2000) 'The legal and policy context for children's services in Scotland and Northern Ireland', in Iwaniec D and Hill M (eds), *Child Welfare Policy and Practice*, London: Jesica Kingsley.

Social Work Services Group (1993) *Scotland's Children*, Edinburgh: HMSO.

Social Work Services Inspectorate (1998) *Report on the Inspection of Barnardo's Adoption Service*, Edinburgh: Social Work Services Inspectorate.

Stone J (1995) *Making Positive Moves: Developing short-term fostering services*, London: BAAF.

Thoburn J (1994) *Child Placement: Principles and practice*, Aldershot: Wildwood House.

Tisdall K, Monaghan B and Hill M (eds) (2000) 'Communication, co-operation or collaboration? Voluntary organisations' involvement in the first Scottish Children's Services Plans', in Iwaniec D and Hill M (eds), *Child Welfare Policy and Practice*, London: Jessica Kingsley.

Triseliotis J (1973) *In Search of Origins*, London: Routledge & Kegan Paul.

Triseliotis J (1980) 'Counselling adoptees', in Triseliotis J (ed.), *New Developments in Foster Care and Adoption*, London: Routledge & Kegan Paul.

Triseliotis J (1991) 'Intercountry adoption: a brief overview of the research evidence', *Adoption & Fostering* 15:4, pp 46–52.

Triseliotis J (2002) 'Long-term foster care or adoption? The evidence examined', *Child & Family Social Work* 7:1, pp 23–34.

Triseliotis J, Borland M, Hill M and Lambert L (1995a) *Teenagers and the Social Work Services*, London: HMSO.

Triseliotis J, Sellick C and Short R (1995b) *Foster Care: Theory and practice*, London: BAAF/Batsford.

Triseliotis J, Shireman J and Hundleby M (1997) *Adoption: Theory, policy and practice*, London: Cassell.

Triseliotis J, Borland M and Hill M (2000) *Delivering Foster Care*, London: BAAF.

Van Keppel M (1991) 'Birth parents and negotiated adoption agreements', *Adoption & Fostering* 15:4, pp 81–90.

Walker M, Hill M and Triseliotis J (2002) *Testing the Limits of Foster Care*, London: BAAF.

Ward H (1995) *Looking After Children: Research into practice*, London: HMSO.

Ward H (1998) 'Using a child development model to assess the outcomes for social work interventions with families', *Children & Society* 12:3, pp 202–09.

Ward L and Skuse T (2001) 'Performance targets and stability of placements for children long looked after away from home', *Children & Society* 15:5, pp 333–46.

Wedge P and Mantle G (1991) *Sibling Groups and Social Work*, Aldershot: Avebury/Gower.

Wheelaghan S and Hill M (2000) 'The Looking After Children records system: an evaluation of the Scottish pilot', in Iwaniec D and Hill (eds), *Child Welfare Policy and Practice*, London: Jessica Kingsley.

Winkler R and Van Keppel M (1984) *Relinquishing Mothers in Adoption*, Melbourne: Institute of Family Studies.

Wolkind S (1988) *The Mental Health Needs of Children in Care*, London: E.S.R.C.

About the contributors

Maureen Buist has been a Research Fellow in a number of Scottish universities where her work has focused upon children and families. She is now a freelance research consultant. She is currently working with the Criminal Justice Social Work Development Centre for Scotland at the University of Edinburgh on the audits of youth crime for two Scottish local authorities.

Irene Clark works for Stirling Council as Senior Social Worker for the adoption and fostering services. For the last 30 years she has worked in child care in a variety of settings. Her special interest in adoption stems from her first experience of placing a primary school-age child in the mid-1970s. Since then she has developed and piloted a new method of assessing adoptive parents and is currently working on management arrangements and practice issues in relation to open adoption, in particular to facilitate face-to-face and letterbox contact.

Gary Clapton works as an after-adoption counsellor at Birthlink in Edinburgh. His doctoral thesis was on birth fathers and he has written several papers on birth fathers and their experiences.

Christina Del Priore is Head of Clinical Psychology Service, Yorkhill NHS Trust, Glasgow.

Clare Devine is Lecturer in Social Work at Paisley University, and an independent social work trainer/consultant.

At the time of writing the paper featured here, **Shona Easton** was a social worker with the Lothian Homefinding Team. In 1996 she retired from work and child care for health reasons. After six years working with elderly people in the community at a voluntary day centre in Midlothian, she is going to work with mentally ill adults, setting up a project for self-help with supportive statutory services.

467

Anne Gilchrist is Team Leader of the East Lothian Resource Team. Her career in social work spans the last 30 years, moving from rural and urban community social work in Ireland to local authority generic practice in Scotland in the late 1970s. There followed eight years teaching in Moray House College of Further Education until she moved into family placement work in 1988. Permanency was the initial focus of her practice with Lothian Specialist Family Finding Unit, and this was extended to embrace the whole range of family resources needed when she moved to East Lothian.

Donal Giltinan was Director of BAAF Scotland from 1994 to 1999. He is now retired.

Malcolm Hill is Director of the Centre for the Child & Society, University of Glasgow, and Commissioning Editor of *Adoption & Fostering*. He has written, co-authored and edited numerous books and articles, including two previous journal anthologies, *Signposts in Adoption* (1998) and *Signposts in Fostering* (1999).

Pauline Hoggan used to work for Lothian Regional Council. In 1996 she went to the newly created Argyll & Bute unitary authority as Head of Service for Children and Families. Since 1999 she has been Director of the Independent Adoption Service, an agency which has a particular commitment to finding placements which reflect a child's race, religion and culture, and to helping children overcome difficult early life experiences.

As an adoptive parent, **Sandra Hutton** was Secretary of Lothian Adopters Group and liaised between the Group and Lothian Region Specialist Homefinding Team. In the late 1980s she returned to teaching to her great satisfaction and has recently retired to work on an educational publication.

Marjut Kosonen is originally from Finland and obtained her CQSW and MPhil in Social Work and Social Administration at the University of York. She previously worked as a childcare and family placement social worker, planner and manager, and now works as an independent consultant and trainer, specialising in children's services. She has a special interest in children's sibling relationships. Her PhD thesis, submitted to the University of Glasgow, explored the nature and quality of foster children's sibling relationships in middle childhood.

Lydia Lambert is now retired. Her research contracts in Scotland started in the 1970s and continued while at the National Children's Bureau before becoming a Research Fellow at the University of Edinburgh.

Margaret McKay is Chief Executive of Children 1st in Edinburgh.

Emma McWilliam works for Stirling Council as Service Manager: Policy and Quality Assurance in Children's Services: Social Work. Her current remit includes responsibility for the Council's adoption services. She previously worked for many years in a specialist children and families social worker post in Glasgow undertaking permanency work, and then moved on to manage the fostering and adoption service in Clackmannanshire. While in the latter post, she worked with colleagues to establish post-adoption support and adult adoptee self-help groups in Central Scotland and to develop a new method of adoption assessment. In 2000, she represented COSLA on the Adoption Services Working Group contributing to the production of the National Care Standards.

Helen Minnis is Specialist Registrar and Research Fellow in Child Psychiatry at Yorkhill NHS Trust, Glasgow.

Gerry O'Hara runs his own consultancy business, Hope Management and Consultanty Ltd. He was Director of NCH Scotland until September 2000. He is Chair of the Scottish Adoption Association and a Director of CareVisions.

Diana Part has worked with children and their families over many years. Social work in adult and adolescent psychiatry was followed by time as a reviewing officer in Tayside region. Here she worked alongside families whose children or young people were living away from home and the carers of those children. Time as Assistant Principal Officer in child protection and later in foster care led to her present post as Programme Leader of the BA in Social Work at the University of Dundee, and, in a voluntary capacity, as Chair of Family Mediation, Tayside.

Rena Phillips is currently a freelance practitioner and researcher. She was previously a lecturer in the Social Work Unit, and a research fellow in the Social Work Research Centre at Stirling University. In the 1980s she was Senior Practitioner in Adoption and Fostering in a local authority setting. She was Chair of BAAF's Research Group Advisory Committee and is currently a member of the peer review panel of *Adoption & Fostering* and the US journal, *Adoption Quarterly*. She is the part-time co-ordinator of a post-adoption support service for adoptive families in Central Scotland, and on Stirling Council's Adoption Panel.

Alexandra Plumtree worked as a solicitor in private practice and as a reporter to the children's panel for 25 years. For the last eight years she has been the Legal Consultant to BAAF Scotland, writing, teaching and providing advice and consultancy. In addition she is the independent legal adviser to the Scottish Executive's Adoption Policy Review Group, a trustee of the Scottish Child Law Centre and a member of the Child Protection Committee of the Scottish Episcopal Church.

At the time of writing the paper in this volume, **Stephanie Stone** was responsible for the Centalised Baby Adoption Service, placing children aged 0–2 years from Strathclyde Regional Council. She is now Principal Officer Adoption and Fostering, Glasgow City Council, and responsible for 400 carers and 700 foster children in placement. She is also a trustee on the board of Fostering Network.

Donald Ramsay was formerly a senior social worker in a childcare team and works as a Performance and Evaluation Officer in Fife Council Social Work Service. He obtained an MPhil degree from Edinburgh University in 1998, researching the construction and interpretation of reports for Children's Hearings. His current work includes development of the performance assessment framework for Joint Future in Fife, changes in domiciliary care services and use of Looked After Children materials.

Satnam Singh is a senior practitioner with Barnardo's Family Placement Services in Edinburgh, and an associate lecturer with the Open University, teaching on the NOLP DipsSW programme. Working with Barnardo's Family Placement Services, Satnam Singh has lead responsibility for the Khandan Initiative, a development to promote policy and practice in relation to the provision of same-race placements as placements of choice.

Kay M Tisdall holds a joint post as Lecturer in Social Policy (University of Edinburgh) and Director of Policy & Research (Children in Scotland). Recent and current research, in collaboration with others, includes listening to children whose parent or carer is HIV positive, girls and violent behaviour, and the views of children in family law proceedings.

John Triseliotis is Emeritus Professor at the University of Edinburgh and Visiting Professor at the University of Strathclyde. He has been carrying out research on separated children in the fields of adoption, foster care and residential care for over 35 years. He has co-authored or edited many books and articles including *In Search of Origins* (1973), *Hard to Place* (1984) *Achieving Adoption with Love and Money* (1989), *Freeing Children for Adoption* (1990) and *Delivering Foster Care* (2000). He has presented papers at many national and international conferences and has lectured in child welfare in several countries.

Moira Walker (formerly Borland) is Senior Research Fellow (Children and Young People) at the Social Work Research Centre, Stirling University. She took up her current post in 2001, having previously worked for ten years at the Centre for the Child & Society, University of Glasgow. Prior to that she had spent ten years in social work practice. Her research has encompassed fostering and residential care, children's participation in decision-making, advocacy and the educational experiences of accommodated children and young people.

Other BAAF titles of interest

Testing the Limits of Foster Care
Fostering as an alternative to secure accommodation
Moira Walker, Malcolm Hill and John Triseliotis
Report of an innovative scheme based in Scotland.
2002   £12.95

Adoption Procedure and Practice Scotland
A guide for adoption agencies in Scotland
BAAF Scotland
2001   £5.95

Getting it Right
Social work reports in adoption proceedings in Scotland
Alexandra Plumtree
1999   £3.50

Child Care Law: Scotland
A summary
Alexandra Plumtree
1997   £5.95

Developing Post-Placement Support
A project in Scotland
Lesley Watson with Janice McGhee
1995   £3.95 (previously £6.95)

Statutory Reviews in Practice
A Scottish supplement
1995   £1.95 (previously £2.50)

ADOPTION
& FOSTERING

For further details visit our website at
www.baaf.org.uk, send for BAAF's complete
catalogue (or order from the website), phone
Publications Sales on 020 7593 2072, or email
pubs.sales@baaf.org.uk

Registered Charity 275689